# WINSTON S. CHURCHILL

## VOLUME III

*The Challenge of War*

1914—1916

# MARTIN GILBERT

# WINSTON S. CHURCHILL

VOLUME III

The CHALLENGE of WAR

1914–1916

*Illustrated with Photographs and Maps*

2

HOUGHTON-MIFFLIN COMPANY
BOSTON

First published 1971
© 1971 C & T Publications Limited
Printed in the United States of America

# 15

# Loyalties

---

CHURCHILL'S FALL from power had been sudden and complete. The speed of the crisis had prevented him from seeing all its aspects, and he had been bewildered by the course of events. Only one fact seemed undisputed: the immediate crisis had begun with Fisher's sudden departure from the Admiralty building on the morning of May 15. Most contemporaries believed that Fisher had gone because he opposed the Dardanelles. Churchill's immediate demotion to the Duchy of Lancaster seemed to confirm that the crisis had arisen because the Dardanelles had failed, and that it was because of this failure that Churchill had been removed from the Admiralty. But there had been throughout a deeper grievance in Fisher's mind than the Dardanelles. Ambition and delusion, not strategy, had led him to his ninth, and final, resignation of six and a half months as First Sea Lord. His letter to Asquith of May 19, in which he had set out the conditions upon which he was willing to return to the Admiralty, revealed the absurd, limitless nature of his aspirations. It was not the Dardanelles policy that would have to change, but all policy. It was not Churchill's methods of conducting the operation which would have to be revised, but all methods different from his own. Only a cypher as First Lord would satisfy him. Impulse, not calculations of policy, dictated Fisher's actions during the crisis. It was the impulse of a man determined to test his own strength and advance his own power, believing that he alone understood the needs of the Navy.

The naval situation at the Dardanelles had not worsened significantly, if at all, on May 15. Churchill had already agreed to abandon any immediate plans for a further naval attack. The Navy had already taken a secondary position. The *Queen Elizabeth* had already been recalled. Kitchener was already planning further assaults inland. It was no new development at the Dardanelles, but Fisher's mental state, that brought the crisis to its climax on May 15. Churchill's absence in Paris for the Italian negotiations had put a heavier burden of work and responsibility on Fisher than he had ever borne before. To be temporarily in charge of Admiralty affairs in time of war, worried not only by submarine dangers at the Dardanelles, but also by the threat of a German invasion of Holland and the possibility that a naval action might begin in the North Sea, demanded nerves of steel. Fisher was unable to preserve the necessary calm. He was seventy-four years old, and the strain of war administration was too much for him.

Churchill had seen no reason why Fisher's resignation on May 15 should lead to the disintegration of the Government, or to his own departure from the Admiralty. He believed that had Asquith wanted to make an effort to preserve his Government intact he might have succeeded, if not in averting, then in postponing the day of coalition. But the concerted pressures for coalition, coming at the moment when Asquith's power of decision had broken down, determined the outcome. Asquith had lacked the strength to resist. Henceforth, Churchill blamed Lloyd George for forcing Asquith to form a coalition, and resented what he regarded as Lloyd George's patronizing tone towards his future place in the Government; hence his ill-judged letter to Asquith informing him that Lloyd George would not make a suitable Secretary of State for War.

Lloyd George knew the extent of Churchill's abilities. He also feared his egoism and distrusted his judgement. He knew that Churchill hoped to emerge as a hero of the war; that he wanted to obliterate past political enmities and wear down persistent Press hostility by successful war policies. Before the war he had often listened to Churchill's dreams. A young Treasury official,

Ralph Hawtrey,[1] later wrote to the author of an occasion which he himself witnessed:

When I was private secretary to Lloyd George in 1910–11, he and Churchill drove down one weekend to his house in Brighton, and I in the car had the opportunity of listening. Churchill began to talk about the next war. He described how, at the climax, he himself, in command of the army, would win the decisive victory in the Middle East, and would return to England in triumph. Lloyd George quietly interposed, 'And where do I come in?'

The May crisis had given Lloyd George his chance to 'come in'; the initiative which he was widely believed to have taken in insisting upon coalition gave him a link with the Conservatives which Churchill had always craved. For Clementine Churchill, Lloyd George was henceforth a Judas, whose demand for coalition had destroyed her husband's position, and whose 'Welsh trickiness', as she later described it to the author, had shattered her husband's career. She was not the only member of the family who singled out Lloyd George for censure. The Duke of Marlborough wrote to Churchill on May 24: 'Pro tem LG has done you in.' But once Asquith had accepted coalition, Churchill's position was weakened beyond the point where Lloyd George could strengthen it.

As soon as Churchill had realized that Asquith was not prepared to take any political risk to keep him at the Admiralty, he had appealed to the leaders of the Conservative Party for support. Many of those who watched the crisis believed that the Conservatives had refused to join the Coalition at all unless Churchill were removed from the Admiralty. This was not so. Asquith had decided to move Churchill out several days before he began consultations with the Conservative leaders to discover their preferences and prejudices. Churchill appealed to Bonar Law because, although their relationship had never been good, it had never been so bad as to exclude at least an outside chance of co-

---

[1] Ralph George Hawtrey, 1879–    . Civil Servant, Admiralty, 1903–4; Treasury, 1904–45. Director of Financial Enquiries, Treasury, 1919–45. Knighted, 1956. Author and economist.

operation. Only when Churchill received Bonar Law's negative reply did he realize that the Conservative suspicions built up during ten years of savage political fighting could not be dispelled, and that if the Conservatives were to play a prominent part in the Administration, he could not look to them for high office.

As soon as the Government was reconstructed, Churchill sent his new Conservative colleagues a large number of official documents, outlining his Admiralty record, hoping thereby to show them how wrong they were to believe him to have been an irresponsible First Lord. But Conservative hostility could not be assuaged by such methods, however detailed or well-documented they might be. Coronel, Antwerp and the Dardanelles were the proofs of something they had believed for a long time. Neither the irreverence of his earlier attacks upon them, nor the vitriol of his speeches against the House of Lords could be pardoned. His Irish policy had angered them even more. As one of the most vocal and provocative advocates of Home Rule between 1911 and 1914, Churchill had, in Tory view, betrayed the cause of Ulster. Bonar Law, Carson, Austen Chamberlain and Long, all members of the new Coalition, had been the leading advocates of Ulster. The memories of Churchill's Irish policies were recent and indelible. For the Conservatives, Churchill's career since 1904 had provided repeated proof of his irresponsibility, lack of balance, and loyalty only to himself.

Liberal opinion was divided in its assessment of Churchill's character. 'He never gets fairly alongside the person he is talking to,' Asquith had written to Venetia Stanley on 4 February 1915, 'because he is always so much more interested in himself and his own preoccupations & his own topics than in anything his neighbour has to contribute, that his conversation (unless he is made to succumb either to superior authority or to well-directed chaff) is apt to degenerate into a monologue. It is the same to a certain extent in the Cabinet.' But it was not Churchill's method alone, but his judgement that seemed at fault to those Liberals who did not know him as well as did Asquith. Since the siege of Antwerp in October 1914 the backbenches of the Party had pullulated with growing distrust of Churchill's judgement. This hostility had burst through to Cabinet level early in March 1915 when the editor of the Liberal weekly the *Nation*, H. W. Massingham, had told Asquith that Churchill was the leader of an intrigue aimed at replacing Grey by Balfour at the Foreign Office. At the end of March further suspicions had been voiced by the Home Secretary, Reginald McKenna. Asquith did not treat these rumours seriously, realizing that they were the product of long-standing Liberal suspicions of Churchill's loyalty; but even Asquith could not always shake himself free of doubts. On April 16, following an attack in Cabinet by Lloyd George and Churchill on Kitchener, Asquith, weary of Churchill's outbursts, had written to Venetia Stanley: 'he is impulsive & borne along on the flood of his all too copious tongue'. By May 1915 there were many Liberals, particularly among backbench MPs and junior Ministers, who believed that Churchill was aiming to break the Liberal Government altogether in an attempt to enhance his own powers. Among the stories which Hobhouse sent to Lord Buxton on 10 June 1915 was the statement that Churchill's objective in the May crisis, had been 'a new Ministerial office, a sort of Department of Public Safety' which would give him supreme control of war policy. Churchill knew nothing of this particular charge. But he realized the extent of Liberal hostility. Many Liberals who admired his energy and courage still had doubts as to whether he ought to remain a member of the Government. John Burns,[2] who had resigned from the Cabinet on the outbreak of war, was a typical example. Between 1908 and 1910, while President of the Local Government Board, Burns had been in constant and constructive contact with Churchill at the Board of Trade; nearly twenty years older than Churchill, he had always taken a friendly interest in his career. On May 24 he wrote in his diary:

It looks as if poor Winston was doomed to go. In a way a great pity. He is patriotic (not in Johnsonese sense). He is energetic and at times inspired to great thoughts and noble expression but at heart he is

[2] John Elliot Burns, 1858–1943. Trade union leader. Independent Labour MP, 1892–1910. Liberal MP, 1910–18. President of the Local Government Board, 1905–14. President of the Board of Trade, 1914, resigning on the outbreak of war.

dictatorial and in his temper demoniacal (note his look coming from Admiralty in papers); he alternates in his passions between blood lusts against the foreigner, and brain storms against his rivals which would be better if they burst upon them instead of devouring himself. I have always been fair, at times indulgent, to him and I see his displacement with regret, because he is brave.

Many Liberals shared Burns' alarm at Churchill's 'dictatorial' tendencies. Others were jealous of the extent to which Asquith had come to rely upon a man whom they believed did not share the deepest instincts of Liberalism. Asquith's relationship with Churchill was a complex one. For many years he had been attracted by Churchill's imagination and energy. He had advanced Churchill's career so swiftly that on the outbreak of war, aged only forty, Churchill had reached a peak of political office and influence. When Asquith became Prime Minister in April 1908 he had immediately brought Churchill into his Cabinet as President of the Board of Trade. Each subsequent advancement had been on Asquith's initiative. Churchill's transfer from the Home Office to the Admiralty had been at Asquith's instigation. He supported Churchill's work at the Admiralty against strong Liberal criticism on the backbenches, in the Press and in the Cabinet. On the outbreak of war, Asquith had brought Churchill into the inner sanctum of power. The Prime Minister had deliberately limited his discussion of war policy at the highest level to an even smaller number of Ministers than were in the Cabinet or, from November 1914, on the War Council: Churchill had been one of this number. Asquith had turned to him as a mediator when Cabinet dissensions threatened to disrupt Government unity. He had used him to placate the Press and the House of Commons. He had entrusted him with delicate naval negotiations, first with France, then with Italy.

Churchill had reciprocated Asquith's confidence. He had no other patron of such power in British politics. The Churchills had been taken into Asquith's family circle, and for several years had been frequent guests at 10 Downing Street, The Wharf and Walmer Castle. But by April 1915 Churchill saw in Asquith a man whose powers of concentration were waning, and felt that he lacked the ruthlessness needed to pursue an effective war policy. When the question of a second naval attempt to force the Dardanelles had arisen in March, Churchill believed, as he later wrote in *Great Contemporaries,* that Asquith 'was resolute to continue', but that 'unhappily for himself and for all others he did not thrust to the full length of his convictions'. From that moment Asquith's patronage had been withdrawn. In giving Fisher a veto power over the Dardanelles reinforcements, as he had done on May 12, Asquith had effectively withdrawn his earlier support for Churchill's actions. Without Asquith's support, Churchill was entirely vulnerable. Had Asquith not had doubts about Churchill's reliability, he would have found it easier to reject Fisher's pressure.

In May 1915, despite these recent and growing doubts, Asquith did not welcome the crisis as a means of removing Churchill from the Admiralty. In a single Party government, Asquith knew that he could control Churchill's enthusiasms. But as soon as a coalition had to be formed, Churchill was no longer manageable. The Conservatives would either win him over by their greater zeal for an active war policy, or rebel against his exuberance and thrusting. It was clear to Asquith from the moment that he decided to form his Coalition that Churchill's presence would lead to dissension. He wanted to control his new Government with the maximum authority. He could not risk Churchill's presence in high office.

Churchill saw Asquith as the man ultimately responsible for his fall. Clementine Churchill shared his belief. Her cousin Sylvia Henley[3] later told the author that Clementine Churchill had, during the crisis, declared that her one remaining ambition was to dance on Asquith's grave. For Churchill, the change in Asquith's behaviour towards him rankled far more than Fisher's resignation, Lloyd George's advocacy of coalition, Conservative acrimony, or Liberal innuendo. He resented above all Asquith's refusal to let him defend the Dardanelles policy. Because Asquith had removed Churchill from the Admiralty, critics of the Dardanelles assumed that Asquith shared their criticisms. Churchill's

[3] Sylvia Laura Stanley, 1882–    . Daughter of the 5th Baron Stanley of Alderley. Clementine Churchill's cousin. In 1906 she married Brigadier-General Anthony Morton Henley, who died in 1925.

dismissal was seen as a punishment for launching an enterprise which, although it had not yet failed, was regarded by many as doomed. Kitchener's responsibility for the military landings of April 25, and for all subsequent fighting on the Gallipoli Peninsula, was overlooked. Because Churchill alone had suffered demotion, he alone was thought to be responsible. Asquith's personal support for the Dardanelles expedition was unknown to the public. Yet Asquith, eager for the enormous benefits to be brought by success, had at every stage given the enterprise the support without which it could not have been begun, or been continued. For many months, at the War Council, and at smaller meetings of three or four Ministers, Asquith had encouraged the Dardanelles to go forward as a matter so secret and so urgent that it need not be debated in full Cabinet. It was Asquith who, on January 28, had persuaded Fisher to give up the Zeebrugge operation and support the Dardanelles in its place. But it was not until 1917, when he was no longer Prime Minister, that Asquith publicly revealed his feelings about the Dardanelles. Speaking in the House of Commons on 14 March 1917 he said: 'It saved the position—absolutely saved the position—of Russia in the Caucasus; it prevented for months the defection of Bulgaria to the Central Powers; it kept at least 300,000 Turks immobile; and, what is more important, it cut off, annihilated, a corps d'élite, the whole flower of the Turkish Army. They have never recovered to this moment from the blow inflicted upon them.'

Churchill had taken it for granted that Asquith would support him after Fisher's resignation, and was exceedingly bitter when he did not. He was unaware of the reservations in Asquith's attitude towards him, which had been present even before the war, and which were aggravated and magnified by the war itself. The constant proximity of the two men, their daily political and personal contact, only twice interrupted—during the siege of Antwerp and the Paris negotiations—by more than forty-eight hours' separation, had led by May 1915 to an increasingly sceptical attitude towards Churchill on Asquith's part. The intensity of Churchill's exhortations had begun to tire him. He found Churchill's eagerness to do and dare, his insistent calls for speed and action, his repeated desire to be in the war zone, his changing and exhausting moods, his emotional appeals to the stage of history, too frequent always to be taken seriously.

As the war progressed a more serious charge was levelled against Churchill than that of personal ambition. Many people began to see in him a man of blood. For those who saw him every day he was the 'happy man' at the outbreak of war, the frustrated soldier thirsting for action at Antwerp, the naval enthusiast willing to throw away ships and men in spectacular enterprises, the Cabinet Minister keen to see the war continue in order to provide opportunities for his own fertile imagination. Churchill seemed to have a lust for battle. On 14 September 1914 Asquith had written to Venetia Stanley: 'I am inclined almost to shiver when I hear Winston say that the last thing he would pray for is Peace.'

Despite his enthusiasm for conducting and directing war policy, Churchill was under no illusions about what fighting meant to the soldiers and sailors who bore the brunt of it. 'Much as war attracts me,' he had written to his wife from German Army manoeuvres in 1909, '& fascinates my mind with its tremendous situations—I feel more deeply every year—& can measure the feeling here in the midst of arms—what vile & wicked folly & barbarism it all is.' Churchill had seen the cruel side of action at Antwerp as well as on the distant frontiers of India. During his visit in May to the western front he had heard the piteous cries of savagely wounded men at the casualty clearing station, a sight the horrors of which he was never to forget. But he believed that the war had to be fought until victory was secured, and felt that if victory demanded losses and suffering, they must be accepted. Efficiency, determination and ruthlessness were the qualities he prized. But he had also a sincere desire to prevent needless slaughter. This was not evident to those who were repelled by his enthusiasm for directing war policy.

In the immediate aftermath of his dismissal, Churchill saw how great was the gap between the reality of war policy and public beliefs about it. Watching as rumours about him changed in the telling from near plausibility to complete nonsense, he feared that his many achievements during nine months of war would remain unknown until they could no longer help his career. In later years he looked back with pride upon what he regarded as major achievements: the preparation of the Navy in the years leading up to war, the mobilization of the Fleet, its successful and secret transfer from the Channel to the North Sea, the safe transport of troops from Britain and the Empire to the zones of war, the hunting down of von Spee, the clearing of the German raiders from the oceans, the maintenance of Britain's naval and maritime supremacy, the check to the German advance at Antwerp, the success of the armoured cars and the naval airmen, the confidence provided by his public speeches and the fertility of his private counsel. But in May 1915 all he felt was that he had been thrown over by the Prime Minister cruelly and unnecessarily, that he had been singled out from among his colleagues as a scapegoat for the Dardanelles, and that even over the Dardanelles he was cut off from all the plans on which he had worked, and from any chance to further those plans effectively. The offensive against Germany in the North Sea would be for others to carry out. Others would maintain Britain's naval supremacy. Others would deploy Britain's naval power in search of victory. Others would win the acclaim for victory when it came.

# 16

# The Duchy of Lancaster

CHURCHILL WAS no longer at the centre of war policy. But he could not accept the limitations which his loss of influence entailed. He continued to believe that his opinions would be taken seriously, that if expressed forcefully enough they would prevail, and that the new Conservative Ministers would welcome his advice. In a series of memoranda, in discussion at Cabinet and in his correspondence, he acted as if he still retained some control over war policy. But he was deceiving himself. His was a voice which no longer had to be listened to; for that reason, he found few listeners. At first he did not realize the extent of his isolation and was always hoping that with time he might regain his full former powers.

When news of his demotion to the Duchy of Lancaster was known Churchill received a flood of letters. Admiral Limpus wrote from Malta on June 7: 'We say farewell—for the present—with a heavy heart. But you are yet young & will be needed again.' Rear-Admiral William Pakenham[1] recalled the time when he had been on the Admiralty Board, writing on June 1 that there had been 'no improvement of the conditions of service of officers and men, or in material, which did not emanate from you'.

[1] William Christopher Pakenham, 1861–1933. Entered Navy, 1874. Captain, 1903. Fourth Sea Lord, 1911–13. Rear-Admiral commanding the 3rd Cruiser Squadron, 1913–17. Knighted, 1916. Commanded the Battle Cruiser Fleet, 1917–19. Commander-in-Chief, North America and West Indies, 1920–2.

General Sir John Brabazon,[2] who had been Churchill's first commanding officer, wrote on June 5:

Dear Winston,

I felt much inclined to write to you some days ago, and then I thought it would have the appearance of a letter of condolence and I want you to understand that I am *not* condoling with you, because I with very many others think you did magnificently well.

One can not win battles or campaigns by acting entirely on the defensive and you are the only one who has shown the least initiative.

Moreover you saved the situation, and in my opinion the Nation, at the beginning of the war, or rather before the war began. If other Ministers had been as bold and far seeing as yourself we should have been in a different position today.

It is not pleasant to be superseded by men whom one feels are inferior to oneself but you have never done anything better in your life than in accepting the very inadequate position they offered you.

But you will come out top dog yet, and old as I am I hope to live to see it.

Ever your very sincere old friend<br>J. P. Brabazon

Josiah Wedgwood wrote on May 19 from the Royal Naval Hospital at Malta, where he was recovering from the wound he had received on the Helles front at the beginning of the month:

My dear Churchill,

I cannot tell you with what indignation I learn that you have ceased to be First Lord. The jackals have got you down at last. Don't imagine that I care a damn about you, except as the sharpest weapon available against those German hounds. It is their rejoicing which puts the lid on the folly of the change.

I suppose they will now make you High Commissioner of S Africa or Governor of Queensland, & you will take it for a living. Then they can make peace & kiss Wilhelm's boots. . . .

Of course there is just a chance that you may choose to stick it &

---

[2] John Palmer Brabazon, 1843–1922. Entered Army, 1862. Commanded 4th Hussars, 1893–6. Commanded Imperial Yeomanry in South Africa, 1900. Major-General, 1901. Knighted, 1911. Colonel, 18th Hussars, 1913–22.

keep the non-party humbug up to the scratch in Parliament. If so count me in every time.

Yours very gratefully
Josiah C. Wedgwood
Lt Com

On May 29 Jellicoe wrote to Churchill 'of the whole hearted manner in which you have lived for the navy for 3 years'. Churchill replied on June 1 with his thoughts on Fisher, the Dardanelles and his own work as First Lord:

My dear Jellicoe,

My separation—quarrel there was not—from our august old friend is among the most painful things in my life. I have been looking through all the letters he wrote me, musing regretfully upon the vanished pleasures of his comradeship & society. The Dardanelles has run on like a Greek tragedy—our early successes converting what was originally launched only as an experiment into an undertaking from wh it was impossible to recede; the awful delays of the army, week after week consumed while the Germans taught the Turks to entrench, & submarines seemed ever drawing nearer; his growing anxiety when checks & losses occurred; his increasing dislike of the whole business; the imperious need to go forward to victory—you can fill in the rest. But you see it must be 'Aye' or 'No' in war.

Now the long-dreaded arrival of submarines complicates gravely the situation, & the military operation continually expands. But on the other hand the monitors are approaching, & Mr Balfour with his cool quiet courage will not leave undone any possible thing. And at least we have Italy as a first-fruits.

I have tried not to think of myself in these days, but to keep my mind steadily fixed upon the enemy. Yr vy kind letter gives me much pleasure. I hope my work here taken altogether may stand the test of after-examination. We have not always agreed as you say, but I have always felt quite safe with you at sea. Your patience inexhaustible, yr nerve untired, your practice & experience unequalled. I feel almost entitled to say the gravest & most critical period is past. In a few months anyhow when the new construction flows in all will be well—even according to yr exacting standards.

All good wishes to you in yr great command.

Yours sincerely
Winston S. Churchill

As Chancellor of the Duchy of Lancaster Churchill's only serious duty was to appoint County magistrates, a diminutive patronage following upon his enormous responsibilities at the Admiralty. 'The Duchy of Lancaster has been mobilized,' he wrote to Jack Seely on June 12; 'A strong flotilla of magistrates for the 1915 programme will shortly be laid down.' Even with such an insignificant official task, Churchill received several direct requests from his colleagues. Lewis Harcourt, whose constituency was in Lancashire, wrote to ask whether he could submit a few names for magistrates. Like most of his predecessors at the Duchy, Churchill had no intention of becoming involved in the complex cross currents of local political patronage, replying on June 16 with a letter drafted in the Duchy Office which served for all future patronage seekers. Applications, he wrote, should come 'from a *non-political* source', and should go direct to the Lord-Lieutenant of Lancashire, Lord Shuttleworth.[3] On May 31 Shuttleworth wrote to Churchill, offering to put his 'experience & knowledge of Lancashire & its affairs' at Churchill's disposal. Henceforth all the official work of the Duchy was in Shuttleworth's hands.

After the formation of the Coalition, the War Council became known officially as the Dardanelles Committee, although it continued to discuss the European as well as Asiatic aspects of war policy. Churchill attended all its meetings. But he had little power to influence its decisions. His new office contained no facilities for a Minister at the centre of affairs; there was not even a messenger attached to it. On June 18 he asked Edwin Montagu if the Treasury could let him have 'a room for myself & two smaller rooms for a Private Secretary & shorthand writer with the necessary conveniences. . . . It is also necessary that I should have a messenger.' The Treasury agreed to give him rooms at 19 Abingdon Street, opposite the House of Lords, and much nearer Whitehall than the Duchy Office off the Strand, and to let him retain the services both of Edward Marsh, and of his Admiralty short-

[3] Ughtred James Kay-Shuttleworth, 1844–1939. Liberal MP, 1869–80; 1885–1902. Chancellor of the Duchy of Lancaster, 1886. Created Baron Shuttleworth, 1902. Lord-Lieutenant of Lancashire, 1908–28.

hand writer Henry Beckenham.[4] With this minuscule staff Churchill turned his attention from the affairs of the Duchy to matters of national importance. Despite his diminished influence, he could not abandon his earlier concerns, and still felt the need to push and prompt those who now had power over war policy. On May 29, three days after he had left the Admiralty, he wrote to Masterton-Smith with several important points which he wished to be put to Balfour. These included the proposal to send two extra submarines to de Robeck, over which Fisher had resigned. Balfour agreed with the need to send them to the Dardanelles, and soon decided that even more should be sent. Sir Henry Jackson, who had succeeded Fisher as First Sea Lord, concurred in Balfour's decision. Churchill also wrote to Masterton-Smith about plans for deep-keel pontoons, about which he felt responsible:

It makes me very unhappy to think that this project actually received Treasury approval and that I subsequently allowed myself to be turned from it. If we had these vessels now, as we should have done had the order been given at the time, they would afford a complete protection against submarines to ships bombarding the Gallipoli Peninsula. Six months have been lost and I reproach myself for having abandoned a project about which I felt so strongly; but the moral of this war is not to be afraid of making long plans, and that it is never too late in it to begin making them afresh.

On May 30 Churchill circulated a paper to the Cabinet showing the increase in British naval strength since the outbreak of war, and giving details of the progress that had been made in the manufacture of ammunition and torpedoes, the supply of coal and oil, and the development of the Royal Naval Air Service, which had expanded from 98 officers and 595 men in August 1914 to 895 officers and 8,039 men in May 1915, and which would have 1,200 aircraft by the end of the year. This was his first exer-

[4] Henry Anstead Beckenham, 1890–1937. Entered Admiralty, 1910. Assistant Private Secretary to Churchill, 1912–15; to Sir W. Graham Greene, 1916; to Jellicoe when First Sea Lord, 1917; to Wemyss when First Sea Lord, 1918; to Churchill, 1918–22. Secretary to the British Empire Exhibition, Wembley, 1923–5.

cise since leaving the Admiralty in the defence of his record as
First Lord. 'There is no reason for anxiety,' he declared, 'about
our superiority in the decisive theatre.' On June 1 Churchill sent
leading Ministers a memorandum in which he set out his views
of the futility of renewed frontal assaults on the western front:

Although attacks prepared by immense concentrations of artillery
have been locally successful in causing alterations of the line, the effort
required is so great and the advance so small that the attack and advance, however organised and nourished, are exhausted before pene-
tration deep enough and wide enough to produce a strategic effect
has been made. The enemy must always have some knowledge of the
concentration before the attack. They will always have time to rectify
their line afterwards. At an utterly disproportionate cost the line will
be merely bent; and bendings of the line at particular points do not
appear to compromise other parts. I expect we have lost more than
50,000 men since the beginning of April—two-thirds in attempts at
the offensive—without appreciable results. . . .

We should be ill-advised to squander our new armies in frantic and
sterile efforts to pierce the German lines. To do so is to play the German game. As long as the process of attrition works evenly on both
sides we are on the road to victory. But a few weeks of an attempted
offensive may inflict irreparable injury upon our newly gathered military power.

Churchill could not turn his mind for long from the Dardanelles. He was distressed and angered by what was happening on
the Gallipoli Peninsula. There, he wrote in his memorandum,
the longer the battle lasted, 'the more dangerous it will become'.
He believed that the delays in beginning the military operations,
and the piecemeal manner in which troops had been despatched,
had 'already given time for the Turks to make elaborate defensive preparations'. Churchill warned his colleagues:

If we delay longer in sending the necessary reinforcements, or send
them piecemeal, we shall have in the end to send all, and more than
all, that are now asked for, and we shall run the double risk of fighting the whole Turkish army in relays around the Kilid Bahr plateau,
and of being seriously harassed by numbers of German submarines,

which will certainly be attracted to the spot by the success which has attended the first one. It seems most urgent to try to obtain a decision here and wind up the enterprise in a satisfactory manner as soon as possible.

Churchill then set out his own plan for a rapid conclusion at the Dardanelles. First, the Army was to advance across the Kilid Bahr plateau in order to dominate the Turkish forts on the Asian shore with its artillery. This alone, he now believed, would ensure that the Fleet could enter the Sea of Marmara. Once this was done it would only be 'a few hours steam to Constantinople', and to victory. Churchill ended his memorandum with a survey of how victory could be achieved:

The Turco-German fleet can then certainly be destroyed. Its destruction removes the menace which has hitherto prevented a Russian army from crossing the Black Sea and attacking Constantinople from the north. Although the Russian army which had been held ready to profit by our success has now been drawn away by more urgent interim needs, the Russians certainly will not let Constantinople fall without their participation. Bulgaria cannot remain indifferent to the movement and approach of these events. She will be inevitably forced to march on Adrianople, and with Bulgaria the whole of the Balkans must come out on our side. Any Turkish troops in other parts of the Gallipoli Peninsula will be incidentally cut off as soon as the Fleet severs the water communication with Chanak and closes the Bulair isthmus from both sides.

But the position of all the Turkish forces in Europe, whatever their numbers, is by the same series of events decisively affected. Their homes are in Asia, their food comes from Asia, their Government will have fled to Asia. They must fall into our hands with all their stores and artillery, as a mere by-product of the main operation. And all this depends on the conquest of 3 or 4 miles of ground! Where else in all the theatres of the war can we look during the next three months for a decisive victory, or for results of this extraordinary character?

The Liberal Ministers felt that they had heard these views before. The Conservatives did not want to be distracted by someone whose place in the Cabinet was peripheral. The only

Conservative Minister who circulated a memorandum supporting Churchill was Lord Selborne, a former First Lord whom Asquith had appointed President of the Board of Agriculture and Fisheries. 'At the very worst fortune of the war for us,' Selborne wrote sceptically on June 4, the Gallipoli Peninsula, Constantinople and the Bosphorus could be given to Germany in exchange for the re-establishment of an unoccupied and neutral Belgium.

Churchill no longer regarded victory at the Dardanelles as either easy or inevitable. On June 2, in reply to a friendly letter of farewell from Hankey, Churchill explained what he believed were the reasons for his failure:

No one knows better than you the difficulties of carrying through a positive enterprise with only partial control. If I have erred, it has been in seeking to attempt an initiative without being sure that all the means & powers to make it successful were at my disposal.

The Lost opportunities of this war from Antwerp to the Dardanelles are a tragic catalogue. No where has there been design or decision. I have tried & Fisher with me, but even our comradeship was not proof agst the ugly situations wh circumstances in the control of others have produced.

Now it will be a hard & stern test to carry through the Dardanelles: & without decision & design very terrible catastrophe may ensue.

Hankey replied two days later that he had 'not the smallest desire to shirk any measure of responsibility which can fairly be attributed to me for the Dardanelles operation. Strategically it has always appeared, and still appears, to me to be the right thing to do.'

On June 5 Churchill went to Dundee to make a public speech about his work as First Lord. He devoted much effort to defending past actions. He described how, since going to the Admiralty in 1911, he had borne a 'heavy burden', responsible in the 'real sense' of the word, in that he had had to take 'the blame for everything that has gone wrong'. Nevertheless he believed that he had done everything possible to secure success, and that 'the archives of the Admiralty will show in the utmost detail the part I have played in all the great transactions that have taken place. It is to them that I look for my defence.' Churchill then summarized the Navy's achievement of which, he said, 'I shall always be proud to have had a share.' This was his claim and pride:

The terrible dangers of the beginning of the war are over, the seas have been swept clear; the submarine menace has been fixed within definite limits; the personal ascendancy of our men, the superior quality of our ships on the high seas, have been established beyond doubt or question; our strength has greatly increased, actually and relatively from what it was in the beginning of the war, and it grows continually every day by leaps and bounds in all the classes of vessels needed for the special purpose of the war. Between now and the end of the year, the British navy will receive reinforcements which would be incredible if they were not actual facts. Everything is in perfect order. Nearly everything has been foreseen, all our supplies, stores, ammunition, and appliances of every kind, our supplies and drafts of officers and men—all are there. Nowhere will you be hindered. You have taken the measure of your foe, you have only to go forward with confidence. On the whole surface of the seas of the world no hostile flag is flown.

These were the words which Asquith had not let him speak in the House of Commons on May 17.

Churchill then spoke briefly about the Dardanelles, pointing out that in nearly every case where a ship had been sunk 'the precious lives of the officers and men are saved', and that the naval losses had been 'exaggerated in the minds both of friend and foe'. It was essential, he said, not to forget what victory at the Dardanelles would bring:

When I speak of victory, I am not referring to those victories which crowd the daily placards of any newspaper. I am speaking of victory in the sense of a brilliant and formidable fact, shaping the destinies of nations and shortening the duration of the war. Beyond those few miles of ridge and scrub on which our soldiers, our French comrades, our gallant Australians, and our New Zealand fellow-subjects are now battling, lie the downfall of a hostile empire, the destruction of an

enemy's fleet and army, the fall of a world-famous capital, and probably the accession of powerful Allies. The struggle will be heavy, the
risks numerous, the losses cruel; but victory when it comes will make
amends for all.

There never was a great subsidiary operation of war in which a
more complete harmony of strategic, political and economic advantages has combined, or which stood in truer relation to the main decision which is in the central theatre. Through the narrows of the
Dardanelles and across the ridges of the Gallipoli Peninsula lie some
of the shortest paths to a triumphant peace.

Churchill had been distressed during the May crisis by the
virulent and continuing Press attacks upon himself. To this subject, which had so upset him, he then turned. He believed that
it was wrong for newspapers to be allowed 'to attack the responsible leaders of the nation' or to write in a manner 'which is calculated to spread doubts and want of confidence in them'. If there
was to be criticism, it ought to be in Parliament. If secret matters
had to be criticized, Parliament ought to meet behind closed
doors. But it was essential in the national interest 'that irresponsible or malicious carping should not continue'.

Although a member of the Cabinet and the War Council,
Churchill appealed to the Government to bring to an end what he
believed were the debilities which had cursed Asquith's previous
administration, and hampered his own work as First Lord:

I ask myself this question—What does the nation expect of the new
National Government? I can answer my question. I am going to answer it in one word—action. That is the need, that is the only justifica-
tion, that there should be a stronger national sentiment, a more
powerful driving force, a greater measure of consent in the people, a
greater element of leadership and design in the rulers—that is what all
parties expect and require in return for the many sacrifices which all
parties have after due consideration made from their particular interests and ideals. Action—action, not hesitation; action, not words;
action, not agitation. The nation waits its orders. The duty lies upon
the Government to declare what should be done, to propose to Parliament, and to stand or fall by the result. That is the message which

you wish me to take back to London—Act; act now; act with faith and courage. Trust the people. They have never failed you yet.

Churchill ended with an appeal to the nation:

Above all, let us be of good cheer. . . . I have told you how the Navy's business has been discharged. You see for yourselves how your economic life and energy have been maintained without the slightest check, so that it is certain you can realise the full strength of this vast community. The valour of our soldiers has won general respect in all the Armies of Europe. The word of Britain is now taken as the symbol and the hall mark of international good faith. The loyalty of our Dominions and Colonies vindicates our civilisation, and the hate of our enemies proves the effectiveness of our warfare. Yet I would advise you from time to time, when you are anxious or depressed, to dwell a little on the colour and light of the terrible war pictures now presented to the eye. See Australia and New Zealand smiting down in the last and finest crusade the combined barbarism of Prussia and of Turkey. See General Louis Botha[5] holding South Africa for the King. See Canada defending to the death the last few miles of shattered Belgium. Look further, and, across the smoke and carnage of the immense battlefield, look forward to the vision of a united British Empire on the calm background of a liberated Europe.

Then turn again to your task. Look forward, do not look backward. Gather afresh in heart and spirit all the energies of your being, bend anew together for a supreme effort. The times are harsh, the need is dire, the agony of Europe is infinite, but the might of Britain hurled united into the conflict will be irresistible. We are the grand reserve of the Allied cause, and that grand reserve must now march forward as one man.

Churchill's speech was widely reported. Its final appeal was much praised. According to the Liberal London evening newspaper, the *Star*: 'Mr Churchill has spoken the words the nation wanted to hear. He has swept away the gadflies and blowflies. He has done justice both to the spirit of the nation and to the gallantry of its youth. His words are thrice welcome, seeing that

[5] Louis Botha, 1862–1919. Commandant-General of the Boer forces in the South African war, 1900. First Prime Minister of the Union of South Africa, 1910–19.

the axe-grinding pessimists for weeks have been supreme.' A flood of letters brought Churchill the congratulations of both friends and strangers.

A veteran member of the Liberal Party, Lord Channing of Wellingborough,[6] wrote on June 9:

Dear Churchill,

Though I fear to write to men in the thick of the great work and great anxiety, I must write one word to thank you for your noble, generous and magnificent speech, the best and most inspiring of any speech during this war.

Without intruding on your obvious and generous desire to say nothing, I will say that I cannot comprehend the ungenerous and stupid failure of some of the Press to understand and appreciate your services in giving the Country an invincible fleet, a splendid water plane and air plane service and I will go farther, in showing that touch of genius in facing great risks wh has scared some people.

I know from old talks with great experts the enormous risks you took in the Dardanelles. But if your plan succeeds, as it will, I earnestly hope, it will mean much to the decisive ending of the war. As one of the old hands I venture to send you my warm thanks for all you have done and dared.

Yours very sincerely
Channing of W

Churchill was encouraged by so much praise. 'I am now master of myself & at peace;' he wrote to J. L. Garvin on June 7, '& yesterday I was conscious that I was not powerless.'

Since the outbreak of war the British Army had filled its ranks with volunteers. The New Armies being raised by Lord Kitchener depended entirely upon voluntary enlistment. Many Conservatives believed that only a system of compulsory military service would provide sufficient manpower to win the war. Now that the Conservatives had moved from the obscurity of a silent Opposition to the centre of Government, the conscription issue was

[6] Francis Allston Channing, 1841–1926. Born in the United States of America. Tutor, fellow and lecturer in philosophy at University College, Oxford, 1866–70. Naturalized as a British subject, 1883. Liberal MP, 1885–1910. Created Baron Channing of Wellingborough, 1912. A prominent backbencher, the champion of tenant farmers and agricultural labourers.

likely to be raised in increasingly insistent form within the Cabinet itself. Churchill shared the general Liberal dislike of compulsory service. During his Dundee speech he had pointed to the successful mobilization of millions of British and Empire citizens by the voluntary method, which he described as 'one of the most wonderful and inspiring facts in the whole history of this wonderful island'. If there were to be compulsory service, he felt that it would 'cast away this great moral advantage which adds to the honour of our Armies and to the dignity of our State'. Conscription, he declared, would have the effect 'of hustling into the firing line a comparatively small proportion of persons, themselves not, perhaps, best suited to the job'. Such a policy, he felt, would be 'unwise in the extreme'.

While firmly opposed to military compulsion, Churchill saw another area of national life in which conscription could be of value. 'But service at home,' he said, 'service for home defence and to keep our fighting men abroad properly supplied and maintained' seemed to him to be another matter:

We are locked in a mortal struggle. To fail is to be enslaved, or, at the very best, to be destroyed. Not to win decisively is to have all this misery over again after an uneasy truce, and to fight it over again, probably under less favourable circumstances and, perhaps, alone. Why, after what has happened there could never be peace in Europe until the German military system has been so shattered and torn and trampled that it is unable to resist by any means the will and decision of the conquering Power.

For this purpose our whole nation must be organised, must be socialised if you like the word, must be organised, and mobilised. . . . I think there must be asserted in some form or other by the Government, a reserve power to give the necessary control and organising authority and to make sure that every one of every rank and condition, men and women as well, do, in their own way, their fair share. Democratic principles enjoin it, social justice requires it, national safety demands it, and I shall take back to London, with your authority, the message: Let the Government act according to its faith.

On returning to London from Dundee, Churchill drafted a Parliamentary Bill intended to introduce national service for all non-combatants. Under his Bill, the Government would be empowered 'to direct any person to perform any duty necessary for the prosecution of the war or the safety of the State; and to prescribe the hours and conditions of such a duty'. Churchill circulated this draft Bill to his colleagues on June 9. But Asquith did not think that the time had come for such drastic measures.

On leaving the Admiralty, Churchill's salary dropped immediately from £4,500 to £2,000 a year. Asquith, realizing the financial difficulties which would result, offered to let him go on living at Admiralty House with his family. But Clementine Churchill did not want to be dependent upon the Prime Minister's charity, and they turned down his offer. His cousin Lord Wimborne[7] let him move into 21 Arlington Street for a short while. Churchill decided that it might be prudent to move with his family into his brother's house at 41 Cromwell Road, immediately opposite the Natural History Museum. It was a large house, and with his brother away at the Dardanelles, Lady Gwendeline Churchill was alone there with her two sons. 'It seems to me,' Churchill wrote to his brother on June 12, 'that in the uncertain situation during the war we must not have two establishments and that the families must live together. Clemmie & Goonie are so fond of each other, that this is very attractive & easy.' But the financial difficulties which had threatened to follow the sudden fall in salary were unexpectedly relieved almost at once, for the Coalition Government decided on a new salary system for the duration of the war, whereby Ministerial salaries would be pooled, and shared on an almost equal basis. Under this scheme Churchill received £4,360 a year. But he could not tell how long he would remain a member of the Coalition, and still deemed it prudent for his family and his brother's to join forces. 'We shall probably

[7] Ivor Churchill Guest, 1873–1939. Conservative MP, 1900–6. Liberal MP, 1906–10. Created Baron Ashby St Ledgers, 1910. Paymaster-General 1910–12. Lord in Waiting, 1913–15. 2nd Baron Wimborne, 1914. Lord Lieutenant of Ireland, 1915–18. Created Viscount Wimborne, 1918. In August 1914 Asquith had been much angered when Churchill pressed him to appoint Wimborne a Civil Lord of Admiralty.

all pack into Cromwell Road for economy's sake,' he wrote to his brother on June 19, and he and his family moved there at the end of the month.

Since leaving the Admiralty at the end of May, Churchill had spent his weekends at a Tudor farmhouse in Surrey, which he had rented for the summer. The house had been converted into a country residence by Edwin Lutyens[8] fifteen years before. Known as Hoe Farm, it lay in a secluded wooded valley a few miles from Godalming. Churchill was so attracted by the area that he even thought for a while of buying a nearby farmhouse as a permanent residence. Hoe Farm itself was quiet and remote, providing a refuge from the noise and strains of London. But he could not shake off his depression at the change in his political fortunes; often, alone, he would pace up and down the grass path at the top of the garden, from the copse of young trees at one end to the small wooden summerhouse at the other, stooped in anxious thought.

The Dardanelles Committee held its first meeting in Asquith's room at the House of Commons on June 7. Hankey was not present, and no notes were taken. But at a Cabinet meeting two days later Asquith told his colleagues, as he reported to the King, that the Committee had reached 'a unanimous decision' to reinforce Hamilton with three Divisions from the first of the New Armies, and that these would reach Gallipoli in July. De Robeck was to receive extra cruisers and monitors. The Dardanelles Committee met again at 10 Downing Street on June 12. On the previous day Churchill had sent Asquith, Balfour, Bonar Law and Curzon a memorandum suggesting that a landing on the Bulair Isthmus might be decisive, as an alternative to the frontal attacks at Helles and Anzac, and that it ought to be carried out by fresh troops sent out specially for the purpose. 'It seems vital to us now,' Churchill insisted, 'to consider this operation in detail. . . .

[8] Edwin Landseer Lutyens, 1869–1944. Architect. His best-known work, the design of the Viceroy's house and central buildings of New Delhi, was begun in 1913. Knighted, 1918.

Ought we not now to put these possibilities to Sir Ian Hamilton by telegraph fully and plainly?'

Asquith took the chair at the Dardanelles Committee meetings, as he had done at the War Council. Kitchener, Balfour, Crewe and Churchill were the only other members of the old War Council present. The new Conservative Ministers were represented by Bonar Law, Curzon and Lord Lansdowne. Churchill hoped to influence the new Tory Ministers present in favour of persevering at Gallipoli, and at the meeting he reiterated a view which he had frequently expressed while at the Admiralty, that once Allied troops occupied the high plateau above Kilid Bahr, 'it would mean a great disaster to the Turkish army in Gallipoli and the whole position would fall into our hands'. Once Hamilton's forces had advanced that far, he asserted, the naval attack could be renewed with a much greater chance of success. During the discussion he found that Kitchener was in agreement with his contention that troops should be landed on the Bulair Isthmus. Such a landing, Churchill stressed, would seriously endanger the Turkish supply routes, for Turkish sea communications would already be disrupted once Balfour had carried out a proposal of his own to send eight submarines into the Sea of Marmara. Kitchener agreed with Churchill's suggestion that Hamilton should be consulted; indeed, on the evening of June 11 he had already telegraphed asking him for his views on Bulair, and on the afternoon of June 12 he telegraphed again. But Hamilton did not believe that his troops were capable of the extra effort involved, or that the operation stood any real chance of success. It was therefore abandoned, to Churchill's chagrin.

Churchill realized that whatever contribution he might make to the discussion at the Dardanelles Committee, the future of the expedition itself was firmly in the hands of Kitchener and Balfour. He was already looking beyond the political horizon. 'I remain here for the present in the Cabinet,' he wrote to Jack Seely after the Dardanelles Committee, 'as I seem to be able to influence events in wh I am greatly interested & for wh I bear a burden. But I do not propose to shelter myself in this sinecure indefinitely, fat tho' it be.' Churchill gave Seely an account of the political situation:

LG is making a strong gas attack on GHQ supported by the North-cliffe batteries heavy & light, & hopes to capture the position in the course of the summer. His successive failures in the Marconi, Anti-Navy, Anti-War and Prohibition operations do not seem at all to have affected his prestige or morale. I occupy a detached position en po-tence covering GHQ & maintaining communications with the Belgians who have lately come in to line on our left. I am not at all exposed to fire now and my units are reorganising.

Churchill's interest in a military career was not entirely fanci-ful. On the same day that he wrote to Seely implying that he might give up politics, the Commanding General Southern Com-mand, Lieutenant-General Campbell,[9] wrote to ask him whether he wished to take command of a battalion of the Oxfordshire Hussars. 'Dear Major Churchill,' he wrote from his Headquarters at Salisbury, '. . . You may not be so busy politically just now, and it might suit you.' But Churchill still believed that he could play some part in the political decisions which had yet to be made about the Dardanelles. Despite Bonar Law's rebuff in May, he saw the new Conservative Ministers, the 'Belgians' of his letter to Seely, as potential allies. Even Asquith was making an effort to mitigate the blow of Churchill's loss of influence. On June 12 Churchill wrote to his brother:

My dearest Jack,

. . . The political situation is favourable to me. The Prime Min-ister much concerned to look after me: the new men good & vy friendly: the public sympathetic. It has been resolved to carry Dlles through coute que coute, & the critical period in wh you cd have been injured by pessimism is past. Mind you ask for what is really neces-sary. The might of Britain is behind your enterprise & everyone is determined to carry it through. Meanwhile I sit here at the centre thinking only how I can watch over your interests & make sure that

[9] William Pitcairn Campbell, 1856–1933. Entered Army, 1875. Lieutenant-General commanding Southern Command, 1914–16. Knighted, 1915. Gen-eral Officer Commanding-in-Chief, Western Command, 1916–18.

you are supported & aided and that our friends have full justice done them in all circumstances.

Poor Naval Division.[10] Alas the slaughter has been cruel. All are gone whom I knew. It makes me wish to be with you. But for the present my duty is here where I can influence the course of events.

Your loving brother<br>W

Henceforth Churchill was torn between the desire to be at the front and what he believed to be his watching brief over the Dardanelles. In an effort to ensure that any new offensive would not fail through lack of men, he wrote to Kitchener on June 15 with a strong plea:

. . . Suppose the three fine divisions now under orders do a great deal, but not all, & after 3 or 4 days fighting are brought to a standstill with 10 or 15000 casualties, both they & the enemy being exhausted: suppose two or three fresh divisions are then needed to carry the business through to complete success: & suppose there is nothing nearer than England wh means a month's delay, by the end of wh you wd have to begin all over again! There is my fear.

Prudence now wd surely keep these extra divisions in Egypt under yr own control, so that you can, if they are needed, put them in in a few days: & if not needed how easy to bring them back!

My feeling is that you now have the opportunity & the means of settling this business, but that if this chance fails, it will be very bad for the Govt & for the country.

Kitchener replied on the following day that the troops were being sent out as quickly as ships could be found to take them, and that plans had been made until well into July. 'Later,' he wrote, 'we will make up a further programme, if necessary, but it would be as well to see how things go before doing so.'

The Dardanelles Committee met again on June 17. Balfour explained that it was difficult to find sufficient escort vessels to get

[10] During the second battle of Krithia, from 4 to 6 June 1915, the Royal Naval Division lost forty officers and six hundred men. The losses were so severe that two of the Battalions of the Division, the Benbow and the Collingwood, had to be disbanded, its men being absorbed into the remaining three Battalions, the Hood, the Howe and the Anson.

the necessary men to Gallipoli much before the end of August.
Kitchener, Curzon and Churchill all protested:

LORD CURZON said that this information put the whole operation
in a different perspective. Hitherto we had imagined that the attack
would take place in the second week in July. Now, however, the whole
operation would have to be postponed until the end of August.
LORD KITCHENER said that it might even happen that two divisions would have to be used instead of three for the assumption of the
offensive. He personally would be satisfied if the date could be advanced until the end of July, but waiting until the end of August would
seriously cripple our troops.
MR CHURCHILL said that he could not understand why these delays should be necessary. He knew that there was a very large amount
of transport in the Mediterranean area. At one time there were no less
than five divisions on the water simultaneously. He suggested that
perhaps some French transports might be obtained.

Later in the discussion Churchill warned that 'though he himself was admittedly as impatient as anyone could be to push on,
he would prefer to delay action while sufficient troops and ammunition were accumulated to ensure success, rather than to
risk a premature attack'. He warned his colleagues of his fear
that although good progress would be made at the beginning of
any advance from Anzac, 'the troops would be worn out with
fatigue and that insufficient reserves would be available to carry
the operation to a successful conclusion'. He suggested that two
territorial divisions should be sent to Malta or Alexandria, as
a permanent reserve within forty-eight hours sailing distance of
the Dardanelles. Kitchener supported him, and Balfour promised
to press his expert advisers further on the possibility of accelerat-
ing transport. Later in the discussion Churchill suggested that
until five divisions could be sent to the Dardanelles 'our offensives
should be postponed'. A premature attack with insufficient troops,
he warned again, had no chance of success.

Churchill was not content to express his views in council. He
wanted to give Balfour the advantage of his experience at every
point. But he was nervous of approaching Balfour direct, and
found himself asking Masterton-Smith to put his points for him.

The fears which he had of transport delays leading to a dangerous delay in troops reaching Gallipoli led him to follow up his plea at the Dardanelles Committee with a letter to Masterton-Smith, elaborating a number of detailed schemes for troop movements. He ended on a personal note: 'Be very careful how you use this letter, because I am so anxious not to give any offence; & of course I have not the material for making a true picture of the shipping. Yours ever, W.'

On June 18 Churchill circulated the members of the Dardanelles Committee with a lengthy memorandum arguing once more that it was still possible, with determination, to achieve victory at the Dardanelles. He stressed again the futility of a renewed offensive on the western front, pointing out that in the previous two months the British had lost at Ypres, Aubers Ridge and La Bassée four thousand officers and ninety-six thousand men, and that as a result of such sacrifice, out of 'approximately 19,500 square miles of France and Belgium in German hands we have recovered about 8'. He commented scathingly that during eight months of trench warfare 'ingenuity seems to have had so little success in discovering means of offence and advance'. He reminded his colleagues that it was nearly six months since he, Lloyd George and Hankey, 'all working independently', had pressed upon Asquith the need for an alternate zone of war, or for some mechanical means which would help achieve a break-through.

In his memorandum Churchill emphasized French and Russian weakness. It was necessary for one of the Powers to speak 'with the indispensable prestige of victory', and this Britain alone could do. 'She commands the sea. . . . She wields the power of the purse. She is becoming an important arsenal of munitions. . . . She only requires victory to give her the ascendancy, without which no good common action is to be expected.' Victory could be obtained most rapidly, Churchill concluded, by success at the Dardanelles:

There can be no doubt that we now possess the means and the power to take Constantinople before the end of the summer if we act with decision and with a due sense of proportion. The striking

down of one of the three hostile Empires against which we are con-
tending, and the fall to our arms of one of the most famous capitals
in the world, with the results which must flow therefrom, will, con-
joined with our other advantages, confer upon us a far-reaching influence among the Allies, and enable us to ensure their indispensable
co-operation. Most of all, it will react on Russia. It will give the encouragement so sorely needed. It will give the reward so long desired.
It will render a service to an Ally unparalleled in the history of nations.
It will multiply the resources and open the channel for the re-
equipment of the Russian armies. It will dominate the Balkan situation
and cover Italy. It will resound through Asia. Here is the prize, and
the only prize, which lies within reach this year. It can certainly be
won without unreasonable expense, and within a comparatively short
time. But we must act now, and on a scale which makes speedy success certain.

While Churchill was setting out for his colleagues this plea for
decisive action at the Dardanelles, Sir Ian Hamilton, no longer
feeling bound by his embargo not to write to Churchill on official
policy, sent him a long account of the prospects as he saw them:

My dear Winston,

I have been simply thirsting to write to you ever since my last letter. The time that has elapsed is so long that you must credit me with
a camel's resistance to thirst, but still there it is, you know the perpetual strain on a Commander. Especially in such a show as this.

There may come a moment, for instance, when you have so knocked
the enemy that you are, humanly speaking, certain he will lie quiet
for 2 or 3 days. The sea may be so glassy calm that you feel for 24
hours at least you have, humanly speaking, respite from the deadly
submarine. All's well. You light your pipe, stretch out your legs, and
prepare for the siesta when suddenly—bang!—a Taube[11] has dropped
his cursed egg within less than no distance of your tent!

In all the world's history surely this is the queerest of all military
situations that has ever arisen. We have turned Gallipoli into a cockpit,
whereunto we have drawn to ourselves, as if with a magnet, all the
best available resources of a vast, if decaying, empire.

[11] Taube, the German for 'dove': the name applied to all German
Rumpler biplanes. The design of their wings gave them a dove-like appearance.

The advantages are obvious. We are attacking Constantinople instead of defending Cairo. Were it not for us Basra would have fallen before the Turks and Van would not have fallen before the Russians. The object lesson also to the Balkan States is near at hand and contagious. All these are *broad* considerations. From the *narrow technical* point of view, nothing in the world could suit the Turks better than to have both flanks resting on the sea (yet in ground so conformed that they cannot be bombarded from the sea) so that their stupid, but exceedingly brave, infantry can be set down to fight with perfectly simple orders to stick where they are at all costs, and shoot anyone who advances against them.

The idea has been suggested from home that we might use our reinforcements to make a separate operation on the Asiatic side of the Straits. I have not answered yet. The project is enormously attractive to me seeing there are not many troops on the Asiatic side at present, and that such a move would relieve our backs and right flank from this cursed Asiatic shelling, which is going on at the moment I write to you—one heavy gun per 30 seconds. Men killed in hospital and officers killed in their dug-outs: all this is not too pleasant, though it is as yet on a small scale and therefore not a prime factor. . . .

But, on the other hand, three separate operations with three separate lines of communications and bases from the Naval point of view are not really practical politics, even for a nation like Great Britain, in view of the existence of the submarine. Moreover, by splitting our force into three, I am so afraid the result might be that each of the three operations would get more or less hung up against entanglements etc, and this would be in the last degree vexatious. No, I think I shall stick to my Gallipoli Peninsula, and handle it in a way which I must not commit to paper, even to you. . . .

Hamilton sent Churchill encouraging news about the Royal Naval Division; despite the heavy losses they had suffered, 'you would not recognise the men if you saw them again now. They have filled out and got a splendid, bold, martial appearance that would delight your heart. They are all good, but the best of them are the miners from the north, Durham and York.'

Churchill had assumed that Hamilton would not abandon his ban on correspondence while he was still in the Cabinet. On June 19, before he received Hamilton's letter, he sent his brother a full

account of his feelings about future operations at the Dardanelles, obviously intended to be shown to the General:

The education of the new men proceeds, & most of the important
Unionists are now fully convinced not only of the obligation to carry
the Dardanelles policy through, but of the wisdom of the enterprise
in strategy & politics. But I have had a hard battle all these weeks &
have been fighting every inch of the road. . . .

I was vy much attracted by the Bulair project & I think the naval
objections cd have been overcome: but of course the Anzac line of
attack if it succeeded wd be instantly decisive. My anxiety is lest you
have not enough men to carry it through: & that if a check occurred
another long wait wd be necessary for reinforcements. That is why I
want 2 more divisions, (besides the 2 corps) held in Egypt or somewhere else at hand, to give the added weight & sustained drive to the
attack. It seems to me it will be a vy severe operation, & while delay
is unpleasant, nothing really matters so much as making sure that the
move when it comes will do the trick. K always says the troops in
Egypt are available as a reserve & that they can come over for an
emergency. I hope that every scrap of force that can be laid hands
on will be used when the time comes, and that the General will not
hesitate to ask for all he requires. . . .

We hope great things from the submarine blockade of the Marmara.
One of the points on wh Fisher went was my request for 2 more E
boats. The new Board have however sent 6 or 7: & are trying to get 2
French of large size besides. It shd be vy difficult to feed the Turkish
army via Bulair or from Asia & still more difficult to supply it with
ammunition, if sea transit both with Panderma & Mudania is cut off.
All intelligence reports received here show gt anxiety & depression in
Cple. We must never forget the enemy suffers as well as we do. I
have derived the impression that the pace of the war has been rather
too hot for the Turks. . . .

In a more personal note, Churchill revealed to his brother a growing sense of anxiety:

The war is terrible: the carnage grows apace, & the certainty that
no result will be reached this year fills my mind with melancholy
thoughts. The youth of Europe—almost a whole generation—will be
shorn away. I find it vy painful to be deprived of direct means of action, but I bear the pangs, because I see & feel the value of my in-

fluence on general policy. I do not think the present arrangement
will last for ever, and I hope to regain a fuller measure of control before the end of the year.

The impotence which Churchill felt at being unable to influence
policy gnawed at him day by day. He wanted a ministerial challenge to absorb his wasted energies. He began to advocate the
establishment of a special Air Department, independent of both
the Admiralty and the War Office; a Department which he was
confident he could organize effectively himself. Early in June he
sent Asquith a four-page, type-written memorandum entitled
'Notes on the Formation of an Air Department'. It was a strong
hint for re-employment. Churchill ended with a confident assertion: 'It ought not to be impossible before the end of the year
to make the British Air Service indisputably the largest, most
efficient and most enterprising of any belligerent power.' But
Asquith took no action.

Churchill could not drive Gallipoli from his mind. Only the
weekends offered the chance of a brief escape. 'I am now off to
Hoe Farm for the Sunday,' he wrote to his brother on June 19,
'where I shall see JG & Peregrine[12] disporting themselves with
my flotilla. How I wish you cd be there. It really is a delightful
valley and the garden gleams with summer jewelry. We live vy
simply—but with all the essentials of life well understood & well
provided for—hot baths, cold champagne, new peas, & old
brandy.' But even at Hoe Farm there was no real escape from
anguish. Nothing could distract him. His wife despaired of ever
seeing him unworried. His depression frightened her, and not
even the weekends out of London seemed able to bring him comfort or relaxation. His sister-in-law Gwendeline Churchill stum-
bled upon a possible solution. She had set up her easel in the garden and begun to sketch. Churchill was fascinated. Seeing this,
she realized that if she could persuade him to take up painting, he
might be amused and distracted. That Sunday she suggested that
he use her sons' watercolour paints. He responded at once. Hoe

---

[12] Henry Winston Spencer Churchill, 1913–    . Known as Peregrine.
Jack Churchill's younger son.

Farm provided him with inspiration. There was much to paint: the pond in front of the house, the winding, tree-lined drive, the rambling house itself with its jumble of roofs and chimneys, the dark timbered rooms, the sloping lawns, the pasture rising behind the house, the woods beyond.

Churchill's experiments that Sunday were the beginning of a new experience which was to bring him comfort until the last years of his life. He found that he could concentrate upon painting to the exclusion of politics. He painted in silence, absorbed entirely by the problem of transferring his subject to the canvas. Edward Marsh, who was with him during the first experiments, recalled in *A Number of People* that 'the new enthusiasm . . . was a distraction and a sedative that brought a measure of ease to his frustrated spirit'.

On June 21 Churchill returned to London. Worries about the Dardanelles flooded back. When the Dardanelles Committee met on the following Friday, June 25, he begged Balfour to make arrangements for a reserve of small craft in Egypt which would be invaluable, he insisted, 'if any landing was contemplated at any time'. He also clashed with Kitchener, who argued that the Turkish supplies of small arms ammunition 'were unlimited'. Churchill claimed that this was not so, and 'that the Turks would fire away the whole of their available ammunition' in the course of the Gallipoli campaign. But he repeated his conviction that 'the attack ought to be postponed until there was ample ammunition' for Hamilton's troops.

Churchill had not forgotten the previous weekend's experiment, and decided to try to paint in oils when next he was at Hoe Farm. After the Dardanelles Committee meeting at 10 Downing Street on June 25 he bought his first easel. Four days later he bought a mahogany palette, oil, turpentine, paints and brushes. On July 2 he returned to Hoe Farm. In an article first published in the *Strand Magazine* in December 1921 Churchill recalled the next stage in his new adventure:

The palette gleamed with beads of colour; fair and white rose the canvas; the empty brush hung poised, heavy with destiny, irresolute in the air. My hand seemed arrested by a silent veto. But after all the sky on this occasion was unquestionably blue, and a pale blue at that. There could be no doubt that blue paint mixed with white should be put on the top part of the canvas. One really does not need to have an artist's training to see that. It is a starting-point open to all. So very gingerly I mixed a little blue paint on the palette with a very small brush, and then with infinite precaution made a mark about as big as a bean upon the affronted snow-white shield. It was a challenge, a deliberate challenge; but so subdued, so halting, indeed so cataleptic, that it deserved no response.

The challenge seemed to have failed:

At that moment the loud approaching sound of a motor-car was heard in the drive. From this chariot there stepped swiftly and lightly none other than the gifted wife[13] of Sir John Lavery. 'Painting! But what are you hesitating about? Let me have a brush—the big one.' Splash into the turpentine, wallop into the blue and the white, frantic flourish on the palette—clean no longer—and then several large, fierce strokes and slashes of blue on the absolutely cowering canvas. Anyone could see that it could not hit back. No evil fate avenged the jaunty violence. The canvas grinned in helplessness before me. The spell was broken. The sickly inhibitions rolled away. I seized the largest brush and fell upon my victim with Berserk fury. I have never felt in awe of a canvas since.[14]

The change in Churchill's daily life between May and June was complete. the daily conferences with the heads of a powerful Department of State were over; so also was the incessant interdepartmental activity, the notes and minutes sent across to the

[13] Hazel Trudeau Lavery, c. 1887–1935. Second wife of the painter Sir John Lavery, 1856–1941. The Laverys lived at 5 Cromwell Place, a few yards from the Churchill house at 41 Cromwell Road.

[14] The *Strand Magazine* article was called 'Painting as a Pastime'. It was twice reprinted: in a volume of essays entitled *Thoughts and Adventures* (Thornton Butterworth, 1932), and in *Painting as a Pastime* (Odhams Press and Ernest Benn, 1948). In 1966 David Coombs compiled a catalogue of Churchill's paintings, *Churchill his paintings* (Hamish Hamilton, 1967). This catalogue included four paintings done at Hoe Farm in 1915: number 23 (the inner hall: incorrectly described in the catalogue as 'the inner hall at Breccles c. 1928'), number 146 (Lady Gwendeline Churchill in the garden), number 148 (the drive and pond) and number 149 (view of the house and garden).

Foreign Office and War Office, the scrutiny of plans submitted daily from experts and intermediaries, the challenge of parliamentary questions, the opportunity for important policy speeches. Gone was the thrill and responsibility of daily contact with the inner secrets of war policy: the intercepted German wireless messages, the tantalizing reports from neutral capitals, the information collected by British agents and the planning of attacks too secret to divulge to any but the Prime Minister. For each fifty letters which he had received while First Lord, there were only one or two addressed to him at the Duchy. A few letters still trickled in from Admirals wishing to console their former chief. A few requests for patronage came his way. Bonar Law, who had once pressed the First Lord to give his two nephews an opportunity of serving at the Dardanelles, now asked the Chancellor of the Duchy to appoint a nominee of his to the Bootle Bench. The longest and most frequent letters which Churchill received came from his brother and from Hamilton at the Dardanelles.

On June 26 Jack Churchill sent an account of the continued fighting on the Helles front. The 29th Division had not rested for two months, and 'although the men are still splendid, everybody's nerves have been strained by being always under shell fire'. Jack Churchill shared his brother's frustration at Britain's failure to obtain Balkan allies. 'We had hoped that Greece would have been moving by now. But our diplomacy is rotten,' he wrote. 'If the Balkans are useful to us—why did they not send out good men— the best they could find—to all these places on the declaration of war. Venezelos had come in with a big war majority, but finds his hands tied for some time, because the Germans have bought most of the senior military officials! Surely we ought to be able to compete in the bribing market.' Jack Churchill reported that the Royal Naval Division had once again had 'a very bad time'; their best officers and men had been killed, and the few officers remaining were too sick to fight.

One member of the Coalition who was enthusiastic about the Dardanelles was Lord Robert Cecil, the new Under-Secretary of State at the Foreign Office. He wrote several times to Churchill with information which had been received at the Foreign Office, and with encouragement. On June 20 he sent news of Balkan developments, asking tersely of the Bulgars: 'Why dont they march straight on Constple?' Three days later he wrote again, worried that not enough artillery was being sent to Gallipoli: 'We ought to devote whatever efforts are necessary to success.' On July 3 he sent Churchill a printed sheet giving extracts from intercepted private letters revealing much hardship inside Austria. These letters, Cecil wrote, confirmed his view 'that we should press on our attacks on Austria i.e. the Dardanelles'. But Cecil's encouragement contrasted with a letter which Churchill received from Carson, the new Attorney-General, written on June 21. 'All anticipations in the Dardanelles have been falsified by events,' Carson declared. 'I quite agree,' he went on, 'that to gain a victory in the Dardanelles whilst there is apparently a checkmate in Flanders would give a very helpful and hopeful turn to the War, but I do not want the obvious advantages of this step to influence our judgements in the direction of miscalculating the difficulties.'

Churchill began to tire of arguing about Gallipoli. He wanted to go there; to lead a brigade fighting the Turks, instead of bickering with his colleagues on the Dardanelles Committee. He expressed these thoughts to Gwendeline Churchill, who passed them on to her husband. But Jack Churchill did not approve. 'I hope you will not attempt such a thing,' he wrote on July 3. 'You would sacrifice such a lot and gain so little. You would have a wonderfully interesting 10 days, and then you would have long periods with nothing to do but be shelled. There are no exciting movements—how can there be with a four mile front and the sea on each flank. A brigadier or even a div-general has a poor show. I am quite sure as far as this show is concerned, you would be twice as useful at home as here.' Jack Churchill had another idea. 'Why don't you get 3 weeks leave,' he wrote, 'and get sent out to report on the situation to the Cabinet! I You could see every inch of the position in 3 days. But I suppose it would raise a shriek!' Churchill was attracted to Jack's suggestion and a number of incidents at the end of June and early in July reinforced his distaste for remaining in London.

At the end of June there was a sharp division of opinion among

Cabinet Ministers on what attitude Britain ought to adopt towards Bulgaria. Crewe, who was acting as Foreign Secretary while Grey was ill, doubted very much whether Bulgaria could be brought into active co-operation with the Allies. He felt that far from there being a possibility of a grand Balkan alliance concerting action against Turkey and Austria, it was more likely that a new Balkan war would break out between Serbia and Greece on one side, and Bulgaria on the other. Churchill had always been a pro-Bulgarian. The precipitant Greek reversal of her offer of troops to take part in the Dardanelles operation had destroyed his original plan for a joint military and naval attack on Turkey. He believed that Bulgarian support, could it be obtained, would be more consistent, and indeed more useful. Lloyd George, who shared Churchill's pro-Bulgarian sympathies, was equally frustrated by what appeared to both men to be a lack of initiative on the part of the Foreign Office. 'I am all for playing the game right out to get Bulgaria,' Churchill wrote to Lloyd George on June 25. 'She is the real prize, & it is only if and when we know she will not come that we shd consider Greek & Servian interests.' On the following day Churchill wrote direct to Cecil at the Foreign Office that it would be wrong to threaten Bulgaria in any way by using 'take it or leave it methods'. The Foreign Office should not 'whittle away the definite offers which have been made to her. . . . For the present we are in the Bulgarian camp: let us stay there. She is worth all the rest put together, and she would bring all the rest in too.' At the Cabinet on June 30 Churchill and Lloyd George acted in unison. Asquith sent an account of the discussion to the King on July 1:

Some members of the Cabinet—especially Mr Lloyd George & Mr Churchill—were strongly of opinion that a high price (at the expense mainly of Greece) was worth paying to secure the prompt adhesion of Bulgaria. Others inclined to the Italian proposal to delay any definite answer to the last Bulgarian note until Italy has declared war against Turkey. Finally, it was agreed that a complete dossier of the whole negotiations should be prepared by the Foreign Office, and a definite decision put off until Friday's Cabinet, or the early part of next week.

Churchill hated such delays, knowing them to be but the prelude to further procrastination. At the beginning of July he asked Asquith if he could go with him to the forthcoming discussions on inter-Allied strategy to be held at Calais; but Asquith said no.

On July 4 Balfour asked Fisher to become Chairman of an Admiralty Committee, the Board of Inventions and Research. Churchill learned of Fisher's appointment when he read about it in the newspapers on July 5. He went at once to complain to Balfour, who told him that Asquith had approved. On July 6 he went to see Asquith and to protest. Asquith told him that as Fisher had apologized for his behaviour in May, there was no reason why he should not have been given the new appointment. Churchill returned to the Duchy of Lancaster Office and wrote angrily:

My dear Prime Minister,

Fisher resigned his office without warning or parley. He assigned no reason except inability to work with me. The only points of policy under discussion were of minor consequence, & all have been settled by the new Board as I had proposed. You ordered Fisher to return to his post in the name of the King. He paid no attention to yr order. You declared that he had deserted his post in time of war; & the facts are not open to any other construction. For ten days or more the country was without a First Sea Lord as Fisher did not even do his duty till his successor was appointed; & during that period events occurred wh might have led to the decisive battle of the naval war. You have repeatedly assured me that in view of these facts you wd not consent to this officer's employment under the Admy.

It was therefore with surprise that I read in the newspapers of Monday's appointment, & still more that I heard from Mr Balfour that you had approved it beforehand. Yesterday you explained to me that Fisher had expressed regret for his conduct & had excused himself by saying that his mind was at the time seriously affected, & that in view of his 'contrition' you had thought it possible to give him the appt.

Considering that it was Fisher's unreasonable & extraordinary action that led you to remove me from the Admiralty in time of war, & thus to humiliate me before the whole world & deprive me of the fruits of my work when they were being gathered, I do not think that this light & easy explanation ought to have been so readily accepted by you; & I feel that I as still a colleague deserved at least the consideration of being consulted before it was accepted.

Fisher's expressions of regret & admissions of nervous or mental weakness will remain unpublished. His appointment is all that will be known. Meanwhile I have remained silent & the truth is undisclosed.

Our friendship has been the light in wh I have forced myself to view a very puzzling series of events [largely incomprehensible to me]. But I must now frankly say that I think this last incident required somewhat different treatment, & that if expressions of regret have been tendered by Fisher, some of them at least were due to me.

Churchill crossed out the phrase in square brackets. Then he decided not to send the letter at all. Instead, he wrote to Masterton-Smith of his anger at Fisher's appointment. Masterton-Smith spoke to Balfour, who wrote to Churchill on July 8, pointing out that Churchill himself had often spoken of Fisher's 'great gifts as an inventor' and of his 'originality of mind and his consuming energy'. These qualities were, as Balfour wrote, 'too valuable at such a time as this to be thrown away'. Churchill replied on July 9, repeating the arguments which he had intended to use in his letter to Asquith, and continuing:

On other grounds I am sure the step which has been taken will be productive of inconvenience and unrest, in the Admiralty office and to a less extent in the Fleet. Every officer who is under Fisher's ban—and they are many—or who did not actively support him, will fear that he is shortly to return to power. As the result two parties will be formed in the Admiralty, one of which will count on Fisher's resumption of office, and the others will endeavour to prevent it at their peril. The position of the Third Sea Lord and of the officers of the technical departments will be specially embarrassed. A newspaper campaign will be set on foot—has already begun. Losses when they occur will be used to prove the need of Fisher's return to real control. Successes will be attributed to his influence behind the scenes.

All this must be viewed in relation to a very old man, without the nerve to carry on war, not quite sane in moments of crisis, and perfectly unscrupulous.

In all my conduct in these recent affairs I have tried to act with loyalty and simplicity. I have striven to do everything that care for the public interests could suggest. I therefore am not actuated by personal feelings, when I say that I am very sorry you did not give me an opportunity of being heard before your decision was taken.

Churchill's protest was in vain. Fisher took up his new appointment, presiding over a team of scientists who examined all suggestions put forward, and authorized research on those inventions which impressed them.

The Dardanelles Committee met again at 10 Downing Street on July 5. Churchill took little part in the discussion. The arguments used by his colleagues were those he had often put forward himself. Lloyd George declared that 'he attached the utmost importance to a proper supply of high explosive ammunition at the Dardanelles' and argued that the appropriate quantity of such ammunition ought to be sent to Gallipoli 'even if we could not supply sufficient for the much larger Army in France'. Kitchener said that the war would be over 'as soon as the Gallipoli Peninsula was captured. Once you got to Constantinople the Turkish resistance would collapse.' Curzon advocated sending out a fifth division to the Dardanelles. Lansdowne and Balfour both agreed that further reinforcements were needed.

As a result of several weeks' pressure from Curzon, Lansdowne, Balfour, Lloyd George and Churchill, Kitchener agreed that two territorial divisions should be sent as reinforcements to the eastern Mediterranean. On July 7 Churchill sent Hamilton the good news:

My dear Hamilton,

I rejoice to say that on Monday (after 3 weeks work) the War Council definitely decided to add 2 territorial divisions to your army making in all 6 divisions not yet engaged. I rejoice also at the punishment you are inflicting on the Turks, at the evident distress of their army & their capital, & at the progress made in gaining ground. My confidence in the future & in the wisdom of the policy wh has launched this operation remains unshaken. Well done & with good luck or mistakenly done & with bad luck, if done in the end it will repay all losses & cover all miscalculations in the priceless advantages wh will rise for the Allied cause. Everything in troops & ships that I can think of

or you & de Robeck have asked for has now been given. It seems to
me that whereas hitherto you have been fighting against numerical
superiority & with little HE [high explosive] shell, your next important
effort shd be made with a superiority of nearly 2 to 1 & with plenty
of HE shell; & further that it will be made upon an enemy army much
enfeebled & dispirited by losses & defeats, and short both of food &
ammunition.

In these circumstances, I cannot help feeling hopeful, & that there
are just grounds for hope. Moreover the monitor fleet will have arrived
& will be able to give you a support far more effective than you have
had hitherto.

It has been a remarkable experience to me watching opinion slowly
& steadily consolidating behind this enterprise, & to see the successive
waves of opposition & surrender—feeling baffled & surmounted one
after another. Ignorance, pessimism in high places, the malice of
newspapers, the natural jealousies & carping of the Flanders army, &
of the French soldiers have all failed to prevent the necessary reinforcements by land & sea from being sent. And now you are equipped
with all that you have asked for—& more, the next great effort can be
made.

I never look beyond a battle. It is a culminating event, & like a brick
wall bars all further vision. But the chances seem favourable & the
reward of success will be astonishing. Your daring spirit and the high
qualities of your nature, will enable you to enjoy trials and tests under
wh the fleshly courage of commonplace commanders wd quail. The
superb conduct & achievements of the soldiers wd redeem even a
final failure: but with a final success they will become a military episode not inferior in glory to any that the history of war records.

Then there will be found honour for all who have never flinched
& never wavered. God go with you.

Your sincere friend<br>
Winston S. Churchill

Victory over the Turks continued to excite the mind of an-
nexationists, of whatever politial party. The Report of the Committee on Asiatic Turkey, which Asquith had called for in April,
was made available to members of the Dardanelles Committee
on July 8. Five separate schemes were each considered in detail.
Under the most ambitious of the proposals, Britain would control the whole of the Tigris and Euphrates valley and extend

her sovereignty from Alexandretta in the eastern Mediterranean to Basra at the head of the Persian Gulf. Under each of the five schemes, Russia would annex Constantinople and occupy the Gallipoli Peninsula.

Churchill had lost interest in these discussions. They seemed to him to be a game played by people who were not necessarily prepared to commit themselves to the action needed to see their plans come true. The thought of going out to Gallipoli continued to excite his imagination. At the beginning of the second week of July, to Churchill's surprise, Kitchener suggested that he go on an official visit to the Dardanelles. Asquith and Balfour both gave their approval. Kitchener wanted a senior ministerial opinion on the conditions and prospects of the Gallipoli Peninsula. Asquith and Balfour felt sympathy for Churchill in his political impotence. They realized that a visit to the scene of action would give them an opportunity to hear about the situation from someone who had followed their discussions from the start. It was a task which Churchill welcomed. On July 16 he asked Asquith for a formal letter 'expressing your wish & that of my colleagues that I should go'. Asquith replied the same day:

My dear Winston,

I believe that your visit to the Dardanelles will secure for the Cabinet valuable information & suggestions in regard both to the future of the campaign & to our policy in that theatre of the War.

Your object will be to survey & report upon the situation, after Conference with the Commanding Officers. You will no doubt make it clear to the General & the Admiral that your mission is not dictated by any want of confidence in them, but by a wish to get into closer touch, so far as they are concerned.

They both enjoy, as they have deserved, our gratitude & trust.

Yours always
H. H. Asquith

Churchill proceeded to make the necessary arrangements. First he drafted a telegram to Hamilton, which Kitchener sent under his own name on the following morning: 'Churchill is coming out on behalf of the Cabinet to confer with you generally upon the situation and to watch the impending operations. He will start on Tuesday morning and will bring one officer & a secretary with him.' Hamilton replied to Kitchener on July 18: 'With reference your telegram I had hoped we were too far off for visitors but you know that in all circumstances you can rely on my loyalty to you.' Churchill was not shown this reply.

The Allied positions on the Gallipoli Peninsula were all within range of Turkish artillery. Churchill would therefore need extra insurance cover for the duration of his visit. On July 16 he asked his insurance broker, W. H. Bernau,[15] to call on him at the Duchy of Lancaster Office. During the meeting Bernau took the following notes:

Going to Dardanelles on private mission. No-one to know. Thorough inspection (as a civilian) in order to report fully to the Cabinet on entire position after conference with Sir I H. He undertakes not to take part in any military operations; he will inspect landing of troops and inspect the trenches. He will 'run no risks'. He expects to be gone about 3 or 4 weeks. He suggests the policy should cover two months as he may call at the scene of warfare in France on return journey.

On the following day Churchill wrote to Bernau to reassure him that he would not take 'an active part in the fighting', but adding: 'It is possible however that my mission may in certain circumstances be extended, and that I may have to visit the Balkan States.'

Churchill realized that he might be killed during his visit to Gallipoli. On July 17 he wrote out a letter 'to be sent to Mrs Churchill in the event of my death':

Darling,

Cox holds about £1000 worth of securities of mine (Chiefly Witbank Collieries): Jack has in his name about £1000 worth of Pretoria Cement Shares & Cassel has American Stocks of mine[16] wh shd ex-

[15] William Henry Bernau, 1870–1937. Started work at Cox & Co., bankers, 1889; in charge of the Insurance Department, 1910–35; retired, 1935.

[16] Sir Ernest Cassel's Administration held, on Churchill's behalf, $10,000 United States Steel Corporation 5% Sinking Fund Bonds, and $10,000 Atchison Topeka and Santa Fe Railway 4% Convertible Bonds.

ceed in value my loans from him by about £1000. I believe these will be found sufficient to pay my debts & overdraught. Most of the bills were paid last year. Randolph Payne & Lumley are the only two large ones.[17]

The insurance policies are all kept up & every contingency is covered. You will receive £10,000 and £300 a year in addition until you succeed my mother. The £10,000 can either be used to provide interest ie about £450 a year or even to purchase an annuity against my mother's life, wh wd yield a much larger income at the expense of the capital. Of course it wd be much better to keep the £10,000 and live on the interest than to spend it on the chance of my mother living a long time. But you must judge.

I am anxious that you shd get hold of all my papers, especially those wh refer to my Admiralty administration. I have appointed you my sole literary executor. Masterton Smith will help you to secure all that is necessary for a complete record. There is no hurry; but some day I shd like the truth to be known. Randolph will carry on the lamp. Do not grieve for me too much. I am a spirit confident of my rights. Death is only an incident, & not the most important wh happens to us in this state of being. On the whole, especially since I met you my darling one I have been happy, & you have taught me how noble a woman's heart can be. If there is anywhere else I shall be on the look out for you. Meanwhile look forward, feel free, rejoice in life, cherish the children, guard my memory. God bless you.

Good bye<br>W

On the following day Churchill set out formally, in a letter to Asquith, his reasons for the visit, and also raised the question, which he had mentioned to his solicitor, of a possible extension of his mission:

The two reasons wh have led me to undertake this journey are first: in case the coming attack does not succeed, or succeeds only partially, I wish to be able to advise the Cabinet with the fullest knowledge upon the new & grave situation wh will then arise. I can acquire this knowledge only upon the spot, & no one else will have the same ad-

[17] In July 1915 Churchill owed Randolph Payne & Sons, wine merchants, nearly £500 (having already paid £100 in June). Lumley & Lumley were his solicitors; he owed them £180 (having already paid £100 in April).

vantages for acquiring it. Secondly—if a decisive victory is won, I shall be at hand shd the Govt decide to send a special mission to Sofia or Athens, in order to reap to the fullest extent the fruits of the victory.

Of this you must judge *quickly*, if & when the circumstances arise.

I shall of course be careful to run no unnecessary risks; but it will not be possible for me to appreciate the position without landing on the Gallipoli peninsula & in consequence coming under fire. If any mischance shd occur I consider that my wife shd receive the pension prescribed for a general officer's widow; & I rely on you to see to this.

I am looking forward vy much to this most interesting expedition.

While Churchill's plans went forward, Kitchener was beginning to doubt the wisdom of his going to the Dardanelles unaccompanied. 'I wish you would send Hankey with him,' he wrote to Asquith on July 17; 'I am sure it would be a wise step & very useful to me.' Asquith at once agreed to Kitchener's request. On Sunday July 18 Churchill went to Hoe Farm for a day with his family before leaving. On Monday July 19 he spent his final day in London. Grey sent him a friendly note from the Foreign Office: 'I am so sorry to have been so busy this afternoon. In case I don't see you before you go I send this line to say that all my good wishes & kindest thoughts go with you.' Stamfordham wrote from Windsor Castle that the King was 'glad to hear' of Churchill's mission to the Dardanelles and quite understood that he could not ask for an audience before his departure.

Churchill had reckoned without his new Conservative colleagues. The Cabinet had met on the morning of July 19. When it had ended, Asquith, Kitchener and Grey remained in the Cabinet room, and Churchill said goodbye to them. As he was shaking hands, and being wished good luck, Curzon unexpectedly returned. Where, he asked, was Churchill going, that he needed to be wished good luck? Curzon had to be told; he gave the visit his blessing, but hurried off to inform his fellow Conservative Ministers about it. The visit seemed to them so unwise that Bonar Law informed Asquith that a serious crisis might develop if Churchill went on with it. Confronted by this opposition, Churchill wrote to Asquith that night that he did not feel he could undertake the mission. Hankey would go alone. Asquith replied at once to Churchill:

Private
My dear Winston,

Thanks for your letter. I was under the impression, as I know you were, that your mission was approved with practical unanimity by all our colleagues. I was therefore much surprised (and annoyed) to find last evening that several of them were quite of a contrary opinion. Nor do I think, after what some of them said, that I or others wd succeed in overcoming their objections.

In the circumstances, I think you are right in saying that you would not undertake such a task in the face of any serious division of opinion.

I am *extremely* sorry, believing, as I do, that you would have been able to render a very real service to the Government & the country.

Yours always
HHA

On July 20 Curzon wrote to explain why he had opposed Churchill's departure:

Confid.
My dear Winston,

I would like to be quite above board with you in this as in all things.

Yesterday morning when I learned for the first time that you were going to the Dardanelles on behalf of the Cabinet (who had never been consulted) I gave to you my startled acquiescence in the project. Later in talking it over with several of our colleagues, who knew as little about it as I did, I found that we shared a doubt as to the wisdom of sending out a Cabinet Minister to the scene of war & as to the reception that public opinion might give to such an act, for which the Govt would be held collectively responsible. . . .

Yrs ever
Curzon

On July 21 Kitchener saw Lord Esher, and told him of the Conservative veto. 'He laughed over it a good deal,' Esher wrote in his diary, 'and admitted that he would not have been sorry to get rid of Winston for a while.' Churchill's disappointment was intense. On July 22 he wrote angrily to Balfour about reported aeroplane deficiencies at the Dardanelles, which were, he said, if true, 'very discreditable to the Naval Wing', and showed in his opinion 'a failure on the part of the Air Department to grasp the importance of the aviation service at the Dardanelles and the scale on which they require to be maintained'.

Churchill did not feel confident that Balfour was working at full stretch. He believed that there were better methods of using air power at the Dardanelles than had yet been tried. Without the power to institute action, he thrust his ideas before Balfour with a persistence which annoyed rather than convinced. One idea of which Churchill wrote in his letter of July 22 was for a comprehensive bombing policy:

The field of operations for aircraft in offensive action in the Dardanelles is very wide, and many important objectives are open. It has occurred to me that now that several submarines will be operating in the Marmora it would be easy for seaplanes to fly across from the Gulf of Saros and join the submarines in the Marmora, refill there, and then deliver attacks on Constantinople. The submarines could carry within limits the comparatively small supplies of petrol which seaplanes require, and have appliances to make the simplest repairs in an emergency. We might therefore organise half a dozen seaplanes working in the Marmora in conjunction with our submarines: scouting for them, making bomb attacks on Constantinople, on the munition factories, on bridges, and on the railways supplying Constantinople. There is a reference in the Foreign Office telegrams to the important effect which would be produced by a bomb attack on Constantinople. The 100-lb bombs would be very effective for smashing up railway bridges, and there can be no great quantity of anti-aircraft guns to prevent the machines flying low enough for accurate aim. In the event of a machine breaking down, or having to make a forced landing, the presence of several submarines in the Marmora in touch with the seaplanes would afford safety to the pilots, who could be taken off in the submarines and the seaplanes scuttled in the same way as we have done in the Heligoland Bight on several occasions.

I hope this project will receive your attention and that of your advisers.

At the Dardanelles Committee on July 24 Churchill spoke with bitterness of the failure to reach a clear policy over the future of the Gallipoli campaign:

MR CHURCHILL pointed out that in case the main operation now under preparation did *not* succeed, it was necessary to settle now, *beforehand,* what our course was to be. Were any more troops to be sent? And if so, were the necessary arrangements for their transport being made? On many occasions it was impossible to look beyond the next battle, but contingencies had to be surveyed.

A few moments later he intervened again:

MR CHURCHILL said that to him there seemed a chance of being able to take Constantinople, but that the Turks might have been bringing up reinforcements as well as we. We ought to consider the possibility of making some progress, but of being then checked. Did we mean to take Constantinople? We had the reserves; but if we did not hurry to do so the Germans would before us.

Churchill's questions received no answer. His isolation was complete. It seemed that his chance of controlling a fighting department could never come again. On July 30 he took matters into his own hands, drafting a personal and private telegram which he wished to send to Hankey, who would by then have arrived at the Dardanelles. 'General sh'd not hesitate,' the draft telegram read, 'to ask for more High explosive ammunition in addition to what is now being supplied. . . . More is available here & wd probably be sent overland if he pressed for a larger supply as a precautionary measure.' Kitchener told Balfour that no such exhortation was needed; Hamilton had just been told that three train-loads of guns and ammunition were on their way to him. Masterton-Smith wrote to Edward Marsh later that day: 'Mr Balfour hopes therefore that Winston will agree with him that the proposed message to Hankey is not now necessary.' Churchill held back the telegram. But although Kitchener had agreed to send the ammunition, he did not tell Churchill either when it was sent off, or by what route. Churchill wanted to know, not trusting Kitchener to carry out his promise. On August 2 he wrote to Masterton-Smith, his only contact with Dardanelles policy:

'Your note about the 3 trains of ammunition for Dlles was comforting. But will you please find out if they have really gone or when they are to go. Creedy[18] cd tell you on the telephone, or General Callwell or even Glyn.[19] Probably you know at Admy because of the ship wh meets them. Send me a wire to let me know if it is all right.' On the following day Churchill wrote to his brother:

There are so many 'able men' in this cabinet that it is vy difficult to get anything settled. The parties hold each other in equipoise. The tendency to the negative is vy pronounced. Never mind. They are in the Dardanelles up to their necks now, & you have only to go forward. Afterwards we will talk about it all. I expect this letter will reach you in the midst of events. Well! A battle is a gamble. It cannot be anything else. We must suspend judgement till after the coup. All my heart is with you & your chief. No great offensive in this war ever offered so much to the Allied cause. Never was there a moment when victory wd be sweeter & more timely.

I am soberly hopeful. I think you will have a good superiority: & they have suffered heavily. The losses will no doubt be cruel: but better there when victory will be fruitful than in the profitless slaughter pit of Ypres.

This time last year I was fortunate in getting the Fleet safely into its station; & now I think we ought to have another gleam of sunlight.

It was only three days before Sir Ian Hamilton was to launch a new attack on the Turkish position. Churchill did not believe that

[18] Herbert James Creedy, 1878–    . Entered War Office as a Clerk, 1901. Private Secretary to successive Secretaries of State for War, 1913–20, including Lord Kitchener, August 1914–June 1916, Lloyd George, July–December 1916, and Churchill, January 1919–February 1920. Knighted, 1919. Secretary of the Army Council, 1920–39. Permanent Under-Secretary of State at the War Office, 1924–39. Chairman of the Security Executive, 1943–5.

[19] Ralph George Campbell Glyn, 1885–1960. Lieutenant, Rifle Brigade, 1904. Secretary, Unionist Reorganization Committee, 1911. Employed at the War Office, 1912–14. Captain, on Missions to Serbia and Russia, 1914–15. Liaison Intelligence Officer between the War Office and GHQ France, May–August 1915. Served Gallipoli and Salonika, 1915–16; France, 1917–18. Major, 1918. Conservative MP, 1918–22; 1924–53. Joint Parliamentary Private Secretary to Ramsay MacDonald, 1931–7. Created Baronet, 1934. Created Baron Glyn of Farnborough, 1953.

Balfour was taking all possible steps to ensure that the operation succeeded. On August 3 he wrote again to Masterton-Smith:

I cannot help feeling unhappy about the 12″ Monitors not being at the Dardanelles. The more my mind turns over the situation there, the more I feel that 4 armoured Monitors may prove just not quite enough to pass the forts and dominate the Marmora. There is really no margin for casualties. There must have been a great slowing down in the production of 12″ Monitors, if only 2 are ready now. The department loves to tinker at ships till they are absolutely faultless, forgetting the end in perfecting the means. However, the coup must obviously be played without them now.

On August 5, less than twenty-four hours before the new offensive was to start, Hamilton wrote to Churchill:

My dear Winston,

Standing once more on the brink of the unknown, and about to take a plunge which will be as vital in its consequences as the first landing, I want just to stretch out a hand to one who has been a steadfast patron to this expeditionary force and all that it stands for. Whatever happens; whether we fail or whether we succeed, we have done a big thing. And if, by the help of God, we can carry it one step further then your perspicuity will be vindicated and the world will understand that where the great Achilles once fought and conquered lies the Achilles heel of that horrible German Empire.

All the troops are in good heart, with the possible exception of one Division whose Commander is not the fount of energy and confidence a Commander should be. Still, take it all round, the troops are quite wonderful, and as ready as they were on the first day of landing to storm hostile trenches and redoubts.

. . . We have no castles here or Rolls-Royce motor-cars, or millionaires gratefully pressing exquisite vintages upon their soldier hosts. On the contrary, dust and sand is our portion mixed with flies and French vin ordinaire. . . .

In his postscript Hamilton wrote:

Now is the moment I would have loved you to be here. I am sure you would have done everyone good going down the trenches and cheering up the men. This was my first feeling and is also my last. Between the two phases of thought was a moment when I felt that from your own point of view it was better not seeing the handle your many venomous rivals might manufacture out of the visit—However—there it is!

Churchill was convinced of the need to persevere at Gallipoli; but he was pessimistic about the planning and the outcome. In his letter of August 2 to Masterton-Smith he had recalled the very different circumstances of the previous August:

We were in the middle of it a year ago: & how tremendous it seemed. Now slaughter is commonplace, & destruction has become the order of the day.

I am anxious about the D'Iles, because the delay of 3 weeks taken in making up the mind of the new Cabinet has enabled the Turks to bring up large reinforcements. History will hold a strict account of every days indecision.

# 17

# Unheeded Counsel

Sir Ian Hamilton's renewed attack at the Gallipoli Peninsula was launched on August 6. Its purpose was to capture the ridge of Sari Bair which rises up to nearly a thousand feet in the centre of the Peninsula and holds a dominant position overlooking the Dardanelles. Hamilton hoped that once his troops were astride the ridge they would plunge down to the northern shore of the Dardanelles. The Turks on the Helles front would be cut off. The Navy would be able to renew its assault on the Narrows without fear of artillery opposition from the European shore. None of these benefits came to pass. After six days of savage fighting the Turks still held the commanding heights. Churchill received a detailed account of the battle from his brother. Two days after the landings at Suvla Bay, Jack Churchill had gone ashore with Hankey and Colonel Aspinall[1] in search of Sir Frederick Stopford,[2] who was in charge of that sector. Neither the General nor his Chief-of-

[1] Cecil Faber Aspinall, 1878–1959. Entered Army, 1900. Major, May 1915. Served on Sir Ian Hamilton's Staff at Gallipoli. Chief General Staff Officer during the evacuation of the Peninsula, 1915–16. Chief Staff Officer to the Royal Naval Division in France, 1916–17. Retired with rank of Brigadier-General, 1920. Assumed surname of Aspinall-Oglander, 1927. His official history, *Military Operations Gallipoli,* was published in 2 volumes, 1929 and 1932.

[2] Frederick William Stopford, 1854–1929. Entered Army, 1871. Knighted, 1900. Major-General commanding London District, 1906–9; received no further military command until 1915. Lieutenant-General commanding the IX Corps in the landing at Suvla Bay, 6 August 1915. Relieved of his command, 16 August 1915.

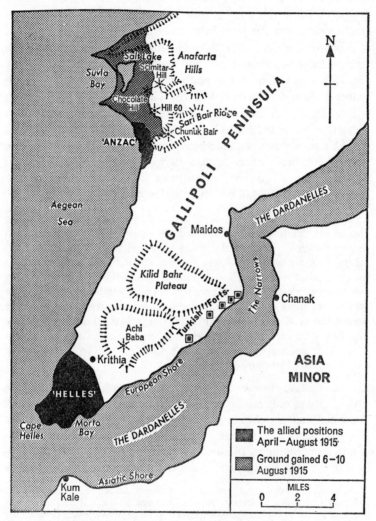

THE MILITARY LANDINGS ON THE GALLIPOLI
PENINSULA, 6–10 AUGUST 1915

Staff, General Reed,[3] had yet been on shore. Throughout August 7 and 8, while the army fought its way across the dry salt lake and towards the Anafarta hills, its senior commanders remained on board ship in Suvla Bay. Having landed successfully, the troops halted. Although at that moment there was hardly any Turkish opposition in the plain or foothills, they had not advanced. Jack Churchill asked the Chief-of-Staff why the men were digging in instead of advancing. 'Reed explained,' Jack Churchill wrote to his brother on August 11, 'that of course troops could not advance without heavy artillery, which could not be landed yet. From where he was—part of the shore was obliterated by the great 14" guns of the monitor & by the cruisers waiting for a target' Jack Churchill had then landed on the plain itself:

There was no musketry anywhere and with the exception of the occasional tick-tok, which reminded me of the advanced guard in S Africa which we used to do; there appeared to be nothing in front of us. In the plain troops were moving about in the open—no shells being fired at them. I talked to one or two regimental officers. They were quite pleased with themselves. They thought there was little in front of them & that an advance would soon take place. . . . We found the GOC 11th div.[4] He seemed apathetic. I understood that the Brigadiers had said that they could not do any more and so on. Everybody seemed to have 'turned it down'. . . . The apathy of the senior officers had spread to the men.

For another twenty-four hours no forward movement was made. It was only on the morning of August 10 that Sir Frederick Stopford and his officers were willing to begin the advance. By then the Turks had taken up positions on all the hills. To the south a small number of allied troops had almost reached the summit of Chunuk Bair. But they did not receive adequate reinforce-

[3] Hamilton Lyster Reed, 1869–1931. Entered Army, 1888. Awarded the Victoria Cross, South African War, 1899–1902. Military Attaché with the Turkish forces in the Balkan War, 1912–13. Brigadier-General, 1914. Senior Staff Officer of the IX Corps at the Dardanelles, 1915. Commanded the 15th (Scottish) Division, 1917–19. Major-General, 1919.

[4] Frederick Hammersley, 1858–1924. Entered Army, 1876. Major-General, 1914. Commanded the 11th Division at the Suvla Bay landing, 6 August 1915. Relieved of his command, 23 August 1915.

ments in time to consolidate their position. Mustafa Kemal, who commanded the Turks on Sari Bair, saw the strategic importance of this summit, and hurled wave after wave of Turkish soldiers against it. By noon the British troops had been driven off by sheer weight of numbers. Jack Churchill wrote:

It has been Spion Kop[5] over again. The same Knob on a ridge—the key of the position taken and held for a short time after terrific fighting. The same lethargy on the plain below. The same fighting on a small narrow front, when a broad advance would have enabled the men at the important point to hold on & make good what they had gained. It is a terrible disappointment. A new advance is being organized. . . . But the splendid surprise has gone and we shall only gain Chunuk Bair again at a terrible cost.

By August 11 it was clear that the attack had failed. Jack Churchill wrote to his brother that day: 'The golden opportunity has gone, and positions that might have been won with a little perspiration would only be gained now by blood.' In his letter, Jack Churchill tried to explain what had gone wrong:

We are all trying to understand what on earth has happened to these men and why they are showing such extraordinary lack of enterprise. They are not cowards—physically they are as fine a body of men as the regular army. I think it is partly on account of their training. They have never seen a shot fired before. For a year they have been soldiers and during that time they have been taught only one thing. Trench warfare. They have been told to dig everywhere and have been led to expect an enemy at 100 yds range. From reading all the stories of the war they have learnt to regard an advance of 100 yards as a matter of the greatest importance. They landed and advanced a mile & thought they had done something wonderful. Then they had no standard to go by—no other troops were there to show them what was right. They seemed not to know what they should do. Was it right to go on so far—might they be cut off or suddenly walk into a trap. Was an occasional bullet only a sniper or was a hidden trench bristling with rifles waiting for them? . . .

[5] A mountain in Natal; on 24 January 1900 the British forces under Sir Redvers Buller were defeated there by the Boers.

The 10th & 11th had nothing to go by. They showed extraordinary ignorance. A shell burst near a working party—at least ½ a mile away. Officers & men stopped work rushed to the low beach cliffs and lay down taking cover! A land mine exploded and the men near all lay flat and remained there thinking they were being shelled! I have just heard that the 53rd are no better. A few shots sent them retreating pell mell from Chocolate hill! Blaming the senior officers must be left to the people who can give effect to their opinions. But there is no doubt that these divisions were completely out of hand.

Jack Churchill reported that as a result of the four days' battle 'all the tricks were lost'; and that Hankey, who had arrived in time to see the battle begin, Hamilton and himself had 'all been going about tearing our hair for the last three days to see such a glorious victory thrown away'. Hamilton was willing to try yet another attack. But, as Jack Churchill wrote, he 'seems to think that it would be dangerous to press them too much at the moment'. On August 12 Jack Churchill added a further page to his letter. 'We still hope to do a lot of good,' he wrote, 'but the chance of a real coup has gone I am afraid.' He was right. Never again were the armies clustering at Helles and Anzac to advance in full force, or to reach any of the objectives which had been set, either for the original landings of April 25 or for the renewed battle of August 6.

On learning of Hamilton's failure, Churchill at once pressed for extra reinforcements to be sent to him. He was convinced that victory could be secured by one further massive effort. At least twenty thousand of the fifty thousand British troops in Egypt, he believed, ought to be sent to Gallipoli for the next offensive. These troops, he wrote to Asquith on August 12, 'could swiftly return the moment the push is over or if an emergency arose in Egypt'. He also believed that 'strong drafts should be sent from here to replace casualties which are, I fear, very heavy'. Churchill had failed to obtain detailed information from Kitchener about what reinforcements were likely to be sent to Gallipoli. 'Kitchener is, I know, doing something in this direction,' he wrote to Asquith, 'how much, I do not know. An enquiry from you would accelerate

and augment the flow, as well as secure the information.' Churchill also pressed Asquith to ensure that three or four train-loads
of ammunition were sent out as quickly as possible to Marseilles,
and thence by sea to the Dardanelles. He ended his letter: 'We
are so near a great victory that nothing humanly possible should
be neglected to secure it.'

Kitchener was as keen as Churchill for a further advance. On
August 14 he wrote to Churchill that he had just learned from
Hamilton that the reason for the failure was that General Stopford and his two Divisional Generals, Hammersley and Mahon,[6]
had done badly. 'It is most annoying,' Kitchener wrote; 'I am taking steps to have these Generals replaced by real fighters as
quickly as possible.[7] Nothing has gone wrong but they have
missed the chance of pushing on & Ian Hamilton says he feels
reluctantly obliged to give them further time for rest and reorganization. It is very disappointing.'

The Dardanelles Committee met on August 19. Kitchener was
absent in France. An acrimonious discussion took place. Bonar
Law declared that Hamilton 'was always *nearly* winning'. When
Churchill pointed out 'the difficulties of the task set him', Grey
remarked tersely 'that we should deal with facts and accept
them'. Asquith said that it 'was not easy to see' why Hamilton
remained confident, despite having lost twenty-three thousand
men. Bonar Law declared 'that a further attack would be a useless sacrifice'; Carson agreed with him. Churchill suggested an
alternative to further attacks, which was 'making a separate peace

[6] Bryan Thomas Mahon, 1862–1930. Entered Army, 1883. Lieutenant-
General, 1912. Knighted, 1912. General Officer commanding the 10th (Irish)
Division, 1914–15. Commanded the Division at the Suvla Bay landing, 6
August 1915. Resigned his command, August 15. Resumed command, Au-
gust 23. Commanded the Salonika Army, 1915–16. Commander-in-Chief,
Ireland, 1916–18. Senator of the Irish Free State, 1922–30.

[7] Sixteen years later, when writing *Military Operations Gallipoli*, Aspinall-
Oglander learned that the Cabinet wished to suppress all critical references
to the Suvla generals. On 23 November 1931 he wrote to Churchill: 'The
truth is that if the generals who failed are whitewashed the blame comes
back (*a*) to you, and (*b*) to the unfortunate troops who, till Stopford & Co
had choked them in a fog of defeatism, were perfectly ready & capable to
do everything required.'

with Turkey'. He proposed that Britain should offer to make
peace on the basis of the Straits being kept open, Turkish independence guaranteed by Britain and the Germans expelled
from Turkey. Grey said the Russians would never agree to such
terms. Later in the discussion Churchill urged that if Hamilton
thought he could still reach the crest of Chunuk Bair, 'he should
be allowed to do it'.

The Dardanelles Committee met again on August 20, after
Kitchener's return from France. The Secretary of State for War
declared that in his opinion Hamilton 'would now be in a position to master the situation'. Discussion turned to the western
front. Kitchener suggested urging upon Joffre the need for an
early offensive, 'as delay was dangerous'. Churchill opposed any
new offensive on the western front:

MR CHURCHILL expressed his regret at such a course. The German
forces on the Western front had not been reduced, and were some
2,000,000 against the Allies 2,500,000. This amounted to a superiority
for the Allies of five to four, which was inadequate for the offensive.
Since our last offensive effort the relative strengths had not altered,
while the German defences had been continually strengthened, and
heavy guns and ammunition had not been correspondingly accumulated by the Allies.

It seemed to him that in the hope of relieving Russia and to gratify
our great and natural desire to do so, the Allies might throw away
200,000 or 300,000 lives and ammunition and might possibly gain a
little ground. The attack of the 9th May (Festubert-Arras) had been a
failure, and the line had not been altered by it. *After* an expenditure
of lives and ammunition in this way by us the Germans would have a
chance worth seizing; and it would be worth their while to bring back
great forces from the East. A superiority of two to one was laid down as
necessary to attack, and we (the Allies) had not got it.

LORD KITCHENER admitted that there was a great deal of truth
in what Mr Churchill had said, but unfortunately we had to make war
as we must, and not as we should like to. There was another point
unconnected with the actual strategy, and that was that trench work
was becoming very irksome to the French troops, and that an offensive was necessary for the *moral* of the French army, amongst the
members of which there was a good deal of discussion about peace.

Once more the fear of a negotiated peace on the part of an ally dictated British war policy. Early in 1915 fears of Russian and French defeatism had been a factor in pressing on with the Dardanelles operation; now they were the stimulus to further frontal attacks against an enemy numerically almost as strong and much more securely dug-in, and to denying to Hamilton the reinforcements which he believed might bring victory on the Gallipoli Peninsula.

On August 21, as Kitchener wished, a further attack was launched towards the high ground dominating the Gallipoli Peninsula. Hamilton had decided to attack in the afternoon so that the infantry could advance with the sun on their backs and the defenders blinded by its glare. But shortly after midday the sun disappeared unexpectedly behind a bank of cloud, and the Turkish positions were hidden by the haze. The preliminary artillery bombardment failed to touch the Turkish front line. At the outset of the advance most battalions lost their officers, and many their guides. The result was confusion. The immediate objectives, Scimitar Hill and Hill 60, were scenes of bitter fighting. Of the 14,300 men who took part in the fighting around Scimitar Hill, over 5,300 were killed or wounded by nightfall. The battle for Hill 60 continued for seven days. Throughout the fighting the crest of the hill remained in Turkish hands. By August 28 it was clear that no further progress could be made. The troops at Anzac and Suvla had exhausted all their energy. No further attack was possible. The Turks remained in complete control of the Sari Bair ridge, and despite their own severe losses, maintained their dominance over the Peninsula.

Writing to Asquith, Kitchener and Balfour on August 21, Churchill had argued that the time had come to look again at the possibility of a renewed naval attack. He begged them to believe that the military operations had failed, and pointed out that Hamilton's army, 'though five times as large as the original force', was in the General's opinion 'inadequate to the essential task'. Churchill feared that 'the possibility of the German Armies overawing Roumania, crushing Servia, and seducing Bulgaria comes nearer every day', and that to maintain a large army on the Gallipoli Peninsula during the winter would be extremely difficult and costly. The naval risks, he argued, would be far smaller:

Even the unfortunate operations of the 18th [March]—foolishly treated as a 'stupendous event'—only entailed to the British the loss of 2 old battleships and about 100 men. The question now arises whether, in view of all the above considerations, the naval operation begun on the 18th March should not be resumed, pressed to a decision, and fought out, as it has never yet been; and in these circumstances it is worth while examining the new facts which have developed in the naval situation.

Churchill stressed three such facts which increased the possibility of a naval success. The first fact was that the Turkish Army on the Gallipoli Peninsula had become so large, and the land route to it so inadequate, that once a squadron of British ships were in the Sea of Marmara 'the Turkish army must either be starved or so reduced that our army can overpower them'. The second fact was that any British squadron which reached the Sea of Marmara would no longer have to be so strong, for the *Beslau* was known to be out of action and the *Goeben* to be in a dilapidated condition. At the same time there were a number of British submarines continually in the Sea of Marmara, making Turkish naval communications with Gallipoli almost impossible, and forcing the Turkish Army to move almost all its stores and men over the land route, which at the Bulair isthmus was largely exposed to naval guns. The third fact was that special naval vessels had been designed by the Admiralty, 'protected against torpedoes by their structure' and so shallow in draught 'that they should be able to pass over the Kephez minefield without danger'. Four of them were ready for action. Churchill then set out in detail how he proposed that the naval operation could take place. 'There is no reason why the losses should be severe,' he concluded. 'But they could not in any case be weighed for a moment against the vast and fatal catastrophe towards which we may be drifting. The risks to be avoided and the prizes to be won, are incomparably greater than the risks and stakes which would be involved. And

before we resign ourselves to the failure of all our hopes, this
effort ought certainly to be made.'

When the Dardanelles Committee met on August 27 Balfour
reported that the Admiralty, 'after a special investigation of the
matter, are adverse to sending monitors or other ships under
existing conditions into the Sea of Marmora'. Kitchener declared
that Hamilton was satisfied that the forty-seven thousand troops
that were being sent to reinforce him were 'sufficient to make it
unnecessary for him to abandon any of his 3 positions [Helles,
Anzac and Suvla] or to contract his lines'. 'For what it was
worth,' Kitchener added, 'the trend of all the reports pointed to
the fact that we should hang on, for the Turks could not last much
longer.' On August 30 Hankey circulated a memorandum to the
members of the Dardanelles Committee reporting on his visit to
the Gallipoli Peninsula, and declaring that in his opinion 'there
is good ground for hoping for another success in the Anzac region'. On the following day he gave the Dardanelles Committee
a verbal report on his visit, reiterating his belief that if Hamilton
were reinforced, a further offensive, and the chance of a victory,
was possible, and that until the offensive, 'we should hang on to
all three landing places'. The Dardanelles Committee met again
on September 3. The discussion ranged over the best means of
helping Hamilton, either by reinforcements or by a further landing, possibly on the Asiatic shore. The French wanted a landing
at Besika Bay. Churchill pressed Kitchener to concentrate on
Gallipoli and 'to discourage, by every means, the prosecution of a
violent offensive in France'. Kitchener replied that such a policy
'would break the Anglo-French alliance'. Lloyd George supported
Churchill with strong remarks, which brought the meeting to a
close:

MR LLOYD GEORGE pointed out that an attempt should be made
at one operation or the other and not at both at the same time. He
thought that we had the men to give our troops a fair chance in the
Dardanelles, but if we frittered away our strength and split them
between two theatres, we ran a great chance of meeting with failure
in both. He thought it was important to persuade the French to post-

pone the offensive in the West, and to send any excess in men and munitions to the Dardanelles, where we already had some superiority.

During early September Churchill began to press his colleagues to make a careful provision for the coming of winter weather at the Dardanelles. In Cabinet he asked Balfour to circulate a report on weather conditions, and Balfour agreed to do so. But when no report was circulated, Churchill was provoked to anger, writing to Balfour on September 5:

Generally, I am very anxious about the provision which is being made for the winter campaign on the Peninsula. The sanitary conditions in the wet weather require extraordinary study and exertion. The trenches and living shelters should have been long ago properly cemented. Good reservoirs should be made, and a complete system of wire-haulage and tramways established. These last are no doubt not your affair, but still I hope they will not be out of your mind.

Neither Balfour nor Kitchener was willing to be influenced by any of Churchill's schemes or anxieties. Since July, Kitchener had been making plans for a further offensive on the western front. On July 6 and 7, at the Anglo-French conference at Calais, the British Ministers present—Asquith, Balfour and Crewe—believed that they had obtained a veto on further attacks in the west in 1915; unknown to them, Kitchener and Joffre had agreed on the necessity of launching a British as well as a French offensive on the western front during September.

Since the middle of August Churchill had been a member of the War Policy Committee of the Cabinet, whose task was to examine Ministers and civil servants in order to report on the need for conscription, and on whether munitions output made conscription possible. Lord Crewe was Chairman of the Committee; Curzon, Austen Chamberlain, Selborne and Arthur Henderson its other members with Churchill. They held twelve meetings. On August 16 they examined Lloyd George, who told them: 'You will not get through without some measure of military compulsion or compulsion for military service. The longer you delay the nearer you will be to disaster. I am certain you cannot get through without it. . . . To send a number of men who are obviously inadequate is just murdering our own countrymen without attaining any purpose at all.'

Churchill had, since June, come to accept Lloyd George's argument, and tried privately to persuade Grey that conscription was needed. But Grey was appalled at the idea, writing to Churchill on August 18:

I cannot understand your passion for uncontrolled Recruiting. It is madness unless I am mad.

The Germans carefully exempt from military service the people necessary to carry on the life of the country: if they had not done so they would have had a break down by now.

We on the other hand recruit without regard to the trades necessary to keep the country alive & even to supply military & naval needs.

There are two possible ways of being beaten in this war: one is to be defeated on land & sea by the enemy: the other is to commit suicide at home. It seems to me that we are heading straight for the latter & quite unnecessarily, for I believe that we cannot in this war be beaten by anybody but ourselves.

Kitchener's frequent denials that compulsory service was needed had been based, not on moral but on military grounds. But Major-General Callwell, Director of Military Operations and Intelligence at the War Office, knew that Kitchener's denials were not based upon the military facts. 'The truth is I am afraid,' Callwell had written to H. A. Gwynne on July 7, 'that K is not letting his colleagues know the state of things, and that he wants to be able to say at the end of the business that he produced an army of so many divisions by the voluntary principle.' The War Policy Committee examined three of Kitchener's subordinates: Major-General Montgomery[8] on August 17, Sir Reginald Brade[9] on August 19 and Callwell on August 20. Each gave assurances that Kitchener's faith in voluntary service was justified by the facts of

[8] Robert Arthur Montgomery, 1848–1931. Entered Royal Artillery, 1868. Major-General, 1902. Commanded the 22nd Division, 1914–15. Director-General of Recruiting, 1915.

[9] Reginald Herbert Brade, 1864–1933. Entered War Office as a Clerk, 1884. Secretary of the War Office and Army Council, 1914–20. Knighted, 1914.

the military situation. Neither Montgomery, Brade nor Callwell felt able to oppose their chief. Callwell had lied to maintain Kitchener's position. He expressed his guilt in a letter, undated, to H. A. Gwynne:

By his opposition to Compulsory service he is antagonising the bulk of the Cabinet and they will, sooner or later, find out the difficulties we are in and the imposture which these 'New Armies' are. We can keep going possibly for a time with three in the field, besides all the old stuff; but after that there must come a collapse it seems to me. . . . At the present moment, when I. Hamilton is far below establishment, we are only dribbling out about half the drafts he requires to make him up to strength, and by the time those are there he is bound to have lost a lot more. In dealing with Cabinet Committees it is very difficult not to expose the business. I am not a good liar— the spirit may be willing but the flesh is weak—and you cannot fool people like Curzon & Winston who know the business. Northcliffe may get hold of the facts because Repington somehow has very useful sources of information, and if he does he may make trouble much more effectually than he did on munitions. K trusts to bluffing them all; but he may not succeed. . . .

On August 24 Kitchener himself appeared before Crewe's Committee. He declared that men could always be obtained by a voluntary appeal. Churchill warned that he might be mistaken:

. . . the time is coming when very heavy taxation will have to be imposed, which will perhaps touch the working classes, and when prices will rise still higher, and when the idea that nobody is to be worse off by the war will long have passed away, and when the war may be very unpopular. A series of unbroken disasters and of very very heavy losses might create a situation such that when you come forward and are ready to stake everything on it, you may find the opposition much greater than it is now, because based upon the general unpopularity of the war.

To this Kitchener replied: 'I do not feel competent to form an opinion on such a subject.'

Lord Crewe reported to Asquith on September 7 that the Committee had been unable to reach a conclusion on the basis of what they had heard. Kitchener and Lloyd George had adopted irreconcilable positions, and their evidence had been contradictory. Churchill, Curzon, Selborne and Chamberlain submitted a dissenting 'Supplementary Memorandum' in which they, a majority of the Committee, declared that 'the times are so grave, and the crisis of our national fortunes so urgent, that it is our duty to set forth in explicit terms . . . the conclusions to which we have come'; these were that conscription was absolutely necessary, and a workable proposition. They quoted Lloyd George's remarks verbatim to prove their point. Asquith took no action on this majority report.

Since joining the Government as Attorney-General, Sir Edward Carson had been appalled by the way in which important war business was conducted. He disliked the casual way in which his colleagues brushed aside carefully prepared arguments, and resented too strong or emotional an appeal on some major war question. Provoked by Kitchener's unwillingness to admit that more troops were needed at Gallipoli to ensure success, and by his refusal to gather together the largest possible number of men available, Carson expressed his anger in a letter to Churchill on September 9. The two men had come into vitriolic conflict on the Irish issue immediately before the outbreak of war. The war itself found them of like mind, and Carson knew that Churchill would be sympathetic:

. . . What I feel so acutely about is that all our calculations (if we can dignify them by that name) are absolutely haphazard—we are always told what we can send & not how many are necessary & this I think leads to minimum calculations so as to get what the general on the spot thinks is the best we can expect—we cannot win on these principles & I feel it criminal to waste insufficient forces simply on the grounds that it is the best we can do under the circumstances.

I have not yet been at any Cabinet when anything was properly or usefully decided ie in such materials as we wd require in deciding the usual questions which arise in ordinary business matters. Nor do I see how it even can be so in a cabinet of 22 meeting for a fixed & definite time & with no plans properly worked out when they are submitted.

Is there no way in which we cd have the whole question of the present system raised? or wd it seem to be a reflection on the PM who has formed the Cabinet? A good war staff working daily at war problems only & submitting to the Cabinet the duty of finding the means is as far as I can see the solution. The Cabinet to be vy small 5 or 6 & sitting daily to consider the problems.

Carson ended his letter on a pessimistic note: 'Personally I look on all our Cabinet Meetings as useless & waste of time & I earnestly wish I could humbly retire.'

Churchill received much news and encouragement from his friends in France. On August 10 Sir John French had written from his Headquarters to say how sorry he was that the Dardanelles visit had not taken place. 'I hope you are coming to see me again some day!' he wrote; 'I often—very often—think of you.' It was exactly three months since Churchill had last visited the western front. During September his thoughts turned to something more challenging than a brief visit to the General Headquarters or a short tour of the trenches. On September 10 he asked Asquith if he could leave the Government and command a Brigade in France. Asquith was sympathetic; he knew how frustrated Churchill felt at the Duchy. But neither of them could overcome Kitchener's hostility. Kitchener did not mind Churchill going on a Cabinet mission to the Dardanelles; he did object to him taking up a permanent post in his own armies. Churchill had therefore to give up the idea, writing to Asquith on September 13: 'I was too much influenced by French who is always so kind to me; & I saw —for a moment—an escape from a situation wh on various grounds public & private I dislike increasingly as the days pass by. Many thanks for the interest which you took in my feelings.'

A senior military command was clearly impossible. Churchill tried instead to arrange for a prolonged visit to the western front. On September 14 he wrote to W. H. Bernau about extra insurance cover. 'I may require to go to France in the near future on the same sort of conditions of liberty as were arranged for my visit to the Dardanelles,' he explained. 'I shd like to pay an extra premium to cover say 15 days actually in the zone of the armies though not serving as a soldier; these days to count as they occur.' Churchill did not give up hopes for some military activity. Kitchener might refuse to give him a senior post. But he could always go out as a major in the Queen's Own Oxfordshire Hussars. 'In the event of my later on in the same year wishing to pay the regular £5.5.0% of full war risk,' he wrote to Bernau, 'I shd like this partial fragment to be counted towards the total. Can this be done?'

That night Churchill dined with Lloyd George and Curzon. His contempt for both Asquith's and Kitchener's direction of war policy was complete. Lloyd George reported the dinner conversation, and his own thoughts, to Frances Stevenson, who recorded in her diary later that week:

They had a most important talk, and Curzon says the Tories are going to approach the PM & say that they cannot proceed any longer under the present state of things. They will demand conscription and the removal of K from the WO, as being incompetent and having failed to grasp the military situation. D [Lloyd George] & Churchill will throw in their lot with Curzon & his followers, for D says he cannot possibly be a party any longer to the shameful mismanagement and slackness. He says that things are simply being allowed to slide, and that it is time someone spoke out. As I said before, however, he hates going against his party, & he fears that the Liberals will hate him violently if he goes against them now. He fears Churchill, too. He is not sure whether Churchill will come too, or whether he will remain & get the PM to put him into D's shoes in the Munitions Office. D says that Churchill is the only man in the Cabinet who has the power to do him harm, and he does not trust him when it comes to a matter of personal interest.

Churchill sensed Lloyd George's distrust. He felt quite friendless in political circles. The trenches seemed to him the only escape. But he did not want his departure for the front line to be interpreted as an escape from criticism of his time as First Lord. He was tired of being the recipient of all the innuendo and odium connected with his wartime months at the Admiralty. On August 10 Josiah Wedgwood had given Churchill the draft of a letter which he had wanted to send to Oliver Locker-Lampson.[10] In his letter Wedgwood described a rumour that was beginning to circulate to the effect 'that Prince Louis of Battenberg did everything that was right & C only what was wrong'. Wedgwood believed that he and Lampson were 'not the only people who are rather "fed up" with this utterly unjust treatment of almost the only man with push enough to be a leader', and had proposed to distribute publicly a memorandum setting out the 'Charge' against Churchill, followed by the 'Facts' of the three cruisers, Antwerp, Coronel and the Dardanelles. For each of the incidents which he mentioned, Wedgwood had written out the facts as he saw them. Churchill kept Wedgwood's proposed letter, and no memorandum was published. Churchill realized that the initiative in any attempt to vindicate him would have to come from the Government. On September 15 he wrote to ask Asquith to publish 'the truth' about Antwerp, the sinking of the three cruisers and the defeat off Coronel:

. . . I am repeatedly made the object of vy serious charges in all these matters, wh have never been contradicted, & seem in some way to be comfirmed by my leaving the Admiralty. Sometimes the charges appear in print . . . but much more are they kept alive by conversation, or by constant references in newspaper articles; & there is no doubt whatever that the belief is widespread that I personally acted in these events wrongfully & foolishly.

You know the facts. I have made them known to some of my colleagues. But that does not help me outside, & I still remain under the shadow of utterly false aspersions wh are a serious injury to me.

For a long time I have been content to do nothing, but I am now convinced that action is necessary. In justice to me, & also I may add to your late Government the truth must be published; & I am determined not to let this session slip away without this being done. I am sure that you wd not wish to treat unfairly one who has been so long yr colleague & friend.

[10] Oliver Stillingfleet Locker-Lampson, 1880–1954. Conservative MP, 1910–45. Lieutenant-Commander, Royal Naval Air Service, December 1914; Commander, July 1915. Commanded the British Armoured Car detachment in Russia, 1916–17. Parliamentary Private Secretary to Austen Chamberlain, 1918–21.

Churchill suggested one of three courses: Parliament could be given a digest of the actual telegrams and minutes; Asquith could give a detailed written answer to a Parliamentary question; or Churchill himself could make a full personal explanation. The Dardanelles presented a particular difficulty, as Churchill explained in his letter.

Here again my only wish is that everything shd be published. These operations are however still proceeding in the same circumstances & on the same ground, & discussion of them might be harmful. There is a clear line of demarcation between past & current operations. It will be all the easier to maintain this line if we show ourselves ready to make a full disclosure of what has happened in the past, & if Parliament sees how good our case is in that respect.

While waiting for Asquith's reply, Churchill received another appeal from Carson on September 19:

Are we going to allow everlasting drift on the policy of the Dardanelles?

I read daily in the dispatches & news the effect which delay & failure is having in Russia & the Balkans & this delay & failure is daily changing the situation & making success more & more difficult. In my opinion we are guilty of criminal folly to the nation in this policy of drift. . . .

Surely outside a Cabinet such delay & want of policy wd not be tolerated in any business.

Now you know I always speak vy plainly—I daresay rudely—but I am going to say that no one is held more responsible for the Dardanelles policy than yrself! Now if the clear policy of certain victory at any cost is adopted by the Cabinet I will back it, but it must be no narrow margins nor estimates framed 'to do the best we can' & for Generals who are only looking to see how far they can please.

I feel every day more inclined to retire altogether, not because of any particular policy but because there is *none*—absolutely *none*, & I feel ashamed when I see the H of C & the country misled about it. . . .

Please do not answer this. I will be in town on Tuesday morning & will see you at another futile Cabinet!

Asquith does not appear to have answered Churchill's letter of September 15. On September 23 Churchill wrote to him again, enclosing 'papers which I have prepared about Cradock and the three cruisers' and urging the publication at least of the Cradock documents, as no secrecy was involved. Over Antwerp, Churchill wrote that as the French Government was involved, and as he regarded their role as rather discreditable, 'I regret that I do not feel able to ask for its publication', although, as he told Asquith, the story of Antwerp was from his point of view '. . . the best of all'. Asquith was unwilling to institute any enquiry about past events. Churchill wanted retrospective vindication. But Kitchener, Grey and the Prime Minister himself still held the positions which they had held then, and any open scrutiny of their actions might lead to loss of public confidence. All Churchill could do, in default of open publication, was to circulate the documents of his Admiralty administration to his Cabinet colleagues as part of his right as a Cabinet Minister. This he proceeded to do. The Conservative Ministers had seen none of these documents before; many of the Liberals had not had access to them at the time. Both had relied upon second-hand reports, or upon the Press, for their information. Churchill proceeded to send them a series of folders. On September 29 he circulated a bulky set of telegrams concerning Antwerp; on October 14 what he described in his covering note as 'the facts about certain episodes of past Admiralty administration which have been the subject of criticism, and with regard to which misconception exists'; on October 29 thirty-three pages of telegrams relating to the Dardanelles; on November 12 a further short set of papers about the Dardanelles, with the pathetic covering note: 'My colleagues may like to have these odd papers for their Gallipoli collection.'

Clementine Churchill had begun war work of her own, helping to set up canteens for munition workers, whom the YMCA provided with cheap meals. She asked her husband to speak at one of her canteens, and he did so, at Enfield Lock, on September 18. It was three months since his previous public speech, at Dundee. He spoke twice, first to the men about to go on the night shift, and then to the men coming off the day shift. Both speeches were reported fully in the national press. Churchill emphasized the many disappointments of the war in the previous months. But of Gallipoli he was confident, 'that we have only to persevere with resolution and unflinching courage, to move forward to a conclusion which, when it is achieved, will repay all the heavy cost and losses we have endured'. He ended his speech with a rousing peroration:

Our situation is a serious one. We have it in our power by our exertions to carry this war to a successful and a decisive conclusion, but we have it in our power to do so only if we exert our strength to the utmost limit of human and national capacity.

After all we did not seek this struggle. We did not desire as a nation, or as a generation, to have imposed upon us this terrible ordeal. We cannot understand the inscrutable purposes which have plunged these evils upon the world, and have involved all the nations of Europe in a catastrophe measureless in its horror. But we know that if in this time of crisis and strain we do our duty, we shall have done all that it is in human power to do—and we shall so bear ourselves in this period —all of us, whatever part we play on the stage of the world's history —we shall bear ourselves so that those who come after us will find amid the signs and scars of this great struggle that the liberties of Europe and of Britain are still intact and inviolate; when those looking back upon our efforts such as they have been, will say of this unhappy but not inglorious generation, placed in a position of extraordinary trial, that it did not fail in the test, and that the torch which it preserved lights the world for us today.

I cannot but express most sincerely my gratitude for all the exertions which are being made, and I earnestly trust you will not flag or slacken in these, so that by your efforts our country may emerge from this period of darkness and peril once more into the sunlight of a peaceful time.

Since the beginning of the war Churchill had been much exercised by the unequal contest between men and machines, to which all his soldier friends bore witness. On 23 September 1914, in a memorandum to Colonel Ollivant and Captain Sueter, he asked for work to be begun on a trench spanning car: it was his first formal proposal for a mechanical device to influence trench warfare. 'It is most important,' he wrote, 'that the motor transport and armed motor-cars should be provided to a certain extent with cars carrying the means of bridging small cuts in the road, and an arrangement of planks capable of bridging a ten- or twelve-feet span quickly and easily should be carried with every ten or twelve machines. A proportion of tools should also be supplied.' Admiral Bacon, at that time Manager of the Coventry Ordnance Works, and a naval gunnery expert, worked on the design. Within two months Bacon had designed a machine such as Churchill envisaged. Unfortunately the bridge device was found unable, after tests at the War Office, to negotiate a double line of trenches, and was abandoned. Colonel Swinton,[11] the War Office Eyewitness at the Headquarters of the British Expeditionary Force in France, had come independently to the same conclusion that Churchill had reached. He too believed that a trench-crossing weapon might be decisive in securing victory for the side which possessed it. Swinton had taken his idea to Hankey, who at the end of December 1914 circulated several members of the Cabinet, including Churchill, with a paper on the need for some trench-crossing mechanical device. As soon as Churchill read Hankey's memorandum he wrote to Asquith, on 5 January 1915, urging him in the strongest possible language to take immediate action:

It would be quite easy in a short time to fit up a number of steam tractors with small armoured shelters, in which men and machine guns could be placed, which would be bullet-proof. Used at night, they would not be affected by artillery fire to any extent. The caterpillar system would enable trenches to be crossed quite easily, and the weight of the machine would destroy all wire entanglements.

Forty or fifty of these engines, prepared secretly and brought into positions at nightfall, could advance quite certainly into the enemy's trenches, smashing away all the obstructions, and sweeping the trenches with their machine-gun fire, and with grenades thrown out

[11] Ernest Dunlop Swinton, 1868–1951. Entered Army, 1888. Assistant-Secretary to the Committee of Imperial Defence, 1913–14, and to the War Council, 1915. Colonel, 1916. Raised Heavy Section, Machine Gun Corps (tanks), 1916–17. Major-General, 1918. Knighted, 1923. Chichele Professor of Military History, Oxford, 1925–39. Colonel Commandant, Royal Tank Corps, 1934–8.

of the top. They would then make so many *points d'appuis* for the British supporting infantry to rush forward and rally on them. They can then move forward to attack the second line of trenches.

Churchill had wanted Asquith to authorize the necessary expenditure to prepare a prototype. 'The cost would be small,' he wrote. 'If the experiment did not answer, what harm would be done? An obvious measure of prudence would have been to have started something like this two months ago. It should certainly be done now.' Asquith sent Churchill's letter to Kitchener, who set in motion a certain amount of design work at the War Office. But this did not satisfy Churchill, who felt that the military authorities were not really convinced either that the machine could be made, or that it would be of much value once it was completed.

In February 1915 Churchill had dined with his friend the Duke of Westminster. Among the guests were some officers of the Armoured Car Division of the Royal Naval Air Service, in which the Duke was then serving. One of these officers, Major Hetherington,[12] who knew something of the experiments which had already been carried on at the War Office, declared his complete conviction, not only that such vehicles could be made but that they would win the war. During the dinner he told Churchill that he believed a very large cross-country armoured car could be designed which could carry guns, and be able to surmount most obstacles. Churchill instructed Hetherington to submit his plans to him. On the following morning he sent for one of his leading ship designers at the Admiralty, Captain Eustace Tennyson D'Eyncourt,[13] and showed him Hetherington's proposals.

[12] Thomas Gerard Hetherington, 1886–1951. Joined Royal Flying Corps on its formation, May 1912. Attached to the Royal Naval Air Service for experimental work, 1914–15. Air Attaché, Washington, 1926–30; Rome, 1931–5.

[13] Eustace Henry William Tennyson-d'Enycourt, 1868–1951. A naval architect, 1898–1912. Director of Naval Construction and Chief Technical Adviser at the Admiralty, 1912–23. Knighted, 1917. Vice-President of the Tank Board, 1918. Managing Director of Armstrong Whitworth's shipyards at Newcastle, 1924–8. Director of the Parsons Marine Steam Turbine Company, 1928–48. Created Baronet, 1930.

Churchill asked D'Eyncourt to go into the question exhaustively, and try to design 'a land ship'. Captain Sueter was also brought into the discussion. Hetherington and Sueter examined the possibility of a caterpillar type of propulsion. To mystify those who might see the designs or early experiments in progress, the new weapons were called 'water carriers for Russia' and it was put about that they were some new method of bringing water forward in large quantities to the troops in the battle area. Colonel Swinton, seeing that they would probably be abbreviated in the War Office to 'WCs for Russia', suggested that they should be called 'tanks'.

The first formal Admiralty conference to discuss the best methods of proceeding with the tank was held on 20 February 1915, in Churchill's bedroom, as he was suffering from a bad attack of influenza. As a result of this meeting a Land Ship Committee was formed with D'Eyncourt as Chairman. It held its first meeting on February 22, and submitted its proposals to Churchill, who accepted their recommendations, minuting on February 24: 'As proposed & with all despatch.' An order for the first tank was placed with Messrs Fosters of Lincoln, a firm of agricultural engineers, one of whose Directors, William Tritton,[14] joined the Land Ship Committee. It was Tritton who suggested using a tractor as the model for the new machine.

By the end of February Churchill, having obtained Asquith's approval for his experimental activities, gave the Committee £70,000 from Admiralty funds to pursue its developments with as much speed as possible. The first designs were submitted to Churchill by the Committee on March 9, and he minuted: 'Press on.' Twelve days later he received a further progress report and a request from D'Eyncourt to proceed with the construction of eighteen separate prototypes. Churchill minuted on March 20: 'Most urgent. Special report to me in case of delay. . . .'

When Balfour succeeded Churchill as First Lord a new mood

[14] William Ashbee Tritton, 1875–1946. Member of the Firm of Tritton, Foster & Co. of Lincoln. Knighted, 1917, for his part in the development of the tank.

descended upon the Admiralty. Churchill described this in a letter to the Royal Commission on War Inventions in 1919:

The new Board of Admiralty included three out of the four naval members of the Old Board. They appear to have viewed the financial commitments which had already been incurred to an extent of about £45,000 either as undesirable or wholly beyond the sphere of Admiralty interests. They, therefore, proposed to terminate the contracts and scrap the whole project.

In his memoirs, *A Shipbuilder's Yarn,* published in 1948, D'Eyncourt recalled how Balfour summoned him and said: 'Have not you and your Department enough to do in looking after the design and construction of ships, without concerning yourself about material for the Army?' But D'Eyncourt did not despair. He went at once to Churchill and warned him of what was about to happen. Churchill immediately appealed directly to Balfour, who agreed to allow experiments to continue.[15] But the enthusiasm which Churchill had imparted to the project was gone. On 23 September 1915 he wrote to Arthur Steel-Maitland,[16] the Under-Secretary of State for the Colonies, expressing his mounting frustration:

[15] In its Report of 17 November 1919, the Royal Commission on War Inventions stated that 'it was primarily due to the receptivity, courage and driving force' of Churchill that the idea of using the tank as an instrument of war 'was converted into a practical shape'. Churchill refused any monetary payment. The Commission granted £1,000 to Swinton, £1,000 to Tennyson d'Eyncourt, and £7,500 to Tritton, as well as making several other payments. Its Report concluded with a note about the claim of Mr L. E. de Mole: '. . . We consider that he is entitled to the greatest credit for having made and reduced to practical shape as far back as the year 1912 a very brilliant invention which anticipated and in some respects surpassed that actually put into use in the year 1916. It was this claimant's misfortune and not his fault that his invention was in advance of his time, and failed to be appreciated and was put aside because the occasion for its use had not then arisen. We regret exceedingly that we are unable to recommend any award to him. . . .'

[16] Arthur Herbert Drummond Ramsay Steel-Maitland, 1876–1935. Conservative MP, 1910–29. Parliamentary Under-Secretary for the Colonies, 1915–17. Created Baronet, 1917. Joint Parliamentary Under-Secretary of State, Foreign Office, and Parliamentary Secretary, Board of Trade, 1917–19. Minister of Labour 1924–9.

My dear Maitland,

I ordered a dozen of these machines as an experiment when I was at the Admiralty—tho' they were no business of mine. I believe that they are *one* way of taking trenches. There are parts of the Dlles terrain in wh they cd be used.

But the effect now of fostering the idea is I fear beyond my present resources. If you want to help you shd study the problem for yourself or ask Captain Hetherington of the RNAS to tell you about it, & then if you are still pleased with the project, you shd try to convince your Chief.

Remember the elephants of Roman times. These are mechanical elephants to break wire & earthwork phalanges.

I am intimately acquainted with the general aspect of the machine. Its merits will be appreciated after the war is over.

Yours vy truly
Winston S. Churchill

'It is odious to me,' Churchill had written to Jack Seely three days before, 'to remain here watching sloth & folly with full knowledge & no occupation.'

The Dardanelles Committee met on September 23. Its members discussed the imminent danger of an Austro-German attack on Serbia, and whether there was anything Britain could do. Lloyd George suggested holding on to Anzac and Helles, but withdrawing from Suvla Bay, and sending the forty-five thousand troops there to Salonika. Britain, he insisted, 'must not make the same mistake that we had always made so far in dealing with the Near East, that is, of being too late with our proposals'. Churchill supported Lloyd George, believing that 'by sending four divisions now rotting at Suvla we might be able to prevent the Austro-German incursion'. But later in the discussion he spoke with bitterness against Lloyd George:

MR CHURCHILL said that both Mr Lloyd George and Mr Bonar Law wished to abandon the Dardanelles, and this was their real aim in the proposal to move four divisions from Suvla Bay. Not to send the promised four French divisions and two British divisions meant throwing up the sponge at the Dardanelles. It would be very hard to explain, particularly in the case of Australia, a sacrifice which had been incurred with no result, and to decide to do so in a hurry would be fatal. There was also to be considered the fate of the troops at the Dardanelles. He inquired if the operations based on Salonica were to take the place of those suggested on the Asiatic side of the Dardanelles.

MR LLOYD GEORGE said that the operation based on Salonica had no point if the Austro-Germans did not attack; and if the Austro-Germans did attack in Europe, what was the good of having troops in Asia? By holding Anzac and Helles we would, on the other hand, keep some of the Turks in occupation.

MR CHURCHILL said that he would not be a party to abandoning the Dardanelles.

On the following day the Dardanelles Committee met again. The six Conservative Ministers present, Lansdowne, Curzon, Bonar Law, Balfour, Selborne and Carson, and the five Liberals, Asquith, Crewe, Churchill, Grey and Lloyd George, with Kitchener's approval, agreed on 'the importance of pushing on arrangements for a winter campaign in the Gallipoli Peninsula'. That day Kitchener telegraphed to Hamilton: 'I need hardly say there is no intention of abandoning Dardanelles.'

The British offensive on the western front, against which the Calais conference in July had seemingly decided, and against which Churchill had warned, began on September 25. The objective was the village of Loos, and the high ground a mile beyond. Within two days, more than fifteen thousand British soldiers had been killed. The Germans lost five thousand. The offensive had failed; the German line was intact.

On September 10 an officer on Sir Ian Hamilton's staff, Captain Dawnay, had arrived in London from the Dardanelles. He was at once asked his opinion about the chances of victory on the Gallipoli Peninsula, not only by Kitchener but also by Churchill and other Ministers. On September 14 Dawnay saw Churchill, recording in his diary that Churchill had said 'that the resources of the Admiralty in small craft, etc—were ample to meet any demands that might be made. He also raised the question of the evacuation of Suvla Bay, and expressed himself as very much averse to the adoption of this measure.' On September 16 Dawnay breakfasted with Steel-Maitland and Bonar Law, recording in his diary that he 'contradicted Bonar Law's pessimism about Suvla and the situation generally'. On September 21 he discussed the military situation with Carson and Churchill at the War Office, recording:

Sir Edward Carson and Mr Churchill pressed the question of the prospects of a renewed offensive. . . .

Mr Churchill pressed the project of an expedition on the Asiatic side of the Straits. By this time, information from French Headquarters had been received, which made it begin to appear improbable that the French would after all undertake an expedition there. Mr Churchill, therefore, proposed to tell the French that if they did not undertake the task we would do so—even to the point of withdrawing a number of divisions from France. His view and that of Sir Edward Carson was that, if done at all, it should be done on the amplest scale. Mr Churchill proposed that 10 divisions should be landed, completely mobile, so as to ensure that the force should be sufficient to sweep aside all possible opposition to a dash on Chanak, in combination with a renewal of our attack on the Sari Bair and towards Maidos.

Callwell, who was present, pointed out the great amount of time that would be needed to land up to 200,000 men on an open beach, but no detailed discussion took place. Dawnay saw Churchill again three days later, when they discussed the new 'Stokes trench Mortar' which Dawnay believed could be effective at Gallipoli. On the following day, September 25, Callwell informed Churchill that Dawnay had seen the Stokes gun in action 'and came back immensely impressed with its capabilities, especially for work in the Dardanelles . . .'. Callwell added that 'there seems to be a good deal of delay about adopting this weapon'. Churchill promised to use his influence to hasten its production, entering into a long and at times acrimonious correspondence with Lloyd George's Parliamentary Secretary at the Ministry of Munitions, Dr Christopher Addison.[17] On September 30 Daw-

[17] Christopher Addison, 1869–1951. Hunterian Professor of Anatomy, 1901. Liberal MP, 1910–22. Parliamentary Secretary to the Board of Education, 1914–15. Parliamentary Secretary, Ministry of Munitions, 1915–16.

nay saw Churchill for the last time before returning to Gallipoli, and recorded in his diary Churchill's bitter comment: 'He said that he thought the operations in Champagne had definitely failed to achieve any vital success, and said that with one quarter of the military effort which has been needed to take the village of Loos, we should have been able to get through the Narrows.' Churchill's belief that the Gallipoli campaign had not yet failed was reinforced by all that Dawnay told him.

On October 1 Churchill lunched with Lloyd George. The comparison between the western and Gallipoli fronts was uppermost in his mind. The editor of the *Manchester Guardian*, C. P. Scott,[18] who was present at the lunch, made a note of their conversation immediately afterwards:

Both very hostile to the policy of attack now being carried out on Western front, any considerable success from which they regard as impossible. The whole of Cabinet had been opposed to it except one man—Kitchener. . . .

Both Lloyd George and Churchill insisted on the far greater possibilities of the Eastern front. As Churchill put it the same effort and expenditure which had given us the village of Loos would have given us Constantinople and the command of the Eastern world. Our policy in the Balkans had been persistently futile. We had missed some six excellent diplomatic chances. Even now we were without a considered policy and merely waiting on events. Bulgaria was obviously only playing for time till the Central powers were ready to attack.

When the lunch was over, Churchill took Scott back to the Duchy of Lancaster Office, where they had a further talk. Scott noted:

---

Minister of Munitions, 1916–17. Minister in Charge of Reconstruction, 1917. President of the Local Government Board, 1919. Minister of Health, 1919–21. Minister without Portfolio, 1921. Labour MP, 1929–31; 1934–5. Minister of Agriculture and Fisheries, 1930–1. Created Baron, 1937; Viscount, 1945. Secretary of State for Commonwealth Relations, 1945–7. Paymaster-General, 1948–9. Lord Privy Seal, 1947–51.

18 Charles Prestwich Scott, 1846–1932. Editor of the *Manchester Guardian*, 1872–1929. Liberal MP, 1895–1906. A friend of Lloyd George, who often sought his advice.

. . . spent an hour with him in going through the confidential papers relating to (1) the loss of the 3 cruisers in the North Sea (2) Cradock's defeat in the Pacific (3) the Antwerp expedition (4) the attack by sea on the Dardanelles. He made out a conclusive case for himself on the first two and a fairly good defence on the other two. At first he offered to let me take away the papers to study, but thought better of it. He is chafing desperately at having virtually no work to do and spoke of perhaps resigning and joining his regiment. He said that so far as his difference with Lord Fisher was concerned the Prime Minister had promised to back him, but when at the same time, in face of the munitions scandal, Lloyd George forced on a coalition Government it was inevitable that he should be sacrificed. He did not complain of that—it was the fortune of war. What he did strongly resent was that he should be held responsible for errors which he had done his best to prevent and he longed for the day when he could publish the whole of the facts.

Since leaving the Admiralty, Churchill had continually pressed upon Balfour the need to accelerate the despatch of Monitors to the Dardanelles. His greatest faith lay in Monitors armed with 14-inch guns, which he believed would be able to force the Narrows without difficulty. While First Lord he had sent de Robeck two 14-inch-gun Monitors, believing that they would exert a decisive influence on the naval campaign. On September 29 Balfour asked Masterton-Smith to send Edward Marsh an extract from a letter he had received from de Robeck, commenting on the Monitors. 'Mr Balfour thinks that Winston should see the enclosed,' Masterton-Smith wrote to Marsh that day. The extract from the letter, which was undated, read:

Each class of monitor has her own particular trouble; 14″, the steering engines are too weak; 9.2″, the exhaust fumes in the funnel; 6″, weakness of decks under the guns; but they are mostly being successfully dealt with by 'Reliance', where Engineer-Captain Humphreys[19] is worth his weight in gold and never makes a difficulty.

We must not expect too much from these monitors, especially the

[19] Henry Humphreys, 1864–1924. Entered Navy, 1884. Engineer-Captain, 1913. Served at the Dardanelles, 1915. Engineer Rear-Admiral, 1918. Knighted, 1919.

14″, which could not navigate the Dardanelles without tugs, so the question of forcing the Narrows with monitors is, I am afraid, for the present not a workable proposition.

This was depressing information, made all the more galling by Churchill's realization that Balfour had no intention of taking him into his confidence, and was content to use de Robeck's letter to increase his sense of isolation.

Churchill could not make up his mind whether to abandon politics or not. Asquith was contemplating setting up a smaller war policy group, and told Churchill that he would try to find a place on it for him. When he wrote to his brother on October 2, he was therefore more optimistic about his power to influence events. 'I am slowly gathering strength & influence in council,' he wrote, 'in spite of the sombre course of your Dardanelles operations. I shall do my best to see you through.' Churchill passed on one complaint which, 'if just', he felt should be put right, 'viz that the General is not enough seen by his troops on the mainland & remains a remote figure on an island'. The war overshadowed all other considerations. 'Alas, the world is getting vy grey,' he ended. 'Courage we shall not fail, but at every cost to this generation & to ourselves will conquer. Also I am sure we shall carry the Dardanelles to ultimate victory. Do not despair whatever happens, or let others do so. I wish I were with you so much. Here with full knowledge & now lots of time on my hands it is damnable. But for the present this is my post.'

There was little Churchill could do in his 'post' but write a series of lengthy memoranda and closely argued letters. On October 4 he sent Asquith a series of 'definite proposals for action' against Turkey through a new zone of attack, based either on Salonika or the Asiatic coast of Turkey. He feared that nothing would be done while Kitchener remained at the War Office, informing Asquith that in his opinion:

1. Kitchener shd command the British armies in France.
2. French shd command the British armies against the Turks.
3. A French General of proved reputation shd command the army operating with the Greeks & Serbians in the Balkan peninsula.

Churchill went on to warn Asquith of the danger of defeat unless new policies were adopted:

The time has clearly come when nothing but bold & drastic changes in persons and broad regroupings of armies in accordance with a coherent & positive plan will save the allies from disaster & probable defeat. We must first make up our own minds & then come to a complete agreement with the French Government. But every day that passes without a policy carries us nearer to a fatal conclusion.

I feel it my duty to write to you upon Lord Kitchener's position from another point of view which is also a vy grave one.

The experiment of putting a great soldier at the head of the War Office in time of war has not been advantageous. In the result we have neither a Minister responsible to Parliament nor a General making a plan. In spite of his splendid qualities wh in their proper sphere wd achieve success, we have suffered most terribly during the war from his control of the War Office. The composition of our new armies, the preparation of munitions, the strategic & professional advice at the disposal of the Cabinet are three salient examples. Nearly all our principal colleagues including those who have joined us from the Conservative party are convinced that the present arrangement is thoroughly bad: and you had yourself determined to change it as long ago as the formation of the Coalition. These are not times when one is at liberty to shrink from most disagreeable tasks, or when vital state policy can be conducted upon what is known to be an unsound foundation by all who are acquainted with the facts. I therefore feel bound, unpleasant though it is, to put my conviction plainly before you—being anxious to do my duty as I see it now. I urge you to revert to the intention you told me of when the new Government was formed and to put Lloyd George at the War Office as Secretary of State with the best & strongest general staff that can be found. [Sir Douglas Haig[20] in spite of his feeble powers of speech is incontestably the most highly educated & intellectually gifted soldier we possess; & he has solid achievements in the field behind him. His science with

[20] Douglas Haig, 1861–1928. Entered the Army, 1885. Knighted, 1909. Chief of Staff, India, 1909–11. Lieutenant-General, 1910. Commander of the 1st Army Corps, 1914–15. His successful defence of Ypres, 19 October–22 November 1914, made him a national figure. Commanded the 1st Army at Loos, November 1915. Succeeded Sir John French as Commander-in-Chief, British Expeditionary Force, 19 December 1915. Field-Marshal, 1917. Created Earl, 1919.

Lloyd George's drive and penetrating insight wd make what] we now
lack altogether—viz an efficient *composite* brain for war direction of
military affairs.

In his draft Churchill then crossed out the passage in square
brackets; later he decided to hold back these final three para-
graphs altogether. His views were expressed with conviction,
but he knew that they would not influence Asquith. He therefore
concentrated upon more practical suggestions, writing to Asquith
again on October 5 proposing four separate possible alternative
attacks which, in the event, as then seemed likely, of Bulgaria
invading Serbia, he believed should be examined and compared
by the General Staff of the War Office:

(i) Entry into action on the left of the Greek Army. Objective: the
Bulgarian Army, Sofia, & the railway communications between
Austria & Turkey. Base Salonica.

(ii) Entry into action on the right of the Greek Army, ie the seaward
flank. Objective: the Bulgarian Army, the Turkish Army in Thrace
& the railway communications between Tirnova & Kuleli-Burgas.
Bases: Salonica & Cavalla, & later Dedeagatch and Enos.

(iii) An operation detached from the Greek Army by direct landings
at Dedeagatch & Enos. Objective: the Turkish Army in Thrace
& the railway communications between Adrianople & Constantinople, & secondarily the land communications in Thrace with the
Bulair Isthmus.

(iv) A landing on the Asiatic shore. Objective: Chanak, or some point
on the Dardanelles, & the Turkish Army in the Gallipoli Peninsula.

Churchill found it galling to be making proposals for war
against Bulgaria. He and Lloyd George had both believed, from
the early days of the war, that of all the Balkan States, Bulgaria
could most easily be brought into the Allied orbit. Such was his
anger at what he regarded as a major failure of British diplomacy
that on October 6 he circulated to the Cabinet a memorandum
which he had written the previous July, insisting upon the need to
win Bulgarian support. 'We must get Bulgaria now,' he had written; 'Bulgaria is strong, her army is ready.' But none of the
territorial offers which Churchill had then outlined in his memorandum to win Bulgaria had been offered, and Bulgaria had

CHURCHILL'S FOUR-POINT PLAN OF ATTACK AGAINST
BULGARIA, 5 OCTOBER 1915

turned to Germany for patronage. Churchill felt that the Bulgarian failure was but a single example of overall neglect. In a bitter covering note he lashed out at the Government for its inept war policy:

The enclosed memorandum was written by me in the middle of July. I showed it to Curzon and Mr Lloyd George; but did not circulate it generally, because I felt it would be useless then to add to the views I had already expressed in Council. Since then, from the 6th to 9th August, the battle in Gallipoli has been fought without success. This battle could have been fought a month earlier if the decisions ultimately come to had been taken in time. The loss of a month enabled at least five fresh Turkish divisions to reach the Peninsula, and thus our reinforcements were countervailed before they arrived. On the 12th August Sir Ian Hamilton reported the failure of his attempt and asked for large reinforcements, and for drafts to raise his units to full strength. It is now the 6th October.

Nearly three months have passed since the plan of sending Allied troops to the Vardar [i.e. to Salonika] was favourably entertained by the Cabinet. But the four Powers were still corresponding on the point when the Bulgarian mobilisation occurred. Every suggestion made by any one of them has been pulled to pieces by the others; and the obvious remedy for this state of things, viz., that we should send a person of the highest consequence as an envoy to the Balkans—so often urged—was never adopted.

In July we were assured that the Germans were about to begin a great offensive in the west, and were actually concentrating large armies for that purpose in the neighbourhood of Cologne. So far from this being true, it is we who have taken the offensive. The wise decisions of the Calais conference were thrown to the winds by the generals. Our action in the Balkans and at Gallipoli has been paralysed at the very moment when it was most urgent and would have been most fruitful. It will soon be possible to measure what we have gained instead in France, and what those gains have cost in life and limb.

When the new Government was formed the belief was widely held that some form of national service would be introduced. More than 4½ months have passed and the Cabinet has never yet ventured to discuss the subject. During the last two months our losses have greatly exceeded our recruiting, and the total of the British armies instead of growing has already begun rapidly to dwindle.

My object in now circulating this paper is not to make reproaches nor to boast superior foresight, but to implore my colleagues to rouse themselves to effective and energetic action before it is too late.

In a further memorandum written on October 6, entitled 'Gallipoli', Churchill tried to put his colleagues' minds at rest about reports of growing Turkish ammunition supplies reaching the Dardanelles. He believed that these reports were exaggerated, and that it was well within the Army's powers to deal with an increased artillery bombardment. He was particularly scathing at how little had been done on the Peninsula to meet such a contingency: 'Had the Germans held the positions we have been holding for all these months, a system of subterranean habitations, lighted by electric light, lined with concrete, and properly warmed and drained, would have been in existence.' Churchill believed that the prospects at Gallipoli were still hopeful, that the artillery danger was less than in the Ypres salient, 'where positions subject to every military vice . . . have been held month after month in spite of the fire of batteries incomparably heavier and more numerous, and far more abundantly supplied with ammunition . . .'. He felt that the artillery danger would be reduced by the use of smoke screens, and that, as the rains came, greater efforts should be made to trap and conserve the water. Churchill did not prejudge the question of evacuation: 'Whether it is desirable to leave an army of these dimensions indefinitely to waste by fire and sickness on the Gallipoli Peninsula, without hope of an offensive or any plan to relieve it, is another question. But if it is decided to take that course, there is no reason at the present time to doubt our ability to maintain ourselves, in spite of losses, for an almost indefinite period.' Churchill ended his argument by warning against allowing the artillery threat to dictate a premature policy of withdrawal:

When dangers are a long way off and it is desired to emphasise the need for immediate action, one is often led to speak of those dangers in exaggerated and too sweeping terms. For instance, the approach of the submarine was regarded by me with the utmost dread, and I had even gone so far as to write that their arrival would be fatal. In fact, however, when the danger came, it was successfully grappled with by the Admiralty and reduced to its proper dimensions. The landing and supply of far larger armies on the Gallipoli Peninsula has been successfully accomplished since the arrival of the German submarines than we had ever attempted beforehand. Our own resources grew with the resources of the enemy, and the warfare in this theatre gets more thoroughly understood. We must not be in a hurry to yield to the prospect of dangers and difficulties which, when stoutly confronted, will not be found to contain any decisive element.

In his third letter to Asquith in three days, Churchill suggested on October 6 that he and Lloyd George should be appointed as a special sub-committee of the Committee of Imperial Defence, with Hankey as their secretary, to report to the Dardanelles Committee about the whole future of the Gallipoli operation. He feared that the War Office was neglecting its duty to the troops on the Peninsula. 'Kitchener is far too busy to make a special study of these things,' he wrote. 'Subordinates do not know what data to work on nor what weight to assign to each part of them. I believe LG is seeking the truth on this point, & although we approach it from different poles, I think we cd together thrash it out thoroughly. You cannot do this in the War Council. What is required is the patient canvassing & study of the whole case as presented by the soldiers, by 2 of us.' Churchill asked Asquith to propose this arrangement when the Dardanelles Committee met on October 7. But Asquith refused to support it.

Churchill's desire to see a renewed naval attack had been stimulated by a letter which his brother-in-law, William Hozier[21] had sent him from Mudros on September 21. Hozier reported that 'it is the opinion of some senior officers here that a well organized attempt would meet with success in forcing the narrows'. Hozier then outlined a possible plan of attack, whereby 'the Bosphorus would be forced and a junction made with the Russian Fleet & Constantinople raised to the ground by half a dozen ships left for that purpose'. He argued that 'things so far have been half done & have therefore failed'. A renewed attempt, he declared, 'would be gladly welcomed out here. There is a feeling of despair at present owing to our helpless inactivity.'

On October 6 Churchill wrote to Balfour pleading for an examination of the possibility of a renewed naval attack, and telling him not to give too much weight to de Robeck's hesitations:

. . . You should not overlook the fact that Admiral de Robeck is deeply committed against this by what has taken place, and his resolu-

---

[21] William Ogilvy Hozier, 1888–1921. Clementine Churchill's brother. Entered Navy, 1904. Lieutenant, 1909. Commanded the Torpedo Boat Destroyers *Thorn*, 1914–15, and *Nubian*, 1915. 1st Lieutenant on board the Cruiser *Edgar*, 1915–16. Commanded the *Clematis*, 1916–18. Lieutenant-Commander, 1917.

tion and courage which in other matters are beyond dispute, are in this case prejudiced by the line he has taken since the beginning. Could he have foreseen after the 18th the terrible course and vast expansion of the military operations, it is inconceivable that we would not have renewed the attack. But in those days the loss of four or five thousand men was the most expected and a swift victory was counted upon. Since then probably 150 thousand French and British troops have been killed or wounded on the Peninsula. The Admiral is therefore in a very difficult position. The naval attack is admittedly a great hazard. If it fails there is a heavy loss; if it succeeds he would be stultified. Is it not natural that in these circumstances his opposition to it should be deep-seated?

The Cabinet met that day. The discussion was dominated by Gallipoli. After heated arguments, Asquith agreed to set up a committee of naval and military experts[22] to examine, as a matter of extreme urgency, the respective merits of the western and Gallipoli fronts. The Committee sat throughout the weekend, and on Monday October 9 circulated its conclusion to the Cabinet, recommending that all military effort should be concentrated on the western front. On that same Monday, events in the Balkans made this conclusion worthless. German and Austrian forces crossed the Danube and entered Belgrade. Serbia's days of independence seemed numbered. Two days later the Bulgarians abandoned their neutrality and mobilized their army on Serbia's eastern border. On October 11, the day of Bulgarian mobilization, the Dardanelles Committee met at 10 Downing Street. Bulgaria's action destroyed any lingering hopes that the unified Balkan States could be persuaded to join the Allied cause. With Bulgaria committed to the Central Powers, Turkey had little to fear of a stab in the back in Thrace or on the Gallipoli Peninsula. Greece had every reason to refuse to succumb to Allied blandishments. Rumania, flanked on all but her northern border by hostile powers, had even greater cause to cling to her neutrality. At the Dardanelles Committee Carson asked scathingly

---

[22] The Committee consisted of members of the Admiralty and War Office Staffs headed by the First Sea Lord, Sir Henry Jackson, and the Director of Military Operations and Intelligence, Major-General Callwell.

what the British forces were now supposed to do at Gallipoli:
'Was it to hold on and to prepare to resist the Bulgarians, Germans and Turks?' Grey suggested that whatever happened,
Gallipoli must be evacuated: 'One way was to advance and carry
the Peninsula, and then having saved our prestige, we might
withdraw without danger. The second way was to evacuate the
Peninsula whatever the cost.' Churchill asked 'whether we had
the force' to capture the Gallipoli Peninsula; if not, he too favoured evacuation. But Kitchener was appalled at the thought
of leaving the Gallipoli Peninsula:

LORD KITCHENER said . . . that abandonment would be the most
disastrous event in the history of the Empire. We should lose about
25,000 men and many guns. He thought also that Egypt would not
stand long. The troops along the canal would not be able to hold on;
the Western borders were open to attack anywhere. He considered
that the dangers of abandonment were, therefore, very grave, but he
would like to liquidate the situation.

Carson wanted troops to be sent at once to help Serbia. Curzon
was also anxious to help the Serbs, hoping that a rapid British
decision might even then cause the Bulgarians to hesitate in
their advance. The strongest plea for Serbia came from Lloyd
George:

MR LLOYD GEORGE . . . wanted to know why the Roumanians
and Greeks had hesitated so far. He thought it was the reputation we
had gained for neglecting our Allies and friends. It was only necessary
to look at Belgium, whose safety we had guaranteed, lying trampled
on in the mud, and it seemed as if Serbia would be treated in the
same way. He thought that if Great Britain abandoned Serbia, the
whole of the East would point to the way she abandoned her friends,
and that Germany was the country to be followed. He did not think
that people who thought and said these things were to blame. It was
a question of self-preservation for them. It seemed to him a very serious thing to abandon Serbia; it also seemed that it would be a great
disaster to withdraw from Gallipoli, but at the same time if we made
another effort there which failed, it would double the number of men
we might lose.

The question turned upon how long it would take to send British troops to Salonika. Lloyd George spoke with passion that 'we had always been two or three weeks late for everything. . . . He thought that the Germans would have reached Gallipoli by the third week in November.' When Asquith pointed out that the Germans, too, might be late, Lloyd George replied, 'that it so happened that the Germans were not often late'.[23] Churchill said little during the long and acrimonious discussion which proceeded between Lloyd George and the Prime Minister. Curzon suggested a third alternative to the Salonika or Gallipoli plans, that Britain might 'come to terms' with the Turks'. He thought that despite the British promise of Constantinople to Russia, 'we might guarantee the Young Turk Party the retention' of their capital. Curzon reminded his colleagues that the immense sacrifice made by the British on the Gallipoli Peninsula had been made 'partly on Russia's account' but that they had now come to such a stage 'that it was unavoidable that we should endeavour to make some arrangement with the Turks'. The discussion then veered away from the question of peace to the question of reinforcements. Towards the end of the discussion Churchill tried to focus his colleagues' attention upon the three points which he felt needed urgent decisions:

1. Whether to send an army to Salonica to help the Serbians.
2. Whether to send a force to Gallipoli.
3. Whether to abandon the whole proposition in Gallipoli.

Asquith, declaring that he 'was of an open mind', told his colleagues that two of these proposals seemed 'out of the question': to abandon Gallipoli, and to throw a body of troops into Serbia. The only conclusion that the Dardanelles Committee was able to

[23] Two months after this outburst, speaking in the House of Commons on 20 December 1915, Lloyd George repeated this theme of 'too late' with great effect: 'Too late in moving here!' he declared. 'Too late in arriving there! Too late in coming to this decision! Too late in starting with enterprises! Too late in preparing! In this war the footsteps of the Allied forces have been dogged by the mocking spectre of "Too Late"; and unless we quicken our movements damnation will fall on the sacred cause for which so much gallant blood has flowed. I beg employers and workmen not to have "Too Late" inscribed upon the portals of their workshops!'

reach was that 'a specially selected General' should proceed without delay to the Near East 'to consider and report as to which particular sphere and with what particular objective, we should direct our attention'. Lloyd George felt that Churchill had used unfair pressures to influence Asquith in favour of remaining on the Gallipoli Peninsula. 'He is sick with Churchill,' Frances Stevenson wrote in her diary that night, 'who will not acknowledge the futility of the Dardanelles campaign. He (Churchill) prevents the Prime Minister from facing the facts, too, by reminding him that he too is implicated in the campaign, & tells him that if the thing is acknowledged to be a failure, he (the PM) as well as Churchill will be blamed.'

On the following day Lloyd George told Frances Stevenson of a further attempt, in which he believed Churchill was implicated, to influence the Gallipoli policy by unfair means. The Dardanelles Committee of October 11 had been circulated a War Office General Staff memorandum which advocated sending a further 150,000 men to Gallipoli. But Frances Stevenson recorded in her diary on October 12 that 'Carson was told by a member of the General Staff that this plan was not approved by them, that it was not in the memorandum and that it must therefore have been inserted by the Prime Minister at the instigation of Churchill'.

Lord Esher recorded in his diary on the same day another version of the same story:

Last night, Lloyd George and Winston swooped down on Lord K with a telegram to Greece and Rumania that they were very anxious to send. The gist of the telegram was this, that if they would come in on the side of the Allies, we would send at once 150,000 men to Salonika. They then added the interesting information that we are giving 500,000 rifles to Russia, and that the Russians will be ready immediately to attack the Bulgarians. Lord K was tired, and would not struggle with them. They then went on to Asquith, and obtained his sanction.

Churchill persevered in the inconclusive daily discussions, in which he could only advise on policy, not initiate it. He believed that if he could argue clearly in favour of a particular course of action, his colleagues might be convinced. But throughout this period there were those who advised him to leave the Government. 'If you can not see your way clear to help the country in the capacity of a minister,' Frederick Guest had written to him on July 21, 'why not leave the Government and become its saviour as a free lance and a powerful patriot critic?' On October 10 Guest wrote again, asking him to consider four points that Lord Rothermere[24] had put to him on the telephone that morning:

1. That some sort of a collapse or fall of the Government will take place this week and that you will not only go down with it but will be irretrievably out of future business—
2. That you will be made the scapegoat for the failure of foreign diplomacy by being saddled with the Dardanelles from which (they will still say) all our Eastern troubles have come.—
3. That you have only 2 or 3 days in which to clear your self of all the misrepresentation that has been showered upon you—
4. That if you do so now & leave the Government on grounds of general mushiness & want of confidence in the War Office, that in less than 6 months you may be at the head of the state.

Guest believed that Rothermere's brother, Lord Northcliffe, shared these alarmist views. His letter continued:

It is not too late to break away now as the ship is not sinking actually—only it has a heavy list. Later on when things get much worse you perhaps could not do it—

I dont know why he thinks a collapse inevitable—He must know something to have rung me up here this morning.

To my mind the whole thing is pitiable, every body knows but no one will say & so I fear it will go on to the end. How unfair it is on all those gallant, trusting, men who hold the trenches and assault impossible places, that so much should be rotten behind them at home; and

[24] Harold Sidney Harmsworth, 1868–1940. Younger brother of Lord Northcliffe, with whom he had helped to establish the *Daily Mail* and *Evening News*. Created Baronet, 1912. Proprietor of the *Daily Mirror*, 1914. Created Baron Rothermere, 1914. Launched the *Sunday Pictorial*, 1915. Director-General of the Royal Army Clothing Factory, 1916. President of the Air Council, 1917–18. Created Viscount, 1919.

how uncomfortable must or should be the conscience of anyone who knows it & has the power to remedy & yet does not do so.!

Truth is indestructible & always wins eventually, nothing else matters now.

Churchill rejected this advice. He knew that Asquith was in no serious danger, and still hoped to influence the Cabinet from within.

Early on the morning of October 14 Bulgarian troops crossed into Serbia, advancing rapidly. When the Dardanelles Committee met at 10 Downing Street that day it discussed at length what Britain's reaction should be. The former British Military Attaché at Sofia, Colonel Napier,[25] proposed a landing of British troops at the Turkish port of Enos, from which they might, after by-passing the Turks, attack Bulgaria, a plan similar to one of those which Churchill had suggested to Asquith nine days before. Grey declared that in the Foreign Office's opinion, 'we were entitled to commence hostilities' against Bulgaria. Sir Henry Jackson, who had succeeded Fisher as First Sea Lord at the end of May, proposed a direct bombardment of the Bulgarian port of Dedeagatch. Kitchener stated that such a bombardment 'might be of some value'. Bonar Law felt we should bombard the Bulgarian port 'at once and show definitely that we were at war'. But Balfour said that he would prefer to let Russia take the lead against Bulgaria. Kitchener then proposed simultaneous action by Russia against Varna and by the British against Dedeagatch. No decision was reached.

Churchill only entered the Committee's discussion when Asquith raised the question of recalling Sir Ian Hamilton on the grounds that he 'had lost the confidence of the troops under him'. In a letter to Curzon on October 2 Churchill had opposed Hamilton's recall on the grounds that the failures at Gallipoli had been largely due to the 'unnecessary delays in supplying him with rein-

[25] Henry Dundas Napier, 1864–1941. Entered Army, 1884. Military Attaché, Sofia and Belgrade, 1908–11. Lieutenant-Colonel, 1912. Military Attaché, Sofia, 1914; Bucharest, 1915. Captured by a German submarine in the Adriatic, 1915. Prisoner of war in Austria, 1915–16. Military Representative, Sofia, 1918.

forcements . . . the failure to keep his units up to their proper strength by the supply of drafts, the poor quality of the troops sent him, the lack of any proper proportion of regular troops, and lastly, the character of the subordinate Generals'. But by October 14 these considerations had been set aside, and no Minister was willing to insist that Hamilton be retained in his command. Churchill acknowledged that Hamilton had lost the confidence of his men, but intervened briefly on his friend's behalf:

MR CHURCHILL said that it must not be forgotten what appalling difficulties Sir I. Hamilton had had to contend with, in the task of landing a small army and maintaining himself in the face of the growing strength of the enemy. Though he had failed to retain confidence, he had never failed to plan the *coup* and to attempt what was demanded of him. The failure was partly due to inexperienced officers, to the fact that he had under him only one Regular division, and that he had been prevailed upon by his staff to keep aloof. He had made most strenuous efforts and Mr Churchill trusted that his recall would be effected without casting a slur on him.

It was decided to recall Hamilton from the Dardanelles. On October 16 he received his orders to return to England. He left the Dardanelles on the following day, handing over his command temporarily to Birdwood until his successor, Sir Charles Monro,[26] reached Mudros on October 28.

The discussion at the Dardanelles Committee of October 14 returned to the repeated question of what should be the next military development on the Gallipoli Peninsula. Churchill accused Kitchener of having done 'practically nothing' to send out the troops which the Dardanelles Committee had agreed to send. Kitchener protested 'that no time had been lost and that everything had been done except the actual despatch of troops'. He defended himself by explaining that he had 'asked Sir J. French

[26] Charles Carmichael Monro, 1860–1929. Entered Army, 1879. Lieutenant-General commanding the Third Army in France, 1915. Knighted, 1915. Commanded the Mediterranean Expeditionary Force, October 1915 to January 1916. Commanded the First Army in France, 1916. Commander-in-Chief, India, 1916–20. Created Baronet, 1921. Governor and Commander-in-Chief, Gibraltar, 1923–8.

to send off six divisions and two Indian divisions as soon as possible, and had asked General Joffre to take over the extent of
line now held by the two southern British divisions as soon as
his offensive was over. There had been no delay.'

Later in the discussion Churchill told his colleagues that 'he
personally would not for a moment shrink from the evacuation
of Gallipoli if he was certain that everything else had been tried'.
Lloyd George believed that everything had been tried. 'The no-
tion that we are satisfying the needs of this critical situation by
making another attack on the Gallipoli Peninsula is, to my mind,'
he wrote in a memorandum that evening, 'an insane one. We
have failed repeatedly when the Turks were short of ammunition. Are we now to succeed when they are reinforced with heavy
German guns and abundance of ammunition? It is by no means
improbable that the Turks, thus re-equipped, might drive us into
the sea before reinforcement ever reached our army on that
Peninsula.' Churchill could not make up his mind as to whether
Lloyd George's argument was entirely valid. On the following
day, October 15, he drafted a lengthy memorandum dealing with
the whole question of evacuation, pleading for a decision one
way or the other:

Nothing leads more surely to disaster than that a military plan
should be pursued with crippled steps and in a lukewarm spirit in the
face of continual nagging within the executive circle. United ought
not to mean that a number of gentlemen are willing to sit together on
condition either that the evil day of decision is postponed, or that not
more than a half-decision should be provisionally adopted. Even in
politics such methods are unhealthy. In war they are a crime.

There is no disgrace in honest and loyal decisions, however the
incalculable event may subsequently fall. Even withdrawals and capit-
ulations if they are necessary should not be flinched from. But there
would be enduring shame in impeding a decision, in hampering military action when it is decided on, in denying a fair chance to a war-
like enterprise to which the troops have been committed, or in so
acting, even unconsciously and unintentionally, that an executive
stalemate is maintained until disaster supervenes.

Every war decision must be forced to a clear-cut issue, and no

thought of personal friendship or political unity can find any place
in such a process. The soldiers who are ordered to their deaths have a
right to a plan, as well as a cause.

I have done my utmost to co-operate with those who seek to bring
effective aid to Serbia, and I believe that the gaining of Greece and
Roumania to our side now is a more urgent and a more important
objective than forcing the Dardanelles—would indeed, if attained,
carry the Dardanelles with it. But whether this plan will succeed will
be settled in a few days. Then we must make up our minds one way
or the other about Gallipoli, without compromise of any kind.

Churchill's instinct remained in favour of continuing the attack
at Gallipoli. He was concerned about the effect of withdrawal
upon Russian morale, and Russia's ability to continue the war.
'The one great prize and reward which Russia can gain,' he
wrote, 'is Constantinople. The surest means of re-equipping her,
the one way of encouraging her efforts, is the opening of the
Dardanelles and the Bosphorus. With the evacuation of the Gallipoli Peninsula that hope dies.' Churchill decided not to circulate this memorandum to his Cabinet colleagues. He knew that
support for remaining at Gallipoli was waning. But in an attempt
to influence one Liberal newspaper, the *Westminster Gazette*,
he sent his memorandum to its editor, J. A. Spender.[27] But
Spender was unimpressed, replying on October 18: 'The main
point is that we failed with the August offensive . . . the war
will be ended by killing Germans & in no other way.'

On October 20 Churchill circulated a further memorandum to
the Dardanelles Committee pointing out that large German installations of poison gas had arrived at Constantinople. It was a
matter of urgency, he wrote, 'to send out a complete new outfit
of the latest [gas] helmets' to Gallipoli. He also argued in favour
of the Allies themselves using poison gas against the Turks, a
policy which had been opposed at the Dardanelles Committee
on the grounds that the Turks, being Muslims, would find this
method of warfare repellent. Churchill drew no distinction between Christians and Muslims. In his memorandum, he gave his

[27] John Alfred Spender, 1862–1942. Editor of the *Westminster Gazette*,
1896–1922.

reasons for wanting to extend the practice of the western front
to Gallipoli.

I trust that the unreasonable prejudice against the use by us of gas
upon the Turks will now cease. The massacres by the Turks of Arme-
nians and the fact that practically no British prisoners have been taken
on the Peninsula, though there are many thousands of missing, should
surely remove all false sentiment on this point, indulged in as it is only
at the expense of our own men. Large installations of British gas
should be sent out without delay. The winter season is frequently
marked by south-westerly gales, which would afford a perfect opportunity for the employment of gas by us.

During October Kitchener became the object of a sustained
attack by those Ministers who were outraged at his apparent
neglect of military policy, both at Gallipoli and on the western
front. Conscription became the issue on which his opponents decided to challenge him. Kitchener had declared himself entirely
opposed to any system of compulsion. His recruiting policy had
relied for over a year on the personal appeal to the patriotic
conscience of every able-bodied man with posters insisting: 'Your
country needs YOU.' When the Cabinet had met on October 12,
Kitchener had defended the adequacy of voluntary recruitment.
Five Ministers had argued that the voluntary system was inadequate: Lansdowne, Curzon, Lloyd George, Walter Long and
Churchill. 'Very odd position,' Hankey wrote in his diary after
the Cabinet meeting, 'Churchill, Curzon, Selborne & the other
conscriptionists, who have for a long time been attacking Lord
K, are now basing a tremendous National Service push in the
Cabinet on a Memo of Lord K's.' This memorandum was a survey
by Kitchener of military needs, which he claimed proved his
case, and which the advocates of conscription were convinced
sustained theirs. On October 15 Margot Asquith wrote to Hankey
warning him against a 'plot' led by Lloyd George, Churchill and
Curzon:

Dearest Col Hankey,
    Does Arthur Balfour realize what is happening? It is clear as day
that LlG, Curzon & Winston are going to try & wreck the Gov.

. . . *Inside* we know LlG, Winston & Curzon—outside the same lot led by Northcliffe who loathes our Lib Gov—are they to break the Coalition? ?

Do be brave & go & see Balfour. Directly you get this & just say to him: 'You've read LlG's, & Winston's, & K's memorandums, it must be clear to you that things are rocking—if you don't support the PM & stand close to Grey, Crewe & the PM you play into the hands of LlG & Co.'

You are the only person who can do this—you shd also see K or Fitz-Gerald on this subject. . . .

Yours affectionately
MA

Three days later Margot Asquith wrote direct to Kitchener:

. . . Remember you, Henry, Grey, Crewe, Arthur Balfour, McKenna & Runciman can beat Curzon, F. E. Smith, Winston & Ll George if you show courage & above all do it at once. Get hold of them & talk it all out.

This is what I hear Curzon is going to do. He is going to bring it before the Cabinet backed by Ll George & Winston (the country campaign paid for & organised by Northcliffe). If the Cabinet go against them they threaten to resign. Now there is only one thing to do which is to make it quite clear to *everyone* what you & the Prime Minister wish over the question of conscription. If you wish it then LlG, Curzon & Co will have triumphed, it is for you to say to my husband 'There is no need in *my* mind for conscription now everything possible is being done & I will back you'. . . .

The Ministers who were challenging Kitchener's authority did so because they believed that he was no longer fit to hold a responsible position at the centre of Government policy. His secretiveness appalled them. Often, at meetings of the Dardanelles Committee, he took up contradictory positions almost simultaneously. He had a tendency of ascribing to his Generals opinions which they did not always hold. He was often reluctant to divulge important statistics, without which the Dardanelles Committee could not possibly form a clear opinion. He did not always seem to consult, or fully to understand, the telegrams

which were arriving from the western and Gallipoli fronts. At the
Cabinet meeting immediately after the German and Austrian
armies had invaded Serbia, several Ministers had asked Kitchener
whether the attacking force had actually crossed the Danube.
Kitchener said that he had received no news. But when Asquith's
secretary telephoned the War Office to ask if news had been
received since Kitchener had left for the Cabinet, it emerged that
the War Office had learned twenty hours previously that the
Danube had been crossed. Carson wrote to Lloyd George across
the Cabinet table: 'K does not read the telegrams—& we don't
see them—it's intolerable.'

On October 12 Carson resigned, angered by Britain's failure
to help Serbia, and convinced that Kitchener's tenure of the War
Office was leading to disaster. But Carson's resignation did not
precipitate the Government's collapse, nor were the conscriptionists able to use his resignation as a lever against Asquith. On
October 5 Asquith had appointed Lord Derby[28] as Director of
Recruiting, with instructions to find an alternative to compulsory
service, and Derby's plan was ready by October 15. It completely
undermined the position adopted by those who were trying to
use Kitchener's faith in voluntary recruiting as a means of ousting
him. Under the Derby scheme every man between the age of
eighteen and forty-one was asked to 'attest'; that is, to pledge
himself to volunteer when his 'class' was called for. There were
two classes, single and married men, each class subdivided into
twenty-three age groups. Kitchener believed that as a result of
this scheme, the voluntary system which he so prized could be
preserved, and would provide sufficient men to meet all the
needs of war. His critics could not prevent the scheme from being given its chance, and Churchill had to acquiesce in something
which he believed could not succeed.

[28] Edward George Villiers Stanley, 1865–1948. Conservative MP, 1892–
1906. Postmaster General, 1903–5. 17th Earl of Derby, 1908. Director-
General of Recruiting, October 1915. Under-Secretary of State at the War
Office, July–December 1916. Secretary of State for War, December 1916–18.
Ambassador to France, 1918–20. Secretary of State for War, 1922–4.

Churchill was finding it increasingly difficult to obtain information from Kitchener which, as a member of the Dardanelles Committee, he needed in order to join in its discussions effectively.
On October 19 he sent Kitchener a long and terse note asking
for specific details which until then Kitchener had failed to provide, about the troops being sent to Salonika.[29] 'What operation
does the General Staff advise?' Churchill ended curtly. Kitchener
did not reply. When the Cabinet met on October 21 the atmosphere was tense. Asquith was unwell, and Crewe presided. It
was felt by all present that the Dardanelles Committee was too
large to be effective. The need for a series of rapid decisions
on war policy demanded a much smaller group. After the Cabinet meeting, all the members of the Dardanelles Committee except Kitchener remained behind. They came to the conclusion
that Kitchener was no longer fit to remain Secretary of State for
War. On October 22 Churchill prepared an account of the discussion for Asquith. On reflection, he did not send it, but it expressed his angry feelings:

My dear Asquith,
    Crewe will have written to you about the opinion unanimously
expressed in Cabinet yesterday that the executive conduct of the war
shd be vested forthwith & publicly in a vy small committee of Ministers, & of our sincere wish that no personal claims or considerations
shd stand in the way of this being done. After the Cabinet the members of the War Committee remained behind to settle some points
left over from our morning meeting, & Mr Balfour then informed us
that he could not serve upon a Committee so small as three because
of Kitchener's unsuitability to the duties of Secretary of State for War.
The reasons wh Mr Balfour gave were most serious & were not dis-
puted by any one present. They are well known to you. They seem
to me to apply with equal force to a Committee of five or six. There
is no doubt whatever that the present Administration of the War
Office does not command the confidence of any of your principal colleagues, & that a speedy change is required in the highest interests of

    [29] On October 5 an Anglo-French expedition had landed at Salonika. The
French troops were commanded by General Sarrail, the British by Sir Bryan
Mahon. The force advanced northwards towards the Bulgarian border, but
by mid-December had been pushed back almost to Salonika.

the State. You were yourself of this opinion as far back as the date of the formation of the Coalition. You know how much the same feeling influenced Sir Edward Carson in his decision to resign. This is not a time when disagreeable duties must be flinched from. The peril to our cause & natural fortunes is grave in the extreme & does not permit us to build upon unsound foundations. There are no doubt other steps wh shd be taken, but all of these are of minor importance compared with this prime necessity viz a competent civilian Secretary of State for War responsible in a real sense to Parliament & sustained by the strongest General Staff wh can be formed.

Churchill felt so strongly that Kitchener ought to be removed that he had intended to end his letter by making his own Cabinet position dependent upon Kitchener's departure:

In these circumstances I feel it my duty to inform you that I for one cannot continue in the Government unless a change in the control of the War Office is made or is about to be made.

It is with the greatest sorrow on personal grounds that I shd take leave of you. Our close friendship has never been disturbed by the political stresses & storms of nearly ten years official work at your side & under your leadership. That friendship was specially prized by me because it revived the older one wh existed between you & my father. I am sure that the course to wh I now feel bound by the strongest sense of duty & wh I must pursue no matter at what cost to myself will not impair it. . . .

Yours always
Winston S.C.

Asquith refused to dismiss Kitchener, even on the recommendation of so many senior Ministers. He had no intention of leaving the War Office open for Lloyd George. Margot Asquith discussed the crisis with Eric Drummond, her husband's former Private Secretary, and since May 1915 Secretary to Grey at the Foreign Office. Drummond wrote to her on November 1, setting out several points which he felt should be borne in mind, and suggesting that Asquith take over the War Office:

1. That K's position in the country is still quite inassailable. He may be a wooden idol but he is still worshipped, and if Lloyd George

tries an attack on him even with Tory support, he will fail as badly as Northcliffe did. It follows from this that he can only be induced to leave the War Office entirely of his own free will and any idea of pressure is very dangerous. He can, I am afraid, almost dictate his own terms to the Cabinet and the Prime Minister must therefore keep his own side.

2. L.G. in War Office is fatal. He destroyed the Treasury and the Munitions office is chaos. The ideal solution is that he should have some job like the Duchy of Lancaster and be on the War Committee, where he would be of value because his brain is very fertile.

. . . I believe the best solution for the W.O. would be that the P.M. should take it over with Bob Cecil and Edwin Montagu under him—one for military and the other for financial questions. . . .

Asquith curbed the criticisms of Government inefficiency by announcing his intention to end the Dardanelles Committee almost at once, to set up in its place a small policy-making Committee of three—himself, and the heads of the two military Departments, Kitchener and Balfour. Balfour agreed to serve with Kitchener.

Once the Dardanelles Committee were no longer in existence, Churchill would lack all contact with war policy. In Cabinet he spoke openly of resignation. 'I hope you may still decide to stay,' Harcourt wrote to him during one Cabinet meeting. This was also the advice of the Conservative MP, Sir Edward Goulding,[30] a close friend of F. E. Smith, who wrote to him on October 24: 'You are wanted in England. Stick to your guns and remember your Father's great mistake.'[31] Carson's resignation, Goulding pointed out, was 'a failure—24 hrs talk & no permanent effect'. But Churchill was determined to go unless he could have fuller powers. Hankey thought up one job he might do, writing

[30] Edward Alfred Goulding, 1862–1936. Known as 'Paddy'. Conservative MP, 1895–1906; 1908–22. Created Baronet, June 1915. Created Baron Wargrave, 1922.

[31] Lord Randolph Henry Spencer-Churchill, 1849–95. Secretary of State for India, 1885–6. Appointed Chancellor of the Exchequer, June 1886. He resigned in December 1886 and received no further political office.

in his diary on the evening of October 22: 'Suggested to PM to send Winston Churchill to Russia to buck up communications of Archangel & Vladivostok for importation of rifles and munitions.' But nothing came of this suggestion.

For a week Churchill waited to see whether Asquith might offer him some worthwhile employment. No such offer was forthcoming. In the last week of October Churchill wrote a 1,400-word statement of his air policy when First Lord, as an answer to what he described as 'inaccurate or partial accounts' circulating; he was bitter that Balfour had not corrected these accounts. He believed that his work with the Royal Naval Air Service clearly showed his abilities, and that these should not now be discarded. 'When the whole story,' he wrote in his statement, 'of the wonderful creation in so short a space of time of an entirely new arm on the largest possible scale can be told, the country will not deny to those concerned in it the recognition and goodwill which are their due.' He sent the statement to Balfour for his comments. 'Mr Balfour has read the statement . . .' Masterton-Smith wrote to Edward Marsh on October 25, 'and has no objection whatever to Winston making any use of it he intends.' Churchill did nothing further with it. No appeal to history could help him to regain the influence he had lost in May. On October 25 Churchill wrote a further memorandum on the Dardanelles, pleading yet again for a renewed naval attack against the Narrows. 'Mere sentiment in regard to the loss of vessels,' he wrote, 'is exercising an altogether undue influence.' Failure at the Dardanelles, he concluded, 'may easily be the decisive struggle between England and Germany'. On October 27 Churchill sent Asquith, Kitchener and Balfour a 'most secret' seven-point proposal 'for recovering the initiative in the Near East'. He wanted an immediate advance against Turkey and Bulgaria by an Anglo-French force, reinforced by 150,000 Russians, armed by Britain with Japanese rifles. No other Cabinet minister sought either to champion or to contest Churchill's suggestions. On October 30, realizing he had no means of asserting his claims to take part in determining war policy, he wrote to Asquith resigning his office:

My dear Asquith,

I had hoped to see you yesterday, to tell you that our ten years work in office together must now end.

I agree with the principle of a war executive composed of the Prime Minister & the heads of the two Military Departments; but the change necessarily deprives me of rendering useful service.

After leaving the Admiralty five months ago I have only remained in the Government at your request in order to take part in the work of the War Council. It would not be right for me at this time to remain in a sinecure. The views I have expressed on war policy are on record, and I have seen with deep regret the course which has been followed. Nor could I conscientiously accept responsibility without power. The long delays in coming to decisions have not been the only cause of our misfortunes. The faulty & lethargic execution and lack of scheme and combination over all military affairs, & of any effective concert with our Allies are evils wh will be not cured merely by the changes indicated in yr memorandum—good though these are in themselves.

I therefore take my leave of you not without many regrets on personal grounds but without any doubts. There is one point however on which it would perhaps be well for us to have a talk. It is now necessary for the truth to be made public about the initiation of the Dardanelles expedition.

Asquith had planned to make a policy statement to Parliament on November 2. On the grounds that this would include a full explanation of the Dardanelles, he persuaded Churchill to withhold his resignation at least until then. Churchill hoped that Asquith would rebut the charges that had been made against him. At the same time, Kitchener's removal was again the subject of much discussion, and this too might affect his decision. On November 1 Hankey recorded in his diary that Asquith told him 'that the Cabinet were unanimous that Lord K ought to leave War Office, principal reason being that he will not tell them the whole truth'. Asquith decided to ask Kitchener to go to the Near East as Commander-in-Chief of all British forces outside France. Kitchener refused. It was finally decided, by Asquith, Balfour and Kitchener himself, that Kitchener, while remaining Secretary of State for War, should go to Egypt and Gallipoli to report on the situation.

On the evening of November 1 Churchill telephoned Hankey and asked if he would come and see him, to help him draft a statement about the Dardanelles operation which Asquith could deliver in Parliament on the following day. 'He was in a very excited state,' Hankey recorded in his diary, 'and told me he had only stayed in the Government for this.' On November 2 Asquith made his statement to the House of Commons. In it he defended the Dardanelles operation in general terms. He did not use the material Churchill had provided, nor did he defend Churchill from the charges levelled against him. It was the removal of Kitchener, if only for a short while, which was Asquith's overriding worry. By sending him to the Dardanelles and Egypt, Asquith explained to Lloyd George on November 3, they were avoiding 'the immediate supersession of K as War Minister, while attaining the same result'.

Ministerial discussion centered upon the question of the evacuation of the Gallipoli Peninsula. The arguments were turning against any further effort to remain. On October 31 Sir Charles Monro, who had taken up his command at the Dardanelles three days previously, had telegraphed to Kitchener that he could see no military advantage in remaining on the Peninsula, and that steps ought to be taken to evacuate it.[32] 'It must be remembered,' he added, 'that the whole of the troops on the Peninsula have been very seriously affected in the matter of health, and that few of them could now be regarded as really strong men capable of great physical exertion.' On November 2 Monro had telegraphed again, at Kitchener's request. His advice was unchanged. 'The longer the troops remain on the Peninsula,' he asserted, 'the less efficient they will become.' Bonar Law, who was a leading advocate of immediate evacuation, wrote to Asquith on November

[32] Churchill wrote scathingly of Monro in *The World Crisis:* 'General Monro was an officer of swift decision. He came, he saw, he capitulated.' Keyes recorded in his *Naval Memoirs* that Monro had told him that 'every man not employed in killing Germans in France and Flanders is wasted'.

5 echoing these views. The Gallipoli positions, he wrote, were 'untenable' and the delay in reaching a decision which Kitchener's visit involved 'is in my opinion a fatal error'.

The Dardanelles Committee met for the last time on November 6. No conclusion was reached about Gallipoli, and the Committee's work was over. Churchill was excluded from its successor, the Cabinet War Committee. He realized that he could no longer exercise any influence upon war policy. That evening Hankey recorded in his diary a conversation with Balfour:

Winston Churchill had asked the PM to make him Governor-General and British Commander-in-Chief in British East Africa and had given him a scheme for attacking the Germans with armoured cars. He added that perhaps if he succeeded in this the military objections to his resigning a high post of command would disappear. All this tickled Mr Balfour so much that he positively pirouetted on one foot, looking very odd in his long frock coat, so that Masterton-Smith and I fairly roared with laughter.

On November 11 Asquith informed the King that a new Cabinet War Committee had been set up. It would have five members, not three: himself, Lloyd George, Balfour, Bonar Law and McKenna. Kitchener was not to be a member. He had left London on his special Cabinet mission to the Dardanelles, to report on whether or not the Gallipoli campaign should continue. There were no changes in the composition of the Cabinet. That same day Churchill sent off his second and final letter of resignation:

My dear Asquith,

When I left the Admiralty five months ago, I accepted an office with few duties in order at your request to take part in the work of the War Council, and to assist new Ministers with the knowledge of current operations which I then possessed in a special degree. The counsels which I have offered are upon record in the minutes of the Committee of Imperial Defence, and in the memoranda I have circulated to the Cabinet: and I draw your attention at the present time to these.

I am in cordial agreement with the decision to form a small War Council [i.e. the Cabinet War Committee]. I appreciated the intention you expressed to me six weeks ago to include me among its members. I foresaw then the personal difficulties which you would have to face in its composition, and I make no complaint at all that your scheme should be changed. But with that change my work in the Government comes naturally to a close.

Knowing what I do about the present situation, and the instrument of executive power, I could not accept a position of general responsibility for war policy without any effective share in its guidance and control. Even when decisions of principle are rightly taken, the speed and method of their execution are factors which determine the result. Nor do I feel in times like these able to remain in well-paid inactivity. I therefore ask you to submit my resignation to the King. I am an officer, and I place myself unreservedly at the disposal of the military authorities, observing that my regiment is in France.

I have a clear conscience which enables me to bear my responsibility for past events with composure.

Time will vindicate my administration of the Admiralty, and assign me my due share in the vast series of preparations and operations which have secured us the command of the seas.

With much respect, and unaltered personal friendship, I bid you good-bye.

Yours very sincerely<br>Winston S. Churchill

Asquith accepted Churchill's resignation, replying on November 12:

My dear Churchill,

I hoped that you would reconsider your decision and regret to learn from your letter that you have not felt able to do so.

You have rendered services, both in Council and in Administration, which no one is better able to appreciate than myself, in regard to the conduct and direction of the war, and I am sincerely grieved that you should think it your duty to leave the Cabinet.

I am certain that you will continue to take an active and effective part in the prosecution of the war.

As you know well, on personal grounds I feel acutely the severance of our long association.

Yours always sincerely<br>H. H. Asquith

Churchill's letter of resignation and Asquith's reply were published in the newspapers on November 13. For the first time in ten years Churchill was without political office. He still hoped that he might be offered the command of the British forces fighting against the Germans in East Africa. Balfour had found the idea absurd, but it received support from an unexpected quarter. On November 12 Bonar Law wrote to Asquith:

I wish you would not definitely decide against Churchill going to East Africa without consulting some of your military advisers as to the wisdom of it. I suggest Callwell or Brade or both. I thought of Callwell, to whom of course I have not spoken on the subject, because he quite approved of trying to get Smuts[33] when K was against it.

I am certainly influenced by sympathy with W, but one of the things from all I hear about the operations in France, I feel most strongly is we are suffering from the want of brains in the higher commands; and if the responsibility were mine alone I think I should rather entrust East Africa to Churchill than to any officer whom we are likely to get.

As regards Parliamentary and Press criticism, it is I think true that, while the appointment would be attacked as a job, there is another strong stream of criticism against the incapacity of our generals, and this appointment could be defended on the ground of capacity. I spoke to Carson today about it and he thinks and would say in the House that though when he entered the Cabinet he had the strongest prejudice against Churchill he was so impressed by his ability that he would regard the giving of such an appointment to him as an indication that the Government were trying to make use of available ability and were not bound by red tape.

I only press this idea to the extent of asking you to find out how it would be regarded by some of your intelligent advisers at the WO.

[33] Jan Christian Smuts, 1870–1950. Born in Cape Colony. General, commanding Boer Commando Forces, Cape Colony, 1901. Colonial Secretary, Transvaal, 1907. Minister of Defence, Union of South Africa, 1910–20. Second-in-command of the South African forces that defeated the Germans in South West Africa, July 1915. Honorary Lieutenant-General commanding the imperial forces in East Africa, 1916–17. South African Representative at the Imperial War Cabinet, 1917 and 1918. Prime Minister of South Africa, 1919–24. Minister of Justice, 1933–9. Prime Minister, 1939–48.

News of the possibility of Churchill commanding in East Africa reached the Press. On November 14 the pilot Spenser Grey sent him notes on a Royal Naval Air Service wing which could be set up in East Africa, and hoped that he would soon be serving under Churchill again. 'I imagine,' he wrote, 'and sincerely hope that you are not really going to Flanders as Major of your Regiment. It doesn't seem to offer you a very large scope for your energies.'

Asquith declined to give Churchill the East African appointment, which would undoubtedly have aroused Parliamentary criticism. The only opportunity open to Churchill for active service was therefore to go to France as a Major in the Queen's Own Oxfordshire Hussars. This he decided to do. Among the first letters which he received when his decision to go to France was known was one from Violet Asquith, who wrote from 10 Downing Street on November 13:

Dearest Winston,

. . . Fate has been very blind & very cruel—any day she may veer & change & show us a golden face again—but meanwhile you are going out to France—away from us all & away from the great theatre in which you have played so great a part—to an even greater arena—where perhaps an even greater rôle may await you. *I* trust your star —but star or no—it is a *splendid* thing to do—& for one who knows as you do what he has to offer the world—it is a very great thing to risk it all as you are doing. So fine a risk to take that I can't help rejoicing proudly that you should have done it—tho' I don't for a minute think you should have been allowed to. . . .

Goodbye dearest Winston & God bless you—come back to us very soon & remember that England trusts & needs you.

Always yrs
Violet

On November 15, following the custom of all resigning Ministers, Churchill made a personal statement in the House of Commons. 'No other Minister,' he stated, 'who does not hold a laborious office, and is not on the War Council, has been so closely connected as I have been with the conduct of the War for its first ten months.' He then spoke of each of the episodes

for which he had been criticized during his Admiralty administration. 'I am not the cause of any withholding of papers from
publication,' he pointed out. 'It is not in my interest that they
are withheld.' Referring to Lord Fisher, Churchill told the House:
'I did not receive from the First Sea Lord either the clear guidance before the event or the firm support after which I was entitled to expect.' The essence of his criticism was that 'If the First
Sea Lord had not approved the operations, if he believed they
were unlikely to take the course that was expected of them, if he
thought they would lead to undue losses, it was his duty to refuse
consent. No one could have prevailed against such a refusal. The
operation would never have been begun.' Later in his speech
Churchill turned to strategic considerations:

All through this year I have offered the same counsel to the Government—undertake no operation in the West which is more costly to us
in life than to the enemy; in the East, take Constantinople; take it by
ships if you can; take it by soldiers if you must; take it by whichever
plan, military or naval, commends itself to your military experts, but
take it, and take it soon, and take it while time remains.

The situation is now entirely changed, and I am not called upon to
offer any advice upon its new aspects. But it seems to me that if there
were any operations in the history of the world which, having been
begun, it was worth while to carry through with the utmost vigour
and fury, with a consistent flow of reinforcements, and an utter disre-
gard of life, it was the operations so daringly and brilliantly begun by
Sir Ian Hamilton in the immortal landing of the 25th April.

Towards the end of his speech, Churchill reiterated the belief
which he had held since the start of the war, that the Allies
must win in the end:

There is no reason to be discouraged about the progress of the War.
We are passing through a bad time now, and it will probably be worse
before it is better, but that it will be better, if we only endure and
persevere, I have no doubt whatever. Sir, the old wars were decided
by their episodes rather than by their tendencies. In this War the
tendencies are far more important than the episodes. Without winning any sensational victories, we may win this War. We may win it
even during a continuance of extremely disappointing and vexatious

events. It is not necessary for us to win the War to push the German lines back over all the territory they have absorbed, or to pierce them. While the German lines extend far beyond their frontiers, while their flag flies over conquered capitals and subjugated provinces, while all the appearances of military successes attend their arms, Germany may be defeated more fatally in the second or third year of the War than if the Allied Armies had entered Berlin in the first.

Churchill ended with an appeal to the neutral States which still hesitated to decide whether or not to intervene in the conflict:

It is no doubt disconcerting for us to observe the Government of a State like Bulgaria convinced, on an impartial survey of the chances, that victory will rest with the Central Powers. Some of these small States are hypnotised by German military pomp and precision. They see the glitter, they see the episode; but what they do not see or realise is the capacity of the ancient and mighty nations against whom Germany is warring to endure adversity, to put up with disappointment and mismanagement, to recreate and renew their strength, to toil on with boundless obstinacy through boundless suffering to the achievement of the greatest cause for which men have fought.

Churchill knew that his vindication could not come until Asquith allowed the full story to be told. For over five months he had watched his influence slip away. As Chancellor of the Duchy there had not been a single opportunity for him to speak to Parliament. His resignation speech gave him the occasion to show the House once more his grasp of events. His sense of perspective was unimpaired; his confidence in the outcome clear. Perspective and confidence were two qualities which the House appreciated, and which it seldom received. But this was a speech of farewell. Nothing could be built upon it. Churchill won sympathy by it; but it could not retrieve his lost influence. Asquith gave a brief reply, before passing on to other business:

The House is always accustomed, and properly accustomed, to give great latitude, and even to expect great latitude, to explanations from a Minister of the Crown who has resigned his office, and my right hon Friend has taken advantage of that privilege in a manner which, I think, will be generally appreciated and admired.

I only wish to say two things. I think my right hon Friend has dealt with a very delicate situation not only with ability and eloquence, but also with loyalty and discretion. He has said one or two things which I tell him frankly I had rather he had not said, but, on the other hand, he has necessarily and naturally left unsaid some things which, when the complete estimate of all these transactions has to be taken, will have to be said. But that does not affect his personal position at all. . . .

I desire to say to him and of him, having been associated with him now for ten years in close and daily intimacy, in positions of great responsibility and in situations varied and of extreme difficulty and delicacy, I have always found him a wise counsellor, a brilliant colleague, and a faithful friend.

I am certain, Sir, he takes with him to the new duties which he is going to assume, having with great insistency abdicated those he has hitherto discharged, the universal goodwill, hopes, and confident expectations of this House and of all his colleagues.

During the debate that followed, a number of members referred to Churchill's resignation. Bonar Law spoke with evident sympathy:

I entered the Cabinet, to put it mildly, with no prejudice in favour of the right hon Gentleman. I have now been his colleague for five months. He has the defects of his qualities, and as his qualities are large the shadow which they throw is fairly large also, but I say deliberately, in my judgment, in mental power and vital force he is one of the foremost men in our country. . . .

He is a man still young who has had some little experience of the Army, and who is resuming his old profession. We know his capacity, and I for one trust that the Commander-in-Chief will find some means of utilising his great ability.

The Irish Nationalist MP, T. P. O'Connor,[34] declared that it was a 'national tragedy' to remove from the Government's counsels 'a man with such courage, genius and insight as my right hon Friend the Member for Dundee'. That night Frances Stevenson wrote in her diary: 'I am rather sorry for him, as it must be a terrible experience for one who has had so much power in his hands. But all the same I think he deserved it.'

[34] Thomas Power O'Connor, 1848–1929, Irish Nationalist MP, 1885–1929. Journalist and biographer.

During his speech Churchill had referred to the Dardanelles as 'a legitimate gamble'. This phrase horrified some MPs, and became the subject of continuing critical comment in the Press in later months. The phrase 'legitimate gamble' was frequently quoted by those who thought that he lacked moderation and shunned caution; for them his departure was acceptable, and indeed welcome.

On the morning following Churchill's speech, J. A. Spender, the editor of the *Westminster Gazette*, wrote to Lord Esher: 'Winston was less mischievous than was expected &, if the egotism can be pardoned, the performance was effective though essentially unfair to Jackie & the experts. It is all very well to say that "discussions were frequent & no adverse opinions were expressed", but we all know who discussed & what happened to the exponents of adverse opinions.'

Following his resignation, Churchill received a great number of letters of sympathy and encouragement. Most of them were from strangers. Sir Charles Coke,[35] who had commanded the British squadron on the coast of Ireland while Churchill was First Lord, wrote from his home in Exeter on November 13:

Two days ago I was returning from London, in the train was a young Flying officer who did not know I was an Admiral, he remarked 'Where would the Naval Flying Service have been but for Mr Churchill's energy & foresight' & went on to say how the whole Naval Flying Corps owed you a deep debt of gratitude; It is not often that I enter into conversation in the train, but could not help cordially agreeing & remarked that—'Mr Churchill not only deserved the gratitude of the RN Air Service, but that of the entire service & the country, for his untiring efforts both before & after war was declared'.

Lloyd George wrote on November 16:

Dear Winston,
. . . Your speech yesterday was amazingly clever both in substance & tone.
Under the circumstances you are right to go. All the same it is a

[35] Charles Henry Coke, 1854–1945. Entered Navy, 1868. Rear-Admiral, 1908. Knighted, 1911. Vice-Admiral commanding on the coast of Ireland, 1911–15.

blunder—a stupid blunder—to let you off. Here your special knowledge & gifts would be invaluable. I cannot help thinking that you must
soon return.

In a hurry. Good luck to you.

Yours sincerely<br>D. Lloyd George

Violet Asquith, who had heard the speech, also wrote on November 16:

Dearest Winston,

One line to say I thought your speech *quite* flawless—I have seldom
been more moved—It was a fine and generous speech—*How* thankful
I am you said what you did about that wicked old lunatic.

Is there anything you *haven't* got for the Front? Compass? Lumin-
ous wristwatch? Muffler & Tinderlighter? If there is any lacuna in
your equipment let me fill it.

Goodbye and good luck—God bless you—

Yours<br>Violet

Grey also wrote on November 13, expressing his own feeling
about the war. 'Your going is a great wrench,' he wrote, 'it adds
to my hatred of the war—I shall look back upon it if I survive it,
as a time of horrible memory. I hated it beforehand & I hate it
now, though I do not see how it could have been avoided. . . .'

Churchill decided to go at once to join his regiment in France.
He knew that he would be made welcome in the Oxfordshire
Hussars, and that some position would be found for him in the
regiment. On November 16 he gave a farewell luncheon at 41
Cromwell Road. Violet and Margot Asquith, Gwendeline Church-
ill, Nellie Hozier[36] and Edward Marsh were among the guests.
Violet Bonham Carter later recorded her impressions in *Winston
Churchill As I Knew Him:*

Clemmie was admirably calm and brave, poor Eddie blinking back
his tears, the rest of us trying to 'play up' and hide our leaden hearts.

[36] Nellie Hozier, 1888–1957. Clementine Churchill's sister. Served as a
nurse in Belgium, 1914. Captured by the Germans but released almost immediately. She married Colonel Bertram Romilly in 1915.

Winston alone was at his gayest and his best, and he and Margot held the table between them. . . .

For most of us it was a kind of wake. My heart ached for Clemmie, and Eddie was very pathetic. Winston was not unmindful of his plight and had asked my father to take him on as an extra Private Secretary as he could not bear to think of poor Eddie being plunged back into the bowels of the Colonial Office, sans personal function, sans friends, sans anything. So he was coming to us at No 10 to be put in charge of Civil List Pensions, which we hoped would make him feel a little less of a motherless child.

On the following evening Max Aitken called at 41 Cromwell Road. 'The whole household was upside down while the soldier-statesman was buckling on his sword,' he later wrote in *Politicians and the War*. 'Downstairs, Mr "Eddie" Marsh, his faithful secretary, was in tears. . . . Upstairs, Lady Randolph was in a state of despair at the idea of her brilliant son being relegated to the trenches. Mrs Churchill seemed to be the only person who remained calm, collected and efficient.' On the morning of Thursday November 18 Churchill crossed to France. That evening James Masterton-Smith, who had been his Naval Secretary throughout his three and a half years as First Lord, wrote to Clementine Churchill from the Admiralty:

It is half after ten of the clock and the shutters of the old familiar Private Office are just going up, but I cannot let this day pass without telling you that you no less than Winston have been much in the thoughts of many of us. Not even the high gods (whether their home be Fleet Street or Mount Olympus) can make things that have been as if they had never been, and to those of us who know and understand, Winston is the greatest First Lord this old Admiralty has ever had—or is likely to have.

With those of us who shared his life here he has left an inspiring memory of high courage and tireless industry, and he carries with him to Flanders all that we have to give him—our good wishes.

# 18

# 'The Escaped Scapegoat'

CHURCHILL CROSSED over to France on 18 November 1915 to join the Oxfordshire Hussars. No sooner had he reached Boulogne than higher authorities intervened, for Sir John French had sent a car to meet him, and take him to the General Headquarters of the British Expeditionary Force at St Omer. This summons was totally unexpected. On the way to GHQ Churchill persuaded the driver to take him to the Regimental Headquarters of the Oxfordshire Hussars at Bléquin, where he spent a few hours. That night he dined with the Commander-in-Chief at St Omer.

French suggested that Churchill should either become one of his ADC's at St Omer, or that he should take command of a Brigade. Churchill at once opted for the Brigade, and the Commander-in-Chief said he would arrange it as soon as he could. The offer of a Brigade meant much to Churchill. Here was the military responsibility for which he had often longed. Before accepting a Brigade, Churchill asked to have some experience of trench warfare, and suggested that if French could arrange it, he would like to have his training with the Guards. That night Churchill wrote to his wife:

. . . I am staying tonight at GHQ in a fine chateau, with hot baths, beds, champagne & all the conveniences. Redmond[1] has been dining here—very agreeable, & admits I am absolutely right to leave the Govt. They are descending into the abyss. I am sure I am going to be en-

[1] John Edward Redmond, 1851–1918. MP, 1881–1918. Chairman of the Irish Parliamentary Party at Westminster.

tirely happy out here & at peace. I must try to win my way as a good
& sincere soldier. But do not suppose I shall run any foolish risks or
do anything wh is not obviously required.

I will write to you again tomorrow my dearest pet as soon as my
plans are finally settled.

On November 19 Sir John French asked Lord Cavan,[2] the
Commander of the Guards Division, to come to St Omer, and
put Churchill's request to him. Cavan agreed that Churchill
should have his training with the Grenadier Guards. During the
day Churchill wrote to his brother, who was still at the Dardanelles, explaining why he had decided to abandon politics, which
were still much on his mind:

My position at home since I left the Admiralty has been one of such
responsibility without control & I have watched all these weary
months folly, sloth & indecision ruining large conceptions. I have made
up my mind not to return to any Govt during the war except with
plenary & effective executive power: & this is a condition not likely
to be satisfied. So I propose to do my utmost to win my way in the
Army wh is my old profession & where as you know my heart has
long been. . . .

I am extremely happy & have regained a peace of mind to wh I had
long been a stranger.

On November 19 Churchill drove the twelve miles from St
Omer to La Gorgue, the headquarters of the Guards Division,
where he was introduced to the senior officers of the Division.
He returned to St Omer for the night, writing to his wife:

Midnight
My dearest soul,
    (this is what the gt d of Marlborough used to write from the low
countries to his cat) All is vy well arranged . . . but as I do not know
to wh battalion I am to be sent, I cannot tell the rota in wh we shall

[2] Frederick Rudolph Lambart, 1865–1946. Entered Army, 1885. 10th
Earl of Cavan, 1900. Major-General commanding the 4th (Guards) Brigade,
September 1914–June 1915. Commanded the Guards Division, August 1915–
January 1916. Commanded the XIV Corps in France and Italy, January
1916–18. Commander-in-Chief, Aldershot, 1920–2. Chief of the Imperial
General Staff, 1922–6. Field-Marshal, 1932.

go into the trenches. But I do hope you will realise what a vy harmless thing this is. To my surprise I learn they only have about 15 killed & wounded each day out of 8,000 men exposed! It will make me vy sulky if I think you are allowing yourself to be made anxious by any risk like that. You wished me to write & tell you & therefore I do—to satisfy you, & not because I attach any importance to so ordinary & average an experience. I went this afternoon to see my regt: also my Brigadier.[3] They were caressing. They highly approved of my course of action & thought it vy right & proper. Altogether I see that the Army is willing to receive me back as 'the prodigal son'. Anyhow I know what they think right, and mean to do it. . . .

I am vy happy here. I did not know what release from care meant. It is a blessed peace. How I ever cd have wasted so many months in impotent misery, wh might have been spent in war, I cannot tell.

In the intervals between going into the trenches I shall come back for hot baths etc to GHQ where I have been told to consider a place always open. French tells me he has written to you today. He is a good friend.

Always your loving husband<br>W

Sir John French's letter was brief but sympathetic:

Dear Mrs Churchill,

I am just sending a line to tell you that Winston has come out and that I am going to do all I can to help him. I want you to know that I will do all I can for him & to take care of him.

Forgive me for writing to you but I know how you must have felt parting with him and I am hoping this line may make you feel happier.

Yours very sincerely<br>J. French

Churchill spent the morning of November 20 at GHQ and then returned to La Gorgue for lunch with Lord Cavan, who told him that he had been attached to the 2nd Battalion of the

---

[3] Geoffrey Percy Thynne Feilding, 1866–1932. 2nd Lieutenant, Coldstream Guards, 1888. Lieutenant-Colonel, 1912. Wounded during retreat from Mons, October 1914. Brigadier-General commanding 1st (Guards) Brigade, August 1915–January 1916. Major-General commanding Guards Division, January 1916–October 1918. General Officer Commanding, London District, 1918–29. Knighted, 1919.

Grenadier Guards, commanded by Lieutenant-Colonel Jeffreys.[4]
The Battalion was to go into the line near Neuve Chapelle that
afternoon. Churchill drove with Cavan to Jeffreys' headquarters.
Most of the Battalion was already on its way to the front. Cavan
returned to La Gorgue; Churchill set off with the officers of the
Battalion's headquarter staff to the front. In *Thoughts and Adventures* he recalled:

It was a dull November afternoon, and an icy drizzle fell over the
darkening plain. As we approached the line, the red flashes of the
guns stabbed the sombre landscape on either side of the road, to
the sound of an intermittent cannonade. We paced onwards for about
an hour without a word being spoken on either side.

Then the Colonel: 'I think I ought to tell you that we were not at all
consulted in the matter of your coming to join us.'

I replied respectfully that I had had no idea myself which Battalion I was to be sent to, but that I dared say it would be all right.
Anyhow we must make the best of it.

There was another prolonged silence.

Then the Adjutant:[5] 'I am afraid we have had to cut down your kit
rather, Major. There are no communication trenches here. We are
doing all our reliefs over the top. The men have little more than what
they stand up in. We have found a servant for you, who is carrying a
spare pair of socks and your shaving gear. We have had to leave the
rest behind.'

I said that was quite all right and that I was sure I should be very
comfortable.

We continued to progress in the same sombre silence.

[4] George Darell Jeffreys, 1878–1960. Known as 'Ma'. 2nd Lieutenant, Grenadier Guards, 1897. Lieutenant-Colonel commanding the 2nd Battalion,
Grenadier Guards, 1915. Commanded the 58th, 57th and 1st Guards Brigades, 1916–17, and the 19th Division, 1917–19. Major-General, 1919. Commanded London District, 1920–4. Knighted, 1924. General Officer
Commanding-in-Chief, Southern Command, India, 1932–6. General, 1935.
Created Baron, 1952. Colonel of the Grenadier Guards, 1952–60.

[5] Wilfred Russell Bailey, 1891–1948. 2nd Lieutenant, Grenadier Guards,
1911. Lieutenant, 2nd Battalion Grenadier Guards, October 1914; Adjutant,
November 1914. Captain, September 1915. Lieutenant-Colonel commanding
the 1st Battalion, Grenadier Guards, October 1918. Succeeded his father as
3rd Baron Glanusk, 1928. Commanded the Training Battalion of the Welsh
Guards, 1939–42. Colonel, 1942.

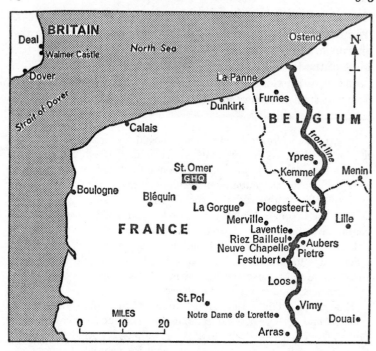

THE OSTEND TO ARRAS SECTOR OF THE WESTERN
FRONT, NOVEMBER AND DECEMBER 1915

The 2nd Battalion of the Grenadier Guards had suffered greatly
during the first year of the war. Of the twenty-four officers of the
Battalion who had fought in the first Battle of Ypres at the end of
October 1914, eight had been killed and six wounded by the
time the battle had ended in mid-November. When Churchill
joined them a year later Jeffreys was almost the only surviving
officer of the original band.

At dusk on the evening of November 20 the Battalion reached
the front line. Battalion headquarters was situated in what
Churchill described in *Thoughts and Adventures* as 'a pulverized
ruin called Ebenezer Farm', behind whose broken walls a few
sandbagged rooms had been constructed. He recalled that at

dinner that night in Ebenezer Farm the officers drank 'strong tea with condensed milk', not a drink to which he was addicted; and that under Jeffreys' stern gaze there was little conversation: 'His subordinates evidently stood in the gravest awe of their Commanding Officer, and very few remarks were made except on topics which he himself initiated.' 'At about eight o'clock,' Churchill recalled, 'a dead Grenadier was brought in and laid out in the ruined farmhouse for burial next day.' When dinner was over, Churchill had to decide where to sleep. He was offered first a place in the signal office at Ebenezer Farm. On inspection, he found that the office was only eight feet square, stifling hot, and already 'occupied by four busy Morse signallers'. The only alternative was a rough dugout two hundred yards from the farm. This, he discovered, was 'a sort of pit four feet deep, containing about one foot of water'. He therefore decided to sleep in the signal office.

It was not a comfortable existence, even in a static line. For most of November the ground had been hard with frost. With each brief thaw, it was clogged up with mud and water. A surfeit of rats added to the discomfort.

'The trenches here have been damnably neglected by the troops whom we succeeded,' Churchill wrote to his wife on November 21, 'and the Guards are working hard to make the defences strong and safe.' He himself had been put to hard work. A young Machine Gun officer, Ralph Bingham,[6] later recorded, in a letter to the author, the impression Churchill's arrival made on the Guards:

I was a MG officer in the 1st Guards Brigade MG Company. We were in the front line near—I think—Laventie. It was winter and cold and wet; if I remember rightly. Churchill came out to the front to learn the routine of trench warfare, and was attached to the 2nd Bn Grenadier Guards for instruction. As soon as they heard that Churchill

[6] Ralph Charles Bingham, 1885–    . Lieutenant, First Life Guards Reserve of Officers, July 1914. Captain, Machine Gun Corps, October 1915. Wounded on the Somme, September 1916. Lieutenant-Colonel commanding 4th Battalion City of London Regiment, 1934–7. Clerk of the Cheque and Adjutant of the Yeoman of the Guard, 1950–5.

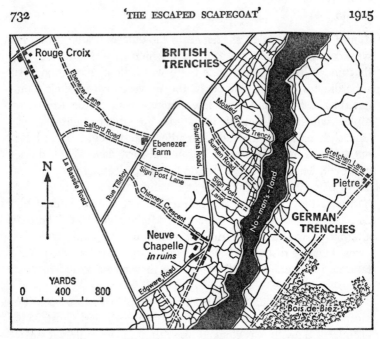

BRITISH AND GERMAN TRENCHES, NEUVE CHAPELLE
NOVEMBER AND DECEMBER 1915

was coming to them, they rubbed their hands together and said 'By Jove we're getting one of those damned politicians to teach. We'll walk him off his so-and-so feet!' Which they did. They walked poor Winston round and round the Trench system until he was practically stone cold—it was a somewhat tiring job unless you were used to it—especially in the winter. Of course, the Grenadiers quickly got over their 'damned politician' point of view.

In his letter of November 21 Churchill gave his wife an account of his experiences in the trenches, and of the opinion he had formed of Jeffreys:

My darling,
Here I am in the line. Except for heavy cannonading the results of wh do not come near us, everything is vy quiet. A few men are hit now & again by stray bullets skimming over the trenches, or accurate snip-

ing. But we are able to walk right into the trenches without crawling along a sap, & even in the fwd trenches of the front line there is gt tranquillity. We came in last night on a 48 hours spell, then 48 hours in support, & then into the front line again up to a total of 12 days at the end of wh we are entitled to 6 days rest in Divisional reserve. I am attd to the 2nd Battalion of the Grenadier Guards, wh once the gt d of Marlborough served in & commanded. I get on vy well with the officers—though they were rather suspicious at first—& all the generals are most civil & kind. I am not going to be in any hurry to leave this regt while it is in the 1 line, as its Colonel is one of the vy best in the army & his knowledge of trench warfare is complete & profound. All his comments and instructions to his men are pregnant with military wisdom; & the system of the Guards—discipline & hard work—must be seen at close quarters to be admired as it deserves. Altogether I look forward to an extremely profitable spell of education.

The conditions of life though hard are not unhealthy, & there is certainly nothing to complain about in them—except for cold feet. . . .

The artillery fire is dying away now as the light fades; & per contra there is a certain amount of maxim & rifle fire beginning. I am writing from a dugout a few hundred yards behind the trench where the Colonel & Adjutant are. . . .

Churchill appealed to his wife for supplies, sending her a numbered list of the things which he wanted her to despatch *with the utmost speed* to St Omer. The list was comprehensive:

1. A warm brown leather waistcoat.
2. A pair of trench wading boots. Brown leather bottom, & water proof canvas tops coming right up to the thigh.
3. A periscope (most important).
4. A sheepskin sleeping bag; that will either carry kit, or let me sleep in it. . . . In addition Please send me
5. 2 pairs of Khaki trousers (wh Messrs Tautz forgot to pack).
6. 1 pair of my brown buttoned boots.
7. 3 small face towels.
   Voila tout!
   Your little pillow is a boon & a pet.

Churchill's one night in the signal office at Ebenezer Farm had been enough for him. He had not come to the western front to listen to the noise of signallers tapping out their morse messages, or to partake of the restrained regime of a Battalion headquarters. He wanted to be where the action was, and decided to spend the next night in the trenches. Edward Grigg,[7] whom he had known before the war, was commanding the Battalion's Number One Company in a forward trench. Churchill asked Grigg if he could spend the night in his dugout. Grigg was delighted, as indeed was Churchill, for among the other contrasts with Ebenezer Farm, whisky was allowed in the forward trenches as a comfort in such cold conditions. Churchill spent the night of Sunday November 21 with Grigg's Company. 'This gives me the opportunity,' he wrote to his wife two days later, 'of seeing & learning thoroughly. It is not more dangerous than at battalion headquarters, because frequent walks to & from the trenches over an area where stray bullets are skimming are avoided.' But the front line was, he told her, 'a wild scene'; the trenches which Grigg's Company were holding had been built along the ruins of older trench lines taken from the Germans, and then built up again without too much care. A great deal of time was spent, Churchill wrote, 'cleaning everything up' and trying to strengthen the trenches and parapets. This was unpleasant work, made more difficult by increasing shelling and firing, by cold winds and intermittent snow. 'Filth & rubbish everywhere,' Churchill wrote to his wife, 'graves built into the defences & scattered about promiscuously, feet & clothing breaking through the soil, water & muck on all sides; & about this scene in the dazzling moonlight troops of enormous bats creep & glide, to the unceasing accompaniment of rifle & machine guns & the venomous whining & whirring of the bullets wh pass over head.' 'Amid these surround-

[7] Edward William Macleay Grigg, 1879–1955. Editorial staff of *The Times*, 1903–5; 1908–13. Served in the Grenadier Guards, 1914–18. Military Secretary to the Prince of Wales, 1919. Knighted, 1920. Private Secretary to Lloyd George, 1921–2. National Liberal MP, 1922–5. Governor of Kenya, 1925–31. National Conservative MP, 1933–45. Parliamentary Secretary, Ministry of Information, 1939–40. Financial Secretary, War Office, 1940. Joint Parliamentary Under-Secretary of State for War, 1940–4. Minister Resident in the Middle East, 1944–5. Created Baron Altrincham, 1945. Editor of the *National Review*, 1948–55.

ings,' he continued, 'aided by wet & cold, & every minor discomfort, I have found happiness & content such as I have not known for many months.'

During Churchill's first forty-eight hours in the trenches, two men were killed and two wounded. There was spasmodic shelling and sniping. From both sides of no-man's-land snipers watched intently to catch the slightest movement, and to fire. The Battalion held a front seven hundred yards long, from Moated Grange Trench to Sign Post Lane. Between these two positions a maze of trenches nearly four hundred yards long transformed what had once been farmland into a sunken chaos of dugouts and strong points which gave the men whose task was to kill a brief and uncertain safety.

On the evening of November 22 the Battalion marched to its reserve billets at Bout Deville, three miles behind the line. On November 23 the Battalion's war diary recorded laconically: 'Wet and muddy. Poor billets.' Churchill sent his wife a fuller description of his new surroundings: 'We are near enough to hear rifle fire but out of range of everything except the artillery, wh will not be likely to bother about the cottages & farms in wh we are living. I have spent the morning on my toilet & a hot bath—engineered with some difficulty. . . .' He was becoming increasingly absorbed in Battalion life: 'I have lost all interest in the outer world and no longer worry about it or its stupid newspapers.' That afternoon he had been to see Asquith's son Raymond[8] who was in billets about six miles away. 'We had a pleasant talk & some tea,' Churchill told his wife; 'he is quite a soldier now, & much improved by the experience.' Returning to his Battalion's reserve billets, Churchill sent her his further reflections about the Guards:

I am making friends with the officers & the Colonel, and it is pleasant to see their original doubts & prejudices fading away. The discipline & organisation of their battalions are admirable. In spite of losses which have left scarcely a dozen of the original personnel re-

[8] Raymond Asquith, 1878–1916. Asquith's eldest son. Called to the Bar, 1904. Lieutenant, Grenadier Guards, 1915–16. Killed in action, 18 September 1916.

maining, and repeated refills from various sources, the tradition & the system of the Guards asserts itself in hard work, smartness & soldierly behaviour. It will always be a memorable experience to me to have served with them.

It was sixteen years since Churchill had submitted to the rigours of military cooking. Since then he had become accustomed to eating well. He had no intention of accepting army food without also trying to summon help from home. In his letter of November 22 he had asked his wife to help satisfy his culinary demands: 'Will you send now regularly once a week a *small* box of food to supplement the rations. Sardines, chocolate, potted meats, and other things wh may strike your fancy. Begin as soon as possible.' This letter ended with a reflection on his new status: 'Do you realize what a vy important person a Major is? 99 people out of every 100 in this gt army have to touch their hats to me. With this inspiring reflection let me sign myself, Your loving & devoted husband, W.' In his postscript Churchill wrote: 'Kiss Randolph, Diana & that golden Sarah for me.'

In London the Cabinet had decided to evacuate the Gallipoli Peninsula. 'Personally I felt desperately depressed at this decision,' Hankey wrote in his diary on November 23. 'I believe it to be an entirely wrong one. Since Churchill left the Cabinet and the War Council we have lacked courage more than ever.'

On November 24, while still in reserve, Churchill wrote to his mother. It was the first personal letter he had written to her for some time. It marked a renewal of their correspondence, which had languished since his marriage seven years before. During his earlier army days he had found his mother's letters the principal source of that encouragement which he so much needed when cut off from the people who made up the world in which he moved. By his note to her he seemed to invite her once more to write to him as of old:

Dearest Mamma,

Clemmie will I am sure have shown you my letters to her, so that I only write a few lines by way of supplement.

I am vy happy here & have made good friends with everybody now. I always get on with soldiers, & these are about the finest.

I do not certainly regret the step I took. I am sure it was right from every point of view. Also I know I am doing the right thing out here. Mind you write to me & tell me all your news & what plans you are making with Clemmie & Goonie. Keep in touch with people who can be useful & are friendly.

With fondest love.

Your loving son<br>
Winston

In his postscript Churchill wrote: 'Do you know I am quite young again.' Lady Randolph had not needed his letter in order to take up her pen. She not only wrote to her son frequently while he was at the front, sending him her strange blend of good cheer and gossip, but also began to busy herself on his behalf. In London she brought together at her dinner table a small group of politicians and friends who still believed that her son's true place was not in the trenches but in Parliament. On November 21 she wrote to him with news of Kitchener, who was still on his Cabinet mission to the Dardanelles, and with a favourable report of her son's resignation letter of November 11 and his House of Commons speech four days later. Only a week had passed since his last Parliamentary appearance:

My dearest Winston,

You venturesome fellow! But I might have known that 50 miles behind the firing line was not your particular style—I can understand that you want to study sur place this new phase of warfare. It is no use my saying 'be careful'. It is all in the hands of God—I can only pray & hope for the best. . . . I have no doubt you have found plenty of friends & they are making a fuss over you—but that was a certainty. . . .

They tell a story of K of K telegraphing that as his job was finished, he wd now return—but the whole Govt frantically looked for something else to keep him out there.

Clemmie will have told you of our arrangements for the moment. I am trying to let the house for 6 months or a year—I have some one coming to see it tomorrow but unless I let it for a certain sum it wd not repay me—Meanwhile until I do I propose to contribute towards the housekeeping at C Rd [Cromwell Road] as much as I can. I had tea there today with all the children—Great darlings.

While I have the house I mean now & then to have a dinner. Goonie is coming on Thursday & I have asked Bonar Law & George Curzon. I wish you were going to be here—it is like Hamlet without Hamlet. I will write to you how it all goes off.

Ld Ribblesdale[9] came to see me today. I reproached him for making a rash speech in the H of L—on the evacuation of Gallipoli. He thought yr letter & speech splendid & thought you were quite right to defend yrself and until yr speech he—like many others blamed you. . . .

I saw the Laverys today—I haven't seen as yet your chef d'oeuvre of Goonie. She tells me that Jack is now at Salonika. . . .

Best love—write to me sometimes & let me know if you want anything—or want me to find out anything—Bless you

Your loving
Mother

Lady Randolph's letters were enthusiastic and gossipy, but hardly gave Churchill the support he needed; it was his wife's letters that provided him with the information, advice and comfort upon which he depended, and helped to reduce his sense of isolation.

Writing from 41 Cromwell Road on November 21, Clementine Churchill sent an account of all she was thinking, and of the many things that she had done. 'I long for you to have a Brigade,' she wrote, '& yet not too soon for fear of partly dimming the "blaze of glory" in which you have left the country.' She reported that wherever she went, 'I find people awestruck at your sacrifice'. She was particularly worried that he was going into the trenches too quickly, and 'that you may get pneumonia or an internal chill unless you get gradually hardened'. At the end of the letter, above the sketch of a cat, she signed herself, 'your loving lonely Clemmie'. On the following day she wrote again, warning him that he must be inoculated '*as soon as possible* . . . as it would be terrible if you had typhoid or enteric'. Edward Marsh had lunched with her that day, and was, she wrote, 'much excited at your going with the Guards'. On November 23 she wrote again to say that she had received his second list of requirements, and had sent

9 Thomas Lister, 1854–1925. 4th Baron Ribblesdale, 1876. Lord-in-Waiting to Queen Victoria, 1880–5. Master of the Queen's Buckhounds, 1892–5.

them all off 'with the exception (alas) of the trench wading boots.
London seems to be emptied of these, but I am going to make a
fresh try this morning & if I fail I shall send you pro tem a pair of
rubber waders which they say is the next best thing.' It made her
so miserable, she continued, to wake up at night and think of
him shivering in the trenches. She also told him that his son Randolph wanted to buy a spade so that if a bomb fell on his father's
trench he could dig himself out sideways.

Three days earlier Clementine Churchill had dined with her
cousin Venetia Montagu. Everyone at the dinner, she continued,
'was thrilled at your having joined the Grenadiers'. Augustine
Birrell,[10] who was present, 'was most sympathetic & has invited
me to dine with him tonight which is I know a great honour as
he does not ask many people'. She also reported that J. L. Garvin
was dining that night with Lady Randolph, and that she herself
was disappointed not to have been asked in time. Nevertheless,
she had arranged to see Garvin soon at 41 Cromwell Road, to
enlist his support for her husband's actions. She wrote also of a
young soldier who had just returned from the front, and had told
her sister Nellie Hozier 'that it was common knowledge that you
had refused a Brigade & wished to go in the trenches'. The young
man had told Nellie Hozier that 'everyone thought this splendid
as the general expectation among the rank & file of officers was
that you would join your regiment for a week or a fortnight; that
you would then be put on some staff while the regiment was
given some interesting work & that you would then be given a
Brigade'. Clementine Churchill's letter ended on a sad note, for
this was the beginning of an unhappy time for her. 'My darling,'
she wrote, 'I think of you constantly & I do hope that when you
think of me, it is not a picture of a harsh arguing scold, but your
loving & sad Clemmie. I love you very much more even than I
thought I did—for Seven years you have filled my whole life & now
I feel more than half my life has vanished across the channel. . . .'
There had been many occasions during their seven years of marriage when Churchill and his wife had not been together. Church-

[10] Augustine Birrell, 1850–1933. Liberal MP, 1889–1900; 1906–18. Chief
Secretary to the Lord Lieutenant of Ireland, 1907–16.

ill's work had often called him away from London. But this was the first time that they had been apart for any length of time. Both knew that they might never meet again.

On November 26 Churchill's career nearly came to an abrupt end. He had returned to the trenches the previous day, and was sitting in the headquarters dugout of No 1 Company with Edward Grigg eating some lunch, when an urgent message arrived from far behind the lines. It read: 'The Corps Commander wishes to see Major Churchill at four o'clock at Merville. A car will be waiting at the Rouge Croix crossroads at three fifteen.' The Corps Commander was Lieutenant-General Haking,[11] whom Churchill had known for many years. If he were to be appointed to the command of a Brigade, it might well be one under Haking's command. Churchill described what then happened in a letter to his wife on the following day:

. . . I thought it rather a strong order to bring me out of the trenches by daylight—a 3 miles walk across sopping fields on wh stray bullets are always falling, along tracks periodically shelled. But I assumed it was something important and anyhow I had no choice. So having made myself as clean as possible, I started off just as the enemy began to shell the roads & trenches in revenge for the shelling he had been receiving from our provocative and well fed artillery.

I just missed a whole bunch of shells wh fell on the track a hundred yards behind me; and arrived after an hour's walking, muddy wet & sweating at the rendezvous where I was to meet the motor. No motor! Presently a Staff Colonel turned up—saying he had lost the motor wh had been driven off by shells. He added that the general had wanted to have a talk with me but that it was only about things in general & that another day wd do equally well. I said that I was obeying an order, that I regretted leaving the trenches at a moment when they were under bombardment, that if I was not wanted for any official duty I wd return at once. And this I did—another hour across the sop-

[11] Richard Cyril Byrne Haking, 1862–1945. Entered Army, 1881. Brigadier-General commanding the XI Corps, 1915–18. Knighted, 1916. Commanded British Military Mission to Russia and the Baltic Provinces, 1919. High Commissioner, League of Nations, Danzig, 1921–3. General Officer commanding the British troops in Egypt, 1923–7.

ping fields now plunged in darkness. As I walked I cd see our trenches in the distance with great red brilliant shells flaring over them in fours & fives & cd hear the shriek of the projectiles rising like the sound of a storm. It looked fierce & formidable but by the time I got near silence had descended. You may imagine how I abused to myself the complacency of this General—though no doubt kindly meant—dragging me about in rain & wind for nothing.

I reached the trenches without mishap & then learned that a quarter of an hour after I had left, the dugout in wh I was living had been struck by a shell which burst a few feet from where I wd have been sitting; smashing the structure & killing the mess orderly who was inside. Another orderly and one officer who were inside were shaken & rattled, & all our effects buried in mud & debris. When I saw the ruin I was not so angry with the General after all.

My servant too was probably saved by the fact that I took him with me to carry my coat. Now see from this how vain it is to worry about things. It is all chance and our wayward footsteps are best planted without too much calculation. One must yield oneself simply & naturally to the mood of the game and trust in God wh is another way of saying the same thing.

These are commonplace experiences out here wh do not excite wonder or even interest. . . .

This near escape from death was one on which Churchill often reflected. 'In war,' he later wrote in *Thoughts and Adventures,* 'chance casts aside all veils and disguises and presents herself nakedly from moment to moment as the direct arbiter over all persons and events. . . . You may walk to the right or to the left of a particular tree, and it makes the difference whether you rise to command an Army Corps or are sent home crippled or paralysed for life.'

Churchill remained with the Guards for another four days. He spent a further forty-eight hours in the front line, exploring the trench system, learning how saps were constructed and parapets strengthened, gaining an impression of the power of snipers and the force of exploding shells, watching men under stress, and sharing their dangers. 'I continue to make friends with these Grenadiers,' he wrote to his wife on November 26, 'and really I have had no time to think of larger things than those I see.' He found himself drawn towards leniency and towards compassion. 'I keep watch during part of the night so that others may sleep. Last night I found a sentry asleep on his post. I frightened him dreadfully but did not charge him with the crime. He was only a lad, & I am not an officer of the regiment. The penalty is death or at least 2 years.' The hazards of war did not disturb him unduly. 'This morning we were shelled & I expect there will be more tonight,' he wrote to his wife on November 26. 'It has not caused me any sense of anxiety or apprehension, nor does the approach of a shell quicken my pulse, or try my nerves or make me about to bob as do so many. It is satisfactory to find that so many years of luxury have in no way impaired the tone of my system. At this game I hope I shall be as good as any.'

Churchill felt that he had learned a great deal in five days, and that his experiences would serve him well once he had been given a Brigade. 'I feel I understand the conditions and shall not be at sea if I take a command,' he wrote to his wife. 'Nothing but direct personal experience as a company officer cd have given me the knowledge. Few generals have drawn their water from this deep spring.' The Battalion marched to its reserve billets on the evening of November 26. In that brief period of holding the line two men had been killed outright, two had died of wounds and eight others had been wounded. The wintry conditions had not abated: 'Cold and raw with a little snow during the night,' the Battalion's war diarist had recorded on November 25. Writing from reserve billets at Riez Bailleul, Churchill tried to reassure his wife that he was not disturbed by his new surroundings: 'I do not mind the discomfort at all & do not think it will affect my health in any way. . . . I feel vy much master of myself & superior to the ordinary material considerations.' Two days later, on November 28, he wrote again:

. . . We came out of the line last night without mishap, & marched in under brilliant moonlight while the men sang 'Tipperary' & 'The Farmer's boy' and the guns boomed applause. It is like getting to a jolly good tavern after a long day's hunting, wet & cold & hungry, but not without having had sport. The discipline of this battalion is vy strict. For the slightest offence—a sulky word, a single crouch under the parapet at the wrong time, a small untidiness, men are sharply punished. But the results are good. The spirit is admirable. The men are better than most of the officers. The officers are quite up to the mark.

A total indifference to death or casualties prevails. What has to be done is done, & the losses accepted without fuss or comment. But for the fact that I ought to do what is most useful, I cd be quite content with a company in this fine regiment.

In reserve, Churchill had time to reflect, for the first time since he had left London, on politics, and on his own future. 'I do not feel the least revolt at the turn of events,' he had written to his wife in his letter of November 27. 'LG & McK [McKenna] & the old block [Asquith] are far away & look like mandarins of some remote province of China. If I survive the war, I shall have no difficulty in taking my place in the House of Commons & it must ever be a good one.' He had a number of commissions for her to carry out: 'Garvin, Scott, Rothermere & others shd be cultivated. They are loyal friends of quality & power. Keep in touch with the Government. Show complete confidence in our fortunes. Hold your head vy high. You always do.' There followed a more personal reflection: 'Above all don't be worried about me. If my destiny has not already been accomplished I shall be guarded surely. If it has been there is nothing that Randolph will need to be ashamed of in what I have done for the country.'

During his forty-eight hours in reserve, Churchill received a letter from Lord Lansdowne, who had written on November 20: 'If I had a regiment to rejoin I should very likely have followed your example, but having none I suppose I must remain where I am. It cannot be for long, and when you come back to political life you will find me—if still in any sense alive—beyond all doubt politically extinct.' Churchill replied on November 27, encouraging Lansdowne not to resign:

Your vy kind letter has just reached me on coming out of the trenches, & I take advantage of a day in support to answer it—& to thank you for it.

It was a gt pleasure to me to find that we were so often in agreement on the questions of the war; & I feel that you understood fully &

to a large extent shared my point of view. I hope you will not think of leaving the Government. My position & commitments were quite different to those of any other Minister. I took pains to point this out when I spoke in Parliament. It wd be a cause of regret to many out here if you were to stand aside—without a reason of supreme importance. The only thing that really matters is to persevere obstinately in the war. For that you stand as the representative of the Conservative party more than any one else. Method & policy are quite subordinate to this.

I am being vy kindly received & treated by the soldiers, & am happy to be free from cares, serving in the line with the Grenadiers. Later on they may find something else for me to do, but it is only possible to learn the conditions of trench warfare by living under them.

This was the first political letter Churchill had written for over a week.

On November 28 Lord Cavan asked Churchill to lunch with him at his Headquarters at La Gorgue. 'He talked everything over quite freely,' Churchill wrote to his wife that night, '& invited me to do the same.' Cavan told Churchill that it was no longer necessary for him to return to the trenches, that after a week's concentrated experience of the front line—most unusual for a man of his age—the time had come for him to remain at Brigade headquarters until he was appointed to command a Brigade of his own. But Churchill refused this offer. 'I said I wouldn't miss a day of it,' he wrote to his wife. 'Nor did I. I also scorned the modest comforts of Battalion HQ & lived in the wet & the mud with the men in the firing line. My physique is such that I support these conditions without the slightest ill effect. Of course I have seen vy little, but I have seen enough to be quite at my ease about all the ordinary things.'

On the night of November 28 the 2nd Battalion returned to the trenches. Once more Churchill slept in a front line dugout with Grigg's Company. 'A quiet night. Casualties one man slightly wounded,' the Battalion diarist reported. Very little happened throughout the next day, except rain. On the morning of November 30 there was more activity. It was Churchill's forty-first birthday. 'We had a good deal of shelling . . .' he wrote to his wife,

'& for about 3 hours the trenches were under bombardment at about 2 shells a minute. I had a splendid view of the whole entertainment. Splinters & debris came vy close—*inches*—but we only had 2 men hurt in the company. They were all vy glad to be relieved however, & on our return celebrated my birthday with a most cheery dinner.'

The 2nd Battalion spent the next eight days in reserve billets at Merville. Churchill accepted Sir John French's invitation to return to St Omer as his guest.

Edward Grigg had found Churchill absorbed by army life. On December 2 he wrote to his mother:[12]

Winston was attached to the Company again for all the last period in the firing line. It was very cold and very wet—first a bitter frost, and then rain, sleet and thaw, which put us up to the calf in mud and slime. That part of the line is in bad order, too, and we had nothing but a small dug-out about 2 ft 6 high with a wet mud floor to live and sleep in, and we all got kinks in our spines getting in and out of the beastly thing. But Winston accepted the situation with great cheerfulness and we had quite a good time. He has forgotten his political legacy from Lord Randolph, and thinks much more, I am sure, of the military instincts which have descended to him from the great Duke of Marlborough. The result is that he is strictly amenable to discipline, and salutes the Commanding Officer as smartly as any of us when he comes round. It's a funny world.

Churchill reached St Omer on the evening of December 1. Lord Esher,[13] who arrived earlier on the same day, wrote in his

---

[12] Elizabeth Deas Thomson, 1836–1920. Married, 1870, Henry Grigg, Indian Civil Service, who died in 1895, aged 54.

[13] Esher's status in France was obscure. 'Nobody knows what he does here exactly,' Northcliffe later wrote to Geoffrey Robinson from Paris, on 8 August 1916. 'The Ambassador does not know, and asked me. He is dressed as a colonel and wears the Grand Cross of the Legion of Honour all day long and probably all night too. He is always going backward and forward between Paris and the French G.H.Q., writes for the papers, sees everybody who comes to Paris directly they arrive, is mixed up with some very queer Jews, but is really, I believe, only a busybody. Still what he says, as the Americans say, "goes" among the French. His visiting card is a most extraordinary production; it is in French—"Le Vicomte Esher, Member of the War Council (or some such words), Governor of Windsor Castle, Commissioner of the Red Cross." There are about seven lines of it.'

diary that night that Churchill had amused the inhabitants of GHQ by referring to himself as 'the escaped scapegoat!'. The atmosphere at Sir John French's headquarters was tense. The Commander-in-Chief had just been recalled to London, and for several days those who believed themselves privy to the secrets of Government spoke openly of his imminent removal from his high command. 'Sir John is in a state of dégommé,' wrote Sir Henry Wilson in his diary on November 30. Both Wilson and Esher gave Churchill their views on the political situation, and were pleased to find someone new with whom they could exchange confidences. But Churchill was disturbed by all they told him. He had hoped to be able to forget politics and to become a soldier. Their information would not allow him to do so. Esher told Churchill about the latest situation on the Gallipoli Peninsula, recounting further details about the incident of which his mother had written; of how Kitchener, despatched to the East by the Cabinet in order to report personally on the situation, had returned precipitately to London, having first demanded and then opposed an end to the whole Gallipoli enterprise. London and Paris were buzzing with rumours of the imminent departure of the whole Allied force from the Gallipoli Peninsula. 'The idea of evacuating Gallipoli infuriates him,' Esher recorded in his diary, 'and he declares that if this is decided upon, he will go back to the House of Commons and denounce his colleagues. Of these, without exception, he has no great opinion. Apropos of the War Council, from which he was excluded, he said, "I was one of HM's servants, but not one of his upper servants." He has lost nothing by being in the trenches, not even his brilliant conversational powers.'

A day at St Omer surrounded by political talk wrenched Churchill's thoughts from parapets to politics. Not only the Gallipoli evacuation, but the difficulties on both the Salonika and Mesopotamian fronts upset him. He also learned of the appointment of Sir Horace Smith-Dorrien[14] to the East African com-

---

[14] Horace Lockwood Smith-Dorrien, 1858–1930. Entered Army, 1876. Served on Lord Kitchener's Staff at Omdurman, 1898. Major-General, 1901. Knighted, 1904. General commanding the IInd Corps, 1914–15; the 2nd

mand which he had so wanted. Two days later, on December 3, he wrote to his wife:

> . . . The news I get here from the generals & Esher reveals a continuance of the same utter inability to take a decision on the part of the Government. What they settle one day is upset the next. Months have now passed in this condition: & now the great twin disasters at Gallipoli & Salonika are drawing near. The story when told, as told it shall be, will be incredible to the world: & the guilt of criminality attaches to those responsible. . . . There is I fear no doubt that the Baghdad operation has been heavily checked. There again 4 precious weeks were wasted making up the Cabinet mind after the victory of Kut-el-Amara.[15]
>
> Kitchener returns after 25 days of futile banging about the Near East and making silly proposals. It seems likely that to get rid of him a large number of troops will be diverted to Egypt & locked up there. Old Smith-Dorrien for East Africa! Bravo Henry!

Rumour placed Churchill at the centre of many cabalistic combinations. A journalist, James Douglas, wrote to Fisher on December 2: 'I hear that Beresford & Carson are forming a "National" Party to provide an Opposition and an alternative Government. This is Churchill's pet scheme, and the idea is that he would come back and join the cabal. Churchill and Beresford would be a dangerous combination with Carson. May heaven preserve us from that!'

Churchill was not privy to such eccentric plots. On the morning of December 2 he rode with Sir Henry Wilson. 'We have made friends again after some serious differences in the past,' Churchill wrote to his wife on December 3. 'He was much impressed with my ideas & at his suggestion I have spent today

---

Army, 1915. Removed from his command by Sir John French, May 1915. Commanded the 1st Army for Home Defence, May–November 1915. Appointed to command the forces in East Africa, December 1915, but invalided home with pneumonia on reaching Cape Town. (The command was given to General Smuts.) Governor of Gibraltar, 1918–23.

[15] In July 1915 a British Expeditionary Force advanced from Basra towards Bagdad. Kut-el-Amara, 100 miles from Bagdad, was captured on September 29. Advancing to Ctesiphon, 13 miles from Bagdad, the Force was defeated on November 24, and retreated to Kut, having lost in killed or wounded over one-tenth of its men.

embodying them in a paper. . . .' Wilson drew Churchill into
talk of an anti-Asquith movement. 'I asked him why he did not
go home, join forces with Milner[16] & Carson, & knock Squiff off
his perch,' Wilson wrote in his diary on December 2: 'He was
quite open about these things. He was going to wait for Gallipoli
and Salonica disasters & then try to jump in.' This was an incomplete interpretation of Churchill's feelings. Although he was not
averse to denouncing Asquith's conduct of the war should it seem
to be leading to disaster, he did not believe that an outsider could
ever overthrow a Prime Minister so well entrenched as Asquith.
Only widespread popular revulsion with the war policy, based
upon genuine concern, could lead, in his opinion, to effective political change, and tempt him home. Wide-ranging power, not
partial involvement, was what he wanted, as he had explained to
his brother two weeks before. Milner and Carson could not give
him that. He therefore turned his attention to the mechanics of
war.

The ideas which he had discussed with Wilson were centred
upon his search for something to break the deadlock on the western front; preferably some mechanical means which would end
the stalemate and offer swift victory, while at the same time re-
ducing considerably the loss of life which trench warfare entailed. Churchill wrote down his ideas that evening and during
most of the following day. He then had them typed out at GHQ
in the form of a memorandum which he called 'Variants of the
Offensive'. His memorandum examined methodically a series of
possible attacks other than by the 'bare breasts of men'. His first
proposal was for shields: 'For the specific object of protecting
men from machine gun bullets during the short walk across from
trench to trench *shields*[17] are indispensable.' These shields could

[16] Alfred Milner, 1854–1925.    Under-Secretary for Finance, Egypt,
1889–92. Chairman of the Board of Inland Revenue, 1892–7. Knighted,
1895. High Commissioner for South Africa, 1897–1905. Created Baron, 1901.
Created Viscount, 1902. Member of the War Cabinet, December 1916–18.
Secretary of State for War, 1918–19; for the Colonies, 1919–21.

[17] In 1914 Sir Frederick Hamilton, the Second Sea Lord, designed a model
steel screen 12 ft long by 6 ft high which would take six infantrymen abreast
and give protection to at least twenty-five men as they advanced. On 2 Janu-

be carried by single men 'or pushed by several men'; they would be 'lined along the parapet and picked up by the men on the signal to advance'. Churchill suggested the use of a collective shield, capable of covering between five and fifteen men, 'pushed along either on a wheel or still better on a Caterpillar'. This collective shield on Caterpillar tracks would be fifteen feet broad and four feet high. Faced in the direction of German machine-guns, which would fire at it in vain, the men behind it would complete any cutting of the German barbed wire which the artillery had failed to demolish. Churchill wanted five such composite shields used in front of a Battalion during the attack, and 'slewed around to face the fire' forty or fifty yards in front of the attacking units.

Churchill suggested that some seventy shields should be completed before a single one was used in battle. Then they would be 'disposed secretly along the whole attacking front two or three hundred yards apart. Ten or fifteen minutes before the assault these engines should move forward over the best line of advance open, passing through or across our trenches at prepared points. They are capable of traversing any ordinary obstacle, ditch, breastwork or trench. They carry two or three maxims each and can be fitted with flame apparatus. Nothing but a direct hit from a field gun will stop them.'

The memorandum went on to examine what the Caterpillar could do once it reached the German wire; its tracks could turn to left or right, running parallel to the trench, sweeping its parapet with fire, crushing and cutting its barbed wire, and making the gaps through which 'the shield-bearing infantry will advance'. The Caterpillars could also be designed so that they could cross the trenches, climb slopes and, with armoured machine-guns on top of them, act as an offensive as well as a protective weapon. The Caterpillar trench-cutting and firing machine would be used suddenly and unexpectedly, but it should not be used alone. The collective shield and individual shields should be used simultane-

---

ary 1915 he wrote to Churchill: 'As I have been an advocate of this principle & have been trying to find any flaw in it for the last 20 years I make no apologies for indicating how I think they should be used.'

ously. While the Caterpillar machine was cutting the wire, individual soldiers would be at work with special wire-cutting implements. In a footnote to his memorandum Churchill commented:

In the dockyards one frequently sees men cutting steel plates with a jet of flame as if they were brown paper. Could not a rod be made which a soldier could carry with the necessary gas cylinder which would enable him to fuse *instantly* the wire in his front? If so, no invention would appear to be more urgently required.

Churchill also envisaged what he called 'the attack by the spade'. Instead of isolated saps pushed out in front of particular trench lines, the soldiers of several Battalions would dig, on a two- to three-mile front, some three hundred saps, dug simultaneously towards the enemy lines, and themselves interconnected. Once they reached within sixty yards of the enemy's parapet, they would be immune from his artillery.

Churchill discussed his ideas with all those within range. Having spent the morning riding with Sir Henry Wilson on December 2, he then drove out for lunch with his friend Jack Seely, at the headquarters of the Canadian Cavalry Division near Kemmel, and after the lunch, he, Seely and Seely's ADC Sir Archibald Sinclair examined the cavalry positions. That same night, back at St Omer, Valentine Fleming came to dinner, and once more Churchill expounded his ideas. Absorbing himself in these technical problems, Churchill did not let himself be over troubled by so much talk of politics. He had made up his mind to have no part in the schemes of those he met. 'I am jolly glad to be out of it,' he wrote to his wife on December 3. 'It has indeed distressed & unsettled me to come again for a few days into the area of secret information. The able soldiers there are miserable at the Government's drifting. Some urge me to return and try to break them up. I reply no—I will not go back unless I am wounded; or unless I have effective control.'

Clementine Churchill continued to write to her husband while he was at St Omer, comforting, advising and warning him as best she could. 'Poodle darling,' he had written to her on November 27, 'I love yr letters and it is a delightful thought to me that you are there at home with your 3 kittens thinking of me & feeling that I am doing right.' On November 28 she was still worried that he was 'staying longer in the trenches than your duty requires', and that he might suffer from having gone 'at one swoop from an atmosphere of hot rooms, sedentary work & Turkish baths to a life of the most cruel hardships & exposure'. She was worried too about how his reputation might be affected should his trench experiences end in disaster: 'If you were killed & you had over exposed yourself the world might think that you had sought death out of grief for your share in the Dardanelles. It is your duty to the country to try & live (consistent with your honour as a soldier).' She was disturbed by his description of the rats which swarmed everywhere in the front line. 'I should mind the rats even more than the bullets,' she wrote; 'Can you kill them or would that be wasting good ammunition?' She was also sad that 'for the first time for seven years besides being parted from you I am cut off from the stream of private news & have to rely upon the newspapers and *rumour,* so that I am in a state of suspended animation'. The only political news she could impart was on December 1, when she reported that 'Simon yesterday made a long attack on Northcliffe which would certainly have been very damaging if it had not been made by a prig and a bore'. Her principal pride was that he was on active service: 'Since you have re-become a soldier I look upon civilians of high or low degree with pity & indulgence. The wives of men over military age may be lucky but I am sorry for them being married to feeble & incompetent old men.'

These sturdy sentiments hid a deeper anguish. In her letter of November 28, which she hoped would reach him on his birthday, but which in fact arrived a day late, she wrote of how lonely she was without him. Not even their daughter Sarah, who looked so like him, could fill the gap caused by his absence. Nor could her fears be dispersed by his own self-confidence, or her forebodings by his optimism. It was a terrible time for her, uncertain, cold and overshadowed by the knowledge of the dangers of the front-line. Too many of their relations and friends were dead already, too much mutilation had occurred, too many lives made unbearable by sudden loss, for her to shake off the desperate fear which so many women had now to live with.

On November 30 Violet Asquith married Maurice Bonham Carter, her father's Private Secretary. To everyone's surprise, for they all believed that he was still in the eastern Mediterranean, Kitchener arrived to sign the register. The Churchills were also represented at the ceremony. Clementine Churchill reported the next day: 'Randolph officiated as one of the pages and looked *quite* beautiful in a little Russian velvet suit with fur. His looks made quite a sensation & at Downing Street afterwards he was surrounded & kissed & admired by dozens of lovely women.'

On November 27 Churchill's mother sent him a long account of her activities. She reported dinner gossip to the effect that Churchill had been offered the command of a Brigade, but had refused it; that she had dined with Garvin and Curzon on the previous Thursday; that she was trying to arrange a further dinner for Bonar Law and Balfour; that Curzon 'was full of you, he wants to write to you & I gave him yr address'. She also told her son that she was writing literary articles which brought her £50 a month, and that she would give all her earnings to her two daughters-in-law. She was concerned about her son's welfare. 'I am sending you a pair of oil silk stockings,' she wrote, 'to be worn sandwiched between two woolly ones. They say they keep yr feet at the same temperature as when you put on the stockings—*not* very healthy but better than frost bites. Let me know how they do and I will send you some more—I hope this will reach you in time for your birthday. . . .' Her faith in her son's future was unshaken:

Please be sensible. I think you ought to take the trenches in small doses after 10 years of a more or less sedentary life—But I am sure you won't 'play the fool'—remember you are destined for greater things than even in the past. I am a greater believer in your star—& I know that you are doing absolutely the right thing. We shall all of us 'hot up' your friends & keep the ball rolling. . . .

Churchill replied to his mother on December 1: 'The return of K delights me. What a world of shams it is! Well I am thank God only a spectator now, so I am better situated to see the humour of the play.' Of her offer to 'hot up' his friends, he wrote: 'You are quite right to keep in touch with our friends—also with our pseudo-friends. My attitude towards the Government is independent not hostile, & yr tone sh'd be salt not bitter.'

At the end of November Edward Marsh had written to Churchill reporting that a Duchy of Lancaster key was missing. 'Eddie dear,' Churchill replied on December 1, 'I have no split key—nor any key—except the key to heaven.' His letter continued: 'Tout va bien ici. I am now "resting" after 10 days in the line. I had a lot to live down with the Grenadiers, having been so long in the Government: but I parted from them this morning for two or three days as if from home. . . . You would enjoy yourself out here, if I could find you a coign. . . . Best love. Write sometimes.'

On December 3, Clementine Churchill received a visit at 41 Cromwell Road from General Bridges, who had just seen her husband at GHQ and spoke appreciatively of his military future. 'It is nectar to me,' she wrote after Bridges had gone, 'to feel & see generous admiration & appreciation of you, which for so long have been denied unjustly.' Her scorn for Asquith was undiminished. On December 3 she reported how, after Violet Asquith's wedding, she had been standing with Haldane in the hall at 10 Downing Street, when Asquith appeared: he merely 'muttered a few civil words & shuffled off sniffing nervously'. There was also family news from home. On December 4 her sister Nellie Hozier married Bertram Romilly.[18] On the previous day she had reported that 'Randolph, Diana and Johnny are terribly excited as they are to carry Nellie's train arrayed in white satin'. But there

[18] Bertram Henry Samuel Romilly, 1878–1940. 2nd Lieutenant, Scots Guards, 1898. Colonel, attached to the Egyptian Camel Corps, 1914–17. Military Governor, Province of Galilee, 1919–20. Chief Instructor, Cairo Military School, 1925–8.

was sad news too. No family could escape the toll of war. Churchill's first cousin, Clare Sheridan,[19] had lost her husband,[20] and was distraught. Clementine Churchill wrote in anguish: 'My darling I don't know how one bears such things. I feel I could not weather such a blow. She has a beautiful little son 8 weeks old, but her poor "black puss" sleeps in Flanders. You *must* come back to me my dear one—(you are now my orange pug again . . .).'

[19] Clare Consuelo Frewen, 1885–1970. Sculptress.
[20] William Frederick Sheridan, 1879–1915. Known as Wilfred. Grandson of Richard Brinsley Sheridan. Businessman. Married Clare Frewen, 1910. 2nd Lieutenant, 11th London Regiment, September 1914. Captain, 2nd Rifle Brigade, 1915. Killed in action at the battle of Loos, 25 September 1915, five days after the birth of his son.

# 19

# The Seven-day General

***

CHURCHILL SPENT December 3 at St Omer, confident that when Sir John French returned that evening he would be given a formal offer of higher military employment. He was relieved to have left the hostile atmosphere of London, but did not intend to neglect his few supporters. After he resigned, C. P. Scott had sent him a note of encouragement. 'It is something of a calamity,' Scott had written on December 1, 'that you should be lost to our politics at the time when they stand most in need of your qualities.' Churchill welcomed the *Manchester Guardian* as an ally. The *Observer* had been his most consistent supporter; to its editor, J. L. Garvin, Churchill wrote on December 4, telling him of Scott's letter and adding: 'I hope you will keep in touch with him. Two virtuous pens may save the nation. Who else is there?'

Like the others who had gathered at GHQ, Churchill was concerned to learn the future of Sir John French himself—for it was common knowledge at GHQ that the Commander-in-Chief no longer had the confidence of the Cabinet, and his dismissal was believed to be imminent. But when French returned to St Omer that Friday evening, he was still in command of the British forces in France. As such, he remained responsible for all promotion, and was Churchill's patron. That night Churchill dined at GHQ as the Commander-in-Chief's guest, and learned of what had passed in London. 'Asquith clearly wants him to go, & go without any kind of friction,' Churchill reported to his wife. 'French wants to stay but also to behave with dignity. Asquith has so left the case that French is free to stay & is all the time tortured by the sense of utter insecurity. For three weeks no one has thought of the enemy. 'Tis cruel. Anyhow I don't expect any immediate change.'

French pressed Churchill to accept a Brigade at once. He already had full confidence in Churchill's abilities to take one; but he also had a further reason for wanting to settle the matter quickly, knowing that within three weeks he would no longer be Commander-in-Chief. 'I have acquiesced,' Churchill wrote to his wife on December 4. It was now certain that in a week or two he would be a Brigadier-General. Meanwhile he decided to stay on at St Omer, to visit other sectors of the front, and to go into the line once more with the Grenadiers before taking up his command. In his letter of December 4 he continued:

. . . I have just got back from a vy long walk with French—talking about all things in heaven & earth. I am so sorry for him. No man can sustain two different kinds of separate worries—a tremendous army in the face of the enemy: a gnawing intrigue at the back. He seems to have told a good many people of my refusal of a Brigade and insistence on going to the trenches. He said the PM spoke with emotion about me. But Asquith's sentiments are always governed by his interests. They are vy hearty & warm within limits wh cost nothing.

While at St Omer Churchill had made friends with a young cavalry captain, Edward Louis Spiers,[1] whom he had first met before the war at the home of Venetia Stanley's sister, Sylvia Henley. Spiers, who was serving as liaison officer between GHQ and the French 10th Army, offered to take Churchill to the 10th Army's sector of the line in front of Arras on December 5. During the journey he was stimulated by Spiers' interest in him. The

[1] Edward Louis Spiers, 1886–    . Joined Kildare Militia, 1905. Captain, 11th Hussars, 1914. Four times wounded, 1914–15. Liaison officer with French 10th Army, 1915–16. Head of the British Military Mission to Paris, 1917–20. In 1918 he changed the spelling of his name to Spears. National Liberal MP, 1922–4; Conservative MP, 1931–45. Churchill's Personal Representative with French Prime Minister and Minister of Defence, May–June 1940. Head of British Mission to General de Gaulle, 1940. Head of Spears Mission to Syria and the Lebanon, 1941. First Minister to Syria and the Lebanon, 1942–4.

admiration of this young man, whose bravery Sir John French had praised, encouraged him to spill out his bitter thoughts about the Dardanelles, the conduct of the war and Grey's Balkan diplomacy. Spiers recorded in his diary that evening:

. . . WC talked of everything. . . . Failure in Aug in Gallipoli was due to our thinking one div was as good as another one—we were within a few 100 yards of the ridge which meant success & 16 or 17 Divs prisoners. Says Serbia was non accommodating & refused to give Bulgaria Bulgarian country even against heavy compensations elsewhere. Believes it is a war of men & therefore we must not lose men fighting Bulgaria etc. Told me we had achieved the impossible, i.e. a union between Bulgar & Turk with a fair chance of Greece chipping in against us as well. All due to our hesitations. Believes we ought to leave Salonika at once as news bad. . . . Thinks we will have disasters in Serbia, Dardanelles & Bagdad—but we will win in end as ruin is better, so all England thinks, than a bad peace—and above all Russia has been given breathing space.

Churchill and Spiers reached the French front line at noon. 'I was received with much attention,' Churchill wrote to his wife that night, 'more so in fact than when I went as 1st Lord.' Spiers showed him round the battlefields where, in the fighting two months before, a hundred thousand men had been killed. Churchill wanted to set her mind at rest about the danger. The Germans, he wrote, 'considerately refrained from shelling as usual, & I was able to visit all the celebrated spots'. He was photographed, at the French General's[2] insistence, against a background of German prisoners, and for the photograph he wore a French steel helmet, which General Fayolle had given him. He kept the helmet, whose superior safety virtues he at once recognized. 'I have been given,' he told his wife, 'a true steel helmet by the French wh I am going to wear, as it looks so nice & will perhaps protect my valuable cranium.' The two men then drove

[2] Marie Emile Fayolle, 1852–1928. Entered the French Army, 1875. Professor, Ecole de Guerre, 1897–1907. General of Brigade, 1910. Commanded the 33rd Corps, 1915–16; the 6th Army, 1916–17; the Centre Group of Armies, 1917; the Group of Armies of Reserve, 1917–18; the French occupation Forces on the Rhine, 1918–20. Marshal of France, 1921.

off. Once again Churchill confided in Spiers, who recorded in his diary:

. . . On return journey WC said French spoke v highly of me to him. Said I was most gallant & able. He told me Sir John wd probably go & be replaced by Robertson. Sir J might get big job in London as adviser to the government. Meanwhile had offered WC a Brigade! WC said he wd prefer a Bn but Sir J advised him to take what he offered. WC consulted me & all things considered I advised a Bde— after all Seely has one. He then said he had asked Sir J for me as Bde Major! ! Sir J said I had been wounded twice & [had no] right to expect more, further that I cd ill be spared. WC put the question to me. Well I said I was anxious enough to fight—& because it was put to me that it was a come down to accept, wd not say no. Flattered in a way but anxious & don't quite think it right.

Later that evening Spiers had further thoughts:

On thinking it over think it wd be absurd—a politician as Brigadier, a cavalry man as Bde Major! Poor Brigade. I know nothing of what wd be required, no details—& yet I wd practically have 6 Bns to command. . . .
WC has no doubts. Quietly spoke of it having been proposed he should command the force going to E. Africa.

Although Sir John French had persuaded Churchill to bypass the humbler sphere of Battalion Commander, Clementine Churchill did not think this was a wise move. On December 6, as soon as she heard of the proposed promotion, she wrote to dissuade him:

. . . I hope so much my Darling that you may *still* decide to take a battalion first, much as I long for you to be not so much in the trenches. I am absolutely certain that whoever is C in C, you will rise to high commands. I'm sure everyone feels that anything else would be wasting a valuable instrument. But everyone who *really* loves you & has your interest at heart wants you to go step by step whereas I notice the Downing Street tone is 'of course Winston will have a brigade in a fortnight'—Thus do they hope to ease their conscience from the wrong they have done you, and then hope to hear no more of you. I have the fear that if you are now suddenly given a brigade & Sir John shortly afterwards goes, you might perhaps stick there as his successor might feel stodgy & that enough has been done for you. Sir John loves you & wants *himself* to have the joy of doing something for you, but I believe in Lord Cavan's advice—you & he should make a very strong combination & if he gets a corps I feel sure you wld soon get a division under him. Do get a battalion *now* & a brigade later.

Churchill had already made up his mind to take a Brigade. While at St Omer he had talked several times to Sir John French about his future staff. He was determined to have Spiers as his Brigade Major, and Sinclair as his ADC. The Commander-in-Chief argued that Spiers might not think Brigade Major a promotion. But on December 6 Churchill wrote to his wife that 'Spiers yesterday of his own initiative asked me to let him come to me in any command I obtained: & if they will let him go I shall certainly get him'. On December 7 Sir John French was in Paris. There was still no definite news of Churchill's promotion. 'General Instability is in command,' Churchill wrote to his wife on December 8. He had decided to spend another day with Spiers, and on December 7 they had gone to La Panne on the Belgian coast, to see the extreme sea-flank of the Allied line. During the drive they had discussed a variety of topics. Spiers recorded in his diary that night:

Met W Churchill at C in C's house at 8. W angry at my own car being late. Set off in one of C in C's Rolls Royces to La Panne. Lovely day & pleasant run. Told WC of my lack of experience as a Bde Major, of how important it was etc. He poo-hooed the idea—if it comes off & I fail he was warned.

We talked literature. Mostly French & politics—I made out a case for the house of Lords & he downed it—no agreement reached. He said some fine things about democracies, their answer to finer calls. Talk on religion—told him my views & he his—he believes he is a spirit which will live, without memory of the present, in the future.

When they reached La Panne, Churchill and Spiers were met by General Bridges, who took them to see the trenches running down to the sea. On returning from the coast Churchill and

Spiers visited Maxine Elliot,[3] Churchill's friend of many years, who was supervising a reception centre for Belgian refugees from a barge which she had made her headquarters and her home. Spiers was fascinated by this diversion from the rigours of military life. 'Tea with Maxine Elliot on her barge,' Spiers wrote in his diary, 'nice clever woman, must have been v beautiful. . . . Played 3 handed bridge. WC lost 20 f & I 11 f. WC v entertaining. Full of stories. Has one for every event. Dwelt on his cleverness in leaving Cabinet when they meant to sacrifice him & before the disasters he foretells occur—Salonika, Dardanelles & Bagdad.' Churchill had greatly enjoyed the visit. 'Such a jolly place,' he wrote to his wife, '& Spiers after so many months of war weariness & danger found it quite hard to climb the ladder wh led out into the night. . . . Maxine was absolutely alone—& vy lonely. She has done good work & is a really fine woman—tho' she must be judged by special standards.'

Churchill and Spiers drove back to St Omer. 'I like him vy much,' Churchill told his wife, '& he is entirely captivated.' In Spiers, Churchill found something that he greatly needed; someone who would listen to his plans without trying to denigrate them; someone who would be excited to hear of what he had done as First Lord, and would not belittle the things which he believed were achievements; someone who could give him the affection which he so needed at this moment of uncertainty and loneliness. It had been a tiring day; but throughout the return journey Churchill continued to tell Spiers of the plans and stratagems which he had devised when he was First Lord:

. . . WC said when we got to sea we shd have understood we had turned G's flank. Clever. Said we shd have forced Holland in at beginning & landed troops there. Said it had been thought of landing at Borkum & making naval & submarine base there to watch G fleet, our short range submarines wd then have come in & 1 Div wd have been landed forcing enemy to garrison whole coast & forced G fleet to fight.

[3] Jessie Dermot, 1868–1940. Born in Maine, USA. She adopted the name 'Maxine Elliot' for her stage career. In 1914 she organized a Belgian Relief Barge, from which, in fifteen months, she fed and clothed some 350,000 refugees.

Forgets Borkum within range of land & water shelling. Wd be true of
Heligoland but disastrous there. Said we cd then have put a few big
ships in Baltic not to fight a fleet but destroy units & joining hand with
Russians. Spoke of torpedoes fired from seaplanes.

Late that night Churchill and Spiers reached St Omer, but the
day was not over. For some while Lord Curzon had been pester-
ing Clementine Churchill about the apparent non-arrival of a letter which he had sent Churchill on November 30, together with
some apparently indiscreet enclosures. When she had told him
that there was nothing in her husband's letters to indicate he had
received it, Curzon was alarmed, and afraid that it had been intercepted by the military censor, a serious matter, as it contained
an account of the Government's dilemma over the evacuation of
Gallipoli. But the letter was not lost. On returning to GHQ with
Spiers, Churchill found it waiting for him.

In the letter, which Churchill opened in front of Spiers, Curzon revealed a number of disturbing and extraordinary things:
that the Cabinet had been divided by the issue of whether or not
to evacuate the Gallipoli Peninsula; that a serious political crisis
threatened; that Asquith had favoured evacuation; that Curzon
had led the protest against it; that Lansdowne, Selborne and
Crewe had supported Curzon; that a forceful report had been
circulated to the Cabinet from Admiral Wemyss in which he insisted that a further naval attack, on the scale of that of 18 March
1915, could turn the balance in favour of a combined military
and naval victory. Curzon reported that Bonar Law, 'who with
Lloyd George is the leader of the Scuttle', had demanded immediate evacuation. But that the combined influence of Lansdowne, Selborne, Crewe and Curzon had forced Asquith to give
a pledge of a week's delay before any decision was reached. Curzon believed that this delay, though short, was 'a powerful factor
operating against abandonment'. But he also told Churchill that
'B. Law and Ll George will fight to the finish'. Of Balfour's
attitude he wrote with acerbity: 'Balfour is as usual an inscrutable factor, sitting silent and detached as though he were a spectator on Mars, observing through a powerful telescope a fight

between the astral inhabitants of Saturn.' Most extraordinary of all, according to Curzon, were Kitchener's antics:

. . . A new and uncertain factor has been introduced on to the scene by the reappearance of Kitchener. It now transpires that he took away with him the Seals of Office, apprehending that they would be taken in his absence and transferred to Ll George! He is said to have scented a conspiracy against him and to have returned deliberately in order to defeat it. The most pathetic telegrams were sent to him by the PM pointing out how urgently his services were required to steady Egypt and straighten out Salonica or inspire some third place. But he always managed to receive these telegrams just too late to act upon them. And after a characteristic tour in which he hobnobbed with the various warrior kings and was cheered at the Continental railway stations, he reappeared last night, just in time to sign the register at Violet Asquith's wedding today.

His telegrams from the Aegean were almost fatuous, being contradictory, unbalanced and destitute of grasp or foresight. Starting from pronouncements against evacuation, he then wobbled, proposed a great Alexandretta move, and when this was refused became obsessed with an Egyptian nightmare, under the stress of which he came down on the side of evacuation at Gallipoli. I expect, if he were sent back again to carry it out, he would sing to a different tune. In the meantime his friends (or is it his enemies?) say that he is conscious that his days as S of S are numbered, and is resolved on getting out, through the Viceroyalty of India. Asquith took advantage of his absence to appoint Smith Dorrien to British E. Africa, and to hand over the remaining ordnance departments to Ll George [as Minister of Munitions], which I do not suppose will have sweetened his temper. . . .

Curzon ended his letter on an expectant note, hinting at Churchill's return to politics: 'I miss you very much—and so I am sure do many others. For as regards the Dardanelles I have only caught your mantle, as it fell from the fiery car of Elisha; and as regards Compulsion—we shall stand in urgent need of your advocacy and alliance.' This was the first time since Churchill's departure that a colleague had implied that there was still a place for him at the centre of political discussions. His first instinct was to return at once. Spiers, to whom he showed Curzon's letter and read Wemyss' report, was astonished at Churchill's reaction. 'Seemed furious,' he wrote in his diary, '. . . said things were moving fast and he might have to go to London.' But when morning came Churchill was less certain that his opportunity had come. He was thrilled that Wemyss had advocated a renewed naval attack, which he himself had always believed could be decisive. But he did not see how his personal position could really be rescued by his return. That evening he wrote to his wife:

. . . It wd not have been any good my joining in these discussions. A fresh uncompromised champion like Curzon had a better chance than I cd ever have had: & he has started the case as well as I cd have done. Please lock up all these papers after reading them, & never say you have seen them. Also keep in touch with Curzon & others. Don't fail to keep the threads in yr fingers. Let me know who you see. Curzon's letter & enclosures have of course revived distressing thoughts. My scorn for Kitchener is intense. If they evacuate in disaster—all the facts shall come out. They will be incredible to the world. The reckoning will be heavy & I shall make sure it is exacted.

Churchill knew that there was no part for him in the renewed Gallipoli discussions. All he could do was to try to encourage Curzon to persevere, and to rehearse his own reasons for remaining in France, writing to him on December 8:

My dear George,
I have read yr papers (wh reached me last night only) & as you may imagine with deep emotion. You have fought a splendid fight, & coming into it fresh & uncompromised, were better armed than I cd ever have been. I am absolutely content with your advocacy & do not desire to add or alter a word. By now I expect the decision will have been taken; but yr story breaks off at the climax & I must wait for the sequel.
The situation is no longer capable of the good solutions wh were open some months ago: but I do not think the right decisions wd be difficult, if any one had the necessary authority. Broadly speaking my views are yours: withdraw from Salonica: hold on at Gallipoli: use the Salonica and Egyptian forces to renew the attack by land both at Suvla & on the Asiatic side at the earliest moment, in conjunction with a resolute effort by the Fleet. I shd also persevere with the Bagdad ex-

pedition and make a further *barrage* there to the Oriental ambitions of Germany. It is needless to say that energy & efficiency in *execution* are as important as good decisions in principle.

I do not feel any prick of conscience at being out here. I did not go because I wished to disinterest myself in the great situation or because I feared the burden or the blow: but because I was and am sure that for the time being my usefulness was exhausted & that I cd only recover it by a definite & perhaps prolonged withdrawal. Had I seen the slightest prospect of being able to govern the event I wd have stayed. But in the circumstances I was not only free but bound to claim release.

And what a release! Except for the distressing thoughts wh yr papers & letter revive I have been entirely happy & free from care. I do not know when I have passed a more joyous three weeks; & to let that tremendous melancholy situation of our affairs all over the world slide from one's mind after having fixed it so long in mental gaze, has felt exactly like laying down a physical load. . . .

It is a jolly life with nice people; & one does not seem to mind the cold & wet & general discomfort; nor do I seem to be affected by them. Also as one may be killed at any moment—tho' I hope not—worries great & small recede to remote & shadowy distances.

I am not far away: but vy good reasons wd be required before I cd return. If such a break up on conscription as you indicate were to occur I cd not refuse my aid to an opposition, if it were desired. But I hope & believe this corner will be turned without a smash. I shall be painfully interested in your letters, but vy grateful for the kindness wh impels & inspires them. Give them to Creedy who will put them in French's bag—as long as there is a French! The uncertainty of the command out here & the rumours of change do great harm, & paralyse military thought. It wd be better to let things alone.

Yours ever<br>W

Curzon's letter had given Churchill a night of anticipation and uncertainty. But he soon realized that it was impracticable to act upon it. Clementine Churchill had also been thrilled to learn that Curzon had emerged in Cabinet as an advocate of renewed effort at Gallipoli. She had always fervently believed in the importance of victory at the Dardanelles. Writing to Curzon from 41 Cromwell Road on December 9, she took the initiative in trying to strengthen the new friendship:

My dear Lord Curzon,

I have just heard from Winston—a long letter telling me of your letter to him.

All you have told him has revived distressing thoughts & agitated him. But he says:—'It would not have been any good my joining in these discussions: a fresh uncompromised champion like Curzon had a better chance than I could ever have had.' He adds that you have stated the case better than he could have done. I should much like to see you—I wonder if you would lunch with me here on Saturday at 1.30?

I have always felt you liked Winston, but now that I know you both think alike it is another bond in common.

Yours always sincerely<br>Clementine S. Churchill

In her postscript Clementine Churchill wrote: 'The news in W's letter has moved me deeply; since he went away I have heard nothing of what has been going on in your councils, & have tried not to think or feel too much.' Although Churchill's thoughts of politics had been stirred by Curzon, the call to London never came. Nor was he entirely certain that it really would, or that he was not better off in France. When he wrote to his mother on December 8, urging her to 'keep in good touch with all my friends'—including Curzon and Garvin—he declared emphatically that 'All I hear confirms me in my satisfaction to be freed from my share in the present proceedings.' To J. L. Garvin he wrote with acerbity that same day:

K. is unspeakable & I thought I took leave of a comrade & a hero—whatever his blunders. I am glad not to have been present at the return of a booby.

Events will now take charge in both these theatres; & these events it seems to me must be decisive in the case of A & K. I suppose a system a la L.G. will have its trial then. There is no virtue there: but at least there will be an effort and a plan. I do not like holding Salonika, even if it is not impossible as many declare. . . . The Balkans must be left to stew in their own bitter juice. Germany will not find them tractable or harmonious. . . . But you must erect a barrage further east against the German advance; & I consider the Bagdad operation shd be vigorously persisted in.

. . . The military indictment wh cd be made on the operations of
the last 6 months wd be—shall I say—will be—incredible to the world.
There is also no equal to it in the history of war; & those who have
wielded the power must bear the burden. At the right time, Parliament will have to be informed of the whole sequence of events. . . .
Keep in touch with Scott.

During December 8 Churchill was able  to telephone the Admiralty from GHQ. Helped by Masterton-Smith, he had managed to speak for a few moments to his wife. 'I rejoiced to hear
your voice over the telephone,' he wrote two days later; but as a
Staff Officer had stayed in the room, 'I cd not say much & even
feared you might think I was abrupt. One cannot really talk down
it.' 'It was wonderful . . . to hear your voice on the telephone,' she
had written on December 9, 'but very tantalising, as there is so
much I want to say to you which cannot be shouted into an unsympathetic receiver!' It had been a strange experience for her,
returning to the Admiralty after six months' absence. 'Masterton
very nice & amiable—I think he manages the whole show,' she
wrote. 'Colonel Hankey came out of "your" room where he had
been speaking to Mr Balfour & was then wending his way to
Downing  Street. He said to me "In these moments of anxiety &
difficulty I miss your Husband's courage & power to take a
decision." '

On December 9 Churchill left St Omer and returned to the
Grenadiers in their front-line trenches near Neuve Chapelle.
'Ma' Jeffreys offered to make him acting second-in-command of
the Battalion. He was flattered; but his hopes for higher things
had been so stimulated by Sir John French's request that he stay
on at GHQ, that he returned to St Omer that evening. There he
learned exciting news. He was definitely to become a Brigadier-
General. Sir John French had chosen the Brigade, and his friend
Tom Bridges was to be his Divisional General. In his letter of
December 10 he wrote:

I am to be given the command of the 56th Brigade in the 19th
Division. Bridges will command the Division—having risen from a
squadron at the beginning of the war. The 19th Division is a regular

Division in the second new army, & the Bde I shall command comprises 4 Lancashire Battalions. The division has a good reputation, has been out here some time, & is now in the line, next to the guards. It forms a part of the same Army corps—the 11th wh I hope will soon be commanded by Cavan; but is at present under General Haking (the corps commander who led me on such a lucky wild goose chase). Altogether it is a vy satisfactory arrangement.

Churchill feared that his wife would not approve of so swift a promotion, and tried to anticipate the reasons which she would use in urging delay: 'Of course there will be criticism & carping. But it is no good paying any attention to that. If I had taken a battalion for a few weeks, it must equally have been said "he has used it merely as a stepping stone etc". I am satisfied this is the right thing to do in the circumstances, & for the rest my attention will concentrate upon the Germans.' But Clementine Churchill no longer argued against the promotion, replying on December 15 that she was 'thrilled' by the news; but she was also worried that, while the danger from rifle fire would be less, that from shellfire would be greater. Not everyone at GHQ was impressed by Churchill's impending promotion. Sir Henry Wilson recorded in his diary on December 11:

Winston came up this morning to my room & had a long talk. I advised him *not* to take a Brigade as it would be bad for Sir John, Winston and the Brigade, but I did not convince him. He said Squiff had promised him a Division! and that as French's tenure was uncertain he would not adopt my proposal of taking a Battalion first, but would take the Brigade while he could get it.

On December 11 Churchill returned to the Grenadiers for the last time before joining his Brigade. On December 12 he wrote to his wife from the Battalion's reserve billets at Laventie:

I am out here now with the Guards again in a shell torn township whose name need not be mentioned. We go into the trenches tomorrow, & I shall continue doing duty with them till I get other directions. I saw Cavan today & told him what was settled. He seemed quite pleased & has arranged for me to study the supply system tomorrow morning—what they call the Q side of the work—I am to follow the

course of a biscuit from the base to the trenches etc. He has written a
long memo on my 'Variants of the Offensive' generally in cordial agreement & urging action. If only French were staying—all these thoughts
wd take shape and have their fruition in some fine event. That odious
Asquith, & his pack of incompetents & intriguers ruin everything.

I am now quite cut off from information and am content to be. I
thought it more seemly to come out here, than to wait about at GHQ
—comfortable as it was, & civil as was everyone. Really they are nice
to me here, & delighted to see me. I rode over to the Divisional HQ
this morning, had a talk with Cavan, lunched with the 2nd Guards
Brigade. . . . Went to see Raymond [Asquith] whose battalion is in
reserve, & then back here, to spend a pleasant evening singing songs
(some of a vy sultry character) with Grigg's company & other officers.
I dined with Grigg. We had a few casualties yesterday afternoon from
shell fire, otherwise all is vy quiet in this section of the front: and the
mining game seems to have reached no climax yet. The ground is
soaked with water; but the breastworks are not uninhabitable; & we
can still go in & out through communication trenches wh saves loss
of life.

My Darling the most divine & glorious sleeping bag has arrived, & I
spent last night in it in one long purr. Also food boxes are now flowing
steadily; & I get daily evidences of the Cat's untiring zeal on my behalf.
The periscope was the exact type I wanted. How clever of you to hit
it off. My steel helmet is the cause of much envy. I look most martial
in it—like a Cromwellian. I always intend to wear it under fire—but
chiefly for the appearance.

My dearest one—I have your little photograph up here now—and
kiss it each night before I go to bed. . . .

On December 13 the Battalion went into the front-line
trenches for forty-eight hours. While they were in the line an
extraordinary incident occurred, which Churchill reported to his
wife on December 15, after he had returned to St Omer:

10 Grenadiers under a kid[4] went across by night to the German
Trench wh they found largely deserted & water logged. They fell upon

[4] William Alastair Damer Parnell, 1894–1916. Joined 2nd Battalion Grenadier Guards as a 2nd Lieutenant, 21 August 1915. He was awarded the
Military Cross for the raid. Killed in action on the Somme, 25 September
1916. His eldest brother, the 5th Baron Congleton (born 1890) was killed
at Ypres in November 1914.

a picket of Germans, beat the brains out of two of them with clubs &
dragged a third home triumphantly as a prisoner. The young officer
by accident let off his pistol & shot one of his own Grenadiers dead:
but the others kept this secret and pretended it was done by the
enemy—do likewise. Such men you never saw. The scene in the little
dugout when the prisoner was brought in surrounded by these terrific
warriors, in jerkins & steel helmets with their bloody clubs in hand—
looking pictures of ruthless war—was one to stay in the memory. *C'est
tres bon.* They petted the prisoner and gave him cigarettes & tried to
cheer him up. He was not vy unhappy to be taken & to know he wd
be safe & well fed till the end of the war.

The Grenadiers had heard of Churchill's promotion before he
had reached them. Their reaction pleased him. 'Colonel Jeffreys
had heard of my impending move,' he wrote to his wife, '& with
a total absence of justifiable jealousy, said he had absolute confidence & really seemed to rejoice in it. I was touched because of
all men in the army none had claims so good.' Higher things even
than a Brigade were being spoken of at Laventie: 'In the Grenadiers the opinion is that I am to have a division. This they
seemed to consider quite reasonable.' Although he was on the
verge of generalship, Churchill believed that there would still be
a place in it for him in politics when the crisis came. 'The hour of
Asquith's punishment & K's exposure draws nearer,' he told his
wife. 'The wretched men have nearly wrecked our chances. It
may fall to me to strike the blow. I shall do it without compunction.'

London was filled with much hostile comment when news of
Churchill's impending Brigade became known. A question had
been put down on the House of Commons' Order Paper by a Conservative MP, Sir Charles Hunter,[5] which the Government would
have to answer on December 16. Hunter reflected the growing
backbench hostility to Churchill's new sphere of activity, for he
intended, 'To ask the Under-Secretary of State for War if Major

[5] Charles Roderick Hunter, 1858–1924. 3rd Baronet, 1890. Inspector of
Musketry, Imperial Yeomanry, 1900. Conservative MP, 1910–18. Divisional
musketry and machine gun officer, 1914–16.

Winston Churchill has been promised the command of an Infantry brigade; if this officer has ever commanded a battalion of Infantry; and for how many weeks he has served at the front as an Infantry Officer.' It was not only parliamentary backbenchers who were critical of Churchill's promotion to the command of a Brigade. When Lord Esher, who had returned to London from St Omer, lunched with Clementine Churchill at the Berkeley Hotel in Piccadilly, she was shocked and disturbed by his outspoken criticisms, which she held back until her letter of December 17:

My darling,

. . . I will tell you (for what it is worth) what Lord E said. Of course you will know better than I can whether he is in touch with feeling in the Army or not & whether to attach importance & weight to his opinion. He said 'Of course you know Winston is taking a Brigade & as a personal friend of his I am very sorry about it; as I think he is making a great mistake. Of course it's not his fault, Sir John forced it upon him. All W's friends are very distressed about it as they had all hoped he would take a battalion first.'

He said how tremendously popular & respected you had become in the short time you had been there & repeated to me the story you told me of the Colonel of the Grenadiers receiving you so disagreeably & then being entirely won over.

This interview took place in the crowded grill-room of the Berkeley. I preserved a calm & composed demeanour, but I was astonished & hurt at his blurting all this out to me. He repeated again & again that the thing was a mistake; I tried at last to head him off by asking him personal questions about you, how you were looking, if you were well.

He then launched forth again, saying that you had been in the greatest danger, in more than was necessary etc & that French had determined to give you this Brigade as he was convinced you wld otherwise be killed. After this I crawled home quite stunned & heartbroken. . . .

Esher's arguments were crudely stated. It is not surprising that they led Clementine Churchill once again to doubt whether her husband was wise to accept the rapid advancement on which he had decided. But she no longer felt the strength to challenge him. 'My Darling Love,' she wrote in the same letter, 'I live from day to day in suspense and anguish. At night when I lie down I say to myself Thank God he is still alive. The 4 weeks of your absence seem to me like 4 years. If only My Dear you had no military ambitions. If only you would stay with the Oxfordshire Hussars in their billets.' Churchill's new career was a daily source of torment for her. 'I can just bear it,' she wrote, 'feeling that you are really happy. I have ceased to have ambitions for you. Just come back to me alive that's all. Your loving Clemmie.'

Churchill returned late on the night of December 14 to St Omer. Sir John French was no longer there. He had been summoned to London, where Asquith had informed him that his dismissal could no longer be delayed. Churchill already knew that French's fate was virtually sealed. On the following morning a letter from Spiers brought good news: 'Nothing could please me more than to be your Brigade Major,' Spiers wrote. 'Once in the way of it I believe I cd be useful to you & I sd love it.' That morning Churchill wrote to Edward Marsh; the decision to evacuate Gallipoli, a decision he was powerless to influence in any way, had much upset him:

My dear Eddie,
My information is only good in parts; but distressing letters from various quarters had already apprised me of the decisions wh have at last been reached. You know only too well what I think about them. I was vy glad to be able to occupy my mind with the practical trifles of trench warfare & the bickerings of the rival artilleries. The tale has yet to be told to its conclusion. . . .

Churchill could not be certain whether French's imminent dismissal would affect his appointment as a Brigadier-General or not. 'I do not know what effect the unhappy recall of my friend will have on my local fortunes,' he wrote to Marsh, 'but I feel superior to them. A Brigade or a company in the Guards is the same or almost the same to me—during the present interlude. I have fallen back reposefully into the arms of fate; but with an underlying instinct that all will be well and that my greatest work is to hand.' Marsh's absence, after nine years of daily inti-

macy, added to Churchill's sense of isolation. He hoped that once
he were formally appointed a Brigadier-General, Marsh would
join him:

> I should like to set you free from your present surroundings and if
> it were in my power to find you a little island here I should not hesi-
> tate to propose it to you. Brigades have an 'interpreter' who has a jolly
> time. Let me know what you feel. I am very glad you found a ciga-
> rette case among those wh Clemmie produced wh appealed to you.
> 'Tis but the poor symbol of a deep affection.
>
> Yours always<br>W

This letter sealed, Churchill then wrote to his wife:

> I am back here at GHQ to see the last of my poor friend who re-
> turns to pack up tomorrow. I don't know what effect this change of
> command will produce upon my local fortunes: possibly it will throw
> everything into the melting pot again. Believe me I am superior to
> anything that can happen to me out here. My conviction that the
> greatest of my work is still to be done is strong within me: & I ride
> reposefully along the gale. I expect it will be my duty in the early
> months of next year—If I am all right—to stand up in my place in
> Parliament and endeavour to procure the dismissal of Asquith &
> Kitchener: & when I am sure that the hour has come I shall not flinch
> from any exertion or strife. I feel a gt assurance of my power: & now
> —naked—nothing can assail me. . . .

This letter too was sealed, and Churchill waited for the arrival
of the King's Messenger who was expected at St Omer that morning, and would take both letters back with him to London during
the afternoon. While waiting for the Messenger, he was called
to the telephone. It was Sir John French himself, speaking from
London. He had something extremely unpleasant to say. That
morning he had received a letter from Asquith vetoing Churchill's promotion. The blow was unexpected and severe. At first
Churchill could hardly believe it. 'Do not allow the PM to discuss
my affairs with you,' he wrote to his wife, after having reopened
his letter to add the bad news. 'Be vy cool & detached and avoid
any sign of acquiescence in anything he may say.'

Asquith's direct intervention had brought seven days of expectation to an end. Churchill was bewildered by what had happened. 'You will cancel the order for the tunic!' he wrote to his wife in his postscript. That evening he dined at Sir John French's house at St Omer. He had asked Spiers to dine with him, not knowing when he had invited him that his hopes would be so suddenly smashed. On the telephone Sir John French had told him that Asquith had actually written in his letter: 'Perhaps you might give him a Battalion.' Churchill did not want such a narrow sphere of command but if he had to, he would accept. In his diary Spiers described the evening:

Dined at C in C's house. . . . Winston had long talk with me. He likes telling me his affairs. . . . Says things always turn out for best. . . . Spoke of various things. Of danger we all run, of how we wd probably all be killed in next offensive. . . .

At dinner he was brilliant, really fascinating. Told me in private Holland was the only Rd open to us, in public that the Gs wd first use Egypt & attack India by the Turks. Told me Asquith was a man of warm friendship but never let it interfere with duty or even comfort. Told me K of K was played out. Churchill told me he had thought, when still in Government, of going to Russia[6] & taking me! He is of course selfish, likes me but wants to make use of me. He is all right. . . .

By December 17 Churchill felt the full enormity of Asquith's veto. Twice that day he wrote to his wife, with the black thoughts that had taken control of him; a day later he asked her to burn the letters, telling her: 'I was depressed & my thought was not organised. Everyone has hours of reaction, & there is no reason why written record shd remain.' Nor does it.

Desperate to learn the full story of Asquith's abrupt decision, Churchill stayed at St Omer throughout December 17. French returned that evening with orders to hand over his command to

[6] Perhaps a reference to the mission to Vladivostock and Archangel which, two months earlier, Hankey had suggested to Asquith as a possible outlet for Churchill's energies. This entry in Spiers' diary is the only contemporary evidence I have found that Churchill may have taken the idea seriously.

his successor, Sir Douglas Haig. As soon as he reached his head-quarters he gave Churchill an account of what had happened in London. On the following day Churchill sent his wife an account of what French had reported:

The position is as follows. He saw Asquith, told him that he had given me a Brigade & Asquith said he was delighted. A few hours later, being I suppose frightened by the question in the House, Asquith wrote a note to French (wh French showed me *vy privately*) saying that 'with regard to our conversation about our friend—the appointment might cause some criticism'—& should not therefore be made—adding 'Perhaps you might give him a battalion'. The almost contemptuous indifference of this note was a revelation to me. French was astonished; but in his weak position he cd do nothing, & now he is no longer C in C. Meanwhile he had told everyone that he had given me a Brigade & is of course deeply distressed at the turn of events.

Churchill could not restrain his bitterness against the Prime Minister:

To measure Asquith's performance one has to remember that on my leaving the Admiralty he offered me a Brigade: & that when I told him three months ago of the offers that French had made to me if I came out to the front, he advised me to go & assured me that any advancement wh was thought fitting by the C in C would have his hearty concurrence. One has to remember all the rest too of a long story of my work & connexion with him.

Altogether I am inclined to think that his conduct reaches the limit of meanness & ungenerousness. Sentiments of friendship expressed in extravagant terms; coupled with a resolve not to incur the slightest criticism or encounter the smallest opposition—even from the most unworthy quarter. Personally I feel that every link is severed: & while I do not wish to decide in a hurry—my feeling is that all relationship shd cease.

Churchill was not enthusiastic about taking command of a Battalion, and was angered by the suggestion that an appointment to a Battalion involved any generosity on Asquith's part:

With regard to my taking the command of a battalion: there is no use in my doing so unless under a C in C who believes in me & means in a few weeks to promote me. The risk & labour of such a task are vy heavy, & I am a special target for criticism. The appointment is no gift. With my rank & war services I cd have obtained it quite easily had I been an ordinary unknown officer. I shd be practically alone with 1000 amateur officers and untrained men, in a situation of much anxiety and no real scope. I have not asked for anything out here & have only accepted the brigade after considerable hesitation & delay. But having done so, I do not feel called upon to undertake the duties of a batallion commander, unless they are pressed upon me in a manner that leaves me no choice.

The uncertainties of the higher command put Churchill's military future at risk, and he could not tell whether Haig would be helpful:

This afternoon French is to see Haig & intends to tell him the whole story. My action will necessarily depend on the new man's view & disposition. Unless he is inclined to make himself responsible for the decision to wh French had come and takes clearly a favourable & friendly view, I shall remain with the Grenadier Guards as a company officer. I think they will be willing to make an exception to their rule about only Guards commanding Guards & will let me do the work in a regular way. This at any rate is the place of honour and as they will be continuously in the line till the 25th Jany I shd find the service of great interest.

Churchill did not dismiss from his mind the possibility, however remote, that he might return to London without taking up any further military duties. 'I do not think any difficulty would be placed in my way,' he ended his letter, 'if I required to return home for Parliamentary duties if the situation needed my presence.'

In later months and years Churchill was often to brood on his failure to secure a Brigade, and on Asquith's veto. The threat of Parliamentary criticisms had been decisive. During a month in which many members of Parliament believed that the Government was in difficulty over the question of conscription, the Prime Minister did not want to create any opportunity, however trivial, for backbench unrest. When Sir John French informed

Asquith of Churchill's impending promotion on December 14, the Prime Minister sensed danger. He acted accordingly, thereby protecting himself from an irritating attack in Parliament. On December 16, when Sir Charles Hunter asked his hostile question, the Parliamentary Under-Secretary of State for War, H. J. Tennant, was able to reply with disingenuous confidence: 'I have no knowledge myself, and have not been able to obtain any, of a promise of command of an Infantry brigade having been made to my right hon and gallant Friend referred to in the question.' Hunter then asked whether Churchill had been promised command of a Battalion, to which several unidentified MPs called out—'Why not?' A former Indian Army officer, Sir George Scott Robertson,[7] spoke up in Churchill's defence: 'Is not the question absurd on the face of it . . . ?' he asked pointing out that as a serving officer under sixty Churchill was qualified to command a battalion. But the last comment was a hostile one. A Conservative MP, Evelyn Cecil,[8] asked: 'Is the right hon Gentleman aware that if this appointment were made it would be thought by very many persons both inside and outside this House a grave scandal?'

At noon on December 18, Sir John French's last day at St Omer, he and Churchill set out from the town by car. Finding a small, secluded cottage in the countryside, they picnicked together. On the drive back they talked at length, as Churchill wrote to his wife, 'about every sort of thing'. They reached St Omer only a short while before Sir Douglas Haig, who was to take over formal command of the British Army in France on the following day. French appealed at once to Haig on Churchill's behalf. Haig wrote in his diary:

[7] George Scott Robertson, 1852–1916. Indian Medical Service, 1878–88. Indian Foreign Office, 1888–95. Knighted, 1895. Liberal MP, 1906–16.

[8] Evelyn Cecil, 1865–1941. Grandson of the 2nd Marquess of Salisbury. Conservative MP, 1898–1929. Chairman of the Committee on Public Retrenchment, 1915. Member of the Inter-Allied Parliamentary Committee, 1916–18. Created Baron Rockley, 1934.

. . . I saw Sir John French at 3 pm. He did not look very well and seemed short of breath at times.

He expressed a wish to help me and the Army in France to the best of his power at home. Then he said that 'there was a delicate personal matter' which he wished to speak about. This was that he had wanted to give Winston Churchill an Infantry Brigade. This had been vetoed but he was anxious that Winston should have a Battalion. I replied that I had no objection because Winston had done good work in the trenches, and we were short of Battalion CO's. I then said goodbye.

Haig asked to see Churchill, telling him that there was no chance of an immediate Brigade, but offering him a Battalion. Churchill accepted. That evening he wrote to his wife of the interview:

. . . He treated me with the utmost kindness of manner & consideration, assured me that nothing wd give him greater pleasure than to give me a Brigade, that his only wish was that able men shd come to the front, & that I might count on his sympathy in every way. He had heard from Cavan of the 'excellent work' I had done in the trenches. Altogether it was quite clear that he will give me a fair chance. In these circumstances I consented to take a battalion—wh one is not yet settled—but it will be one going in the line. I asked for an officer—Archie or Spiers—and he went off and arranged at once that I was to have what I wanted. It is possible even that I shall get the two in a short time. The need of a few competent professionals is really vy great, and every step I take is watched by curious eyes. I must be well supported. I was greatly reassured by his manner wh was affectionate almost. He took me by the arm and made the greatest fuss. I used to know him pretty well in the old days when he was a Major & I a young MP. But I am bound to say the warmth of his greeting surprised me. . . .

Stimulated by Haig's warmth, Churchill decided to ask him if he would be interested to read his memorandum on trench warfare. 'I asked him if he wd like to see "Variants of the Offensive" & he said he wd be "honoured"—! So I am back on my porch again with my feathers stroked down.' That same day Haig told Churchill that he could command the 9th Battalion of the King's Royal Rifle

Corps. Later in the afternoon he discovered that the Battalion was about to leave France almost immediately, and wrote apologetically:

Dear Winston,

V many thanks for the notes which I will read with much interest.

I had no idea the Battn was about to go abroad.—Please ask the Mil Sec to cancel your posting to the 9th KRR & I'll see to it personally when I have taken over.

Meantime good luck to you—Excuse hurried line and Believe me,

Yrs vy truly

D. Haig

Churchill's anger towards Asquith intensified in the weeks to come. He did not know whom he could trust, or who would give him confidence in the future. F. E. Smith was the only friend then in the Cabinet to whom he felt he could turn.[9] On December 18 he sent him a sad appeal for support and encouragement:

My dear,

I am awfully disappointed and so is French. What ill-fortune.

It is becoming important for me to see you and I trust you will not fail me. I do not know where I shall be; but a rendez-vous can easily be arranged without exposing your uninsured person to danger.

A week ago French gave me the command of the 56th Brigade XIXth Division. The Prime Minister however being frighted of the question in the House got this cancelled. Quel homme! The departure of French is a gt blow to me and threatened to leave me vy much en l'air. In these circumstances I had resolved to take a company in the Grenadiers, where I have my footing. But Haig who I saw this afternoon with French treated me with the utmost cordiality and consideration, assured me of his desire to give me a Brigade and to further my interests, and in the circumstances I have consented to take a battalion in the front line. I wd not have done this except under a sympathetic C in C: preferring a company in the Guards, if no advancement were open, to a long spell with strangers, and imperfectly trained men.

Early next week I shall be in the line; and there will be no nice

[9] F. E. Smith had entered the Cabinet on 3 November 1915 as Attorney-General, following Carson's resignation.

dinners sitting next to the C in C like tonight, which I can offer you; but come and we will make shift somehow.

I have many things to say to you and some to hear from you: and I do hope you will be able to come. GHQ will I am sure facilitate your movements, and you can telegraph to me through Brade. I am suspending certain political action till I see you.

I find myself treated here with good will and I think respect on all sides: though I am usually urged to go home and smash the bloody Government.

Yours always<br>W

'As for Asquith,' Churchill wrote to his wife in his letter that evening, 'make no change except a greater reserve about me & my affairs. The incident is best ignored; but it need not be forgotten. Don't you tell me he was quite right—or let him persuade you. Esher talks foolishly. It wd not have been a great mistake for me to take a Brigade. There was something to be said either way. But on the whole it was worth taking.'

Churchill asked his wife to comfort Sir John French in his distress, writing in the same letter: 'He is a dear friend. I want you & Goonie to get him to come & dine with you and cherish him properly: & write him a nice letter. My heart bled for him in this wrench.' French spent his last morning at St Omer on December 19. Churchill described the final scene to his wife on the following day:

French's departure was affecting. He saw a long succession of generals etc & then opened his door & said 'Winston, it is fitting that my last quarter of an hour here shd be spent with you'. Then off he went with a guard of honour, saluting officers, cheering soldiers & townsfolk —stepping swiftly from the stage of history into the dull humdrum of ordinary life. I felt deeply his departure on every ground—public & private. It was not I think necessary or right. The French are rather unhappy about it: the army have no real opinion. But Asquith will throw anyone to the wolves to keep himself in office. . . .

Churchill had gone to France to escape the anxieties of political impotence. For four weeks he had found an escape, amid the daily activities of the Grenadiers and the challenge of trying to devise new weapons which could lead to new war tactics. But Asquith's unexpected intervention, ending his chances of a Brigade, brought politics once more to the forefront of his thoughts and worries. It was clear that there could be no escape from political pressures and jealousies; that no military environment could shield him from the ever-clamant demands of political life; and that he himself, however keen to participate in the world of divisions, brigades, battalions and companies, could never really be satisfied by army life. From that moment Churchill aspired, not to advance his military career, but to rebuild his political one. From the isolation of the war zone, from the danger of the front line, from the uncertainties of a crashed career, he turned his energies and introspection to a political objective. A return to Cabinet Office was certainly remote, and probably unobtainable. But for twelve months he sought to return. Sometimes he acted alone, sometimes with colleagues. But wherever he was, however weak his political position, however demanding his military duties, a drastic change in the methods of war-making became his target.

Waiting at St Omer to learn which Battalion he was to command, Churchill received several letters in which politics predominated. F. E. Smith wrote on December 19 with an account of events in the Cabinet:

My dear Winston,

. . . We fought (Curzon, Selborne, Lansdowne & myself) for the Dardanelles as long as possible & only gave up when every single soldier abandoned us including K and we were told that it was impossible this weather to send the Salonika troops then if we decided that the evacuation at Salonika shd be made to reinforce the Dardanelles.

I am so disappointed at not seeing you. It was a combination of tragic mishaps. You may absolutely rely on seeing me in a fortnight or so and I will make friends with Haig in your interest. BL's star is much in the ascendant & he continues most friendly.

Yours affectionately
F

Lady Randolph also wrote on December 19, with news and questions. She had just spoken to one of Fisher's friends, the journalist Lovat Fraser:[10] 'He says there is much grumbling in the Navy against AJB—they say he has gone to sleep & everything is left to slide. Fraser also said that K—was the stumbling block at the beginning, & is still so. He ended by saying that you must return at the first good opportunity. . . . Do you know Haig? I mean fairly well? I remember him in the old days. . . . A hard man—& a bit of a bounder—but I imagine a fine soldier. . . .'

The fullest political news came from J. L. Garvin, who hoped to act as a focus of unity for those Liberals and Conservatives who were dissatisfied with Asquith's leadership. He believed that Churchill had an important part to play in any such group. The main reason for dissent during December 1915 was conscription. Asquith was still trying to preserve the voluntary system. But the increasing demand for more men at the front had placed a heavy strain upon voluntary recruitment; a strain which Kitchener could no longer conceal. Lord Derby had been brought in to effect a compromise. But many critics of the Government, led by Curzon inside the Cabinet and Carson outside it, believed no compromise would work, and that if the war were not to be lost, compulsion must be brought in at once. Asquith feared the anger of many Liberals if he abandoned the voluntary system. But it seemed to his critics that it was no longer a question of military tradition or Liberal ethics, but of the urgent needs of war. On December 20 Garvin, himself a compulsionist, wrote to Churchill:

. . . It is impossible to say yet what will happen at home. I think Asquith's confidence in being able to hold on is very considerably shaken. The worst disasters anticipated won't come from all I hear; so that the chance that events themselves might force a drastic solution is deferred, and you have still the situation as unsatisfactory as possible yet it's not difficult to change.

Of course without LG there can be no sufficient change, but he is

[10] Lovat Fraser, 1871–1926. Editor, *Times of India*, 1902–6. On his return to London in 1907 he joined the Editorial Staff of *The Times*, remaining with the paper until 1922. Chief Literary Adviser, *Sunday Pictorial* and *Daily Mirror*, 1922–6.

still singularly isolated on the one hand, while on the other resolved not to jump until he is certain to land on sound ground. His greatest mistake was the breach with you, and sooner or later that estrangement must be composed if only on the principles of a marriage de convenance. He needs alliances. He will get them somehow because others need him as much as he needs them. His power in Opposition would at any time be enormous but specially under unmuzzled conditions after the war. But I think he will 'pig' it with irksome but tenacious patience until he sees the real big chance.

When will it come? Not now as was anticipated by some last week. Asquith is much more likely to come to an agreement with Derby to deal with the residue of single men by a peremptory call that may save the face of voluntaryism.

Garvin informed Churchill of the first stage of the end of the Gallipoli story: 'The news that Anzac troops have been evacuated at last comes today, and the War Office claim that the casualties have been insignificant and that the guns and stores have been saved. . . . It is a bitter amputator of hopes that were as much part of us as limbs, but now we must look right forward, and set our teeth.' Only the troops at Helles remained on the Peninsula.

Jack Churchill, who had witnessed the evacuation from Anzac, sent his brother an account of it on December 22:

My dear,

The arrangements were perfect—but we had to have wonderful good fortune to get away as we did. The enemy suspected nothing, and the embarkation was absolutely unmolested. But the weather was the most important feature. During the operation it remained dead calm—but as soon as it was over a South Westerly gale sprang up, which must have smashed all the old piers and which would have sunk all the small boats & lighters had it occurred a few hours before. As it was—the large army was all withdrawn. With the loss of 2 men wounded! Almost all the munitions and guns were brought away and nothing of value to enemy was left intact. Birdwood carried out the whole operation and I think the Govt & Ld K owe him a great deal. A disaster would have settled the Govt I should imagine, but this will give them a new lease of life.

It was a great feat—but we are all very depressed at having to come away. The Anzacs feel it very much. One man expressed himself 'We have a lot of fellows sleeping in those valleys, and we should never have been told to leave them'.

Best love<br>Jack S.C.

On 19 December 1915 Sir Douglas Haig took up formal command of the British forces in France. At dinner that evening with Spiers and Sinclair, Churchill spoke optimistically of his own military future. Spiers wrote in his diary: 'Dined with Churchill & his friend Archy Sinclair a particularly nice fellow at Rest Vincente. 2 bottles of Champagne, 2 glasses of Brandy. Rather nice talk. He is to get a Bn & is having Sinclair attached & asking for me as 2nd in Command. . . . WC has Douglas Haig to heel. DH is ready to do anything for him.'

On December 20 Churchill moved from GHQ a few doors further down the street, taking up quarters with his friend Sir Max Aitken, who had temporarily left London to take up the post of Canadian Eyewitness at the Front. It was the beginning of a lifelong intimacy between the two men. At St Omer, Aitken gave Churchill renewed hope in his future. Churchill's anger with Asquith over his lost Brigade had swung his mind violently back to politics; Aitken encouraged him to believe in his political future. It was a time when Churchill desperately needed such encouragement. He never forgot how at that moment, when almost everyone else seemed against him, Aitken held out the hand of hospitality and hope.

Churchill waited at St Omer for the offer of another vacant Battalion. Haig had agreed to let him have Sinclair as his ADC. Whether he would be allowed to have Spiers was still uncertain. On December 20 Churchill and Spiers had tea together at St Omer, Spiers recording in his diary:

He v interesting describing battle of Coronel & Falkland, how it happened, Craddock disobeying orders & insisting on fighting & how at the Falklands the 1st message was that v Spee had come up & that the Brit fleet was coaling. How Fisher objected to the fast cruisers leaving England on Friday the 13th. Fascinating. Also dodges to catch submarines, the boat which pretends to surrender, the crew tumbling overboard & then guns unmasking. . . .

That same afternoon Churchill wrote to his wife, whom he had hoped would be able to meet him in Paris after Christmas:

. . . I shall know today or tomorrow wh battalion I am to have, & where it is posted in the line. Archie comes with me, tho I have not yet settled how to fit him in. I must first see how they all look in their jobs. Afterwards I may get Spiers. This will be a vy arduous and anxious piece of work, requiring the whole of my attention. It is not more dangerous than I shd have made a Brigade command: but of course much depends on the part of the line we are in. . . .

I am sure there is no chance of Paris for some time yet. I have at least six weeks of the most strenuous work before me—& that direct responsibility—like a ship's captain—for the safety of all in my charge.

That evening Churchill received a letter from his wife, dated December 18, in which she wrote that she was 'astounded at the PM not backing you for a brigade'. She hoped that Asquith had asked Haig to give him one 'later on after you have commanded a battalion for a little while'. 'My own Darling,' her letter ended: 'I feel such absolute confidence in your future—it is your present which causes me agony—I feel as if I had a tight band of pain round my heart. It fills me with great pride to think that you have won the love & respect of those splendid Grenadiers & their austere Colonel: in happier times you must let me see them all. Perhaps if any of them come home on leave they would come & see me.' Churchill replied at once:

Your 1 a.m. 18th letter has just arrived, & stimulates me to add a little to what I wrote this morning. . . . I am simply waiting d'un pied a l'autre for orders. It is odd to pass these days of absolute idleness— waiting 3 or 4 hours together in tranquil vegetation, when one looks back to the long years of unceasing labour & hustle through wh I have passed. It does not fret me. In war one takes everything as it comes, & I seem to have quite different standards to measure by. As one's fortunes are reduced, one's spirit must expand to fill the void.

I think of all the things that are being left undone & of my own

energies & capacities to do them & drive them along all wasted—
without any real pain. I watch—as far as I can—the weak, irresolute &
incompetent drift of Government policy and turn over what ought to
be done in my mind, & then let it all slide away without a wrench. I
shall be profoundly absorbed in the tremendous little tasks wh my
new work will give me. I hope to come to these men like a breeze. I
hope they will rejoice to be led by me, & fall back with real confidence
into my hands. I shall give them my vy best.

No battalion command had become vacant by December 22.
Churchill took advantage of the delay to make a brief visit to
London to see his wife and family.

While Churchill was in London he was caught up briefly but
deeply in political speculation, seeing both J. L. Garvin and Lloyd
George. At dinner with Garvin the subject of his working once
more with Fisher was raised. Garvin sent Fisher an account of
the discussion in a letter dated 'Christmas 1915':

Winston is home for a few days leave. I dined with him and went
at my old aim with him and you—union for the country's sake. He is
willing to bury the hatchet and is out and out for your wonder-ship.
Why not reopen the old firm ON AN AGREED PROGRAMME to the accompaniment of throwing up hats throughout the country? There
would be glory enough there for two and to spare but to have you
and him working under the same administration somehow again is
vital. Lloyd George, you, Carson and Winston are a fighting quartette
(or Super-Dreadnought Squadron) which can save this country and
the allies. I am not sure anything else can. This is the best and most
affectionate Christmas card that could be sent to you by yours ever
                                                    J. L. Garvin.

Garvin also wrote to Lloyd George on Christmas Day. 'You, Carson, Winston, Fisher,' he declared, 'working together can win this
war. Haldane (as I know having dined with him) would join
you. . . .'

In a conversation with Lloyd George, Churchill discussed the
political crisis which had again arisen over conscription. Lloyd
George was bitter against Asquith for the delay in bringing in
national service, and held out hopes for a change of government

which would enable Churchill to return. On December 27, having returned to France, Churchill wrote to Lloyd Geroge: 'I shall be glad to hear how things go. . . . Don't miss yr opportunity. The time has come.' On his return to St Omer, Churchill could not contain his excitement. On December 28 he saw Spiers, who recorded in his diary:

Dined with WC at Canadian office, after dinner he v interesting. He thinks there is going to be a political crisis on compulsion. He saw Lloyd George who is going to try & smash the Government when either Bonar Law or LG wd be PM & Churchill get Munitions or Admiralty, the remaining one getting the WO.

He showed me all the Government minutes on the war. Some of his really prophetic & really clever & sound.

Bed after 1. . . .

Clementine Churchill was less certain that the time had come for anti-Government action. 'I know nothing, but I feel the break-up is not yet,' she wrote to her husband on December 28. 'This futile government,' she added, 'will fumble on for a few more months.' On the following day she wrote again, having heard that the conscription crisis was apparently over: 'I feel very sad but not exactly disappointed as I never allowed myself to *really* hope for a break-up.' On December 29 Lloyd George lunched with her at 41 Cromwell Road. That afternoon she sent her husband an account of their conversation:

LlG has been & gone. As I feared the crisis is over with 'no change' except the extremely unlikely resignations of Runciman & Simon. The PM appeared at the Cabinet yesterday & did *all* the fighting *for* compulsion. LlG & Curzon hardly opened their mouths. Runciman and McKenna argued against it on the ground of injuring the trade of the country, but finally all agreed with exception of Simon & Runciman who are 're-considering' their positions. I asked LlG if he & the other die hards had tried to break the Government; he said there wasn't a chance as the PM had come right over on to their side. He expressed great distress at you not being in the Government. He said repeatedly 'We must get Winston back'. He asked me if you would come back & manage the heavy gun department of the Munitions Office. He has just been told that 100 of them due in March will not be delivered till later owing to want of drive of the man in charge, 'a first class 2nd rate man' who before the war was earning £15,000 a year with a big armament firm.[11]

Clementine Churchill was surprised at how quickly Lloyd George's pugnacious ardour had cooled. 'LlG is a strange man,' she wrote. 'He was very polite & civil & most friendly, but for the moment the chance of working with you is gone & so his fire is gone and he is more detached than the other day. . . .' On December 30 she wrote again with more political news. Her enthusiasm for Lloyd George had dwindled further:

. . . I forgot to tell you in yesterday's letter that McKenna absented himself from the War Council and sulked down at Munstead which caused a mild flutter, but LlG said that a little flattery and cajolery from the PM would bring him round. I suppose that if compulsion is carried without a single resignation (which seems likely) it will be a feather in the PM's cap & a vindication of his slow state-craft. I am very much afraid this is going to be a 'personal triumph' for him.

I think my Darling you will have to be very patient. Do not burn any boats. The PM has not treated you worse than LlG has done, in fact not so badly for he is not as much in your debt as the other man (i.e. Marconi).[12] On the other hand are the Dardanelles. I feel sure that if the choice were equal you would prefer to work with the PM

[11] Charles Edward Ellis, 1852–1937. Director, John Brown & Co., Shipbuilders, 1890. Entered Ministry of Munitions, July 1915. Deputy Director-General, Guns and Equipment, 1915–16; Director-General, Ordnance Supply, 1916–17. Knighted, 1917. Head of Paris Establishment, Ministry of Munitions, 1917–18; Liquidator of Contracts, France, Italy, Switzerland, 1919. Member, Royal Commission on Awards to Inventors, 1919.

[12] In 1912, during the 'Marconi affair', Churchill had rendered Lloyd George—who, with Rufus Isaacs, was much implicated—a triple service. He had prevailed on Lord Northcliffe to play the scandal down as much as possible in *The Times* and the *Daily Mail;* he had persuaded F. E. Smith and Sir Edward Carson to appear for Lloyd George and Isaacs in their libel action against *Le Matin;* and he had influenced Asquith, in the Debate on the Report of the Select Committee of the House of Commons, not to use any phrase which might provoke Lloyd George's resignation. Churchill shared his wife's view that Lloyd George was in his debt as a result of this help. Later he was to try to get Lloyd George to redeem his debt, but in vain.

than with LlG. It's true that when association ceases with the PM he
cools & congeals visibly, but all the time you were at the Admiralty he
was loyal & steadfast while the other would barter you away at any
time in any place. I assure you he is the direct descendent of Judas
Iscariot. At this moment although I hate the PM, if he held out his
hand I could take it, (though I would give it a nasty twist) but before
taking LlG's I would have to safeguard myself with charms, touch-
woods, exorcisms & by crossing myself. I always can get on with him &
yesterday I had a good talk, but you can't hold his eyes, they shift
away.

You know I'm not good at pretending but I am going to put my
pride in my pocket and reconnoitre Downing Street. . . .

While Clementine Churchill prepared to visit 10 Downing
Street, her husband was back in the warzone, from which it
seemed he would not easily escape. On December 30 he sent her
an account of his three days back in France:

We had a rough passage on the destroyer and I was forced to surrender first my lunch and subsequently my breakfast. In the midst of
these preoccupations the coxswain arrived on behalf of the ship's
company to wish me the compliments of the season & express gratitude for past favours to the Lower Deck. A clumsy skipper failed to
get us ashore in Dunkirk till after 4 hours of trying—the wind was vy
strong—& finally we settled down on a mudbank. Luckily close enough
to the quay for me to escape to the land.

The next day I went to see Bridges. . . . I lunched with him &
afterwards was taken by his Chief of Staff[13] to see Neuve Chapelle.
The Germans obligingly stopped shelling it as we arrived & I was able
without much risk to see this part of the line, wh fills in a gap in my
now extensive examination of the front. I also saw my old friends of
the 2nd Battalion.

Spiers came over and dined with me in the evening, & yesterday
we made an expedition to the French lines. I was able to go to the
very farthest point we hold on the Vimy Ridge, from which a fair view
of the plain of Douai was obtainable.

I believe Spiers & I are the only Englishmen who have ever been on

[13] Archie Stewart Buckle, 1868–1916. 2nd Lieutenant, Royal Artillery,
1888. Lieutenant-Colonel, 1914. Explosives expert. Chief-of-Staff, 19th Division, January 1915–January 1916.

this battle-torn ground. It was pretty quiet. The lines are in places only a few yards apart, but a much less spiteful temper prevails than on the part of the Guards. There you cannot show a whisker without grave risk of death. Here the sentries looked at each other over the top of the parapet: & while we were in the trench the Germans passed the word to the French to take cover as their officer was going to order some shelling. This duly arrived; but luckily it was directed upon the boyau [communication trench] up wh we had just come & not on that by wh we were returning.

Dinner with the corps, and prolonged earnest discussion of the possibilities of the offensive. They *all* agree with me. These men who have suffered the whole terrible experience of these vain attacks, repeated almost word for word the arguments wh I so unsuccessfully addressed to that weak & foolish Cabinet. My mind is making its way steadily through the vast problem of 'how to do it': without prejudice to my present conviction the 'it might not be done'. I am going to write something soon about it all, wh perhaps may be of use. So far as I can tell from the papers Asquith has had no great difficulty in choosing between his office & his principles, & now I daresay things will run on for some time.

Fifty-five years later, in conversation with the author, Spears recalled the expedition of December 29:

I tried to show him what would interest him. I took him to look down on the plain of Douai. The French would be polite—they always were. But they never took him seriously. He played no part in the military hierarchy, which was the one thing that mattered in the French army.

We were both very struck by the rats that we saw. They were appalling things; they were huge. Winston pointed out that they played a very useful role by eating human bodies—it was quite true. At the time of the German retreat to the Hindenburg line there were 15 to 20 miles of trenches left empty. The rats were everywhere. I have driven over roads where you squashed rats as you went along. Had you fallen in a trench you would never have got out alive. They would have devoured you. One heard them all night running about in the barbed wire.

Mostly Winston looked. If there was a question to be put, he put it. There was a place I took him to at Notre Dame de Lorette. It was a ridge and a declivity. The French kept attacking it, but nobody had ever been known to come back alive. This interested Winston considerably. He wanted to know why, why, why. The Germans had realized the importance of the counter-slope, of having trenches within 15 yards of the top of the hill on the far side, and shooting like rabbits at anyone who popped over the top. It was a terrible place. I got wounded there myself. Winston had an inquiring mind of rare quality. He always turned up with some new invention—once it was a bullet-proof waistcoat. On another occasion a bullet-proof raincoat which would have sunk anyone wearing it in any sea.

Winston was very curious, very inquisitive to see what the French were doing. It was a time when they were experimenting with all sorts of devices, like a moving shield which you pushed along in front of the infantry. But when Winston mentioned the idea of tanks the French said: 'Wouldn't it be simpler to flood Artois and get your fleet here?'

Churchill continued his letter to his wife of December 30 with a request that she buy a silver cigar box which he wanted to present to the Headquarters Staff of the Guards Division. As well as an inscription, he wanted her to get for it 'a photograph of the Blücher[14] turning turtle (you know the one) and have this mounted on the top of the cigar-cigarette box—under glass'. As he explained:

I have made great friends with them & am anxious to give them a token. Get this done as soon as possible.

Also, my dearest one, send over my hot water bottle. I always forget it.

Today I am off to Boulogne to meet Archie & to pass the time. You will be glad to know I am making a safer expedition.

No Christmas parcels or food have reached me yet. I am not in immediate want of them: but they seem to have gone astray.

Churchill ended his letter 'Tender love my darling, do not be lonely or low-spirited. Everything will come out right in the end:

[14] The German battle-cruiser *Blücher* was sunk during the action of the Dogger Bank, 24 January 1915. One thousand of her crew were drowned; two hundred and fifty rescued by British ships.

and we shall look back upon these days with satisfaction—even pride. . . .'

Clementine Churchill continued her side of the correspondence, answering all his queries, carrying out all his requests, acting as a moderating influence on his wilder whims, and trying to cheer him. 'In an hour the Cabinet meets,' she wrote on December 27, 'I hope the season of peace & goodwill will not have infected its members'; and on the following day: 'It seems centuries since you have left & a thick pall of fog has settled round me thro' which I can neither hear nor see the conflict. . . . I am absolutely worn out with emotions & the excitement of seeing you & I must have a few days' rest. I can't sleep for anxiety. . . .'[15]

On December 30 Clementine Churchill wrote from Lord Stanley of Alderley's[16] house, Alderley Park in Cheshire: 'I hoped to find Venetia here but she passed me in the train, summoned back to town by the imperious Montagu.' On New Year's Day, while still at Alderley Park she wrote again: 'Venetia the prosperous and the happy, arrived this evening to enliven us & to lift us out of the doldrums. . . . She entertained the PM on New Year's Eve to Beer & Skittles.' Of her husband's request for a photograph of the sinking German battleship to go on the silver cigarette box, Clementine Churchill was not at all certain that this would be a wise present. It was, she wrote, 'a very ghastly picture with all those wretched scorched singed Germans clinging to her & rolling off her'. Another reason against it, she explained, was that it had already been widely published. Had it been a secret, unknown photograph, he might have had an excuse to use it. She was willing, if he still insisted on a gruesome picture, to find a less well known one. But she ended her letter by suggesting that it would be more sensible to use a plain inscription on the box. Churchill bowed to her advice. The photograph of the *Blücher* was abandoned. But he was unconvinced by her letter of Decem-

[15] This letter is reproduced in full in facsimile, pp. 1036–7.
[16] Edward Lyulph Stanley, 1839–1925. Liberal MP, 1880–5. 4th Baron Stanley of Alderley and 4th Baron Sheffield. Clementine Churchill's uncle. Father of Venetia (Mrs Edwin Montagu) and Sylvia (Mrs Anthony Henley).

ber 30 in which she had tried to say a good word for Asquith, replying on January 2:

. . . You are a vy sapient cat to write as you do in yr last letter. But I feel that my work with Asquith has come to an end. I have found him a weak and disloyal chief. I hope I shall not ever have to serve under him again. After the 'Perhaps he might have a battalion' letter I cannot feel the slightest regard for him any more. LG is no doubt all you say: but his interests are not divorced from mine and in those circumstances we can work together if occasion arises. After all he always disagreed about D'Iles. He was not like HHA, a co-adventurer—approving & agreeing at every stage. And he had the power to put things right with us as regards my policy & myself. But his slothfulness & procrastination ruined the policy, & his political nippiness squandered his credit. However there is no reason why ordinary relations shd not be preserved.

As 1915 came to an end there was still no news of which Battalion he was to go to. Churchill remained at St Omer at Max Aitken's headquarters, brooding on politics and anxious to take up his command.

# 20

# In Training

WHILE HE WAS at St Omer on New Year's Day 1916 Churchill
learned that he had been appointed to the command of an Infantry Battalion, the 6th Royal Scots Fusiliers. Military security
would not permit him to tell his wife either where his Battalion
was to train, or to which part of the front it would be sent; all he
could say was that the trenches would be 'a few miles to the left
of where I was before'. He told her how glad he was to be leaving St Omer, 'a desert' since French's departure.

The 6th Battalion of the Royal Scots Fusiliers consisted of thirty
officers and seven hundred men. It formed a part of the Ninth
(Scottish) Division, commanded by Major-General Furse,[1] with
whom Churchill dined on January 1 at his headquarters at Merris.
The evening was a success, more so than his first evening with the
Grenadiers, for, as he wrote to his wife: 'They evidently will like
vy much to have me. The general—Furse—is extremely well
thought of here and is a thoroughly frank & broadminded man.
. . . Most of the staff had met me soldiering somewhere or other,
& we had a pleasant evening.' During the dinner Churchill asked
about the condition and history of his Battalion. He heard of its

[1] William Thomas Furse, 1865–1953. Entered Army, 1884. ADC to Lord
Roberts when Commander-in-Chief, India, 1890–3. Brigadier-General commanding the II Corps in France, 1915. General Officer commanding the
9th (Scottish) Division, 1915–16. Knighted, 1917. Lieutenant-General,
1917; Member of the Army Council, 1920.

gallantry at the Battle of Loos in September 1915, and of its heavy losses, writing to his wife:

More than half the men, & ¾rs of the officers were shot, & these terrible gaps have been filled up by recruits of good quality, & quite young inexperienced officers. I shd therefore be able to bring in my two good officers Spiers & Archie & put them where I like. They will be sorely needed. In spite of its crippled condition the regiment has been for two months in the worst part of the line; but now they are resting & do not go in again till the 20th: & then to an easier post. Thus I will have at least a fortnight to pull them together and get them into my hand.

Churchill's hope of having Spiers with him as his principal support was dashed a few days later when he learned that he could not take him to the Battalion. The work of training seven hundred men and taking them into the line was considered inappropriate for an officer of Spiers' experience, whose liaison activities were assuming increasing significance.[2] But Haig agreed to let Sir Archibald Sinclair join Churchill as his second-in-command.

Churchill entered into his duties as a Battalion Commander with enthusiasm, writing to his wife on January 3, before he had even met his men: 'Now that I shall be commanding a Scottish battalion, I shd like you to send me a copy in one volume of Burns. I will soothe & cheer their spirits by quotations from it. I shall have to be careful not to drop into a mimicry of their accent! You know I am a vy gt admirer of that race. A wife, a constituency, & now a regiment attest the sincerity of my choice!'

[2] The friendship built up between Churchill and Spiers during December continued to flourish, and Churchill followed Spiers' career closely. 'I read your name this morning in the casualty list for the 4th time with keen emotion . . .' Churchill wrote to him on 27 October 1916. 'I cannot tell you how much I admire and reverence the brilliant & noble service you are doing & have done for the country. You are indeed a Paladin worthy to rank with the truest knights of the great days of romance. Thank God you are alive. Some good angel has guarded you amid such innumerable perils, & brought you safely thus far along this terrible & never ending road. . . . Thank you so much for the helmet you sent me. It is a fine trophy. But my dear why don't you write. I shd so value yr letters and it wd be such a pleasure to me to receive them.'

A day later, on January 4, Churchill was formally appointed to his command. He knew that it would not be an easy task, commanding a Battalion which had suffered so severely, and all of whose senior officers had been killed in battle. 'It will be an exhausting labour,' he wrote to his wife, 'but I expect I shall succeed. I am vy glad to have some work to do: after this long appalling waste of my energies; tho' perhaps some more appropriate outlet cd have been found.' Lieutenant Hakewill Smith,[3] the Battalion's only regular officer in 1915, recalled fifty years later in conversation with the author, the 'horror' with which the news of Churchill's impending arrival was greeted. Another regimental officer, Captain Gibb,[4] recorded in *With Winston Churchill at the Front* the reaction of officers and men alike:

When the news spread, a mutinous spirit grew. . . . Why could not Churchill have gone to the Argylls if he must have a Scottish regiment! We should all have been greatly interested to see him in a kilt and, besides, the Argylls were accustomed to celebrities in their ranks since Ian Hay[5] had celebrated their deeds in his remunerative volume. Or again, we should all have been glad to see him once for all oust and utterly displace the Brigade Commander,[6] who had jarred upon us since

[3] Edmund Hakewill Smith, 1896– . Born in South Africa. Served Cape Town Highlanders, August–September 1914. Royal Military College, Sandhurst, November 1914–June 1915. 2nd Lieutenant, Royal Scots Fusiliers, June 1915. On active service, 1915–18; twice wounded. Major-General, 1942. Director of Organization, War Office, 1942–3. Commanded 52nd Lowland Division, 1943–6. Governor, Military Knights of Windsor, 1951. Deputy Constable and Lieutenant-Governor, Windsor Castle, 1964. Knighted, 1967.

[4] Andrew Dewar Gibb, 1888– . Called to the Bar, 1914. Officer commanding D Company, 6th Royal Scots Fusiliers, 1915–16, Captain and Adjutant, 1916. He published *With Winston Churchill at the Front* in 1924. Regius Professor of Law, Glasgow University, 1934–58. Chairman of the Scottish National Party, 1936–40.

[5] John Hay Beith, 1876–1952. Novelist, playwright and historian; penname, Ian Hay. Captain, Argyll and Sutherland Highlanders, 1914–16. Published *The First Hundred Thousand* in 1915. Member of the British War Mission to the United States, 1916–18. Published *Carrying On* in 1917; several chapters were set in Ploegsteert. Director of Public Relations at the War Office, 1938–41.

[6] Henry Ernest Walshe, 1866–1947. Entered Army, 1889. Crossed to France, 13 August 1914, as a Major with the 2nd Battalion South Staffordshire Regiment. Brigadier-General Commanding the 27th Infantry Brigade, September 1915–April 1916.

the day he stopped the Battalion's leave for a fortnight on finding in our front line a well-rusted bayonet, the property of some migratory and irresponsible sapper. We should even have been glad to see him replace the Divisional General [Furse] who, although popular, was always unduly anxious to involve us in unpleasant and dangerous brawls with the Germans opposite. Indeed, any position at all in the Expeditionary Force seemed not too exalted for Winston if only he had left us our own CO and refrained from disturbing the peace of the pastures of Moolenacker.

On January 5 Churchill set off from St Omer to join his Battalion in its reserve billets near the town of Meteren. He and his small staff were billeted in the village of Moolenacker, which for the next three weeks was to be their home. The gently undulating terrain reminded some of the young Scottish officers of Caithness; 'flat and uninteresting', as Lieutenant McDavid[7] later recalled in a letter to the author, 'with croft like farms scattered all around. Buildings were dilapidated, occupying three sides of a muddy square, with the inevitable dung-heap in the middle. . . . I can't remember seeing any livestock, other than somewhat decrepit nags and a few mules probably discarded by a remount section previously billeted in the district.' The Battalion was in need of rest. After its severe losses at the Battle of Loos, it had spent some months in the front-line trenches of the Ypres salient before being sent into reserve. 'We had a frightfully bad time at Ypres,' Hakewill Smith recalled, 'with water up to the waist. We were observed and watched by the Boche all the time; they were oppressively close.'

Before he reached the village of Moolenacker Churchill sent a message forward to say that he wished to meet all the officers at luncheon, after which he would inspect the whole Battalion. 'Just before noon,' Hakewill Smith recalled, 'an imposing cavalcade arrived. Churchill on a black charger, Archie Sinclair on a black

---

[7] Jock McDavid, 1897–    . Enlisted in the Royal Scots Fusiliers, October 1914. 2nd Lieutenant, April 1915. Acting Adjutant, 6th Royal Scots Fusiliers, November 1915. Promoted Lieutenant while serving as Adjutant, December 1915. Gassed, August 1918. Demobilized, October 1919. Area-Manager, Shell-Mex Ltd. 1919–28; Divisional Manager, 1928–34. Subsequently in the brewing and distilling industry.

THE WYTSCHAETE TO ARMENTIÈRES SECTOR OF THE
WESTERN FRONT, JANUARY 1916

charger, two grooms on black chargers followed by a limber
filled with Churchill's luggage—much more than the 35 lbs allowed weight. In the rear half we saw a curious contraption: a
long bath and a boiler for heating the bath water.' Churchill
proceeded to his headquarters at Moolenacker Farm, a farm
which, Gibb wrote, was 'a more than usually dirty farm', whose
farm people were 'more than usually dirty and unprepossessing'.
Some of them had gathered in the orderly room to witness the
arrival of the new Commanding Officer. Gibb described the en-
suing scene:

Whether by means of the sign-language, or by dint of that reiteration which works such wonders, the dirty ladies of the house had come
to understand that the new Colonel was somebody. Winston therefore made fitting entry on this his formal accession to power, for not
only was there much clicking and saluting on the part of
　　　　(a) the officers,
　　　　(b) the Sergeant-Major, and
　　　　(c) the prisoners,
but the ladies rose up to the accompaniment of loud whispers of
*'Monsieur le ministre!' 'Monsieur le Colonel!' 'Ah, c'est lui?' 'C'est votre
ministre?'* and in this way imparted to the proceedings at once an
irregular air of friendliness, and an international colour, which produced a most happy effect and one worthy of the occasion.

Churchill then lunched with the officers of his headquarters staff. Hakewill Smith later recalled:

It was quite the most uncomfortable lunch I had ever been at. Churchill didn't say a word: he went right round the table staring each officer out of countenance. We had disliked the idea of Churchill being in command; now, having seen him, we disliked the idea even more. At the end of the lunch, he made a short speech: 'Gentlemen, I am now your Commanding Officer. Those who support me I will look after. Those who go against me I will break. Good afternoon gentlemen.' Everyone was agreed that we were in for a pretty rotten time.

There followed a parade of the whole Battalion, of which Hakewill Smith was again a witness:

The after lunch parade was a farce. The men were at the slope when Churchill appeared on his charger. Captain Gibb reported that all were present. While the troops were still at the slope, Churchill called out: 'Royal Scots Fusiliers! Fix Bayonets!' The command could not possibly be carried out from the slope position. A couple of the chaps put their rifles on the ground and pulled out their bayonets; the rest were merely mystified. Eventually, Gibb persuaded Churchill to call 'Order Arms' and to fix their bayonets in the normal way.

Winston then inspected the men. Having done so, he gave a cavalry order: 'Sections Right!' This meant nothing to the Jocks, who had the sense to stand still and do nothing.

Such were the impressions that Churchill made in his first hours as a Commanding Officer. His own impressions were mixed. There was a more successful drill parade on the following morning. When Churchill wrote to his wife he was enthusiastic and hopeful: 'The young officers are all small middle class Scotsmen —vy brave & willing & intelligent: but of course all quite new to soldiering. All the seniors & all the professionals have fallen. I have spent the morning watching each company in turn drill & handle their arms. They are vy good. . . . The regiment is full of life & strength, & I believe I shall be a help to them.' McDavid was conscious that the Royal Scots Fusiliers had not made quite the same impact upon Churchill as the Grenadiers had done. Later he recalled, in conversation with the author:

The immediate impression which Churchill formed when he reached us was a poor one. He had come from a guards battalion which consisted almost entirely of regular soldiers. These Guardsmen spent only 48 hours in the trenches at any one time, while we were 6 days in and 6 days out. When Churchill joined the 6th Royal Scots Fusiliers he joined a conglomerated mess of young civilians and old reservists, both of whom had experienced hell since they arrived in France in the spring of 1915; the demoralising effects of the Battle of Loos. After Loos there had only been an extremely brief period of rest, followed by the most disastrous winter of the war over in the Ypres Salient. At Ypres we had to walk four miles from our rest billet to the front line, and over half of this was in the slimy mud with exploding shells as a constant danger. Morale was low, understandably so because of the absolutely hellish condition of the Salient trudging mile after mile with mud up to one's thighs, severe frost, poor equipment, and continual bombardment. When Churchill reached us we had only had a week's rest following these demoralising conditions. No wonder we made a poor impression on him.

It was Churchill's task, as Colonel, to rally these men and prepare them for their return to the front line two weeks later. It was a short time and a heavy task. 'I am now deeply immersed in the very small things which fall to my lot,' he wrote to his wife on January 6. 'I do all I can with zest.' On January 7 he sent his wife an account of his first efforts to gain his men's confidence. They were still puzzled by the appearance of a popular politician in their midst:

. . . I made my battalion parade this morning & drilled them myself all together. They have not done this before and I am anxious to make them feel their corporate identity & the sense of my personal control. A colonel within his own sphere is an autocrat who punishes & promotes & displaces at his discretion. The Brigadier is leaving me to myself for these first days in order that I may get all the threads in my hand. It is not hard for me to give orders as you know. . . .

I am quite comfortable, & the mess, as I told you, is clean & well supplied. Everyone is filled with the desire to obey & assist and I feel a growing confidence in the way the machine will work when I take it into action. Although the fortnight's further 'repose' is vy valuable for training & gaining control, of course I look forward to its conclusion.

'I am settling down here and gaining control & confidence,' he wrote to his wife again on the following day. 'The young officers are so keen, plucky & intelligent, so ready to obey & to be led, that I feel increasingly sure that we shall stand any ordinary test without discredit.' Two days later, on January 10, he wrote:

. . . I continue to work at the details of my battalion wh is officered entirely by quite young boys. Archie does a mass of housekeeping work, & I try to make good arrangements & give them all the feeling that there is something behind them & that they are strongly commanded. Of course they yield implicit loyalty & obedience & endeavour to meet or forestall every wish. I am fairly confident of being able to help them to do well, in spite of the woefully attenuated state of the regiment's officers.

After a week with his Battalion, Churchill felt that he had begun to win their confidence. Nor was Brigadier-General Walshe, his immediate superior, dissatisfied. On January 13 Churchill wrote to his wife:

. . . The Brigadier-General has left me quite alone, tho' civil. He has not meddled at all in my affairs wh I am conducting with confidence. I am pressing hard for the proper promotion of officers wh is shockingly neglected & delayed. I am filling up all the non-commissioned officers vacancies. Yesterday I spent seeing all the officers & NCO's, company by company, & explaining to them how I wish things to be done. It was odd to see these politicians of a year ago—Glasgow grocers, fitters, miners—all Trade Unionists probably, who I have harangued in bygone days in the St Andrews Hall—now all transformed into Sergeants & corporals stiffened by discipline and hardened by war into a fine set of warriors.

Churchill was not enamoured of the reserve billets; 'squalid little French farms', he described them to his wife, 'rising from a sea of sopping fields & muddy lanes'. Even in reserve the war was never far away: 'The guns boom away in the distance,' he told her, '& at night the sky to the Northward blinks & flickers with the wicked lights of war.' On January 13 he gave her an account of the training which he himself was having:

. . . In the morning Archie & I practised bomb-throwing. It is a job to be approached gingerly. You pull out the safety pin, & then as long as you hold the bomb in your hand nothing happens. But the moment you throw it—or release your hand—the fuse begins to burn & then 5 seconds afterwards there is real good bang & splinters fly all over the place. As soon as you have thrown it, you bob down behind the parapet, until the explosion has occurred. Sometimes the men are stupid— drop the bomb in the trench or close to it—then the bombing officer —a young Sandhurst kid—deftly picks it up & throws it away with perhaps 2 seconds to spare. Everyone has to learn. It is perfectly safe as long as you do it right.

The 'young Sandhurst kid' was Hakewill Smith, whom Churchill soon renamed the 'bomb boy'. He too recalled the Colonel's training on that cold January morning: 'Churchill wasn't very accurate in his throwing.[8] He threw one bomb and said "That's enough".'

The efforts which Churchill made to fit himself into the military routine made a strong impression upon the men under his command. McDavid recalled:

After a very brief period he had accelerated the morale of officers and men to an almost unbelievable degree. It was sheer personality. We laughed at lots of things he did, but there were other things we did not laugh at for we knew they were sound. He had a unique approach which did wonders to us. He let everyone under his command see that he was responsible, from the very moment he arrived, that they understood not only *what* they were supposed to do, but *why* they had to do it. . . .

No detail of our daily life was too small for him to ignore. He overlooked nothing. . . . Instead of a quick glance at what was being done he would stop and talk with everyone and probe to the bottom

[8] In 1896, when going ashore at the Sassoon Dock, Bombay, Churchill had dislocated his shoulder, an injury which inconvenienced him for the rest of his life. He was unable to raise his right arm sharply, and had always to play polo with the upper part of his arm strapped to his body.

of every activity. I have never known an officer take such pains to inspire confidence or to gain confidence; indeed he inspired confidence in gaining it.

The Battalion was due to go forward on about January 20. It had been allocated a sector of the front line near the village of Ploegsteert, on the Belgian side of the Franco-Belgian border. Churchill was surprised to learn that the men of the Ninth Division spent longer in the trenches than the Guards had done. He explained the routine to his wife in his letter of January 13: 'Unlike Cavan's—this division do 6 days in the front line, 6 days in the support line (just as unhealthy) 6 days more in the front line, & then some of them 6 days rest—& begin again. No wonder they wear them out. Compare this with 48 hours in & 48 hours out, 3 times repeated, & then 6 days rest.' On the following day he was able to send her more information about the Ploegsteert sector. 'It is a vy quiet part of the line at present,' he wrote, 'though the general (Furse) means to stir them up. The casualties run only to 5 or 6 a day on the front of the division: wh is no more than are lost in one battalion of the Guards. Also I hear good reports of the trenches—dugouts etc. Not too muddy, & good communications to get into them by.'

On January 13, when less than a week remained before the Battalion was due to go into the trenches, Churchill learned they were to have an extra week in training: 'I am sorry there is this further delay,' he wrote to his wife, 'for a war without action is really a dreary affair. But these boys were evidently delighted. . . .' On the following day he replied to a letter from his brother by sending him an account of life as a Commanding Officer. His Battalion, he said, consisted 'entirely of young boy officers—willing, plucky, intelligent—but of course almost untrained and quite inexperienced'. Their average age, he had calculated, was twenty-three. His brother's news about the evacuation of the Gallipoli Peninsula caused him to brood for a while on the past. Of the Dardanelles he wrote: 'History will vindicate the conception, & the errors in execution will on the whole leave me clear. My one fatal mistake was trying to achieve a gt enterprise without having the plenary authority wh cd so easily have carried it to success.' But now, he wrote, 'the days slip away quickly in the transaction of small things'. Churchill told his brother that after two or three months as a Battalion Commander he expected to be appointed to command a Brigade. But he was no longer worried about attaining the position which had so cruelly mocked him in the previous month; 'I shall be proud to lead this shattered battalion to the assault,' he wrote. He was concerned about his brother's future. After Hamilton's departure from Gallipoli in October 1915, Jack Churchill had been taken on to General Birdwood's staff. 'I often think of you,' Churchill wrote, 'and rejoice you are on the whole not ill-placed in these times. Stick to Birdwood, & don't go into unnecessary danger.' As for the future, he wrote, 'The war plods on slowly & I think it will be all right in the end. But what a weary toil for the millions! After it is over politics will be interesting; & we shall find a clear field. . . . If I am killed, the insurances are quite good & Clemmie & Goonie must hold together till peace comes—not—please God—one day before undoubted victory.'

While his Battalion was at Moolenacker, Churchill rode to Kemmel to see Major-General Lipsett,[9] of the Royal Irish Regiment, who had been at Sandhurst with him, and was attached to the Canadian forces. Lipsett was the inventor of the 'raid'; a means of taking offensive action within the strictly limited confines of trench warfare. In the first of these 'raids' a group of Canadians had left their front-line trenches, crossed no-man's-land, entered the German trenches facing them, and with the loss of only one of their own men had killed forty Germans. They then returned to their own trenches. Lipsett was keen to show Churchill how his 'raids' worked. 'He is full of ruses and stratagems,' Churchill wrote to his wife on January 14, 'and his revealing his secrets to

[9] Louis James Lipsett, 1874–1918. 2nd Lieutenant, Royal Irish Regiment, 1894. Major, attached to the Canadian Army, 1911–14. Brigadier-General, attached to the Canadian Expeditionary Force, 1914–16; Lieutenant-Colonel, Royal Irish Regiment, 1917–18.

me is a compliment.' After a day with Lipsett he wrote to her
again:

He made a realistic attack with his bombs on a section of our reserve trenches. The splinters flew all over the place. It was like a
skirmish: but no one was hurt. Lucky! The Canadians grinned from
ear to ear to see me. Wonderful fellows: like leopards. I was made to
make them a speech & produced a really good one on the spur of the
moment. Meanwhile the Germans threw occasional shrapnel shells wh
burst a short distance off without anyone taking the slightest notice.

When Churchill wrote to his wife on January 16 he was under
no illusion about the effort still needed to get the Battalion up to
the mark:

This battalion is the weakest in the brigade & makes the least good
appearance. The young officers have not the command to make their
companies drill & march really well. They can do a plain job all right;
but the polish is at present lacking. Both Furse & the Brigadier realise
fully these difficulties, and I am doing my best to cope with them. Up
to the present however, I have been entirely occupied with practice
points—gas helmets, rifles in good order, trench discipline & routine
etc. As we are going to be a week more out of the line, I shall give
them some vy precise drill & marching. It is all helpful.

Churchill's only serious disagreement with his officers was over
the question of military discipline. His mind turned instinctively
to leniency. 'My dear,' he wrote to his wife, who worried lest he
was too severe, 'don't be at all anxious about my being hard on
the men. Am I ever hard on anybody? No. I have reduced
punishment both in quantity, & method.' Churchill had been
much moved by the sufferings of the 6th Royal Scots Fusiliers at
Loos. His first question to the first troublemaker who came before
him was: 'Were you in the battle?' When the man replied, 'Yes,'
the charge against him was dismissed. The officers were surprised
by this generous act; and horrified when, as McDavid recalled,
'everyone then said they had been at Loos'. Robert Fox,[10] one of

[10] Robert Fox, 1894–    . Left school at the age of twelve. Worked in
mills, factories and shipyards. Enlisted, Royal Scots Fusiliers, 16 August
1914. Crossed to France with 6th Battalion, 11 May 1915. Wounded at

the Battalion's Lewis gunners, recalled in a radio broadcast in 1964: 'Churchill was scrupulously fair to any man before him on a charge. I remember once, when acting as escort, I heard him cross-examine the NCO giving evidence against the man, with all the skill of a counsel at the Bar. The evidence did not satisfy him, so he dismissed the charge and gave the NCO a homily on the virtues of exactitude.' Gibb believed that Churchill was 'quite wrong' in siding so openly with the rank and file, writing in his book:

It is difficult to see how his ideas on this matter could receive sanction without serious detriment to the one essential of discipline, viz, prompt obedience to orders.

It used to happen that a soldier when ordered say, by a corporal, to perform some duty, did, through laziness or dislike of the corporal or distaste for the order given, refuse to obey that order, at the same time usually inviting the corporal to perform certain notoriously impossible physical feats or proceed to a certain non-existent destination, all in order to show his utter contempt of the corporal and emphasize his determination on no account to do as he was told. Now this is indiscipline in the highest degree, and a man is always 'run in' at once for it, and on the facts being proved against him he is usually heavily punished.

It was however impossible, Gibb recalled, to persuade Churchill to punish such indiscipline according to the rules:

He considered that no man would wittingly incur the serious penalties inevitable in such a case, did he know that his conduct was in fact precisely such conduct as would render him liable to them. In any event, the Colonel used to say, whether or not the man knew, it was only fair to explain the position to him there and then, and there and then to give him a chance to depart from his insubordinate attitude.

Churchill's offer of a second chance appalled the officers. 'I am afraid the men began to realize,' wrote Gibb, 'that they might at

---

Festubert, June 1915. Fought at Loos, September 1915. Wounded on the Somme, August 1916. Wounded near Arras, April 1917. Demobilized, 1919. Subsequently a reporter, proof reader and journalist, working in Paris on the *Chicago Tribune* and the *New York Herald*.

least once indulge themselves in the luxury of telling their
sergeants to go to hell!'

Despite his officers' disapproval, Churchill persevered in what
they considered his unmilitary attitude towards discipline.

While the Battalion was in reserve, Churchill had continued to
badger his wife for supplies. 'Try to get a King's messenger to
bring over my new boots when they are ready,' he had written
on January 2. When some food parcels were delayed he wrote
impatiently, on January 3: 'You must find out from the Post Office
what went wrong & also what is the best route & method.' 'Order
me a new tunic thicker than the last,' he wrote on January 5, 'with
less baggy pockets. . . . Send also 2 spare bits of badge for this
regiment: and a Glengarry cap.' On January 8 he wrote from
Moolenacker Farm; 'Go on sending brandy (my own) & tinned
things of the ordinary types (but good quality). Fantastic tinned
things usually mock me in the end.' On the same day, realizing
that he was going to be with the Battalion for some time, he
wrote: 'Let me have some note paper printed nicely:

### 6TH ROYAL SCOTS FUSILIERS
### IN THE FIELD

It is a good thing to fly the flag at the main.'

On January 13 Clementine Churchill's Christmas hamper finally arrived. He was delighted: 'I never saw such dainties & profusion. We shall eat them sparingly keeping the best for the
trenches. It will be a good thing to start off another case on the
same lines (esp the cheese & the raisins). If you send it now, it
will be here in a fortnight or three weeks & will be vy welcome.'
He was full of praise for the sleeping bag which she had sent him:
'I must admit the warmth of the red hot polar bear is delicious
to sleep in. It wd just suit you as it seems to have a natural
warmth of its own & you cd develop that fierce temperature wh
is good for Kats before they plunge into slumber.'

Churchill did not limit the search for comfort to himself alone.
On his first afternoon with the Battalion he had addressed the
officers with solemn words: 'Gentlemen, we are now going to

make war—on the lice.' And this he was determined to do, for, as Gibb recorded:

With these words did the great scion of the house of Marlborough first address his Scottish Captains assembled in council. And with these words was inaugurated such a discourse on pulex Europaeus, its origin, growth, and nature, its habitat and its importance as a factor in wars ancient and modern, as left one agape with wonder at the erudition and force of its author. . . .

Thereafter he created a committee of company commanders to concert measures for the utter extermination of all the lice in the battalion.

The delousing committee was soon busy. 'It was a terrific moment,' McDavid recalled, 'and by God it worked.' The French officer attached to the 9th Division as liaison officer, Emile Herzog,[11] was sent with McDavid to Bailleul to search for baths for the men. Churchill had suggested that brewery vats might be suitable for his Fusiliers. When Herzog and McDavid found a deserted brewery on the outskirts of the town, the men were marched the two miles from Moolenacker to their improvised bath-house. While the delousing committee was at work, Churchill turned to other aspects of the Battalion's comfort. When he addressed the men on the morning after his arrival he spoke sympathetically. 'You men have had a hard time,' he said. 'Now you're going to have it easy for some time—I hope.' Action soon followed, as Robert Fox recalled:

Huge stocks of clothing arrived at the quartermaster's stores. We all needed new rig-outs. We got them. Steel helmets were by then being issued to the British Army. We were among the first to get them. We found, too, a vast improvement in our rations. Bully beef and biscuits were only memories.

There were no parades after mid-day. The rest of the day was given

[11] Emile Salomon Wilhelm Herzog, 1885–1967. Lieutenant, French Army, 1914–16. Attached as liaison officer to the 9th Division, 1916. He drew upon his experiences for his first novel, *Silences du Colonel Bramble,* published in 1918 under the name André Maurois. Novelist and historian. Honorary knighthood, 1938. Eyewitness attached to the British GHQ in France, 1939–40.

over to rest and recreation. A field was rolled out more or less flat and
goal-posts erected. Jerseys and footballs arrived from somewhere.
Games were arranged against neighbouring units. The Fusiliers won
them all. Churchill took a great pride in his team. He rarely missed
a match.

The culmination of these efforts came on January 16, when
Churchill arranged a combined sports day and concert. 'The officers & men have taken a lively interest in both affairs,' Churchill
wrote to his wife on the great day; 'it is odd no one has got any
up for them before.' A piano had been procured from somewhere, new songs were practised and various games were devised with somewhat macabre local touches, such as 'the bomb
throwers'. 'I will let you know how it goes off,' he told his wife.
'I think they want nursing & encouraging, more than drill-
sergeanting. . . .'

Churchill sent his wife a full account of the day's activities. He
was proud of his efforts, and had invited several guests:

The sports were highly successful & the men were really delighted.
They were most amusing sports—mule races, pillow fights, obstacle
races etc. All well organised, & supported by gt keenness & interest.
After dark we had our first concert in a big barn. Such singing you
never heard. People sang with the greatest courage who had no idea
either of words or tune. Jack Seely and other officers came & Jack
presented the prizes for the sports, & called for three cheers for me &
an extra one for you, all were most heartily given. We had quite a
banquet in the evening. Jack S, Colonel Holland,[12] some of the Bde
staff, 'Ian Hay' & others. Quite a cheery day. The men enjoyed themselves immensely. Poor fellows—nothing like this had ever been done
for them before. They do not get much to brighten their lives—short
though they may be. . . .

On the day after the concert, training had to continue, for on
January 18 all four Battalions were to take part in a route march,

[12] Arthur Edward Aveling Holland, 1862–1927. Known as 'Tom'. Entered Army, 1880. Colonel, 1910. Commanded the Artillery of the 8th Division, 1914–15; of the 1st Division, 1915–16. Major-General commanding
the Artillery of the 3rd Army, 1916. Lieutenant-General commanding the
Artillery of the I Army Corps, 1917–18. Knighted, 1918. Conservative MP,
1924–7.

under Brigadier-General Walshe's critical gaze. 'This morning,' Churchill wrote to his wife on January 17, 'I have been drilling them vy strictly, so that tomorrow they may give most satisfaction to the Brigadier, & work with more style & polish. They seemed to try vy hard & I think they will do better. However they are not grenadiers & I am not a drill sergeant.'

On January 17 Churchill rode into Hazebrouck, just over six miles away, to hear a special lecture by Colonel Holland on the battle of Loos. This battle was a grim memory for all who had been through it; its 'lessons' would obviously have to be learned before any further attempt to break through the German trenches were made. Churchill described the lecture to his wife:

. . . The theatre was crowded with Generals & officers. Jack Seely & I cd not even get a seat, but stood at the wings of the stage. Tom spoke vy well but his tale was one of hopeless failure, of sublime heroism utterly wasted & of splendid Scottish soldiers shorn away in vain . . . with never the ghost of a chance of success. 6,000 k & w out of 10,000 in this Scottish division alone. Alas alas. Afterwards they asked what was the lesson of the lecture. I restrained an impulse to reply 'Don't do it again'. But they will—I have no doubt.

As the days passed, the atmosphere at Moolenacker became more relaxed. The men realized that their commanding officer was not going to make life hell for them, or let them down. The 27th Brigade route march took place on January 18. For the first time since he had taken command Churchill saw his Battalion exposed to the critical gaze of higher authorities. He was confident that the efforts which he had made during the past two weeks would be successful. Among his special concerns was that his men should sing while they were marching. The route march was to be the first public exhibition of their talents. Gibb remembered this aspect of the route march vividly:

We were second company, and in passing through the village of Merris the men were busy inventing adventures and ever fresh adventures in song for their hero and heroine. Afar off I saw the Colonel coming down the column and my heart leaped, for here was our company singing lustily and I felt sure of praise. Winston's large black horse loomed in sight, and then the amazing thing happened. The first platoon—mine—was seized, for the first and last time in its existence, with a devastating attack of modesty and dried up like a mountain rill in summer. The contagion spread and in a moment the company was marching mute—mute of modesty:

'Why are your men not singing, Captain Gibb?' shouted the Colonel to our Company Commander.

'They *were*, sir, but they think—they thought—they're afraid that——' but Winston had passed on down the column shouting 'Sing, sing' as he went.

Despite this setback, Churchill was satisfied by his Battalion's performance. 'The men did vy well,' he wrote to his wife; 'Their equipment & bearing showed a gt advance. The Brigadier was impressed in spite of himself; & said what a gt improvement had taken place.'

On January 19 Churchill went into Hazebrouck again, together with the other three Colonels of the Brigade. Colonels had been summoned from the whole reserve area. 'All the day I have been at the Machine gun school,' he wrote to his wife, 'with scores of Colonels listening to not vy illuminating lectures.' Among those who travelled in with him on the bus was Cameron of Lochiel,[13] who had been at Harrow and Sandhurst with him, and had raised, and was then commanding the 5th Battalion of the Cameron Highlanders. 'He has done heroically out here,' Churchill wrote to his wife; and he described how, at Loos, 'only he & his adjutant & 100 men survived unhit out of 26 officers & 850 men who charged. These stormed the German trench & held it. Where is Balaclava compared to that.[14] Two distinguished conduct medals were given to the men! Glorious system.'

After the lectures Churchill somehow procured a car, and was driven into St Omer, 'to buy a few stores, & see a few potentates'.

[13] Donald Walter Cameron of Lochiel, 1876–1951. Entered Army, 1896. Retired with rank of Captain 1906. Raised and commanded the 5th Battalion of the Cameron Highlanders, 1914–16. Commanded the Lovat Scouts Sharpshooters, 1917–18. Knighted, 1934.

[14] On 25 October 1854, at the battle of Balaclava, the Light Brigade lost over 400 of its 673 men.

On the road to St Omer, he wrote to his wife, 'Quite by chance I met Haig riding on the road 3 miles out. He rode up & shook hands & we exchanged a few banalities.'

On January 20 Churchill paid his first visit to the sector of the line which his Battalion was to hold. This was the area in which he would be living and fighting for several months. He was pleased with what he found:

My beloved,

. . . I have just come back from the line, having had a jolly day. I examined the whole of our front & all its approaches thoroughly. It is much the best bit of line I have yet seen all along the front. Incomparably better on every score than the sector where the Guards were. It is dry—the trenches are boarded & drained. The parapets are thick & bullet-proof. The wire is good. The field of fire clear. There are in most parts plenty of traverses (to localise the effect of shells), good dugouts & good shelter from fire. I think we cd stand a pretty good pounding here with comparatively little loss. Yesterday afternoon in fact hundreds of shells were fired into the trenches, & only *one* got a result. . . .

There was a little shelling today. The weather beautiful in the morning. I shall like this line vy much & shall feel vy proud to take charge of 1000 yards of 'the frontier between right & wrong'. . . .

While returning from his preliminary reconnaissance of his own future sector of the front line, Churchill lunched with Seely. That afternoon they attended one of the many lectures which had become a feature of life behind the lines. This time it was a lecture on the front line, 'illustrated by magic lantern aeroplane photographs,' he wrote to his wife; 'The lecturer was inarticulate, & the photographs indistinguishable, a futile performance'. That night Churchill dined with the Argyll and Sutherland Highlanders with whose Colonel, Henry Pelham Burn,[15] he had already made friends. There were twelve Colonels in the Ninth Division, all of

[15] Henry Pelham Burn, 1882–1958. Entered Army, 1901. Captain, 1910. Adjutant, 1st Battalion the Gordon Highlanders, November 1914. Brigade Major, 8th Infantry Brigade, April 1915. Colonel commanding the 152nd Infantry Brigade, July 1916–April 1918. Served in France and Belgium from 31 October 1914 to 8 April 1918. Brigadier-General, 1918.

whom had met at the machine-gun school on the previous day.
'I looked the youngest of all . . . & felt so too,' Churchill told his
wife, 'yet I was the oldest but 2: & have had more worry than
the lot put together.' Among those invited to the dinner was
Pelham Burn's Divisional General, Arthur Hoskins.[16] He was a
good sort of General,' Churchill wrote to his wife on January 22,
'& like nearly all these fellows had met me campaigning several
times, tho' I had forgotten. We sat jawing till 12.30 and Archie
dropped asleep.'

Churchill was eager to go into action; Clementine Churchill
was less enthusiastic. 'It makes me terribly anxious to feel that
your Battalion is so weak,' she wrote to him on January 20; 'It
will be a great credit to you if you improve it and bring it up to
the mark. Do not think me over-cautious, but don't be too ambitious at first or try your men too high—I wish you were not going so soon with these untried men into the line.' She worried
about him all the time, and wanted so much to see him again.
She even devised a scheme to go over to Dieppe and meet him
there, but nothing came of it. In her letter of January 20 Clementine Churchill wrote of how she often woke up at night thinking
of him, and of all the women in Europe who, equally distraught,
lay awake praying for their husbands' safety. On the following
day his sister-in-law, Lady Gwendeline Churchill, wrote, sharing
Clementine Churchill's concern:

My dear Winston,
   Five more days before you and your battalion go in to the Trenches
—and that fact distresses me—it makes me fidgett on my chair; makes
me toss in my bed, makes me bite my nails at meals—I will be light-
hearted again when you come out—when will that be? . . .
   Keep dodging the bullets—whatever happens don't get shot—you
will be wanted here—& for Godssake I hope it will be before the end
of the War—before the government have brought the Country down

[16] Arthur Reginald Hoskins, 1871–1942. 2nd Lieutenant, 1891. Served
on the Nile Expedition, 1898. Brigadier-General commanding the 8th Infantry Brigade, March–October 1915. Vth Army Corps Staff, October 1915–
December 1916. Commander-in-Chief, East Africa, 1917. Knighted, 1919.
Principal, Bonar Law College, 1929–38.

to a stalemate peace—but even my dear, if you are not back before then, you will be wanted then after the corpses of these mediocre worn out extenuéed ministers have been removed & it won't be too late to be at the head of a still vigorous & healthy nation—it will clamour for such a man as you—you are unique in your generation—you are the only one—so dodge the bullets—one ought not to grudge your sojourn at the Front, as long as you keep out the way of obvious danger—it is doing no harm either to yourself or to the Country FOR THE TIME BEING—you have been out barely 2 months—what are a few months in your crowded life or in the life of the Country—though I know that a few days, a few hours count in a War. . . .

How the injustice of all that has happened since last May smarts one—& you in your innermost thoughts have been right ever since the first days of the War—your instincts were right, your Policy, properly carried out, properly supported was absolutely right—energy, decision, forethought, you had them—isn't it extraordinary that you could not down the mediocrities—of course there were too many of them.

You are in the right place just now as it has all turned out—& if only one could make certain that you were bullet proof, it would be alright. . . .

Much love, Yrs affectionately
Goonie

On January 21 Churchill visited the front line again. When he wrote to his wife about his visit on the following day, his account was hopeful and soothing:

I asked a soldier of the Border Regiment who I found yesterday in the trenches we are to hold whether he was not vy glad after three months in the front line to be going to rest. He replied that he was rather sorry, as they wd never get such a good place again. My second examination of the position confirms me in the favourable view I took at first sight. I think we shall be vy comfortable & dry & the trenches generally are well protected against shelling. The two farms in wh I shall live by turns are not far apart; in fact I shall only move back about ¾s of a mile from the front line when we are in support & supposed to be 'resting'. Therefore for the next 2 or 3 months we shall all dwell continuously in close range of the enemy's artillery. However in this part of the world the houses have not been knocked about much: & the losses have been small.

Do you remember a great wood I told you about when I paid a visit to the front more than a year ago. I did not expect then that my fortunes wd lead me to live alongside it for months. In the spring it will be beautiful & alive with wild flowers, & the leaf will give good cover all over this flat country to our daily movements.

Orders came for the Battalion to start moving forward on January 24. It was to reach the support area immediately behind the front line on January 25, and take over its section of the front on the following day. 'Brandy & cigars wd be welcome,' Churchill wrote to his wife on the day before leaving; 'Also another of those lifeguard periscopes you were so clever in finding.'

The last week in reserve was spent preparing for the inspection of the Brigade by the Corps Commander, General Sir Charles Fergusson.[17] The inspection took place on January 22. Churchill wrote to his wife about it on the following day:

The inspection yesterday was a gt success. The Corps Commander (Fergusson) expressed himself astonished at the improvement in the battalion since he last saw it five weeks ago. The men certainly tried vy hard and my battalion drills have taught them a smartness in handling their arms wh was before lacking.

The general was vy polite & friendly, excused himself for not having come to see me, & asked me to ride in & have tea with him. This I did taking Archie to make friends meanwhile with the senior mammon of unrighteousness. I had a long talk with Fergusson. I had met him & most of his staff in the Omdurman campaign. He said he was very sorry I had been sent to this battalion, wh was such a vy weak & shattered one, & that he wd have found me a much better one 'for my purposes' i.e. to learn about regimental work. I said I might be more useful here, & that as long as the difficulties were recognised, I preferred to have a battalion wh wanted helping along. He said there had been a vy gt improvement, & there was no doubt I had done a gt deal of good. I left him a copy of my Variants to ponder over. There is no

[17] Charles Fergusson, 1865–1951. Entered Army, 1883. Adjutant-General, Egyptian Army, 1901–3. 7th Baronet, 1907. Brigadier-General, 1907. Inspector of Infantry, 1909–13. Lieutenant-General commanding the II Corps, 1915–16. Military Governor, Occupied German Territory, 1918–19. Governor-General and Commander-in-Chief, New Zealand, 1924–30.

doubt he is a friend who will help in every way. He spoke with confidence of my having high command etc. However now that we are going into the line I am quite interested here. . . .

Throughout Sunday January 23 the officers prepared the Battalion for its march into action. Colonel Holland gave Churchill lunch at Divisional Headquarters. Furse, Churchill wrote to his wife, 'had been full of praise. So at any rate we go into the line with a good backing.' That same day, writing from 41 Cromwell Road, Clementine Churchill urged her husband to make a careful record of all his experiences once he was in the trenches. She pointed out that even if he did not want to write for the newspapers, he ought nevertheless to write for posterity. She knew that his experiences were shared by millions of soldiers, but she believed that he was one of the very few people who could write 'with genius' on the war. She therefore urged him to make notes every day, and send them to her for safe keeping. Churchill never found time to make these notes. He did, however, find time to write his first letter to his four-year-old son. He wrote, in capital letters:

My dearest Randolph,

I am living here in a little farm. It is not so pretty as Hoe Farm, and there are no nice flowers and no pond or trees to play gorilla but there are three large fat dirty pigs. Like the ones we saw in the wood.

The Germans are a long way off and cannot shoot at us here. It is too far. So we are quite safe as long as we stay here. But we can hear the cannons booming in the distance and at night when it is all dark we can see their flashes twinkling in the sky. Soon we are going to go close up to the Germans and then we shall shoot back at them and try to kill them. This is because they have done wrong and caused all this war and sorrow.

Give my very best love to Diana and kiss Sarah for me. Write me a letter yourself soon and I will send you an answer back.

Your ever loving father<br>Winston S.C.

On the night of January 23 Churchill entertained all the officers of the Battalion to dinner at the Station Hotel in Hazebrouck. He invited Furse and Holland to the dinner. On the following day he described the scene to his wife:

We sat down 20 & had an elaborate feast beginning with oysters & lots of champagne. . . . I made the officers a little speech & the Bde Major[18] told them all about the regiment in the battle; & the pipers played doleful dirges; & we sang Auld Lang Syne and generally there was a scene of much enjoyment. This is the first time they had ever been brought together round a table. Poor lads, they were really delighted. Altogether things have now gone vy well. I put it to Holland & the General (Furse) not to hustle us into raids etc till we had really got a full knowledge of the *terrain* & the enemy; but to lie *doggo* for a fortnight, & then have a whole batch of small enterprises—five at a time—so that if one or two got chopped the success of the others wd carry us through. They were much taken with this idea; & I think they will adopt it.

At eight in the morning of January 24 Churchill left Moolenacker Farm and rode towards the trenches at the head of his Battalion. For two nights he and his men were billeted in the village of La Crèche, half-way between Moolenacker and the front line. Churchill was in reflective mood. It was exactly twenty-one years since his father's death. 'He was only 4 years older than you are now,' Lady Randolph had written to her son the day before. On January 29 Churchill replied: 'I thought much of my father on Jan 24, & wondered what he wd think of it all. I am sure I am doing right.'

[18] Norman McDonald Teacher, 1878–1917. Brigade Major, 27th Brigade, 1916. Commanding Officer, 2nd Royal Scots, 1917. Killed in action in the Ypres salient, 26 September 1917.

# 21

# Ploegsteert

---

DURING 1915 the Belgian village of Ploegsteert had been transformed by the British into 'Plug Street'. It had become a soldiers' town, a maze of billets and dugouts, canteens and cafés. Eastwards from the village a series of tracks and communication trenches led to the front line, along which the soldiers, moving each day to the trenches, were exposed to a spasmodic ration of German shells and bullets. Going up the line, the men risked death or mutilation long before they had reached their forward trenches. By the time the 6th Royal Scots Fusiliers arrived, several military cemeteries had been opened near the village; the largest, on the Armentières road, was less than a hundred yards from Churchill's headquarters.

The arrival of the 6th Battalion of the Royal Scots Fusiliers at Ploegsteert was a routine matter. Men whom the Army considered fresh were replacing those who were in every way exhausted. The Ninth Division was taking its turn in the forward line. It had done so before, and would do so again. Holding the line at Ploegsteert was not easy or safe work, but it was not 'going over the top'; during the hundred days in which the Battalion was in the trenches under Churchill's command only fifteen men were killed and a hundred and twenty-three wounded. After the horrors of Loos, with its swift, brutal losses, the men accepted Ploegsteert with equanimity, and became attached to it. Those, the majority, who went south to fight on the Somme in July would look back to their time at Ploegsteert with nostalgia.

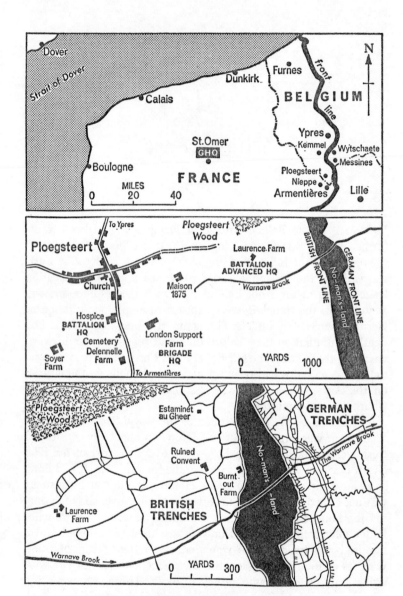

THE PLOEGSTEERT SECTOR OF THE WESTERN FRONT,
JANUARY–MAY 1916

More than a month had passed since Churchill had been in the trenches with the Grenadiers. Now he was going into the line again, in command of men whom he had trained, and who trusted in him. His Battalion headquarters was the former workshop of the Sisters of Charity[1] on the western side of the road which led from Ploegsteert to Armentières. Churchill knew it as the Hospice. It was situated in a good position for the control of a Battalion serving in the line. It was four hundred yards from London Support Farm, in which Brigadier-General Walshe had established Brigade Headquarters.

While in reserve Churchill's companies were lodged in and around three nearby farms. The largest, Soyer Farm, lay directly behind the Hospice, eight hundred yards across the fields. The second, Delennelle Farm, was a thousand yards to the south, beyond the cemetery along the Armentières road. The third, known locally as Maison 1875, was five hundred yards in front of the Hospice on the direct line between Churchill and the trenches. When Churchill arrived at Ploegsteert there had been little serious damage done to any of these farms, and the Hospice was intact.

The enormous military machine of which Churchill was so small a cog did not need his experience, his skill or his courage in order to survive. Sir Douglas Haig, at his headquarters twenty-eight miles away had no reason to be aware of anything more than Churchill's existence.[2] The southern end of Ploegsteert was his home, the fields around his base, the defence of a short section of the trenches in front his ultimate concern.

On January 26, his first night at the Hospice, Churchill sent his

---

[1] A French religious order, they had left France at the time of the anticlerical legislation of 1900. Their mother superior, Mathilde Désirée Foule, was born in Limoges in 1857.

[2] The only reference in Haig's diary to Churchill at this time is on January 15, when he wrote: 'I received a letter from Admiral Bridgeman telling me that I should be on my guard against Winston Churchill acting as a private reporter to the Cabinet. Personally I feel that I can only do what I judge best, and I have no time, even if I had the inclination, to keep an eye on Winston's writings.'

wife an account of life near the trenches, trying, as he knew he must, to put her mind at rest about the dangers:

I am extremely well-lodged here—with a fine bedroom looking out across the fields to the German lines 3,000 yards away. Two nuns remain here and keep up the little chapel which is a part of the building. They received me most graciously when I marched in this morning, saying that we had saved this little piece of Belgium from the Germans, who were actually there for a week before being driven out. I have made the women at all the billets where I have stayed make their excellent soup for us—wh they do most gladly—so we are free for the moment from 'Maggi' & the rest of the tabloid class. On the right & left the guns are booming; & behind us a British field piece barks like a spaniel at frequent intervals. But the women & children still inhabit the little town[3] & laugh at the shells wh occasionally buff into the old church.

It is vy quiet on the front today, & really from your point of view this is an ideal part of the line. It is vy unlikely to be the scene of a big attack by either side. It has no great concentration of German artillery opposite it. The trenches are good, well wired, with a broad interval between the lines. The houses have been little damaged. Some of the men of the battalion we are relieving call it 'The Convalescent Home'. I think instead of being anxious you ought to set your mind gratefully at peace. The Btn we are relieving has lost 70 men only in 4 months: whereas in one day where I was before the Grenadiers lost 20—doing nothing. . . .

Churchill was confident that, despite the reduced size of the Battalion, it would do its duty as well as any:

. . . We take over the trenches before daylight tomorrow. You must not suppose that they will not be adequately defended. Although we have only 700 men instead of 900 wh our predecessors had, 1,050 wh we ought to have, we have more machine guns—so important. Rest assured there will be no part of the line from the Alps to the sea better guarded. It will be watched with the vigilance that mobilised the Fleet. . . .

[3] When, late in 1915, the British military authorities had tried to evacuate the villagers westwards, the villagers petitioned the King of the Belgians to be allowed to stay. Their petition was granted; but in the summer of 1916, after the church had been destroyed and the shelling had intensified, they agreed to move away.

Commanding a Battalion was a far cry from being First Lord. This was not the responsibility he had sought, nor the sphere in which he had wished to exercise it. But he tried not to become too depressed at the far drop in his fortunes. From his room at the Admiralty he used to look out over Horse Guards' Parade, across to the windows of the Cabinet Room at 10 Downing Street; from the window of the Hospice he could see, as he wrote to his wife, '2 bright red pigs rooting about among the shellholes'. That evening the Battalion prepared to move forward to its front-line trenches. Churchill called his officers from their farms and gave them a vivid description of how he believed they should behave. He reported the outline of his 'speech' to his wife in the following day:

. . . Don't be careless about yourselves—on the other hand not too careful. Keep a special pair of boots to sleep in & only get them muddy in a real emergency. Use alcohol in moderation but don't have a great parade of bottles in yr dugouts. Live well but do not flaunt it. Laugh a little, & teach your men to laugh—gt good humour under fire—war is a game that is played with a smile. If you can't smile grin. If you can't grin keep out of the way till you can. . . .

Churchill added in his letter home: 'Since Polonius' advice to Laertes there had been nothing like it. I trust they were edified.' 'It was a good pep talk,' McDavid later recalled; Churchill had been careful to point out that 'although our predecessors had said this was a sanctuary compared with Ypres and Loos, they must not take anything for granted. They had to be on the qui vive in case the Germans discovered that a new Division had come up and lay on at least trench raids for identification purposes.' The officers returned to their companies, and repeated Churchill's warnings to their NCOs.

That night at the Hospice Churchill found it difficult to sleep. A succession of orders about the day's move forward arrived at intervals from midnight onward from Brigade Headquarters. There were last-minute adjustments insisted upon by the Divisional General, and map positions to be co-ordinated with the General in charge of artillery. At 3.30 a.m. the Battalion prepared to move. 'The fever was at a very high level,' McDavid recalled. 'It was possible that word had been put out that the late First Lord of the Admiralty had arrived among us.' The men feared some special German action as they moved forward. But when McDavid put these fears to Churchill, he replied: 'If they thought I was here they would have devastated the country for twenty square miles around.' No German bombardment greeted the Battalion on that tense morning. Shortly after four o'clock the officers moved off from their farms, the men from their out-buildings, shacks and nissen huts. It was dark. Military security forbade lamps or lights. Slowly, in small groups, the companies moved forward along the dark, muddy tracks and into the sodden communication trenches towards the front line. At ten minutes to six, while it was still dark, they relieved the 2nd Battalion of the South Lancashires, and were in place.

Churchill reached his advanced headquarters before dawn. Known as Laurence Farm,[4] it was a small shell-battered farm half-way between the Hospice and the front line. From this farm to the line itself a series of ever-deepening trenches ran forward, whose sandbagged security was protection from all but a direct hit, and which ran so deep that German rifle and machine-gun fire could not interrupt the continual passage of men moving forward into the line. Churchill had sent his wife an impression of Laurence Farm when he had made his brief preliminary visit a week before:

The battalion HQ . . . is about 500 yards only from the trenches in a farmhouse. This is often good quarters. I have a small room to my-self with a little cellar underneath where Archie thinks of establishing himself.

The mess & orderly rooms are clean and waterproof. The place is however a target; & has been hit by perhaps 8 or 10 shells, while many have fallen close around. There is a tolerable shelter in the barn—a corrugated steel-hooped beehive loaded up with sandbags & bags of bricks & able to resist all ordinary shells. In this the HQ popu-lation take refuge when things get lively.

[4] The farm was spelled 'Laurence' on the War Office trench maps of 1916, but 'Lawrence' in the Battalion's war diary.

As soon as Churchill had established himself and his head-quarters' staff in Laurence Farm, and surveyed the position which he was to occupy for each of the six-day periods that his Battalion was in the line, he himself went forward to examine the trenches in which his men had taken up their positions. The line which he and his men were holding stretched two hundred yards from the estaminet at Le Gheer to the Warnarve brook, which ran down from Ploegsteert and through the German lines. The British position consisted of two approximately parallel forward trenches linked by a series of communication trenches. The ground was absolutely flat. On his preliminary visit Churchill had noticed a small shell-shattered convent, and seen some use for it, writing to his wife: 'I am rather attracted by the cellars of a ruined convent right up in the firing line, & if they can be drained & made comfortable they wd be a better and safer HQ especially for fighting purposes than this commodious but conspicuous farm.'

Churchill was proud of the smoothness with which he had moved his Battalion into the line. On January 27, after a busy day both in the sandbagged security of Laurence Farm and in the trenches themselves, looking into the possible uses of the convent cellars, and peering across the front-line parapet at the Germans, he wrote to his wife:

My darling,

The relief was accomplished this morning before daylight with the utmost precision in under 2 hours. I don't think the Grenadiers ever did better. We now hold about 1,000 yards of trenches & I am responsible for this whatever happens. We have so far had no losses—though there has been shelling & sniping & our parapet has at one place been blown in. All is proceeding regularly & the day has been quiet & normal in spite of being the Emperor's birthday. I spent three hours in the trenches this morning deciding on all the improvements I am going to make in them, & looking into the arrangements of the company commanders. It is now dark & we are able to light our fire without being betrayed by the smoke, so that we shall get a hot dinner as usual. Archie is now going round the trenches, & I shall go again after dinner. It takes nearly 2 hours to traverse this labyrinth of mud. . . .

During his first afternoon at Laurence Farm Churchill busied himself with administration. In the evening the Germans began shelling Ploegsteert, and from the Farm he watched the shells pass overhead and explode in the fields well behind him. Writing to his wife that night he described the organization which was under his control, and returned to his culinary demands, for these remained as persistent in the front line as in reserve:

. . . I have telephones to each of my companies, to the brigadier, & to the artillery. In 30 seconds I can turn on a horrid blast of shells—if an attack is made. . . . We are vy careful about gas. That is an odious peril: but I am inclined to think more has been put in on our front by the enemy. We never move an inch without 2 helmets.

About food—the sort of things I want you to send me are these—large slabs of corned beef: stilton cheeses: cream: hams: sardines—dried fruits: you might almost try a big beef steak pie but not tinned grouse or fancy tinned things. The simpler the better: & substantial too; for our ration meat is tough & tasteless: & here we cannot use a fire by daylight. I fear you find me vy expensive to keep. Mind you bill me for all these apart from your housekeeping. . . .

Churchill signed himself: 'You ever loving and devoted—greedy though I fear you will say, W.' Clementine Churchill did her best to satisfy her husband's continuing demands for food, but it was not easy. 'I note your likings as to food,' she replied on January 31, 'but hams are impossible except by the Havre route becos' of weight; the parcel must not be more than 7 lbs. The other day when you asked for Stilton I had to have one cut in half. I will send you a *small* slab of corned beef however—Tell me whether I shall send a ham after all. . . .' Despite the hope of ham and stilton, life at Laurence Farm was far from luxurious. In the trenches the danger of death was ever present. On January 28 he wrote to his wife after having returned from the front:

. . . While I was passing the convent, a good sized shell burst in its ruins (where the cellars are). A fountain of brickbats went up into the air; & I watched them carefully from 50 yards away, to dodge if any fell near me. Suddenly I saw, almost instantaneously with the explosion, 5 or 6 black objects hurtling towards me—You know how quick thought is.

I had time to think they were splinters, to argue that they could not belong to the same explosion, & to reach out for another solution, before I saw that they were frightened birds! . . .

Churchill remained only two days at Laurence Farm, for his Battalion's first spell in the forward line had been kept deliberately short; all subsequent ones were to last for six days. Churchill was proud of his powers of organization in bringing his battalion back to Ploegsteert so smoothly, writing from the Hospice on January 29:

The relief went off like machinery. No casualties; & all over in 4 minutes under the 2 hours I estimated for. Our companies marched into billets in admirable order going through the village in brisk parade step—unheard of outside the Guards. There is no doubt that officers & men try vy hard to do everything I tell them. I am extremely pleased with the officers who are really working splendidly. I got up at 4 am (no rooster) and on coming in here at about 7 we had breakfast & attended Mass in the little chapel. The old *vicaire*[5] was vy gracious. His church is shattered, and the house in wh he lives is freely shelled: but he sticks to his post & 'flies his flag' in the chapel of this hospice. The shelling yesterday evening wh was vy persistent was directed at a battery a few hundred yards away, & was not aimed at any of these houses, though of course the projectiles passed vy near them. It is satisfactory that they ignore the houses, & have ignored them so long: for the artilleryman—particularly the Bosch artilleryman is a creature of habit—& sticks to the target he sets his fancy on. The guns are so accurate that even a hundred yards away one is safe or almost so. . . .

As soon as he was back at the Hospice, Churchill set about arranging the more domestic side of Battalion life:

. . . We have a vy attentive and spruce Belgian[6] officer attached to us as interpreter—well embusquéd. I have set him and the doctor[7]

---

[5] Jules-Jean Vynckier, 1855–1941. Curé, Ploegsteert, 1908–36.
[6] Emile Herzog (André Maurois). The French and Belgian interpreters' caps—with 'floche'—were not dissimilar. Maurois later wrote to the author: 'I cannot hope he noticed that unknown Frenchman who looked at him with admiring eyes and said little.'
[7] I have been unable to discover to which Medical Officer Churchill was referring. 'We had several MOs while Winston was with us,' Captain Gibb

to work to forage for fresh mutton; (I am tired of tough frozen beef); vegetables; & dairy produce: & have seduced the nuns (don't be frightened) . . . into culinary pursuits.

We shall make ourselves vy comfortable here I think when we are settled down. There is a piano too, & several can play it. I have discovered a splendid bath (portable) & a tolerably hot water supply. I am now going to sample it, after 3 days of deprivation of that first of comforts. . . .

There was less repose in reserve than Churchill had hoped for. To his mother, that evening, Churchill wrote of 'a tiresome thing' which had happened during the afternoon, and which showed that it could be as dangerous in reserve as in the front line:

. . . There is a battery in the fields behind our house wh the Germans try to hit; & this afternoon they put a dozen shells over us in search of it, wh burst with loud explosions at no gt distance. I had just had a splendid hot bath—the best for a month & was feeling quite deliciously clean, when suddenly a tremendous bang overhead, & I am covered with soot blown down the chimney by the concussion of a shell these careless Boches have fired too short & wh exploded above our roof, smashing our windows & dirtying me! Well . . . it is an odd world, & I have seen a gt deal of it. . . .

Churchill gave his mother an account of his new existence:

. . . Commanding a battalion is like being captain of a ship. It is a vy searching test and a severe burden. Especially so when all the officers are young & only soldiers of a few months standing: & when a hundred yards away lies the line of the German army with all its devilments & dodges. One wd not have thought it possible a year ago to put a battalion thus composed in the line. But they will give a good account of themselves & no part of the front will be better guarded. . . .

The next two days in reserve at the Hospice were busy ones. Equipment had to be cleaned and repaired, ammunition col-

wrote, 'and he used to discuss them and compare and contrast their points as enthusiastically as though they had been specimens of some wild animals which he collected.'

lected, sandbagging completed, orders from above scrutinized, artillery support arranged, food supplies perfected. 'I have made a treaty with the mess to make excellent soup etc,' he had written to his wife on January 28; and with the arrival two days later of the brandy and cigars which she had sent from London he felt 'well provided'. The mundane tasks of the Battalion pleased him, as he explained on January 31:

. . . I like this sort of work vy much. It occupies me & I hope to be able to do it well. I don't think there is much difference in safety between the trenches & our 'rest billets'. Both HQrs, advanced & support, are registered & shelled. But it takes an awful lot of shells to do much harm; apart from bad luck. On the whole I prefer the trenches where there is always something going on, & where one really is fighting in this gt war for the triumph of right & reason. No doubt about it—one is doing the real thing—wh has to be done by someone. . . .

Politics and his future were also in his mind: 'If I come through all right my strength will be greater than it ever was. I wd much rather go back to the trenches tonight, than go home in any position of mediocre authority. But I *shd* like to see my beloved pussy cat.'

On February 1 the Battalion returned to the trenches for six days: the longest consecutive period Churchill had yet spent in such proximity to the Germans. Captain Gibb recorded in the Battalion's war diary for the whole six days: 'Very quiet period in the trenches. No men killed, 3 wounded'; a typical example of the laconic approach of an experienced soldier to the daily activities of a static line. Churchill was less laconic. For him there was drama in each day's events. On his first day back at Laurence Farm trenches he wrote:

. . . Peace all the morning, but at about 4.30 Shells—chiefly on the convent (where the cellars are). I had just passed through it and was 150 yards to the right when they began. Some were white shrapnel, others big black HE [High Explosive] 'crumps': others 'woolly bears' & some make a tremendous cloud of yellowy white smoke—or even plum

& black, 30 in all. Having luckily wandered down the right turn, Archie & I had a fine view of this exhibition without being at all inconvenienced. We had 4 men hit—one let his own rifle off by accident in jumping nervously when a shell burst overhead. The doctor (not our own) was joyriding in the trenches—did not return when the shelling began—so 2 of the wounded who were rather badly hurt—did not get the prompt attention they required. I have rebuked him. I ordered artillery retaliation for this German aggression & we gave them a good deal stiffer dose than we received. But of course one cannot tell what results are produced.

Darling—Do you like me to write these things to you? They are the ordinary incidents of life here—they are dangerous; but not vy dangerous. The average risk is not great—I wd not write to you about them if I thought the account wd cause you extra anxiety. But I think you like to know the dimensions of the dangers, & what they are like. . . .

That day Churchill spent several hours in the front-line trenches. He seemed to scorn caution. 'I have seen him stand on the fire step in broad daylight,' Lieutenant McDavid later recalled, 'to encourage the Jocks, and to prove to the man on the fire step how little danger there was of being hit.' Churchill decided to go out that night into no-man's-land, across the open fields, to the Battalion's forward posts, which were situated in the shell craters which pitted the landscape between the two armies. McDavid recalled how:

The Colonel's first visitation of our posts in No Man's Land nearly brought the whole British Army into action. Clad in his long trench waterproof, shining knee-high trench boots and blue steel helmet, with his revolver and powerful flash-lamp attached to his web-belt, he preceded me on the journey through the wire. All went well until we were within a few yards of the first post. Then enemy machine-gun fire swept the sphere of operations.

We all made a dive for the shelter of the shell crater, which was now somewhat overcrowded, and consequently we had to keep in a crouching position. Suddenly a blinding glare of light appeared from the depths of the hole and with the CO's muffled request to 'Put out that bloody light!' It was only a matter of seconds before he realised his crouching posture was responsible for pressure on the contact switch of his own flash-lamp, and corrective action quickly followed.

28. Churchill as Chancellor
of the Duchy of Lancaster.
Photograph printed in the
*Bystander*, 2 June 1915

29. Churchill,
Lord Lansdowne and
Lord Curzon, 1915

30. Churchill and
A. J. Balfour, 1915

31. Sir Edward Carson and F. E. Smith, before 1914

32. Andrew Bonar Law

33. Sir Max Aitken, 1916

34. Churchill and his wife
arriving at Enfield

35. Churchill and his wife at Enfield, 18 September 1915, when Churchill addressed munitions workers. During his speech he told them:
'We cannot understand the inscrutable purposes which have plunged these evils upon the world, and have involved all the nations of Europe in a catastrophe measureless in its horror. But we know that if in this time of crisis

and strain we do our duty, we shall have done all that it is in human power to do —
and we shall so bear ourselves in this period — all of us, whatever part we play on the
stage of the world's history — we shall bear ourselves so that those who come after us
will find amid the signs and scars of this great struggle that the liberties of Europe
and of Britain are still intact and inviolate; when those looking back upon our
efforts such as they have been, will say of this unhappy but not inglorious generation, placed in a position of extraordinary trial, that it did not fail in the test, and
that the torch which it preserved lights the world for us today.'

36. A Sopwith biplane which Churchill had just piloted, 1913: biplanes of this type were used on the western front and at the Dardanelles, 1914–16

37. Wing-Commander Samson, 1915. One of Churchill's flying instructors before 1914, he commanded the aeroplane squadron at Dunkirk, 1914–15, and the Dardanelles, 1915

38. Churchill and Lloyd George at Wormwood Scrubs, 28 June 1915, watching a trial of the Killen-Strait barbed-wire cutter, a forerunner of the tank. Churchill is half-hidden behind the post, Lloyd George is in bowler hat

39. Evacuation of a gun and men from the Gallipoli Peninsula, December 1915

40. Lloyd George and Churchill, autumn 1915

This excursion into no-man's-land was not an isolated example of Churchill's apparent tendency to flout safety. Hakewill Smith remembered similar incidents:

He would often go into no-man's-land. It was a nerve-racking experience to go with him. He would call out in his loud, gruff voice—far too loud it seemed to us—'You go that way, I will go this. . . . Come here, I have found a gap in the German wire. Come over here at once!' He was like a baby elephant out in no-man's-land at night. He never fell when a shell went off; he never ducked when a bullet went past with its loud crack. He used to say, after watching me duck: 'It's no damn use ducking; the bullet has gone a long way past you by now.'

Churchill did not seek these dangers for their own sake. He wanted his men to feel that he was one of them, that where the danger was there he would be, that when they needed guidance or good cheer or courage he would be at hand, and that he would not fail them in their hour of need. He knew that many of his men were puzzled to find a politician, whose name and features were familiar to them from their newspapers, commanding them in the line. He was determined that they should trust him. German shells exploded round Laurence Farm almost every day. But Churchill seemed imperturbable. 'He used to sit on one side of the farm,' McDavid recalled. 'Hakewill Smith and Kemp[8] put on the hits of the day on a little portable gramophone. He would sit for a while just beating time, just ruminating.' He even set up his easel in the courtyard of the farm and began painting. The officers were amazed. Hakewill Smith remembered the moment:

Winston started painting the second or third time he went up to the farm. Each time we were in the line he spent some time on his paintings. Gradually, too, the courtyard became more pitted with shellholes. As his painting came nearer to completion, he became morose, angry, and exceedingly difficult to talk to. After five or six days in this mood, he suddenly appeared cheerful and delighted, like

[8] Laurence Kemp, 1891–1956. Signal Officer, 6th Royal Scots Fusiliers, 1916. Invalided home, 1916–17. Served in the Balkans, 1918. Ironmonger. Director of his family's firm, William Kemp & Co, Glasgow, 1929–56 and Chairman, 1949–56.

a small boy at school. I asked him what had happened, and he said
'I have been worried because I couldn't get the shell-hole right in the
painting. However I did it, it looked like a mountain, but yesterday I
discovered that if I put a little bit of white in it, it looked like a hole
after all.'

Churchill persevered with his paintings, and even managed to
preserve some.[9] While providing distraction for himself, he also
remembered his men's needs. Music was the answer, he believed,
and summoned the band of the Ninth Division to Ploegsteert.
Bandsman Fulton[10] had reason to remember the occasion, writing to the author fifty-five years later:

A figure appeared. It was Winston Churchill. He was carrying his
own Chair—it was a .303 Ammunition Box. He says this will do Lads.
We fixed up and started our programme. He sat in the middle. A
young lad from the RAMC sang that beautiful old Ballad 'Sunshine of
your smile'. Then shelling started some well off the mark and some
mighty near accompanied by a few overhead shrapnels. Well with
plenty of ducking and a broad smile on Winston's face we got through
it. At the end he thanked us all. He said 'Lads I am sorry bringing
you into such a precarious position but I am going to let you into a
little secret. Last week the Germans had a band at the back of their
lines playing to them and our artillery got on them and all you saw
was instruments & drums going into the air and I really wanted to see
if their artillery were as good marksmen as ours.'

When General Furse visited the Battalion with Colonel Holland
on February 2, Churchill took them into the forward trenches and
then, as he told his wife, gave them lunch 'in my shattered farmhouse'. It was a quiet day, he wrote, 'profound peace . . . not a

[9] There is a colour reproduction of one of Churchill's paintings of Laurence Farm on page 17 of *Churchill his paintings* (Hamish Hamilton,
1967), compiled by David Coombs, and a black and white reproduction of a
painting of shells exploding over the village (on page 90). The original of
the latter hangs at Chartwell. In 1918 Churchill gave Sir Archibald Sinclair one of his Laurence Farm paintings as a wedding present.

[10] Robert Fulton, 1889–   . Apprentice Ironmoulder, 1904–11. Ironmoulder, 1911–14. Enlisted, Gordon Highlanders, September 1914. Crossed
to France with the 9th Division, May 1915. Fought at Loos, September
1915; and promoted to Lance Corporal. Cornet soloist, 9th Division Band,
1916–19. Worked in an ironfoundry, 1919–57.

shell or a casualty—hardly a bullet'. But on the following day there was further excitement:

My darling one,

Yesterday (3rd) we had a lucky escape. We had just finished an excellent lunch and were all seated round the table at coffee & port wine, when a shell burst at no gt distance making the window jump. Archie said that at the next one we wd go into our dugout in the barn just opposite & we were discussing this when there was a tremendous crash, dust & splinters came flying through the room, plates were smashed, chairs broken. Everyone was covered with debris and the Adjutant [Jock McDavid] (he is only 18) hit on the finger. A shell had struck the roof and burst in the next room—mine & Archie's. We did not take long in reaching our shelter—wh is a good one! My bedroom presented a woe-begone appearance, the nose of the shell passing clean through it smashed the floor and cut a hole in the rear wall. Luckily vy few of my things were damaged. The only serious loss is my milux lamp.[11] . . . I am sending this home as a souvenir, & beg you to send me another *at the vy earliest moment*, as they are indispensable. The wonderful good luck is that the shell (a 4.2) did not— & cd not have—burst properly. Otherwise we shd have had the wall thrown in on us—& some wd surely have been hurt.

I have made them put up another still stronger dugout—quite close, on wh they are now hard at work. I slept peacefully in my tiny war-scarred room last night, after a prolonged tour of the trenches. . . .

There was a respite from shelling on February 4, although Ploegsteert itself was quite heavily bombarded, and some damage was done to the Battalion's supporting billets at Delenelle Farm and Maison 1875. Brigadier-General Ritchie,[12] who commanded

[11] Churchill had a closer escape than he informed his wife. 'Winston had been toying about with his lamp,' McDavid later recalled to the author. 'He was sitting playing with this thing when the shell came along. A piece of shrapnel almost split the battery holder in two—it lodged in the metal of the battery holder. It was less than two inches from his right wrist. If it had been any nearer it certainly would have taken off his wrist.'

[12] Archibald Buchanan Ritchie, 1869–1955. Entered Army, 1889. Served on the Nile Expedition, 1898. Lieutenant-Colonel, 1913. Brigadier-General commanding the 26th Brigade of the 9th Division, 1915–16. Commanded the 11th Division, 1917, and the 16th Division, 1918. Major-General, 1919. Commanded the 51st Highland Division of the Territorial Army, 1923–7. Knighted, 1927.

the neighbouring Brigade, came to lunch at Laurence Farm on February 5 and was, as Churchill wrote to his wife on the following day, 'much impressed at the damage' of the previous day. He and Ritchie had last met in 1898, during the Sudan campaign. It was a quiet day. Churchill worked on a scheme of front-line defence. Under this scheme there was to be more sandbagging, deeper trenches and stronger dugouts. Ministerial papers were not always so easily approved. 'I took lots of pains about it,' he told his wife; 'it was like one of my Cabinet papers, & it carried all before it.'

During the six days in the trenches Churchill had cleared out the water from the cellars of the convent, and these cellars, which he now named 'The Conning Tower', became what he called his 'Battle Headquarters' while he was in the line. They were only a hundred yards from no-man's-land, seven hundred yards closer than his 'Advance Headquarters' at Laurence Farm and only four hundred yards from the nearest German trench. Clementine Churchill worried about the added danger of her husband being so near the Germans. Even Laurence Farm did not seem very safe to her as he had described it. '*Please* leave that wretched farm and find a safer place,' she had written on February 2. Sometimes she wrote of coming to see him: 'It wd be so easy & I cd live with the poor French women in a ruined cottage & hoe turnips'—she had forgotten that her husband was in Belgium. He understood her fears, and while continuing to write graphically of the events he witnessed, insisted that he was not really disturbed by the danger. 'It is one long holiday for me,' he wrote, '. . . like my African journey.'[13]

After five weeks as a Lieutenant-Colonel, Churchill's hopes of Generalship were suddenly and unexpectedly raised again. He had always believed that Haig would give him the promotion once he had gained some front-line experience. On the morning of

[13] In 1908, when Under-Secretary of State for the Colonies, Churchill spent five months travelling with Edward Marsh through Egypt, the Sudan, the Uganda Protectorate and British East Africa. As well as conducting much official business, Churchill hunted rhinoceros, lions and wart-hogs. He wrote an account of his travels for the *Strand Magazine,* later expanded as a book, *My African Journey,* published in December 1908.

February 6 a telegram reached Laurence Farm from St Omer telling him to proceed at once across the fields to London Support Farm and to take over command of the Brigade. Churchill's first reaction was that Asquith's veto had been overcome, and that his future as a Brigade Commander was assured. But it was not in fact so. What had happened, he explained to his wife on February 6, was that 'I am for the moment actually the senior commanding officer, & the Brigadier—Walshe—is expected back tomorrow'. His was merely a brief and transitionary migration to Brigade headquarters: 'I have not therefore attempted to master the detail of the command, but remain here ready to give any broad simple decision that an emergency might (but won't) require. They have now had 4 different men commanding this Brigade in 9 days! Queer folk!' As a result of Walshe's absence, Churchill was temporarily in command of five Battalions—a total of four thousand men—and over two thousand yards of the front line. On reaching Brigade Headquarters on February 6 he received a summons to lunch with General Furse at Divisional Headquarters in Nieppe. To his surprise he found that Curzon was there. It soon emerged that it was only as a result of Curzon's persistent demands to see him that Churchill had been called away from his temporary Brigade duties. Churchill insisted upon showing Curzon the front line. 'I took him out to my shattered farm,' he wrote that night to his wife, '& along my own trenches; & he told me all the news & his view of men & politics in his usual sprightly style. . . . I think he was interested by what he saw. It was vy quiet & we successfully avoided the shells & the machine gun bullets, both of wh came discreetly & tactfully in the places wh we had left or in those wh we had not reached.'

Curzon went back to Carlton House Terrace, Churchill to London Support Farm. Walshe did not return, as had been expected, on February 7, and Churchill remained in command of the Brigade for another day. 'It is not a vy satisfactory arrangement,' he wrote to his wife on February 8, 'as of course I am only a caretaker and cannot attempt to take a grip of the whole machine. I do the office work and have prepared myself to meet any emergency; but otherwise I wait about from hour to hour. The whole

Brigade is now out of the line & in rest billets, so there is nothing going on.' Sinclair telephoned from the Hospice to report heavy shelling on one of the farms which served as a reserve billet, and three men wounded. The Germans had not bombarded the reserve area in this way before. 'They are getting spiteful,' Churchill wrote, '& fire 5 or 6 shells at once without any warning—then wait 20 minutes or so and have another go.'

While he was at Brigade Headquarters, Churchill discovered that the General who had just been appointed to command the Ninth Division artillery, Hugh Tudor,[14] was another friend from the distant past, from subaltern days in Bangalore nineteen years before. On February 7 General Tudor came to see him at London Support Farm. 'We were vy pleased to meet again after so many years—I had not seen him since S. Africa,' Churchill wrote to his wife on February 8. Tudor told Churchill more about the battle of Loos. 'My dear,' Churchill continued, 'what mistakes they made at Loos. You simply cannot believe them possible.' His own thoughts were also critical of the military machine:

. . . there is gt lack of 'drive' throughout the administration of the army. Take the telephone system for instance. It is grotesque. You cannot get through. When you do you cannot hear, there is always a dog fight going on over the wires. They have stuck in the main to the same little field instruments that an army on the move uses instead of making a perfect system wh cd so easily be done. And how vitally important it might be in a battle! If we had been content at the Admiralty to paddle along at that feeble pace, we shd never have mastered the German submarine. Then of course there ought to be 10 times (at least) as many light railways on the front. This war is one of mechanics & brains & mere sacrifice of brave & devoted infantry is no substitute & never will be. By God I wd make them skip if I had the power—even for a month. . . .

Lieutenant McDavid, the young adjutant who had been wounded in the hand at Laurence Farm, went back to England

[14] Henry Hugh Tudor, 1871–1965. 2nd Lieutenant, Royal Artillery, 1890. Brigadier-General commanding the Artillery of the 9th Division, 1916–18. Major-General commanding the 9th Division, 1918. Knighted, 1923.

on leave on February 7. That evening he called at 41 Cromwell Road. 'Such a delightful youth,' Clementine Churchill wrote on the following day, 'bringing with him the nose of the shell which shattered your bedroom, your oiler lamp and photographs of you, also very exciting news, ie that for the present you are a Brigadier—I wonder if you are to be one for good?' Clementine Churchill was worried about the unexpected shelling of the Hospice. 'Write quickly,' she asked, 'and tell me that you have arranged a safer headquarters. I fear so that the Germans in front of you may know you are there.' Churchill had also come to the conclusion that the Hospice was too risky a place for his Battalion headquarters. As soon as he relinquished his temporary command of the Brigade, he moved his Battalion headquarters eight hundred yards further from the front line, to one of his company billets at Soyer Farm.

During his first morning at Soyer Farm Churchill examined the new Battalion arrangements, and inspected the cellar below the entrance hall down which he and his men must dash if the farm were shelled. He hoped they were sufficiently far from Ploegsteert to escape bombardment; but Ploegsteert itself could never escape. From their maps the Germans were able to register their artillery fire with impressive accuracy upon the village crossroads, the church, the curate's house and any other village building which they might choose. That afternoon Churchill, from his study at Soyer Farm, watched the village being bombarded. On the following day, February 10, he wrote to his wife:

The shells hitting the church made enormous clouds of red brick dust wh mingled gaily with their white smoke. Other black & white shrapnel burst over the street & struck the houses. Three of our men who were strolling in the town were hit—one fatally, & another sustained a shock from being near a shell from wh he immediately died. In the last 2 days of 'rest' I have lost 8 men, or more than in 6 days in the front line. I am now reduced to under 600 men instead of 1,000. There are many other battalions like this. . . .

During his first period at Soyer Farm Churchill found time to travel a little behind the lines. On February 10 he and Sinclair went with General Tudor to the far side of Ploegsteert Wood, to watch the progress of a British artillery bombardment. He described it to his wife on the following day:

. . . Two points in the German trenches were selected, & a tremendous fire of 12 inch, 9.2 inch & field guns was suddenly opened on them. This proved a more dangerous expedition than I had expected for I did not think the general commanding all the artillery of a division wd expose himself to undue risks. He took us however (Archie & me) to the front line of our trenches only 100 yards away from the German points attacked, & of course as soon as we began, the enemy replied with vigour. For one hour, by the clock, there was a brief cannonade. Our own guns made so much noise we cd not hear the whistle of the German shells, but they burst all round, striking the parapet, or just skimming over, or bursting in the air with loud explosions & covering us with dirt & debris. It was vy exciting, especially as our own 9.2's put two shells *behind* us by mistake. This was the first really sharp artillery fire I have been under, & certainly it seemed vy dangerous. I was impressed however with the way in wh the trenches gave good protection, & I can quite understand how even the heaviest bombardments can be endured for days on end. Besides the shells, we had bombs from trench mortars thrown at us. These you can see in the air; & after they fall there is an appreciable interval in wh to decide what you will do. I liked these the best of all. I found my nerves in excellent order & I do not think my pulse quickened at any time. But after it was over I felt strangely tired: as if I had done a hard day's work at a speech or article.

That evening Churchill rode over to Divisional Headquarters at Nieppe to dine with Colonel Holland. Even here, three miles from the front line, the German shells could find a target. 'They are in a pretentious chateau surrounded by a moat,' Churchill told his wife. 'It was dusk. Suddenly a loud bang. A shell coming from miles away had fallen in the moat, just outside our window. Presently came 1 more. No one paid the slightest attention to them. It is pure chance, & a shell may come anywhere at any time. . . .'

On February 11 Churchill made a brief excursion across the border into France, when he and Archibald Sinclair rode into

Armentières. 'It is a large town almost deserted, & constantly shelled,' he wrote to his wife on February 12; 'The debris of several hits that had occurred half an hour before was scattered in the streets. And every now & again a shell passed overhead. But there were a fair number of shops open, with women serving in them: & a lot of factories smoking away as if nothing was going on.' Sinclair and he were photographed together: 'I will send you some copies as soon as we get them.' He had also discovered that 'good cakes & sweets' could be bought in Armentières, a further incentive to go again. On February 12, while the Battalion remained in reserve at Soyer Farm, Churchill went forward to the trenches to see what damage had been done since he had been in reserve. He described his expedition to his wife that evening:

. . . Today has brought with it its own risks. I went round the trenches with the Colonel of the Gordons[15] whom we relieve in the line tomorrow morning & saw what work he had done & learned his plans etc. A German aeroplane passed overhead & our guns fired at it. The fragments of the shell as they fell back to earth around us made curious hissing noises quite different from an ordinary projectile. Then on the way back the Gordons' Major[16] (a vy good soldier) insisted on walking across the fields behind the trenches while it was still daylight, & in consequence we were fired upon at no gt distance. Vy foolish I thought, & promptly made for a trench—while Archie & the others scampered about. Finally on the way back to our present HQ the German machine gun 'sprayed' our path with zipping bullets. . . .

There was a further annoyance when he returned that evening to the Hospice: 'And now just as Tudor is coming to dinner in our unprotected but vy comfortable house they have flung 2 shells about 200 yards further up the street. This is a vy bad habit

[15] Alan David Greenhill-Gardyne, 1868–1953. Entered Army, 1888. Lieutenant-Colonel, October 1915. Commanded 8th Battalion, Gordon Highlanders, October 1915–March 1916. Retired invalided, 1920. Big-game hunter and water-colourist.

[16] George J. G. G. Cumine, 1881–1941. 2nd Lieutenant, 1900. Major, 8th Battalion Gordon Highlanders, October 1914–July 1916. Machine Gun Corps, 1917; Tank Corps, 1918. He died in London as a result of enemy action.

for them to start after dark, & if it continues it will sensibly reduce the amenities of this otherwise admirable dwelling.'

On Sunday February 13 the 6th Royal Scots Fusiliers moved forward once more to Laurence Farm. That night Churchill wrote to his wife, who was staying at Walmer Castle as a guest of the Asquiths:

My beloved,

It is odd thinking of you at Walmer now. I remember so well being there at the end of February last, when all was hope at the Dardanelles & I looked forward to a vy wide sphere of triumphant activity. Everything is changed now—only the old block [Asquith] continues solid & supine.

I am now in the line again and am living in the farm I told you of. I am protecting it in various ways by sandbags etc against a renewed incursion of shells; & I have now 2 vy substantial dugouts—sandbags over steel cupolas—wh will at a pinch accommodate our whole population at HQrs—35 or 40.

This afternoon many aeroplanes overhead, & much shooting at them. I was disgusted to watch 1 German aeroplane sailing about scornfully in the midst of 14 British—none of wh cd or worse still perhaps—*wd* bring him to action. Ours seemed to sheer off time after time, & he went where he pleased for at least an hour & a half. As for our guns they fired hundreds of shells without lifting a feather of this hostile bird. . . .

Some of my officers have returned from leave. They are vy homesick. No doubt they feel the weight & burden of this business & long for its conclusion. But it will take a long time, & we must not expect quick results. I think I shall take 8 days leave early in March & come home to see you. I am entitled to it & there will be no difficulty. We must give a few nice dinners. I shall do 2 more tours in the trenches first (including this one now beginning) & come away so as to miss a 6 day rest period. I will let you know the exact dates soon. . . .

Kiss the kittens. I think a gt deal about you all. I never expected to be so completely involved in the military machine. It almost seems to me as if my life in the gt world was a dream, & I have been moving slowly forward in the army all these years from subaltern to colonel. Good night my dearest soul.

Your ever devoted<br>W

That same day Clementine Churchill wrote to her husband from Walmer Castle. She described how 'sitting on the bastion we could distinctly hear the rumble of heavy guns——'; she suspected that it was British ships shelling the Belgian coast. But the contrast with the war zone was complete. She played golf with Asquith, and was annoyed not to have beaten him; it was a victory, she wrote, that she would have relished.

Churchill was back in the forward trenches again on February 14. There was much to do at Laurence Farm:

My darling,

I take up my pen to send you my daily note. Another long day in the trenches has closed, & I sit in a battered wicker chair within this shot scarred dwelling by the glowing coals of a brazier in the light of an acetyline lamp. At 6 I went round my trenches, just as day was breaking and was saluted on my doorstep by a vy sulky bullet. All the morning I laboured in the small business of the battalion & dealt with my Company Commanders & sent off the numerous reports for wh our superiors clamour—patrols, operations, situations, wind, work, fighting strength, enemy's shelling, intelligence etc. . . .

It had been a busy morning, but Churchill's work was not done. For some weeks General Furse had wanted the Ninth Division to take an initiative in trying to break the defensive character of trench warfare. Churchill's sector had been selected for a specially heavy British artillery 'sträfe' organized by his friend General Tudor, who came to lunch at Laurence Farm and explained what was about to happen. As Churchill explained to his wife:

. . . I had arranged to withdraw all my men from those parts of the line & its approaches on wh I thought the enemy's certain retaliation wd fall, & have had them distributed in safe places along the front line—always the safest. We had a hurried lunch—but excellent & wh was terminated by the arrival of a shell 4.2 wh burst close by, obliging us all to adjourn to the new dugout. . . .

Churchill was keen to see Tudor's bombardment clearly. He took the General across the fields to a small ruined farmhouse a hundred yards from his dugouts. The two men clambered on to the roof:

> . . . here we awaited developments. At 2.30 our guns began, & almost immediately the German reply. They fired about 50 shells altogether & we about 150. I had correctly anticipated their intervention & owing to the men having been moved out of the dangerous points and well concealed, *we never lost one*. But several of our trenches were knocked about, particularly a communication trench wh Archie dislikes. It was an odd sensation perched up behind this thin brick wall wh rocked with the mere wind, to see these big shells bursting only a 100 yards away, & to realise that only the caprice of the gunner stood between me and their direct attentions. After half an hour of this we returned to join the others in the dugout: to receive your letter & read it with eager appetite, & to browse about among ungrateful press cuttings & the unfriendly newspapers. . . .
> Finally Archie & I go up again to the trenches to see the damage, & the officers walk about in them for an hour and a half, & on the way down that same communications trench that Archie dislikes we receive (with thanks) 5 shells wh all keep just outside it. . . .

Churchill returned to Laurence Farm; hopefully his day was done: 'darkness has fallen & dinner is almost ready. I shall go round the trenches again tonight, & on the whole when sleep comes, I think I shall have earned my 25 shillings.' The day was not yet over. On February 15 Churchill wrote to his wife of how:

> . . . Last night after writing & after dinner, I had a splendid walk with Archie all over the top of the ground. We left the trenches altogether & made a thorough examination of all the fields, tracks, ruins etc immediately behind our line. You cannot show yourself here by day, but in the bright moonlight it is possible to move about without danger (except from random bullets) & to gain a vy clear impression. Archie was a vy good guide. We also went out in front of our own parapet into the No man's land & prowled about looking at our wire & visiting our listening posts. This is always exciting. Last night also two of my officer patrols went right up to the German wire & cut large strands of it as trophies. One was foolish enough however to leave a Union Jack fastened on to it in bravado. This will only make them more vigilant. Can you imagine such a silly thing. . . .

Churchill got little sleep that night. There was fighting ten miles to the north, just beyond Ypres, and at Laurence Farm, he wrote, 'we cd hear the cannonade splintering & snarling away all through the night'.

Churchill was working out his plans for the leave that was now due to him. He hoped to spend seven days in London, beginning on March 2. 'Of course,' he wrote to his wife on February 15, 'these plans of leave may be altered by my getting a Brigade. . . .' On February 3 his mother had sent him a first-hand report of Asquith himself hinting at a Brigade:

. . . I dined with Cassel last night—16 of us—& who shd take me in to dinner but the PM! He looked very dubious at first, but I exerted myself to put him at his ease, & we got on all right—No use being nasty, it does not help things, & so I made friends with the Mammon of Unrighteousness! Well! of course he asked after you, & I told him you had just come out of the trenches, & repeated the story about the bath & the bomb. He got quite red with emotion. In the bottom of his heart I really think he is very fond of you—but he is so selfish he wd sacrifice anyone to his own convenience. I told him about your batt: & he said 'Of course this is only the beginning & he will get the next step very soon' those were his words. . . .

These hopes were but chimeras. Neither Asquith nor Haig had any plans to give Churchill the promotion for which he hoped.

On February 16 Churchill wrote to his wife from Laurence Farm of the day's dangers:

My darling,
. . . We had only just finished dressing this morning when shells began to arrive in the neighbourhood—just about 200 yards away & then much nearer. Archie & I persevered in our breakfast—till a tremendous bang, clouds of debris & the whizzing of splinters proclaimed our house hit again—this time our dining room was pierced on the other side, & our joint bedroom penetrated in 5 or 6 places. The signal office in the next room completely shattered (mercifully I had just ordered the signallers to take refuge in the dugout). The signal officer, Lieut Kemp, down with 5 wounds (not dangerous) & another man hit. Without knowing all that had happened, we hastily seized our eggs & bacon, bread and marmalade & took refuge in our dugout.

Here we remained while perhaps 20 shells were devoted to our farm & its curtilage. Then the 'strafe' being over we emerged and went about our business. I have now had 2 officers hit out of 5 in my HQ mess: & there is no doubt that we are rather a target. But I do not intend to change these HQrs as they are convenient & it is difficult to find others. Instead I am piling sandbags inside all the walls & on the upper floor & trying to make it proof against the 30 pr shells—if they start with 100 pr I shall have to flit to some hole or other. But till then we remain. . . .

It was odd gobbling bacon & marmalade in the dugout, while the doctor bandaged the gt raw wounds of our poor officer a foot or two away! Archie is vy good—cool, methodical, careful—yet quite fearless. I do not think I mind it vy much. At any rate it does not affect my spirits or my temper. But it is a vy curious life to live.

Your ever loving & devoted<br>W

Clementine Churchill continued with her war work, helping to organize YMCA canteens for munitions workers in north London. On February 16 she sent him a long account of what she had been doing:

. . . Last night, I mean Monday, that nice boy Mr McDavid dined with Goonie & me & we took him to a Music Hall. He is very small & young & rather loveable. I feel sorry for his Mamma. I think he is too young to have a real sweetheart.[17]

The big Ponder's End Canteen . . . flourishes exceedingly, another wing is to be added for the men, & I have just been told that the Manager is engaging 500 girls (diluted labour) & that he expects me to feed them too! At present I am feeding about 650 people a day in my district, in about 2 months I shall be feeding about 1,800, scattered in different places.

With each of the seven years of their married life, Churchill had become more and more involved in politics. Even his weekends had been filled increasingly with public affairs, or, as in the spring of 1914, with weekends away from his wife while he was

[17] He did have a real sweetheart, Harriet Murray (1895–1965); they were married a year later.

learning to fly. She had envied him his capacity to absorb himself so fully in his work that he did not seem to need time with her. She wanted him back, not only from the trenches but also from his obsession with work. In her letter of February 16 she explained her hopes about their future together when the war was over. She longed for the time when they could relax in the country, he painting and playing his 'grizzly bear' game with the children; both of them finding time for leisure. She wanted him to promise that he would put aside for their life together an hour out of every day, a day out of every week and six weeks out of every year.

In her letter Clementine Churchill had gone on to describe how some of his methods had influenced her; how the other women who were organizing the canteens were surprised at the speed with which she got things done, and at her energy in driving forward her fellow-helpers. She began work at nine in the morning and did not finish until seven-thirty at night: 'You have taught me to work outside office hours,' she wrote proudly.

Clementine Churchill's letters meant much to her husband. They made him feel less cut off from London and its daily life. She renewed his vigour; and any delay in the correspondence—inevitable in wartime conditions—depressed him. His own news was almost entirely of shells and sandbags. On February 17 he wrote from Laurence Farm:

My darling,
No letter from you—only one in 4 days has reached me & Mr McDavid who I daresay was the bearer of one as well as of various parcels, is gone in hospital with the effects of anti-tetanus injections.

We were shelled again at this farm at 9, at 11, & at 1 today. Two batteries now take an interest in us—one tries 30 lb & the other 15 pr shells & they shoot from different sides so that they search our weak points vy disagreeably. The house is now much better sandbagged & by tomorrow morning shd be still more so. We were vy punctilious about going into the dugout whenever the bombardment began & waiting for ten minutes without a shell before coming out. No other part of my line has been touched, & no casualties have occurred in the trenches. Other farms in rear of the line are also being made a target—so that there is no reason to suppose there is anything personal in the enemy's attentions. We come out of the line on Saturday morning. These last five days have gone like a flash. The complete absence of worry or strain, of mental work of any serious kind, the good food, & warmth & comfort in wh we live, with lots of open air are vy good for one's health. As a rest cure for the unusual the life is admirable. I expect I am putting on weight.

Some of the others however fret a good deal. The officer who was wounded yesterday morning was given the nose-piece of the shell which wounded him as a *souvenir*. He kissed it! His joy at leaving almost triumphed over the severe pain of his wounds.

I have no more tales to tell you tonight—my dearest soul—so good night & tenderest love

> from yr devoted & ever loving
> W

The evening's letter was but a brief break in the ever-continuing activity. Churchill was determined to check the increased German shelling by some heavy retaliation. He had made special arrangements that day for some shelling of his own, which he directed late that evening by telephone from Laurence Farm. Robert Fox recalled:

When we saw him in the front line accompanied by two naval officers we knew he meant business. Special observers located the concreted German minenwerfer and machine-gun emplacements and sniper's posts. Twelve-inch naval guns on an armoured train six miles away were to be used against them. As the two front lines were only 80 yards apart in places, we evacuated our forward trenches in case of a shell dropping short. With a noise like approaching express trains these huge missiles hurtled over our heads and crashed into the German line. Each impact was like a miniature earthquake.

'I had to sit at the end of the telephone,' Churchill reported to his wife on the following day, 'so that I did not get much fun out of it. But it worked vy well.' On February 18 rain and mist prevented any German retaliation. Churchill had not decided to take the initiative without anticipating the effects. He looked to expertise to counter them. Earlier that month he had sought the advice of the Major who commanded the Royal Engineer section of the Ninth Division. 'Then long pow-wow with Major Hearn[18] —the engineer,' he wrote to his wife on February 14, 'an Indian acquaintance of mine—fat, shrewd, placid, sensible—a regular koi hai:[19] about wh trenches shd be strengthened or drained & where dugouts shd be built etc. He works with me admirably and helps in every way.' Major Hearn—whom Churchill had met in 1898 during the Malakand expedition—had to return to Divisional Headquarters. But he left behind him a young engineer officer, Lieutenant Napier-Clavering,[20] who took charge of the fortifications.

Churchill was impressed with Napier-Clavering's abilities, and soon became absorbed by the work which the Lieutenant and his engineers were doing. Napier-Clavering later recalled, in a conversation with the author, that as soon as he arrived at Laurence Farm, Churchill had remarked: 'The trouble with these dugouts, is they are not whizzbang proof.' The young officer promised to do his best. Churchill's next question was: 'How much earth do you need to stop a bullet?' 'You want at least three feet,' Napier-Clavering replied. 'Well,' said Churchill. 'We'll go up to the front line tonight and have a look. Bring with you a stick three feet long.' After dinner Churchill and Napier-Clavering left Laurence Farm, walked along the communication trench and reached the front line. Once in the forward trench, they climbed up on the parapet and walked along it for the whole length of the Battalion's line. Napier-Clavering had never

[18] Gordon Risley Hearn, 1871–1953. Entered Royal Engineers, 1890. Inspector of Railways for the Government of India, 1904–14. Major, 1910. Commanded the Royal Engineers of the 9th Division, 1914–18. Knighted, 1926.

[19] A Hindustani phrase, used in British India, for someone who had seen long service there; derived from the way in which servants were summoned in a club—'Koi hai?' 'Is there any one there?'

[20] Francis Donald Napier-Clavering, 1892–1969. Lieutenant, 64th Field Company, Royal Engineers, attached to the 9th Division, 1915–16. Major, 1918. Subsequently an engineer with Robert McAlpine & Sons Ltd.

seen an officer take such a passionate interest in the details of trench engineering, but there was more to come, as he recalled:

Up went a Verey Light. Churchill was on his knees measuring the depth of the earth with the stick. The Hun machine guns opened up, belly high. Why the hell we weren't killed I just don't understand. I didn't want to die; I wanted to kill some of the Hun first. 'For God's sake keep still, Sir,' I hissed. But he didn't take the slightest notice. He was a man who had no physical fear of dying.

During the days that followed, under Churchill's constant surveillance, Napier-Clavering continued his work of improving the parapets, fortifying the dugouts and trying to arrange an effective drainage system for the trenches. In the evenings, when they were dining, Churchill often questioned him about his work, and about how the Royal Engineers ought to be run. Hakewill Smith recalled how on one occasion Churchill asked: 'Why haven't we got a trench digger? We want a trench digger. Something that would crawl along and dig out a trench in five minutes.' Not to be outdone, Napier-Clavering decided to ask his own questions:

I said to him one night, after the necessary number of Ports, 'could you tell us, Sir, what advantage it would be to us to win the war?' There was silence for three minutes. Then for the next twenty minutes he gave us a Parliamentary speech. At the end of each paragraph he looked up, and looked at everybody in the room to see what the effect was. His language was so absolutely marvellous. I was only twenty-two at the time. My eyes were standing out like hatpins.

Churchill was equally impressed by Napier-Clavering. 'This young fellow was lunching with us,' McDavid later recalled. 'Winston started giving a dissertation on a new type of vehicle he was keen on. A "Caterpillar" Winston called it; it could get over the humps and over the wire. He used the various condiment sets to explain what he meant. He had this idea that a tracked vehicle could cut the German wire, or drag it through and make a gap. We all thought it an airy fairy idea. "If it amuses him, let him go on talking about it," we thought, "but it is a damned silly idea." It was away up in the clouds. But the young engineer officer took it up with him. He was the only one who encouraged him to talk about it. He realized that it was a possibility. They had quite a discussion together about it.'

The effect of trench life on Churchill was profound. As the weeks passed, the conditions under which his men were living impressed themselves harshly upon his mind. At Laurence Farm he could do nothing to express the anger which he felt at the indignities which the war was imposing upon exuberant boys; transforming them into tired men, driving them to despair or killing them needlessly. By personal intervention, by leniency, by kindness, he tried to lessen in some small way the burden which his men bore. They themselves appreciated the efforts which he made on their behalf. A young private, Reginald Hurt,[21] later recorded two examples of Churchill's attitude in a letter to the author. The first incident took place while the battalion was in the trenches:

I was on sentry duty that night, which meant standing on the fire steps of the front line trench, and looking out towards the enemy lines. It was a bitterly cold, wet night and very quiet as regards action, and in a weak moment I stood my rifle up against the parapet; in a corner of the trench. I then marched up and down on the fire step trying to get some warmth into my arms and legs, when suddenly some-one jumped down behind me from the top of the parapet. Fortunately for me and my sleeping colleagues, it was Sir Winston Churchill and his Adjutant, Sir Archibald Sinclair and not a German patrol. The next five or ten minutes were amongst the unhappiest of my life, all because my rifle *was not* in my possession. I received, and deservedly, the most severe reprimand I can recall. Finally he asked me my age, and on learning that I was one of the youngest soldiers in the Battalion, and had been in the trenches at the age of eighteen, his anger evaporated and he became almost paternal. My punishment was much less severe than that meted out to a Corporal on sentry duty in the next bay, found doing almost the same as myself, who was demoted to the ranks, because he was both a time serving soldier and an NCO, and should have set a better example.

[21] Reginald Hurt, 1896–    . Employed by the Sheffield Electric Supply Department. Enlisted in the Army, May 1915. Crossed to France, September 1915. Severely wounded, May 1916.

The second incident that Private Hurt recalled took place in reserve:

On one occasion, whilst acting as company runner, I was walking along what had been Plugstreet's main road, when I saw the OC coming along in the opposite direction. I gave him the usual smart salute, and had passed along about a dozen paces when he called me back and asked why I was limping. I explained that my feet were sore because of the bad condition of my boots, and that when I had applied for a new pair the quartermaster said they would last another three months. The OC took a letter from his tunic pocket, detached the envelope and wrote on it, 'Quarter-master Sgt. B. Company, supply bearer with one pair of boots *immediately*,' and signed it.

It was not only Churchill's sympathy but also his enthusiasm that caused his men to respond to him. In his book Gibb later wrote:

To see Winston giving a dissertation on the laying of sandbags, with practical illustrations, was to come inevitably to the conclusion that his life-study had been purely of poliorketics and the corresponding counter-measures. You felt sure from his grasp of practice that he must have served apprentice to a bricklayer and a master-mason, while his theoretical knowledge rendered you certain that Wren would have been proud to sit at his feet. . . .

The spectre of a Brigade hovered in front of Churchill throughout February. He was not alone in believing that promotion was still possible. On February 18 Colonel Holland wrote to Clementine Churchill from the Headquarters of the Ninth Division:

Dear Mrs Winston,
   I must just write you a line to say how glad we are to have Winston commanding one of our battalions.
   He is awfully well, better than I have seen him for ages, & full of vigour & vitality & has made his battalion from a moderate one into a d—— good one. He is gradually acquiring the Scotch lingo, which I find very difficult. I always take an interpreter about with me. I hope he will get a brigade soon & have more scope for his energy. . . .

                                                        Yrs sincerely
                                                        A. E. Holland

'I find that everyone has heard of the improvements you have effected in your Battalion,' Clementine Churchill wrote to her husband a few days later. 'Soldiers back from the Front on leave talk about it. This is good, as it prepares the way for a Brigade.'

On February 19 the Battalion moved back into reserve. Gibb, the Battalion diarist, wrote in the war diary for the six days in reserve: 'Nothing of note to record.' But Churchill had much to describe in his letter home on February 20. He had gone to the Hospice to sleep, hoping that it would be less noisy than at Battalion headquarters at Soyer Farm:

My darling,
  . . . We have been hunted by shells during these two days in 'rest' billets—nine men hit this evening and all our farms shelled repeatedly. Archie & I have had a particularly exciting time. I told you how we decided to leave the uncomfortable & crowded farm & go back to delightful quarters in the little town. Yesterday we differed on policy. Archie was for living in one room and darting into a cellar when shelling began. I was for another room next door . . . and was building a strong sandbag protection there. My principle is that one ought to try to make the ordinary place where one lives fairly comfortable & safe & take the chance there. Archie contended that only the cellar was really safe, & he insisted on my following his plan on two occasions yesterday when things became disagreeable. So we all assembled in the cellar—Archie, I, the 3 signallers, two servants, & the people of the house viz an old man, two women & a jolly little flapper. This plan worried me. I hate having repeatedly to skip into a cellar, & wonder where each shell is coming & whether we ought to move in or not.

Also we always got a shell pretty near going across the courtyard & finally I declared that the cellar was not really safe & that a shell at a certain angle wd penetrate it. He said it was 1000 to 1 against it. Well this morning he went out to visit our companies & I stayed in to write a paper on Air, wh may turn out either as a splash or a letter! I had made up my mind to go to the other room & not use the cellar. At about 11 shelling began: and the buildings all around were hit & other shells burst in the courtyard or stopped just short of us across the road. I concentrated my mind on my air argument and wrote on placidly without any feelings of anxiety. After an hour the shelling stopped & I went out to look at the damage. My dear! Archie's pet cellar! A 30 pound shell had entered our bedroom (where I shd have been writ-

ing) passed completely through it, had penetrated the cellar where
all the assembly were huddled—& then mercifully failed to burst.
Otherwise they wd all have been killed. Archie returned from his
walk to abandon his argument. This is now the third time in a fortnight
that our bedroom has been pierced by shells—three different rooms.
Archie says it is the roughest time in billets he has ever had all the
war. You will be glad to hear that I have now moved back 300 yards to
this beastly farm; as I am sure they meant to smash the little town to
pieces. Yet even here shells came in pursuit, & riding across the
ploughed fields shrapnel kept pace with us in the air. One lives calmly
on the brink of the abyss. But I can understand how tired people get
of it if it goes on month after month. All the excitement dies away &
there is only dull resentment.

The church steeple wh had withstood the vicissitudes of 16 months
of fighting came down yesterday at the explosion of a big shell. So
this evening we are smashing up one of their steeples & they are
retaliating by scattering their shells in twos & threes on various points.
Meanwhile the German aeroplanes sail about unmolested overhead
watching the shooting, & scorning our anti-aircraft guns. There is no
doubt who is master of this air! . . .

Goodnight my darling—fondest love<br>
Your devoted<br>
W

Shelled out of the Hospice, Churchill was forced to sleep at
Soyer Farm. The Germans turned their attention elsewhere, and
there followed two quiet days, with snow, and the sound of
heavy shelling somewhere to the south. 'They cannot see to
shoot,' Churchill reported to his wife on February 22. 'This unusual interlude is welcome.' He was excited about his coming
leave, wanting time to relax and to paint. He asked his wife to
make the arrangements: 'I have every hope of coming home on
the 2nd. I propose to come to Dover by destroyer & that you
meet me at the Lord Warden Hotel where we can lunch & go
up to London together. . . . Mind you have a servant ready to
look after me, & let him come in time to have everything ready
on arrival.'

On February 25 Colonel Holland called on Churchill at Soyer
Farm. He had just been promoted to a senior appointment with

the 3rd Army. 'His sphere is extended 12 or 15 times,' Churchill explained to his wife the next day. Holland brought good news, which Churchill passed on: 'He told me that General Furse had spontaneously sent in an official recommendation that I shd be selected for a Brigade command; & that he (Holland) was going to impress this upon GHQ where he stays tonight. It is satisfactory anyhow that my immediate superiors have confidence in my work.' Furse's recommendation came to nought. In London society it was assumed that Churchill was already a Brigadier; on the day after Holland's visit Churchill learned from his wife that at dinner one night the Vice-Chamberlain of Queen Alexandra's household, Lord Gosford,[22] had said that he was 'shocked when he heard you were not yet a Brigadier and said he had been told you really were one but it had not been gazetted'.

On February 26 Churchill returned for the fourth time to Laurence Farm, and to the front-line trenches. Napier-Clavering and his sappers had done their work well. 'Our farm is much more protected,' Churchill wrote to his wife, 'and it wd take 5 9-inch guns to smash it up.' Winter conditions had returned, but the British Army was not without resource, nor was Churchill in any particular discomfort:

Snow covers the ground and we do our scouting in calico gowns—almost invisible at 200 yards. I was up till 1.30 in the trenches, as the night was so dark & the price of safety is eternal vigilance. The artillery co-operation was vy loose last night and we took a vy long time to get a response from them.

I like this farm so much better than the one I am in at 'rest'.

Archie & I have a nice little square room together—the ceiling is propped up by timber, & there are 3 layers of sandbags & brick bags on the top, and all the sides are heavily protected. There are a good many things to burst a shell before it actually hits us, & then the sandbags may be counted on to stop the splinters & to keep out the blast. Inside we have a glowing brazier & two comfortable canvas beds . . . we sleep warm and peaceful.

[22] Archibald Brabazon Sparrow Acheson, 1841–1922. 4th Earl of Gosford, 1864. Vice-Chamberlain to Queen Alexandra, 1901–22.

Confident that his farm was well-nigh impregnable, Churchill had persuaded the artillery to lay on another 'sträfe', which he augmented by front-line fire. All did not go well. The British shells, falling short, killed two men and wounded four. A newly arrived officer, 2nd Lieutenant Buchan,[23] was also slightly wounded. A report of this tragedy was sent the next morning to General Tudor at Artillery headquarters at Steenwerck. 'I found on investigation,' Tudor wrote in his diary, 'that the gunners were entirely to blame.' On the following day Tudor lunched with Churchill at Laurence Farm. Then he saw the artillery officer whose 'offending guns' had caused the tragedy. 'He will arrange something . . .' Tudor wrote in his diary, 'to restore confidence.'

Churchill remained at Laurence Farm for the next three days. He did not write to his wife as he would be seeing her before his letters could arrive. The only record of events is in the Battalion's war diary, which was as usual succinct:

27.2.16 LAWRENCE FM (Bn HQ) shelled at noon with 20–30 7.7 cms. 3 signallers working outside were severely wounded—all three eventually died of their wounds.

28.2.16 Bn HQ shelled twice—once at 1 pm & once at 3 pm. Cupola dugouts afforded complete protection. An orderly who was standing at the mouth of one, however, was severely wounded in the head.

29.2.16 A very quiet day with no shelling. Weather still extremely cold.

1st March 1916 Quiet day. No shelling. One private killed.

At seven in the morning of March 2 the Battalion was relieved by a Battalion of Gordon Highlanders. Churchill left Flanders for London, giving Sinclair command of the Battalion in his absence. He had not been home since Christmas, over two months before. His wife had prepared a careful plan to keep him busy and amused; but it was not a private world that welcomed him back.

[23] Alastair Ebenezer Buchan, 1894–1917. Brother of the novelist John Buchan. 2nd Lieutenant, Cameron Highlanders, 1915. Transferred to the Royal Scots Fusiliers, March 1915. Died 9 April 1917 of wounds received at Arras.

# 22

# 'You can be Prime Minister'

DURING HIS FIRST two months in command of the 6th Royal Scots Fusiliers Churchill had found little time for anything but his military duties. But fifteen years of intense political activity were not to be obliterated by mud or noise or danger. Throughout January and February he had been alerted, not only by the shriek of German shells but by political news from home. On January 1 the Press had announced the resignation of Sir John Simon, the Home Secretary, in protest against the Military Service Bill. Many Liberals feared that the Bill was the first step on the road to conscription. Churchill's meeting with Lloyd George at the end of December had given him the brief hope that the conscription crisis would enable him to rejoin the Government as a leading advocate of compulsory service. But after some reflection he saw little likelihood of Simon's resignation leading to any significant change either in Cabinet policy or personnel. It was a great pity, he wrote to his wife on January 3, that Simon had not been followed 'by others who have not got their hearts in the war'. He realized that by itself Simon's resignation could not weaken Asquith's position; indeed, during February Asquith skilfully emerged as a supporter of the growing conscription lobby. Churchill was not impressed by the Prime Minister's change of view. 'I cannot regard the delay to do what is now shown to be necessary, & the waste of time & energy entailed, as any triumph for Asquith,' he wrote; 'he has simply played the party game as long as he cd, while ruling in the name of the nation.'

The failure of the conscription crisis to develop was not Churchill's only frustration. On the afternoon of January 3 he was summoned to St Omer by the Operation Division of GHQ, and told that they had been instructed by the War Office to follow up his idea of a Caterpillar machine.[1] They 'wanted to know who to apply to in England about them', Churchill wrote to his wife. This made him angry; 'imagine', he continued, that 'after 9 months of actual manufacture and committees unending, there should still be such ignorance and lack of concern'. The combination of Asquith's stratagems over conscription and the War Office's hesitations over the Caterpillar, led him to exclaim to his wife: 'God for a month of power & a good shorthand writer.'

During January Churchill continued to try to overcome his wife's distrust of Lloyd George. 'Keep in touch with LG,' he wrote to her on January 4; 'his necessities will keep him straight if a split occurs. Asquith on the other hand will never have need of me again. It is *need* alone that counts. Nothing else is considered.' After fifteen years in politics, Churchill believed himself a competent judge of political realities. 'I keep turning things over in my mind,' he wrote to his wife on January 6, 'without doing much good. But broadly my conclusion is that nothing but a complete change of regime will require me to return—or be of any use. Asquith will never face the certain demands of opposition hostile to me.' Churchill believed that his chance of Cabinet office depended upon Asquith's overthrow. When this was done, he expected it to be done by others, who would then invite him to return. If it were not done, he could see no future for himself in the political sphere. 'There is little likelihood of my obtaining real power again during the war,' he wrote to Edward Grigg on January 6, '& anything less than that I do not intend to take. It is vexatious to see so many things left undone, or half done, or done too late: but I try with a measure of success to avert my mind from the wide panorama, & close my mental eyes.'

[1] The Colonel who summoned Churchill to St Omer was Hugh Jamieson Elles (1880–1945). Commanded the tanks in action at Cambrai, 1917. Knighted, 1919. Master-General of Ordnance, 1934–7. Colonel Commandant, Royal Tank Regiment, 1934–45. General, 1938.

He had no doubts about the outcome of the war: 'It will all come right in the end,' he told Grigg, 'though not by the shortest or least costly method.'

On January 7, reading of the continuing conscription crisis, Churchill wrote to his wife in a depressed mood. 'I watch in The Times (6th inst) the movement of political things & I must confess it excites & disturbs my mind,' he explained. 'I try however not to look back too much, having not only put my hand but fettered it to the plough. I must rely on you to keep constant touch with the friends & pseudo-friends I have. I do not like to feel forgotten & deconsidéré out here—especially when I am not in the trenches, but only waiting in reserve billets. . . .' Churchill always looked forward to his periods of duty in the trenches. He wanted to escape the depressed moods which came with reading newspapers, and having the time to reflect and brood upon news from England. The trenches provided him with just such an escape. 'I feel vy much bound on the wheel of things out here,' he told his wife in his letter of January 7, 'and when politics calm down again, I shall yield myself to the inexorable motion with suppleness and placidity. But peace out here & crisis at home are disturbing combinations for my mind.'

Churchill needed his wife's encouragement. It was her commentary on political events at home that enabled him to interpret the information which he read in the newspapers or received from others. He wanted too her personal support and her approval for all that he had done. 'You cannot write to me too often or too long—my dearest & sweetest,' he wrote. 'The beauty & strength of your character & the sagacity of yr judgment are more realised by me every day. I ought to have followed yr counsels in my days of prosperity. Only sometimes they were too negative. I shd have made nothing if I had not made mistakes. Ungrateful country.'

Throughout January Clementine Churchill was busy on her husband's behalf. On January 7 she had tea with Margot Asquith at 10 Downing Street, discovering, as she wrote to her husband that evening, 'great relief in that quarter that the division on compulsion went so well'. She had met the Prime Minister in the hall: 'He looked shy when he first saw me, but thought better of it & I had a little talk to him. . . . He asked after you with compunction in his voice.' She remained dubious about Lloyd George. 'I don't think he has managed very well,' she wrote. 'At one time he abused the Dukes to please the working-men, now he has abused the working-men to please the soldiers.[2] He seems to me very isolated. . . .'

On January 7 Churchill received a letter from his mother in which she gave him news of the conscription debate, and told him that by some accounts 'the PM was very badly received', and that the Speaker[3] had doubted whether things would go well 'notwithstanding the crowds of MPs brought back from the front to vote with the Govt'. This news stirred Churchill to further speculation, for he now saw a way in which he could perhaps repair his reputation, if nothing more. On the following day he wrote to his wife: '. . . I am inclined to think that the PM's position is only temporarily strengthened; & that once this conscription corner is turned his utility will be reduced, & his authority stand on a vy lopsided basis. As soon as the Dardanelles episode is finished I propose to invite him to publish papers, including my various forecasts & requests for support.' Churchill believed that if the facts about the Dardanelles were published, they would show that neither the naval failure on March 18 nor the subsequent military disasters had been his responsibility, and that once this were established his political prospects would be

[2] By the end of 1915 many munitions works were far behind with their deliveries. Speaking in Parliament on December 20 Lloyd George, the Minister of Munitions, had linked the deaths at the front with lethargy in the factories at home. On Christmas Eve 1915 he went to Beardmore's Works on the Clyde to urge the men to speed up deliveries of heavy guns. He was met by the singing of the 'Red Flag'. On the following morning in St Andrew's Hall, Glasgow, the Clydeside workers howled him down. The Trade Unions were determined to resist any dilution of labour which might be caused by military conscription. They were also afraid that the Government would introduce some form of industrial compulsion.

[3] James William Lowther, 1855–1949. Conservative MP, 1883–5, 1886–1921. Under-Secretary for Foreign Affairs, 1891. Speaker of the House of Commons, 1905–21. Created Viscount Ullswater, 1921.

much improved. Clementine Churchill did not share this view, replying on January 11:

If you ask the PM to publish the Dardanelles papers let me know what happens. If he refuses or delays I beg you not to do anything without telling me first & giving me time to give you my valuable (!) opinion on it. It is an unequal match between the PM & an officer in the field in war-time—If he dissents I fear you will have to wait. If you insisted on publication against his wish you would have against you all the forces of cohesion and stability including every member of the Cabinet.

On the other hand when the papers are eventually published his refusal to do so earlier will have a very bad effect for him.

But of course the PM may consent. Are you quite certain however that this is the best time for publication, when you are away and not able to speak in the debate which is bound to take place. I am very anxious that you should not blunt this precious weapon prematurely.

Churchill's bitterness against Asquith's treatment of him was unabated. On January 7 he wrote to his mother:

My feeling agst him is due to the fact that knowing my work, & having been a co-adventurer in my enterprises (not merely an approver), he threw me over without the slightest effort even to state the true facts on my behalf; & still more that thereafter in all the plenitude of power he never found for me a useful sphere of acting wh wd have given scope to my energies & knowledge. If I am killed at the humble duties I have found for myself he will no doubt be sorry & shocked. But the fact will remain that he has treated me with injustice, & has wasted qualities wh might have been used in many ways to the public advantage in this time of war.

To his wife, who continued to warn him against Lloyd George, and to beg him not to cut himself off entirely from Asquith, he wrote on January 10:

I cannot see any way in wh Asquith's interests can stand in need of me. However friendly his feelings, his *interests* are best served by my effacement. If I were killed he wd be sorry: but it wd suit his political hand. LG on the other hand wd not be sorry, but it wd not suit his political hand. It is this factor that alone counts in the cruel politics of today. I can feel no sense of loyalty or friendship for Asquith after the revelation of his utter indifference shown by his letter to French. Still here again there is no occasion for a personal breech.

Whenever my mind is not occupied by work, I feel deeply the injustice with wh my work at the Admiralty has been treated. I cannot help it—tho' I try. Then the damnable mismanagement wh has ruined the Dardanelles enterprise & squandered vainly so much life & opportunity cries aloud for retribution: & if I survive, the day will come when I will claim it publicly.

Clementine Churchill continued in her efforts to find out about the political situation, and to give her husband a clear view of what was happening at home. 'To-day, I lunched at Downing Street & for the first time since you resigned talked to the PM,' she wrote on January 9. 'He talked a great deal about you and asked a great many questions. I was perfectly natural (except perhaps that I was a little too buoyant) & he tried to be natural too, but it was an effort. I think it is a good thing to keep up civil relations & it is always interesting to follow the Block's train of thought. He seemed very much pleased at the *Parliamentary* situation, but I expect things must still be very uncertain judging from the fact that this is the 2nd Sunday he has spent in London.' Clementine Churchill was appalled by the lack of serious concern at Downing Street in the conduct of the war. 'The chief topic of social gossip,' she told him, 'is who is to go to India [as Viceroy]. After ranging round the Crewes, Harcourts, McKennas, Islingtons,[4] Sir F. Hopwood etc speculation has narrowed down to two obscurities & it is a dead heat between them —Chelmsford[5] or Balcarres![6] It seems incredible——' On January

[4] John Poynder Dickson-Poynder, 1866–1936. Liberal MP, 1892–1910. Created Baron Islington, 1910. Governor of New Zealand, 1910–12. Under-Secretary of State for the Colonies, 1915–16. Under-Secretary of State for India, 1916–19. Chairman, National Savings Committee, 1920–6. Married, 1896, Anne Dundas, a friend of the Churchill family.

[5] Frederick John Napier Thesiger, 1868–1933. 3rd Baron Chelmsford, 1905. Governor of Queensland, 1905–9; of New South Wales, 1909–13. Viceroy of India, 1916–21. Created Viscount, 1921. Married, 1894, Frances Charlotte Guest, eldest daughter of Churchill's uncle Ivor Guest.

[6] David Alexander Edward Lindsay, 1871–1940. Conservative MP, 1895–1913. 27th Earl of Crawford and 10th Earl of Balcarres, 1913. Enlisted as a Private, Royal Army Medical Corps, August 1914, without disclosing his

11 F. E. Smith sent Churchill discouraging news, declaring that as a result of the conscription crisis: 'The country is overwhelmingly with us & indeed the Bill has a little restored the prestige of the Government.'

Clementine Churchill shared F. E. Smith's interpretation of the conscription crisis, and of Asquith's improved position. 'I'm afraid I can't agree that the PM's position is only temporarily strengthened,' she wrote to her husband on January 11. 'He will always in the end tip down on the side of strong measures after delaying them & devitalising them so as to try and keep everybody together. His method of defeating the enemy is not by well planned lightning strokes, but by presenting to him a large stolid gelatinous mess which he (the enemy) is supposed to pommel in vain.' Clementine Churchill was aware of the terrible pressures which made her husband unhappy. But she believed passionately in his future, and tried always to share his anxieties with him. 'My own Darling,' she wrote on January 12, 'I long so to be able to comfort you. Later on when you are in danger in the trenches you will be equable and contented, while I who am now comparatively at ease will be in mortal anxiety. Try not to brood too much; I would be so unhappy if your naturally open and unsuspicious nature became embittered. Patience is the only grace you need.' She was confident about his future: 'If you are not killed, as sure as day follows night you will come into your own again. I know *you* don't fear death, it is I who dread that. But I am almost glad to be suffering now, becos' I am sure no single soul will be allowed to live thro' this time without sorrow, so perhaps what we are enduring now will be counted and we shall be spared the greatest pain of all.' Recalling August 1914 she wrote: 'I remember quite well when we were at the Admiralty during those wonderful opening weeks of the war, we were both so happy, you with the success of the Naval preparations & with the excitement of swiftly moving events and I with pride at the

identity. President of the Board of Agriculture and Fisheries, July 1916. Lord Privy Seal, 1916–19. Chancellor of the Duchy of Lancaster, 1919–21. First Commissioner of Works, 1921–2. Minister of Transport, 1922. Chairman of the Royal Fine Art Commission, 1924.

glamour surrounding you & the Navy. I remember feeling guilty and ashamed that the terrible casualties of those first battles did not sadden me more. I wondered how long we should continue to tread on air.'

'When it is all over,' she believed, 'we shall be proud that you were a soldier & not a politician for the greater part of the war—soldiers and soldier's wives seem to me now the only real people. . . .' Clementine Churchill's letter continued with some personal advice. She did not want him to tell chance visitors his hostile opinion of Asquith's character and policy, suggesting that he use Archibald Sinclair as a safety-valve for his anger, just as she used her sister-in-law Gwendeline.

For the first two weeks of January Sir John Simon had been much abused for having opposed compulsory military service. By resigning, he drew upon himself the odium of a belligerent society. Many people shared F. E. Smith's view that, as he wrote to Churchill on January 11, Simon was pegging out 'a claim in the garbage' by refusing to compromise his principles. Churchill took a different view. When Jack Seely, who had been at the conscription debate, returned to France, he told Churchill that Simon was much upset; so much so that he thought of joining the Army as an ordinary recruit. Churchill was moved by this news, informing his wife on January 13:

I have written him a note telling him he is vy welcome to come here if he likes. I will look after him & teach him soldiering, & he wd be a pleasant companion to teach me law. I am sorry for him—now he is down. It is vy hard—if one has not the training of a soldier. A cabinet minister can fight in the trenches; but to be drilled by a sergeant in the barrack yard—invests adversity with a squalid air. He cd learn everything out here quite easily.

Seely's account of London politics stimulated Churchill's appetite for political news. 'LG by all accounts is isolated,' he wrote to his wife in the same letter. 'He has been vy foolish in his relations with me, Bonar Law, FE & Curzon. He might have combined us all. As it is he has earned the deep distrust of each, & I who was his friend and had worked with him so long, have now largely by his action been rendered quite powerless for the time being.' Churchill wanted to know more about his wife's meeting with Asquith. '. . . I shd like a *verbatim* report of the Kat's conversation with the old ruffian,' he wrote. 'He has handspiked compulsion as long as he cd, & long after it was needed; & only adopted it in the end, against his deepest convictions, to keep his office—or what is perhaps true—to keep LG out of his office; and for this "statecraft" at the expense of our arms & treasure—he is acclaimed as the saviour of the Nation. . . .'

That evening Churchill read in *The Times* of the previous day, which had just reached Ploegsteert, that the last of the Allied troops at Gallipoli had finally been evacuated from Helles. It was a bitter moment for him. But he was thrilled to learn that Carson had described the Dardanelles as 'admirably conceived' when speaking in the House of Commons on January 11. 'Gradually people will see what I saw so vividly this time last year,' he wrote to his wife on January 14, 'but alas too late forever. Thank God they all got off safe. If things never turn out as well as you expect them, it is also true they never turn out as badly. There is no culminating catastrophe: only a cruel tale of wasted effort, life & treasure, & opportunity—priceless & unique—gone forever.'

Churchill continued to debate in his own mind whether he had been right to leave London for the trenches. On January 16 he wrote to his wife of 'the wisdom & necessity of my coming out here'. It would have been impossible, he explained, to have 'sat still in England—painting to keep my mind quiet & waiting for the wind to change. Here I have to sit still; but somehow dullness does not fret me.' Nevertheless, there were daily reminders of what he could achieve in politics. Writing to his wife on January 17 he described one such incident:

. . . Air fights have been going on overhead this morning, & I think there has been an air raid on some of the neighbouring townships, as a lot of our machines are up. There is no excuse for our not having command of the air.

Since I left the Admiralty, the whole naval air wing has been let down: & all our precious ascendency has been dissipated. If they had

given me control of this service when I left the Admiralty, we shd
have supremacy today. Asquith wanted this, but in contact with the
slightest difficulty & resistance, he as usual shut up.

Churchill told his wife that he was also worried that the large
numbers of British troops at Salonika and Egypt were serving
no purpose, and that these expeditions were welcomed by the
Germans as a means of keeping these troops idle, 'while they
use the Turks to stir up Persia, & later on Afghanistan'; a thought
which led him to exclaim in his postscript: 'Imbecile government,
and purblind Kitchener. Wait & see.' Every letter which reached
him provoked similar painful speculation. Towards the end of
January he received a long account from his brother-in-law, William Hozier, who had been at the Dardanelles on board HMS
*Edgar*. This letter, dated January 17, had a disturbing effect on
Churchill, whose mind was tormented by descriptions of avoid-
able failure and opportunities cast away by inefficiency and lack
of enterprise:

. . . I can now without transgressing the censorship rules give you
some idea of the work carried out by the Edgar class and the monitors
between the beginning of August and the withdrawal on January 8th
and 9th. . . .

The Air Service was not organised sufficiently to cooperate with the
ships and there was no responsible head to direct matters and to confer with us.

There was no interchange of ideas between the Generals at Helles
and ourselves. . . .

Up to the middle of September our orders were to expend a maximum of 25 rounds a day on some section of Achi Baba. This was always done at the same time and was of little value.

The impression therefore prevailed amongst the soldiers that our
only value was a moral one and that naval gunfire was of little use to
support an offensive. . . .

*August 7th* A grand attack by the Helles Army just before the landing at Suvla Bay. RESULT—2,000 casualties: and not an inch of advance. Ships' fire hopelessly ineffective.

*Nov 15th* An attack by the 8th Army Corps. 50 casualties, 200 yards
advance. Supporting ships—Edgar and two 14" monitors. Edgar firing

on twelve different batteries. 14" monitors firing on trenches and earthworks, and our shore artillery on the remaining four hostile batteries.

I am convinced that had it been realised how the naval gunfire would become effective, the 60,000 troops frittered away at Suvla Bay would have been used in the capture of Achi Baba. Of course many more troops would have been needed to beat the Turkish Army but we could have established ourselves for the winter. . . .

Those who are running this war require more 'ruthlessness' or we shall lose it.

Churchill shared his brother-in-law's fear that without 'ruthlessness' there could be defeat. He felt confident that he himself could provide the necessary driving force. But his isolation was complete. 'You do not tell me in yr letter what the PM said,' Churchill had written to his wife on January 11. She replied on January 16:

He talked a great deal about trivialities & femininities which you know he adores and he asked a good many questions about you and about the detail of your life out there—He *wanted* the answers to be reassuring, & my good manners as a guest forbade me making him uncomfortable which of course I could easily have done. He seemed grateful to me for sparing him——! He is a sensualist & if I had depicted you in a tragic and sinister light it would have ruined his meal and I should probably not be bidden again!

Clementine Churchill remained uncertain as to how far Asquith had behaved dishonourably towards her husband. 'I think one might say,' she wrote in her letter, 'that the PM instead of battling bravely with a hurricane is so anxious to avoid ship-wreck that he never minds how often he tacks, so that he frequently describes a complete circle before reaching his object—with consequent loss to our arms & fortunes.' Churchill was not to be deflected from his bitterness against Asquith. His hope of some political development favourable to himself had been stimulated yet again by a letter from F. E. Smith sent from London on January 18. 'If you write any of your able memoranda,' F. E. Smith encouraged him, 'send me one & I will circulate it above my

own august initials to the cabinet.' F. E. Smith wrote that he
was dining shortly with Lloyd George and the editor of the *Daily
Chronicle*, Robert Donald,[7] '& will tell you if anything happens'.
He sent disturbing news about the United States, whose entry
into the war, for which Churchill had so wished when he was
at the Admiralty, seemed increasingly remote: 'The US swine,'
wrote F. E. Smith, 'grow more and more truculent and are
apparently almost prepared to slobber over Brother Bosch.'[8]
F. E. Smith added that he was going to 'make an effort to come
& see you on Friday week if this suits your arrangements. *If not
let me know what weekend will suit you.*' On January 23 Churchill wrote to his wife: 'I am enchanted at the idea of FE coming
out. Tell him to keep it a secret so as to give no handle for political & newspaper gossip.'

Churchill continued to debate with his wife the merits and
failings of the Prime Minister. On January 19 he declared emphatically: 'My precious—I don't take back a word of what I
wrote about Asquith. He has cruelly & needlessly wronged me; &
even in his power & prosperity has had the meanness to strike at
me. No—if I survive—my political life will be apart from him. He
passes from my regard.' His letter continued: 'My mind is now
filling up with ideas & opinions in many military & war matters.
But I have no means of expression. I am impotent to give what
is there to be given—of truth & value & urgency. I must wait in
silence the sombre movement of events. Still it is better to be
gagged than give unheeded counsel.' Dependent upon his wife

[7] Robert Donald, 1861–1933. Editor, *Daily Chronicle*, 1902–18. Chairman,
Empire Press Union, 1915–26. A Director, Department of Information, 1917.
A strong advocate of dropping leaflets over enemy territory. Knighted, 1924.
A friend of the first Labour Prime Minister, Ramsay MacDonald, for whom
he undertook publicity work.

[8] On 2 January 1916 the unarmed British liner *Persia* had been sunk
without warning in the Eastern Mediterranean by an Austrian submarine.
Over half of the 350 passengers and crew were drowned. Among the dead
were many Americans, including the American Consul at Aden. On hearing
the news President Wilson cut short his honeymoon to return to the White
House. But despite what *The Times* described on January 5 as 'excitement in
Washington' against 'Teutonic savageness', the United States accepted a cash
indemnity and remained at peace with the Central Powers.

for almost all the contacts which he wanted to maintain in London, Churchill enlisted his wife's support:

I had a nice letter from Rothermere—saying that 'I had emerged unscathed from Gallipoli'. *Do* I beseech you keep in touch with him, & also through Aitken with Bonar Law. Don't neglect these matters. I have no one but you to act for me. I shd like you to make the seeing of my friends a regular business, like your canteens wh are going so well. It is fatal to let the threads drop. Curzon, FE: BL: Carson; Garvin, Rothermere: Goulding: Alick[9] all these you shd keep in touch with. There is nothing to ask of them—only represent *me* in their circle.

Even while he was writing this letter, Churchill became increasingly disturbed. It was six o'clock in the evening, 'a bad hour for me', he continued; 'I feel the need of power as an outlet worst then; & the energy of mind & body is strong within me.' On the following day he wrote more calmly: 'I expect the Kat will be flustered by my directions to her to keep in touch with so many people. Do only just what comes easily & naturally to you my darling. On the other hand don't simply vanish out of the political circle & plunge into bed & canteens. Do what you can.' Clementine Churchill continued to see her husband's friends and potential allies. She also sent him her own thoughts upon the political scene. 'If tomorrow the PM disappeared Bonar Law would be the successor,' she wrote on January 21. 'He has made a great impression in the House during these last weeks by his skilful handling of delicate topics and this impression will spread to the country—Myself I think Bonar is not a big man, but he is a very skilful one and does not miss his markets. I think Ll-George will remain *perdu* for a bit and then gradually slide away from his "compulsion" attitude towards the working men.' She had just met the new Chancellor of the Duchy of Lancaster and reported: 'Montagu after an absence of 6 months from the Cabinet finds

[9] Alexander William Charles Oliphant Murray, 1870–1920. Liberal MP, 1900–5; 1906–10; 1910–12. Under-Secretary of State for India, 1909. Chief Liberal Whip, 1909–12. Created Baron Murray of Elibank, 1912. Director of Recruiting for Munitions Works, 1915–16.

very little change except a greater disinclination to action, the only Warrior is Curzon.'

On January 23, after lunching with Augustine Birrell, Clementine Churchill wrote again. 'Bonar's growing prestige,' she reported, 'is the common table-talk, & also the disappearance of Ll-G "into quarantine".' On the following day she saw Lloyd George, and hoped that her husband appreciated all her efforts on his behalf. 'Now don't scold your Kat too much for being a hermit,' she wrote on January 24. 'Here in two days I have hobnobbed with Montagu, Birrell, Lloyd George and a South African potentate![10] Tomorrow night I am dining with Cassel. Please send me home the Distinguished Conduct Medal at once & much praise.'

During January Churchill became increasingly distressed at German air superiority on the western front. He often saw German aeroplanes flying over the British trenches, but there was little corresponding activity from the British side. He was excited when his wife reported speculation in London that the Navy and Army air services—the Royal Naval Air Service and the Royal Flying Corps—might be taken away from their respective Ministries and formed into a united Air Ministry, controlled by some political figure who could unify and vitalize them. This was a task for which Churchill believed himself to be ideally suited. The work he had done in building up the Royal Naval Air Service before 1914, his own flying experience, his responsibilities at the outbreak of war for the aerial defence of Britain, had all prepared him for just such a task. Only a few days before he was due to go into the trenches where he hoped to forget such tantalizing political things, he was confronted by the question of his possible return, and felt anew the frustration of lack of power.

In a letter to his wife on January 23 Churchill commented angrily on Britain's weakness in the air, which upset him greatly.

---

[10] Abe Bailey, 1864–1940. One of the principal mine owners of the Transvaal. Knighted, 1911, for his services in promoting South African Union. Served as a Major on the staff of the South African forces which attacked German South-West Africa, 1915. Created Baronet, 1919.

'They have indeed maltreated the Naval Air Service,' he wrote, 'since my protective ring was broken. The way in which these slugs smile & prosper is astonishing.' Clementine Churchill shared her husband's anger and frustration. 'Everyone "in office" seems to be unbelievably smug,' she had written to him two days before. 'Were we like that when you were in power? There is an atmospheric non-conductive barrier between those whose men are in danger & those whose men are in powerful security at home. . . .' Clementine Churchill had also been excited by the Air Ministry rumours: 'Everyone not in office is much disturbed at the gradual ascendency of the German aeroplane,' she wrote. 'If only, when you left the Admiralty you had been given the "air"! I believe if you had really tried for it you might have got it, as in the press there was a movement in that direction—Do you think there is a chance even now tho' "too late"?' 'Of course I wd take an Air Ministry—if it were offered me,' Churchill replied on January 24, 'provided it carried with it a seat on the War Council. But the PM will never face the minor difficulties of such a departure, & I am sure he knows that his interests are best served by my political or other extinction.' Churchill felt that he had nothing to gain by listening to such speculations. 'I think over a gt many plans,' he wrote to his wife; 'but it is better to go on simply here for a while.'

On January 24 Churchill moved forward with his Battalion towards the trenches. That same day his wife lunched with Lloyd George. That afternoon she sent him an account of their conversation. 'He is very anxious to be amiable,' she wrote. 'He talked about current events; just now he is quite out of it—I brought in Bonar Law's name & said how well he had led the House. He didn't like that much & said that he had estranged more Tories than he had conciliated Liberals—He is going to France next week & says he means to seek you out.' Clementine Churchill was most reluctant for the two men to meet. 'I would never like you to be intimately connected,' she wrote, 'becos' tho' he seems to recover again & again from his muddles & mistakes I am not sure his partner would; he would instead be saddled with the whole lot while Ll-G skipped off laughing.'

Churchill was excited by the imminent arrival of both Lloyd George and F. E. Smith at his headquarters. There was much that he wanted to talk about. Every day provided him with examples of the Government's neglect, filling him with anger and contempt. Reading in *The Times* that Harold Tennant, the Under-Secretary of State for War, had told the House of Commons on January 20 that 'nearly every fight in the air takes place on the German side of the trenches', he wrote to his wife on January 26:

Tennant's answer in H of C about German aeroplanes never coming over our lines reads amusingly here. I saw one flaunting himself 20 miles behind the line yesterday; & 4 of them threw bombs within 50 yards of the party of men I sent on to prepare these billets for our reception. The flying officers tell me a sad tale of their difficulties, & the utter want of knowledge & drive that characterises present War Office administration.

Churchill also tried to answer his wife's criticisms of Lloyd George, explaining that although in his view Lloyd George 'has been vy faithless & is now friendless', the Minister of Munitions had nevertheless 'been more on the true trail than anyone else in this war'. In a letter which he wrote to Lloyd George on January 25 he set out his opinions without reserve, but with a certain desperation at his distance from the centre of power:

Secret & Personal
My dear David,

How do you come out of all this? I cannot tell, but from this distance it seems to me that you are even more isolated than when we all dined at Rufus's. Asquith is stronger than ever; K still overlays the War Office; you have enthroned McKenna at the Treasury, in the War Council in the confidence of the Liberal party & press. The coalition wh you made brings to the fore untractable forces & personalities who do not view the world as you do. The Tory dream & intention is a Tory Government. You get the unpopularity of conscription with such elements as oppose it. Others get the credit. Bonar Law particularly has greatly gained & he seems to have effectively assumed the joint Leadership of the House.

Meanwhile what is happening to the war. Germany seeks to present impenetrable fronts in France & Russia, while she raises hell in Asia. She fools us into wasting forces at Salonika & in Egypt while as usual the real movement lies elsewhere. Our initiative seems now to be a choice between two thoroughly unpromising enterprises:—viz either a concerted campaign in gt strength in the Balkans wh means consuming our manhood in killing Bulgars: or more useless slaughter here against fortifications wh daily increase in strength. Even in the air, where at least the defensive has no advantage, we have lost our ascendency. How long ago was it you wrote 'We are slouching to disaster'?

Yet it is true that if you could have had your way last January about Salonika, or in the alternative I cd have had my way last February about the Dardanelles, the whole face of the war wd have been changed. Either plan properly backed would have succeeded. The strategic conceptions were sound and all embracing: & the military forces required at the time were well within our means. The ghosts of Arras, Loos & Champagne cd have altered the history of the world.

Will last years tragedy repeat itself magnified this year? Will a half-measure campaign in the Balkans be the counterpart on a vaster scale of Gallipoli: will the next grand offensive cost us 500,000 instead of only a quarter of a million men. And all this to the tune of Islam triumphant in Asia, and at a cost of five millions a day. There is a will in the conflict. Ponder on these things.

If you come out here on Munition business, come to see me. I cd give you dinner. It is safe enough after dark—unless there is something special on.

Lloyd George did not reply to this appeal. Nor did he accept Churchill's invitation to visit the front line. But he planned to be at St Omer a few days later, and Churchill hoped to see him then. 'I am delighted LG is coming to France,' Churchill wrote to his wife on January 27, 'and I hope we shall meet. I have much to say to him.' At the same time, Churchill learned that F. E. Smith would also be in France, and would make a special effort to go right forward to Laurence Farm on the night of January 28.

Churchill did not hope for any immediate political outcome

from these visits. Both he and his wife were becoming increasingly certain that there would be no place for him in the Government until the war was over. He became more and more depressed. Clementine Churchill tried to comfort him. 'Do not fear your political Estate has now vanished,' she wrote on January 27; 'it is all waiting for you when the right moment comes which (Alas for the country) may not be till after the war—if only you come safely thro'.' On January 28, after he had seen a press report that Enver Pasha had admitted that in March 1915 Turkey had been on the verge of defeat, and could not have withstood a renewed naval attack at the Dardanelles,[11] he wrote to his wife:

. . . It is the truth: & mind you—hereafter Germans & Turks & chancy British naval officers will testify & argue that had we pushed on—we wd have got through. I shall probably get an altogether exaggerated vindication after it is no more good to me—for the purposes of directing this war. However here in the line I am absolutely happy; without care tho' not without caution.

You must not suppose that any of my depressions here have any relation to those terrible and reasonless depressions wh frighten me sometimes. I sorrow only for real things, for gt enterprises cast away needlessly—wantonly—For not having the power wh I cd use better than any other living Englishman to determine the war policy of Britain. It is painful at times: but it is bearable always. . . .

Churchill ended his letter: 'Keep in touch with those smug swine at home'; and wrote in the postscript: 'After the war I shall be friends with *Enver* & will make a gt Turkish policy with him. *Perhaps!*'

F. E. Smith could not get to Laurence Farm on the night of January 28. 'On the whole I was relieved,' Churchill wrote to his wife the next day, 'as the path across the fields to my advanced HQ is not free from random & even sometimes spiteful bullets after dark.' His new plan was to meet both F. E. Smith and Lloyd George in St Omer on Sunday January 30 or the following Mon-

[11] Churchill made no reference to the rest of Enver's statement—quoted in *The Times* on January 27—that 'even had the British ships got to Constantinople, it would not have availed them much. Our plan was to repair our army to the surrounding hills and to Asia Minor.'

day. On January 27 Clementine Churchill dined with F. E. Smith. Two days later she wrote that like Lord Robert Cecil, who had been present at the dinner, F. E. Smith had become 'an absolute mandarin & is enamoured of the Government & all its machinery'. On January 28 she had put on what she described as '3 layers of armour' and went to luncheon in Smith Square with Reginald and Pamela McKenna. Sir Ernest Cassel was among those present and, as Clementine Churchill reported to her husband, she had been 'tickled by the contrast in their attitude towards the war, the red-hot patriotism of the German & the tepid counter-jumping calculation of the Englishman'. She wrote in her letter that she was appalled when McKenna told the assembled guests that 'he wld reduce the size of the present army if he had the power', and that he planned for the future 'to pay our allies to do all the fighting while we do all the manufacturing here'. 'He really is a most noxious creature,' she commented. 'Sir Ernest & I walked away from the house much depressed. . . . I am afraid the war will go on for ever at this rate.'

Although disturbed by the lack of dynamism in high places, Churchill saw no opportunity for his return. 'I am increasingly fatalistic in my moods about things,' he wrote to his mother on January 29, '& do not worry at all at the dangers when they come.' But if the bullets did not trouble him, he could not completely accept political impotence, telling his mother:

I only fret when I think of the many things that ought to be done, & my real powers lying unused at this gt time. But the temper of the country seems admirable; & remember we have only to persevere to conquer. In grt or small station, in Cabinet or in the firing line, alive or dead my policy is 'Fight on'.

I am glad you are keeping in touch with some of my friends. I hope that FE & Ll George will pay me visits here during the next few days, & I shall thus learn how the big game does. But this existence contents me & I am happy & at peace now that we are in the line or near it. . . .

During the afternoon of January 29 a telegram reached Ploegsteert from Haig's headquarters at St Omer, informing Churchill

that F. E. Smith would be coming out to see him on the following evening. The visit went well. 'We had a jolly good meal,'
Hakewill Smith recalled, 'and then sat for hours yarning away.
Winston and FE had consumed a considerable amount of
brandy: Winston seemed all right, but FE was pretty shot when
we went to bed.'

While F. E. Smith and Churchill had been dining at the Hospice, the telephones of GHQ, the 2nd Army, the 9th Division and
the 27th Brigade were all unusually active. The cause of the com-
motion was this: while F. E. Smith had been on his way to Ploegsteert it emerged that he had not received a pass to visit the
forward zone, although he had asked for one a few days before.
Because he was in military uniform, being a Lieutenant-Colonel
in the Queen's Own Oxfordshire Hussars, he was committing a
military offence by proceeding to the front without permission.
During the evening a telegram was sent from GHQ to the Headquarters of the 2nd Army, the gist of which was: 'Sir Frederick
Smith is visiting Lt Colonel Winston Churchill. Ascertain if he has
a pass to enter forward zone. If not then supply him with one.'
Before this telegram reached the 2nd Army Headquarters it had
apparently been altered by some malicious hand, whose identity
has never been traced, and read: 'Sir Frederick Smith is visiting
Lt Colonel Winston Churchill. Ascertain if he has a pass to
enter forward zone. If not then place him under close arrest and
return him to GHQ immediately.'[12]

This order for the arrest of a Cabinet Minister was unique. At
four o'clock that morning a Provost Marshal arrived at Ploegsteert,
located the Hospice and put the Attorney-General under arrest.
F. E. Smith's expostulations were of no avail; he was driven off
to St Omer. Still under arrest, he was taken to the Hotel du Commerce and confined to a bedroom.

Churchill was bewildered by F. E. Smith's arrest. He was also
annoyed at being cheated of the long-awaited opportunity for a
political gossip. As soon as F. E. Smith had been driven off, he

[12] I am grateful to Major-General Sir Edmund Hakewill Smith for recalling the gist of these telegrams, and for much of the account of F. E.
Smith's arrest.

wrote an angry letter to Bonar Law, who had just reached St Omer with Lloyd George:

My dear Bonar,

The arrest of FE in the present circumstances seems to me to be a vy serious event. I received him here in virtue of a telegram from the ADC to the C in C transmitted to me through the HQ of the IXth Division in wh I am serving. Of this I enclose a copy. The act of placing a Cabinet Minister charged with the ultimate appeal in all Court Martial cases in arrest and removing him in conditions of indignity is one wh cannot & will not end here in France. It will become public knowledge and will draw with it many other things. I am of course resolved to take any steps wh the law allows. And I rely on you to give the subject your most earnest & immediate attention as his colleague & friend. You shd show this to Lloyd George.

Yours vy sincerely<br>Winston S.C.

At eight o'clock that morning F. E. Smith woke up at the Hotel du Commerce to find two military policemen outside his door. 'What the Hell are you doing here?' he asked them.

'We are on guard to make sure you don't leave: you are under close arrest.'

'What will you do if I leave?'

'Shoot you, sir.'

F. E. Smith then walked out of the room and left the hotel. Furious, he set about seeking redress. He forced his way into the office of the Adjutant-General, Major-General Macready;[13] but Macready merely asked: 'If you are a civilian, why are you here in uniform? If you are a soldier, why don't you obey the regulations?' F. E. Smith left Macready's headquarters with his temper unabated. He had been technically in the wrong, and was powerless to obtain redress. Nor could he know of the tampered telegram.

[13] Cecil Frederick Nevil Macready, 1862–1946. Entered Army, 1881. Major-General, 1910. Knighted, 1912. General Officer Commanding, Belfast, 1914. Adjutant-General, British Expeditionary Force, 1914–16. Member of the Army Council, 1916. Lieutenant-General, 1916. Adjutant-General to the Forces, 1916–18. General, 1918. Commissioner of the Metropolitan Police, 1918–20. Commanded the Forces in Ireland, 1920–2. Created Baronet, 1923.

Although they were actually at St Omer, Lloyd George and Bonar Law knew nothing of what had occurred during the night. Churchill's letter had not yet arrived. On the previous day they had asked Haig if they could see Churchill, and Haig had agreed. A telegram had been despatched from St Omer asking Churchill if he would meet the Minister of Munitions and the Colonial Secretary at Hazebrouck at ten o'clock that Monday morning. Churchill had for some days been looking forward to meeting Lloyd George; F. E. Smith's arrest added urgency to his journey. Hakewell Smith recalled how, at breakfast:

Winston came in very silent and very angry. There was no sign of FE. Winston demanded a car without delay. I had difficulty in getting one from Divisional HQ. 'Lt Col Winston Churchill is in no mood to be trifled with,' I said. 'It must come in twenty minutes.'

It was a bitterly cold day: about five degrees of frost. To our horror an *open* Vauxhall turned up. Winston was in no mood for badinage. 'Drive as hard as hell to Hazebrouck,' he ordered the driver.

Churchill reached Hazebrouck just before midday. Lloyd George and Bonar Law were waiting for him at Lieutenant-Colonel Newton's[14] extemporized grenade factory, unaware of F. E. Smith's arrest the night before. Churchill told them all he knew. The arrest seemed evidence that GHQ was more prepared to exert itself in order to humiliate a politician than to defeat the Germans.

Lloyd George and Bonar Law, incensed at the treatment which had been meted out to their Cabinet colleague, left the grenade factory and drove back at speed to St Omer, where they found F. E. Smith at Max Aitken's headquarters. Hakewill Smith was present at the meeting, and later recalled how 'FE was there

[14] Henry Newton, 1880–1959. Entered Territorial Force, 1902. Lieutenant-Colonel commanding 2nd Army Royal Engineer Workshops, 1915–17. Deputy Controller, Trench Warfare Department, Ministry of Munitions, 1917. Chief of Design, Mechanical Traction Department, Ministry of Munitions, 1917–19. Among his inventions were the wire-cutting Fuses Nos. 107 and 110; the Newton 6-inch Trench Mortar; the Newton Trench Mortar Bomb; the Newton Pippin rifle and hand grenades; the Newton Universal Military Tractor. Many of these inventions were manufactured at his factory in Hazebrouck.

pacing up and down like a caged lion, in a stinking temper'. Churchill calmed him, and persuaded him to tell them the full story, which he did. 'On hearing this,' Hakewill Smith recalled, 'Winston sat down in a chair and roared with laughter. FE, Bonar Law and Lloyd George then went to lunch with Haig at HQ. They had great difficulty in persuading FE to go as he regarded Haig as the source of his discomfort.' 'He came and sat on my left,' Haig wrote in his diary later that day. 'He did himself very well in the way of liquor and ended up with several glasses of old brandy! After lunch . . . he started a long story which I listened to patiently for three or four minutes, and then asked him what he really wanted. He apologised for having bothered me, and they all agreed it was best to leave the matter as it stood.' Churchill was stirred to make a bitter reflection, writing to his wife on February 1: 'Some of these potentates get more upset about an "incident" of this kind than about sending 1000 men to their deaths.'

In the early afternoon of January 31, Lloyd George, Bonar Law, and F. E. Smith returned to Max Aitken's headquarters, where Churchill awaited them. So many politicians, all of them critics or opponents of Asquith, could not avoid a lengthy political discussion. None of the participants wrote about it afterwards, but Hakewill Smith later recalled that there had been 'full and complete agreement that Asquith had to be got rid of at all costs'. Three of those present were members of Asquith's Cabinet. Lloyd George had hinted that his aim was to become Secretary of State for War. 'I hope he will get it,' Churchill wrote to his wife on February 1, giving as his opinion that the War Office needed 'a civilian's drive & the leadership of a gifted man.' Churchill felt that the politicians who had met accidentally at St Omer were an obvious nucleus of a future government; one in which he believed he would almost certainly find a place. 'The group I want to work with & form into an effective Government instrument,' he wrote to his wife, 'is LG: FE: BL: Carson: & Curzon. Keep that steadily in mind. It is the alternative Government when "wait & see" is over.'

While they were at St Omer, Lloyd George and Bonar Law did

Churchill a service which contrasted with Asquith's earlier action. When they saw Haig they told him, as Churchill reported to his wife, 'that if he saw fit to give me a Brigade there wd be no difficulty at home'. This friendly gesture reinforced Churchill's belief that he could rely on Lloyd George and work with him. He still felt that he could do nothing until Asquith were overthrown; but he now saw the makings of a coalition which might lead to just such an end. Politics remained uppermost in his mind. 'My dislike of Asquith & all his works grows steadily,' he wrote to his wife on February 2; 'He is a fatal drag on our success.' That same day Clementine Churchill lunched with Lloyd George, hoping, she wrote, 'to glean from him news of you'. But she learned little, as there were others present. Her dislike of Lloyd George was unabated. 'I don't trust him one bit,' she wrote; 'fair of speech, shifty of eye, treacherous of heart. . . . You may *have* to work with him but never trust him—If he does not do you in he will at any rate "let you down".'

Lloyd George was to open one of Clementine Churchill's YMCA canteens on the following day, at Ponders End. After lunching with him she sent him some notes about the canteens, to help him with his speech. 'I wanted to ask you so much more about Winston,' she wrote in her postscript, 'but I felt shy before company!' Lloyd George spoke to two thousand munitions workers, 'packed like sardines on the workshop floor', Clementine Churchill reported to her husband on February 4. 'They did not cheer when they saw LlG,' she wrote, 'but (don't say I said so) they gave me a beautiful cheer.' Clementine Churchill complained to her husband about Lloyd George's speech. 'The shabby little tike,' she wrote, 'altho' he said he had just returned from the Front never mentioned your name.' Lloyd George had told her privately that Curzon was anxious to become Air Minister, adding: 'I am so surprised . . . I thought perhaps Winston might have done it—do you think he would have liked it?' To this Clementine Churchill had replied: 'Winston would do it better than anyone else.' But Lloyd George said nothing further on the subject. 'This ungenerous cautious streak in his nature,' Clementine Churchill wrote to her husband, 'will in his old age which is fast approaching leave him lonely & friendless—Ishmael! I do not think *you* will ever need him, *he* will need you when he is on the down gradient—& of course you will help him and he knows it.' Frances Stevenson had accompanied Lloyd George to Ponders End. In her diary she wrote of another visiter to the ceremony:

Much to everyone's surprise, Mrs Bonham Carter (Miss Asquith) turned up, though as far as we can make out she had not been invited. D [Lloyd George] is of the opinion that she turned up expecting to see a row. It appears that even Mrs Churchill was uneasy as to how the meeting would go off, as many of the workers are hostile to him at the present moment. . . . 'The Asquiths and their friends are boasting,' said D to me, 'that Lloyd George cannot hold a meeting with the workers now.' However, she was unpleasantly surprised if she came with that object. One of the speakers referred to D as the man of the moment, & one of the audience shouted: 'Put him in Asquith's place!' . . .

However, Mrs A herself has been heard to declare that 'Nothing but God Almighty himself will drive Herbert out of Downing Street.'[15]

Lloyd George and Clementine Churchill drove back together from Ponders End to London. She sent her husband an account of the drive. Lloyd George had made a poor impression upon her. She contrasted his shabbiness and tiredness with their own strength and vitality. She knew that Lloyd George understood what was in her mind: that he would need her husband in the future, and that in any future scandal such as the Marconi affair, Churchill could be relied upon to help him. The drive with Lloyd George had made her more hopeful about her husband's future. 'I know (DV),' she wrote, 'that you will come back rejuvenated & strengthened from the War & dominate all these decrepit, exhausted politicians.' She ended her letter with a further word for Asquith, still believing that her husband's political future might depend as much upon Asquith's goodwill as upon Lloyd George

[15] A view satirized by Max Beerbohm during 1916:

> Filled through and through with British phlegm
> (than which no phlegm is phlegmier)
> He seems quite likely to be sem-
> piternally our Premier

and the anti-Government forces. 'Don't close your mind to the PM entirely,' she wrote. 'He is lazy but (or perhaps therefore) healthy & anyhow he is not a skunk tho' a wily old tortoise. I must meet him this week and tweak his ear.'

Among Asquith's most vociferous critics in London was Lord Fisher. Churchill knew that Fisher led a faction of discontent, and that he still hoped to return to the Admiralty, for the third time, as First Sea Lord. He believed that if Fisher's opposition were ever to reach serious proportions, Asquith would take effective action. 'I am rather anxious about old Fisher,' he wrote to his wife on February 2. 'I cannot trust the PM not to put him back. He & his press are vy active now. The general apathy at the Admiralty naturally excites dissatisfaction. Fisher without me to manage him wd be disastrous.' Churchill still believed that Fisher could not be trusted to act alone; but in January 1916 the chances of the two men working together again were remote.

Writing to Hankey on January 7, Fisher insisted upon a change of Government as the prerequisite for his return:

I had an illuminating visit here yesterday from George Lambert MP late Civil Lord corroborating two visits from Lord Northcliffe (—the two as you know being as opposite as the poles are asunder!) in anticipating a big uprising of feeling in the country involving big chances in our conduct of the war. . . .

For myself I tell them and many others in reply to multitudes of letters that it appears to me that Asquith & Balfour are such astute Parliamentarians that no one will turn them out & they are irremovable! That's my belief—*and so long as they are in I shall be out!* . . .

There is certainly apathy in the Admiralty and our shipyards are empty and the Germans will give us shortly a Big Naval Surprise I think!

On January 26 Fisher wrote to Hankey again to complain about 'the very sad "INERTIA"' which he saw all about him. 'I am getting very sick of it,' Fisher wrote, 'and am contemplating some action.' In his postscript he added: 'The Prime Minister saw me in the Lobby of the House of Commons 3 days ago. . . . He asked about the Naval Situation! I said what was required was *"Push and Go"!* (NOT *"Wait and See"!*). On that he left me! What a lot of

old women of both sexes are leading us to ruin!' On the following day Fisher wrote yet again:

*Please burn.*
. . . It is no use my talking to the Prime Minister—as he would only
pass me on to Balfour who would involve me in subtle dialectics and
in philosophic doubts! . . . I know perfectly well I could entirely
change the face of the Naval situation! YES. COMPLETELY ENTHUSE
IT! *instead of the present despair!* King Herod was smitten with worms
for bragging so I'm not going to be such an ass! but I have not yet
been wrong in any one little detail since June 10 1902 when I became
Second Sea Lord!

Fisher enlisted two newspaper editors in his quest for action,
J. L. Garvin of the *Observer* and C. P. Scott of the *Manchester
Guardian.* Throughout January and February the Admiral cast
about for some means to return to the centre of naval and national
affairs. 'We want another plan,' he wrote to Lloyd George at the
beginning of January; 'none exists! I am not sure even of our coming sea supremacy!' On January 14 he reported to the former
Civil Lord of Admiralty, George Lambert, that Geoffrey Robinson,
the editor of *The Times,* 'asked to see me urgently yesterday, and
he remained two hours', while Bonar Law also was 'very anxious'
to see him. But Fisher knew, as he told Lambert, that as long as
Asquith and Balfour—'Wait and See' and the 'philosophic
doubter'—were still in office, 'I am out of it!' This did not deflate
his energies. Early in February he wrote to Bonar Law: 'I propose at an early date to take a drastic step to make the country
acquainted with my views. I think I have a case that will necessitate a change.' To C. P. Scott he wrote bitterly on February 2 of
Bonar Law's lethargy, at the same time announcing that '*A BIG
SMASH IS IMMINENT! A FATAL SMASH.*' Fisher was desperate to return to the centre of war-making policy. Inaction was
anathema to him. He felt, he informed Lambert, like Elijah, 'discarded, cast out'. On February 3 he wrote direct to Asquith warning that 'there is grave anxiety and serious misgiving in the Fleet
both as to the conduct of the war at sea as well as in the provision
for the same'. On February 8 he informed Jellicoe that 'yesterday

Hankey came to see me, as he thinks the state of lethargy at the Admiralty is serious'. He also told Jellicoe that he intended to announce 'shortly' in the House of Lords that Balfour's naval administration was 'fraught with vital danger'. In a second letter to Jellicoe on February 8 he used the words: 'If I should become First Lord, which don't seem likely to me (though others think so). . . .'

Fisher believed that it was only Churchill, from whom he had parted so precipitately and with such disastrous results for both of them, who knew his true worth. Churchill's willingness to resign in October 1914 if Fisher were not brought back to the Admiralty had made a deep impression on him. On February 14 he wrote to Lambert that it was the King alone who had stood in his path at that time, and that 'the whole crew, Lloyd George, Bonar Law, Jellicoe, Carson—whatever good intentions—have not the courage of Winston, who said "you be d——d"!'

It was assumed by all that after the disaster of May 1915 neither Churchill nor Fisher would wish to see the other again. Only Clementine Churchill realized that the bond between Fisher and her husband was intimate and indestructible. She dreaded a reunion, knowing how much her husband was excited by Fisher's very presence, and fearing that the old Admiral would poison his judgement, and tempt him to unwise actions. At the beginning of February Churchill had no reason to believe that his path and Fisher's might cross again. He still professed scorn, verging on contempt, for what Fisher had done to him the previous May. He could see no immediate political future for himself, no grouping yet ready to challenge Asquith's control, no sphere in which he might make his mark. 'I wish I could do more,' he wrote to his wife on February 4, 'but after all, I have kept nothing back.' He was at Laurence Farm, drawing up schemes for the defence of his Battalion's front. The needs of his seven hundred men were for the time being uppermost in his mind.

On February 5 Churchill's sister-in-law Nellie Romilly wrote to him of an American schoolboy howler that she had read in the *Daily Mail* on the previous day: ' "Who is Prime Minister of England?" Unanimous reply: "Winston Churchill." ' On February 8

a cutting from a German newspaper, rejoicing that Churchill was
no longer in office, reached him at Laurence Farm. These pieces
of news set him thinking again about his resignation from the
Cabinet in November, and about Fisher. 'While I never doubt the
wisdom of my decision to quit office,' he wrote to his wife on February 8, 'I writhe daily at the lack of power to make things move.
And so I am sure does the old Malay. The time may come when
I shall feel it my duty to go home & make an effective opposition.
But not yet.' The letters he received continued to stir him. 'I
think that the Admiralty has lost all initiative and push since
your departure,' the Duke of Marlborough wrote on February 7,
'and a complete static selfish atmosphere seems to prevail in that
Department. An atmosphere congenial to AJB's temperament. It
is a pity you are not there to give the officials some inspiration.'

Churchill speculated about his political future. It was not very
hopeful. The bulk of the Tory Party remained hostile to him; nor
was there any evidence that his brief encounter with Bonar Law
at Hazebrouck and St Omer had resulted in a change in the Conservative Leader's unsympathetic attitude towards him. The Liberal backbenchers continued to doubt his reliability; many of
them had by February 1916 been convinced, some by Reginald
McKenna, some by the backbencher W. M. R. Pringle, that
Churchill had intrigued with Sir John French to publicize the
'shell scandal' of May 1915. There remained nevertheless a small
group of public men who thought highly of Churchill's abilities,
and wanted them used in Government.

On February 6, J. L. Garvin appealed in the *Observer* for a
rearrangement of the Government and a more effective war-
making Cabinet, giving as his prescription for success that Churchill should become Air Minister and Fisher return to the Admiralty
as First Lord. Garvin believed that Churchill and Fisher could
work together once more. He felt that these two in tandem ought
to be in the Cabinet. He hoped that his suggestion would be
widely enough supported to lead to Balfour's removal from the
Admiralty. Both Churchill and his wife were taken quite by surprise by Garvin's article. Clementine Churchill was worried
because Fisher's name had been linked with her husband's in

Garvin's appeal. For her, this was a disaster, not an opportunity; a threat that her husband's return to politics might take place only in some unsuitable and cabalistic combination rather than on its own merits, and with the minimum of controversy. 'I cannot gauge the Fisher danger,' she wrote on February 8; 'He is certainly very active and has a good press, but neither Asquith nor Balfour can possibly want him back—I expect however that some fancy post will be found for him to satisfy the ignorant and famishing public.'

It was not until February 10 that Churchill was able to read the text of Garvin's appeal in the *Observer*. It did not convince him. 'I do not think they will want me for Air,' he wrote to his wife that day. 'The view I take of my duty, renders me powerless at present, as a critic of the government, & consequently Asquith can afford to let me alone. He knows this & will act quite naturally upon it. Garvin's article was vy friendly & I am touched by his loyalty: but it will not count in the decision.'

Parliament was shortly to reassemble, and in the Debate on the Address it was open to any critic of the Government to challenge Asquith's conduct of the war. Had Churchill wished to take this opportunity, there were undoubtedly those who would have been willing to help him gather the necessary material, naval, military, and diplomatic. He believed that with preparation he could rise in the House of Commons, the soldier returned from the trenches, the 'escaped scapegoat' come to demand retribution, the patriot seeking to save his country from ignominious defeat, and that by his speech he could bring together all the disparate elements of dissatisfaction. 'I have meditated profoundly on whether I shd come home,' he wrote to his wife on February 11; '. . . I have decided against it—tho' sorely tempted. The time has not yet come —nor the occasion.'

From the beginning of the year a number of very different, and previously hostile and competing groups, had united in the hope of gaining political advantage from the public dissatisfaction with the conduct of the war. Many of the leading newspaper proprietors were critical of Asquith's leadership. Lord Northcliffe believed that the war would last for at least another five years if

Asquith remained at the helm. Three leading editors, C. P. Scott, J. L. Garvin and Robert Donald, were tired of trying to criticize the Government while at the same time having no formal opposition behind which they could throw their support. Lloyd George sensed and reflected the discontent. On January 5 Sir George Riddell, who had spent the day with him, recorded in his *War Diary* Lloyd George's remarks: 'Opposition is in the blood of the people. They must conduct their affairs on those lines. At present they want a leader to voice their views.' Who that leader was to be, no one knew. In January it had seemed that Sir Edward Carson might come forward as an opposition figure capable of offering an alternative to Asquith. But the public did not respond readily to Carson, whose support never spread much beyond the Conservative backbenchers in the House of Commons. Nor had Carson shown evidence of executive ability, upon which so much of a successful war administration must depend.

When Lloyd George lunched with Riddell on February 11 he declared that Fisher ought to be brought back into the Government, though he could not see in what capacity. Lloyd George told Riddell: 'Fisher has a genius for war.'

On February 16, in a debate in the House of Commons on air-raid defence, the Government was severely criticized for not taking adequate measures to protect the civilian population against the increasingly frequent German Zeppelin attacks. Lloyd George told Riddell at breakfast the next morning that had a division been taken, the Government would probably have been defeated. He went on to say that he believed that Churchill should have been made head of an air-raid defence department, but that Asquith would not have it.

Stimulated by Garvin's open support, Fisher and his friends continued to search for some means of influencing Government policy. 'We are at the very blackest period of the war,' Fisher wrote to Garvin on February 19. On the same day he informed C. P. Scott that Northcliffe had been to see him a few weeks before, 'and told me it was essential and vital I should be back, and he intended to have me back!' On February 22 Lambert told the House of Commons that it was 'almost a disaster at the Admiralty' to continue without Fisher as First Sea Lord. To Hankey, on March 2 Fisher wrote: 'No amount of Cabinet or War Council instructions are of the slightest use if those who have to carry them out are totally wanting in "push" and initiative. There must be ginger at the top if you want ginger at the bottom!'

Fisher's supporters could not overcome the fact that the Admiral alone did not constitute a political force. The public may still have believed that only Fisher could restore the Navy to its earlier pitch of readiness and resolve. But in the political arena, in Whitehall and in the Houses of Parliament, Fisher had little strength. A politician was needed to bring together the widely scattered forces of discontent. Yet there was no politician willing to take the lead. Asquith's skill in creating his coalition of May 1915 had neutralized the Conservative opposition without alienating any but the fringe of his Liberal majority. When Riddell had tea with Lloyd George on February 26 he learned of Lloyd George's continuing unease at the conduct of the war. 'He says the PM never moves until he is forced, and then it is usually too late,' Riddell recorded in his *War Diary*. 'He fears we shall not improve matters until we get another leader. He says that at a time like this the PM should lead, not follow. . . . He says Asquith will not face unpleasant facts.' Lloyd George spoke of the possibility of resigning, but told Riddell that because of war secrecy he would be unable to give his specific reasons for doing so.

Churchill knew nothing of Fisher's activities and little of Lloyd George's discontent. On February 13, on reading an attack on Fisher in the *Morning Post*, he wrote to his wife: 'I expect the old rogue will realise increasingly as time passes the folly of his action. Together we cd have ridden out every gale, & sure of our strength, we cd have afforded to run those risks wh alone open the gate to victory.' It was two weeks since the St Omer meeting, two weeks of heavy and continual problems in his Battalion's sector: 'I never expected to be so completely involved in the military machine,' he wrote. The news that Curzon might be made Air Minister prompted him to write to his wife on February 14: 'Well I do not care. I cd have done it well. But I am under the vague displeasure

of the press: & Asquith's interests as I told you will best be served
by my disappearance temporary or final. But I must confess it
riles me to see how ungrateful they are. But for my personal
struggles we shd not have had *half* the air service we have today.'

The time had come for Churchill to make arrangements for
leave, which he expected to take when his Battalion left the
trenches on March 2. He would then have seven days, which, he
wrote to his wife on February 15, 'is the only leave I shall get for
another 3 months'. He felt that it was therefore important for
him 'to see various people: and I shall take decisions about my
future plans. . . . I shall review the situation & consider what I
ought to do.' On February 16 he received an account of the first
trial of the 'tank' from the Director of Naval Construction, Eustace Tennyson-d'Eyncourt. 'You see this idea is bearing fruit,' he
wrote to his wife. '. . . But what a toil to get anything done! And
how powerless I am! Are they not fools not to use my mind—or
knaves to wait for its destruction by some flying splinter? I do not
fear death or wounds, & I like the daily life out here; but their
impudence & complaisance makes me quite spiteful sometimes.'
During the week before his leave Churchill received a long
political letter from his cousin Lord Wimborne, written on February 15. It held out no encouragement to him personally. 'I think
this Govt are active and determined,' wrote Wimborne; 'not very
prescient perhaps, but dogged and tenacious and are getting
bolder too.' Wimborne saw no further opening for Churchill in
politics while the war was on. His letter continued: 'But the war
must end some day and then the fun will begin. . . . Then will
be the moment for a real broad national policy and for the *man*
to advocate it.' Churchill did not want to contemplate so distant
a future. His one desire was to be asked to take his part again at
the centre or war policy. In a letter written on February 14, describing the first testing of the tank, Tennyson d'Eyncourt had
explained to Churchill: 'After losing the great advantage of your
influence, I had considerable difficulty in steering the scheme past
the rocks of opposition & the more insidious shoals of apathy,
wh are frequented by red herrings wh cross the main line of

progress at frequent intervals'. Churchill felt stirred by this to write direct to Asquith, for the first time in three months, urging him to give the fullest encouragement to d'Eyncourt's activities. 'It interested me very much,' Asquith replied, not to Churchill but to Churchill's wife, on February 19. 'I have heard a great deal about the Caterpillar from those who have seen it on trial, and we hope great things from it.' There was no encouragement here for someone seeking office and responsibility.

Towards the end of February Churchill became increasingly angry at the repeated criticisms in the *Morning Post*, and other Conservative newspapers, which claimed that it was his neglect while First Lord of the Admiralty that was responsible for the lack of air defence against the Zeppelin. This press criticism revived his idea of making some political speech when he came home on leave, in order to defend himself against these allegations. 'The newspapers not knowing the facts,' he wrote to his wife on February 18, 'continue to carp mechanically about the air & my responsibility. On my return I may perhaps deal fully with the whole subject. I intend to take my seat on the Front Opposition Bench—but shall not decide on any action yet.'

Churchill was disappointed to hear from his wife that on her latest visit to the Prime Minister at Walmer Castle there had been no political talk; Asquith clearly had no intention to ask him back into the Government. Clementine Churchill echoed Lord Wimborne's sentiments when she wrote on February 16, 'I am sure you will return to power after the war with increased prestige.' But Churchill did not wish to wait until the war was over. He was frequently distraught by the fear that the war might actually be lost, and by his profound belief that if the situation worsened, his presence could turn the balance from defeat to victory.

Rather than stimulating his political thoughts, the approach of leave seemed to make Churchill more detached and wistful. Reading a rumour that Balfour was about to abolish the Royal Naval Division, he wrote to his wife on February 22, more in sorrow than in anger, of the activities of his successor as First Lord, 'the old grey tabby', as he called him: 'How easy to destroy. How hard to build. How easy to evacuate, how hard to capture. How easy to do nothing. How hard to achieve anything. War is action, energy & hazard. These sheep only want to browse among the daisies.'

On February 19 Clementine Churchill wrote that if he would send her a list of people, 'I will make some little dinner parties in your honour.' His reply on February 22 was more concerned with his painting and his private life than with politics:

You must parcel out the days as well as possible. I will have one dinner at my mother's, at least 3 at home, 2 plays alone with you & one man's dinner out somewhere. Make up a programme on these lines. Also lunches & try to work in all my friends. You can let people know that I am coming home for a week. I leave it all to you. One night I expect to go to the National Liberal Club for the unveiling of my portrait & here I may make a speech. . . .

I will be vy good & keep all my engagements punctually. Time is so short. . . . I put it all in your hands my dearest soul. Arrange whatever you like to amuse us both the most. I much prefer people coming to dine with me than dining out with them. I want to have at least one day's painting in Lavery's studio. Do you know I think that will be a gt pleasure & resource to me if I come through all right.

Before returning to England Churchill received two letters sent from London on February 25. The first, from his wife, contained an account of the dinner arrangements which she had made to entertain the Prime Minister and his wife that evening at 41 Cromwell Road: 'I have had to work like a beaver to get together the 8 indispensable bridge players which are necessary for their comfort and happiness.' It was to be an entirely social occasion, with Lady Gwendeline Churchill, Lord Wimborne and Sir Ernest Cassel among the guests. The second letter from London was from F. E. Smith. Like Wimborne's letter earlier in the month it did not offer Churchill much political hope. 'The Government,' wrote F. E. Smith, 'is not popular but indispensable & I think that the PM is firmer in the saddle than ever. LG is still very much alone.' F. E. Smith, who did not know that Churchill's leave was almost due, encouraged him to return. 'Do come soon,' he wrote. 'I am sure it is a good thing to turn up at the proper intervals & see people.'

Churchill crossed over to England on the evening of March 2. It was not until he reached London that he discovered that Balfour was to introduce the Naval Estimates in the House of Commons on March 7. Suddenly his path seemed clear to him. He would speak in the debate; he would castigate the naval policy of his successor, defend his own record over aerial defence, and outline an effective policy against the Zeppelin. He would show that it was he, not Balfour, who had a true grasp of what was needed in order to avoid disaster at sea and in the air. Throughout Friday March 3 he worked at his speech. His plans for leisure were put aside. He gave up the idea of unveiling his portrait at the National Liberal Club.[16] That night he dined with his mother, who had invited those whom she thought might help him in his attack on the Government. C. P. Scott had been summoned from Manchester by telegram. Garvin and F. E. Smith were also there. Another guest was Sir Francis Hopwood, who had retained his position as Additional Civil Lord of Admiralty on Balfour's Board. Three months later Hopwood gave his recollection of the dinner to Prince Louis, who noted:

That Friday evening Lady Randolph gave a dinner, which included Hopwood, Garvin and several other public men. To these Churchill delivered his speech, which began by recommending the evacuation of Salonika, suggesting other uses for these troops etc. This part of the speech he afterwards dropped on the advice of friends present. Not one word was said about Fisher in this rehearsal, but to Hopwood, who was the last to leave, C suddenly said that he would teach that d——d old Oriental scoundrel F what it meant to quarrel with him.

In *Winston Churchill As I Knew Him* Violet Bonham Carter recalled that she had heard later that Lady Randolph's guests

[16] The portrait had been painted in the autumn of 1915 by Ernest Townsend, paid for by an anonymous donor. It was ready for presentation on 20 December 1915, and was hung temporarily in a Club Committee Room until such time as Churchill could unveil it. No opportunity was found for the ceremony. In 1921, when Churchill was no longer *persona grata* with the National Liberal Club, the Club decided that his portrait should be 'packed and stored in some dry place'. During the Second World War it was taken out of storage and rehung; almost immediately it was damaged by bomb blast. After being restored, it was finally unveiled by Churchill himself in 1941.

were said to have told Churchill that he was 'the *homme néces-saire* who alone could save a rapidly deteriorating situation' and that they had urged him 'to take action and lead an Opposition in Parliament'. Churchill had intended no such opposition. He wished to make use of the coincidence of his return to warn the House of Commons that all was not well in the naval war, and to defend his own past actions. But for some of those present at Lady Randolph's dinner, Churchill's decision to speak out against the Government seemed an opportunity of a more decisive sort. Garvin and Scott were the partisans of Lord Fisher. They were the men who had for two months urged Fisher's return to the Admiralty, believing that he still possessed energies and insights for which there was no substitute. Churchill's willingness to speak out seemed to them to provide the opportunity for Fisher to emerge again. But Fisher and Churchill had first to be brought together. Churchill's assertion to Hopwood that he would destroy Fisher once and for all was his last hostile outburst. Fisher's friends arranged a meeting between them. To Clementine Churchill's horror, Fisher was invited to lunch at 41 Cromwell Road. F. E. Smith was also present. There is evidence in F. E. Smith's letter of February 25 to Churchill that at the time of his arrest in January the two men had discussed this very possibility of an accommodation with Fisher, and that F. E. Smith himself had acted as an instrument of reconciliation, through his friend Sir Edward Goulding. 'It has not at present been found possible to do anything for our friend,' F. E. Smith had written, 'nor did Garvin, as usual impetuous, help much by premature publicity. . . . I conveyed your wishes I think with discretion about Fisher to Paddy [Goulding] & he tells me all has been made very plain without committing you.'

F. E. Smith told Margot Asquith about the luncheon, and she told Violet Bonham Carter, who wrote in her book: 'I knew what agony this must have been to Clemmie, who had no illusions about Fisher or the ruin he had brought to Winston's fortunes. According to FE she had said to Fisher at luncheon, "Keep your hands off my husband. You have all but ruined him once. Leave him alone now."' On the evening of March 5 Fisher and Churchill met again. Churchill read Fisher the speech which he proposed to make during the Naval Estimates debate. Not only did he intend to attack Balfour's conduct of naval affairs; he had also decided that he would end his speech with an appeal for Fisher's immediate return as First Sea Lord. By this appeal Churchill was determined to show Parliament that he was not a man to harbour rancour or malice; that he could overcome his hostility towards his former opponent in the national interest, and for the sake of the war. Fisher was exhilarated by this extraordinary change in their relationship; for him it was a return to the friendship and excitement of earlier times. Churchill was going to bring him back once more. In the early hours of the following morning he wrote feverishly:

*4 a.m.!! The Early Bird!*
YOU are the *late one!!*
My dear Winston,

I've slept over what you said to me last night—It's THE epoch of your Life!——

I am going to be the humble instrument! So magnificent, a proof OF YOUR SOLE OBJECT BEING THE WAR will have (*justly*) an *immense* effect on your popularity. Ride in on the crest of that Popularity! THE WAR—THE WHOLE WAR—AND NOTHING BUT THE WAR! Do you imagine that if you got up and said '*What are over* half a million of *our* men doing *now* in an unattackable Egypt and in a Salonika where we are being fooled by a few Austrians—*when these half a million men in France are of vital consequence?* Do you imagine you would not topple over the whole present gang? and also ask what a big British Fleet is NOW doing in the Mediterranean? *when the grand Fleet is in danger!!!*' . . .

The Reason the Government are strong is THERE IS NO OPPOSITION LEADER! *Get up every night and batter the box from the Opposition Bench!* No use your sending up one Rocket and then going to have your head '*bashed in*' at the Trenches! Go the whole Hog! *Totus Porcus! Salvation—Here* and *Now!* I repeat what I have said behind your back. *There is no one in it with you to conduct the War—and you can be Prime Minister if you like!*

*'THE NAVY IN DANGER' IS THE CRY!* TAKE YOUR OATH, if I ONCE
GET IN THERE *WILL BE HELL TILL YOU GET IN!*
I say this from *PURE* belief the present mob are absolutely effete!
*Audacity* and *Imagination* are the requirements of successful war—
*THEY DON'T NOW EXIST!* It's *NOT* 'Wait and See' we want but
'*Push and Go!* Not '*Asquith and Balfour*', but *Winston and*—'.
May I criticise?

> ('In angels faults conspicuous grow
> The smallest speck is seen in snow')

I think it's too long—your air portion of your speech—it's too much of
an apology *and not enough of an Attack!* Say this:—
In the 9 months since you left why have not aeroplanes and sea-
planes carried in small craft and submarines been pushed forward?
The Aeroplane is the *ONLY* antidote to the zeppelin. Emphasise the
zeppelin menace to the Grand Fleet. The new Zep. has a radius of
600 miles! So why why why has not the aeroplane been developed?
I don't think you say enough of the frightful menace to the Grand
Fleet of the new Big German submarines—you can be vague and misty
about it but you want to be more mysteriously alarmed!
'Omne ignotum pro magnifico'!
Finally this is absolute fact!
To *win the War and with no other heartfeeling do we two coalesce!
We can do it! Come on!*

Yours as heretofore
Fisher

I am at Berkeley Square the *WHOLE*
day if you want me. I am not          My telephone number
going to leave the house.             is Gerrard 8795

Churchill had one more day to reflect upon the course which
he had decided to take. Among those who encouraged him to
speak in the naval debate were three Liberal MPs who despaired
of Asquith's leadership; Sir Henry Dalziel,[17] Sir Arthur Mark-

[17] James Henry Dalziel, 1868–1935. Radical journalist. Liberal MP, 1892–
1921. Chairman and Managing Director of United Newspapers Ltd; owner
of *Reynolds Weekly Newspaper* and the *Pall Mall Gazette.* Knighted, 1908.
Chairman of the Committee in charge of German prisoners, 1914–18. Helped
Lloyd George to buy the *Daily Chronicle,* 1918. Created Baron Dalziel of
Kirkcaldy, 1921.

ham,[18] and Sir Alfred Mond:[19] all were friends of Lloyd George.

That afternoon Fisher asked C. P. Scott to strengthen Churchill's resolve to make his speech, and to lead the opposition to Balfour. Fisher warned Scott, as the latter noted, that Clementine Churchill differed from her husband and 'insisted' that he should return to France. Scott went to 41 Cromwell Road, where for more than an hour he tried to persuade Churchill that his place was at Westminster. Scott recorded:

I urged that on political grounds there could be no question that he would be more useful in Parliament—that as regards the navy there was not a day to be lost in making the great and acknowledged deficiencies and the whole movement for that and also for vitalising the army, as to which he had strong views, would collapse if he left. He and Lloyd George and Carson were the only three men in the front rank with the instinct for action and capacity for carrying on a great war. Carson was ill, George was for the time being under a cloud and Churchill alone remained. Mrs Churchill was evidently uneasy but acquiesced and Churchill virtually decided to resign his commission.

He then read me the full notes for his speech which wound up dramatically with the demand for the recall of Lord Fisher. He was satisfied with it himself and said if it were the last he was ever to deliver he would be content to stand by it and that was the final test. I found nothing to object to, but Mrs Churchill thought it went at one part rather too much into details which had better not be made public. Churchill said he thought he had better give the Prime Minister notice of what he meant to do (and he would no doubt inform Balfour) so that it might not be said he had taken the Government by surprise. He had asked to see the Prime Minister that afternoon, but had not yet had an answer. In any case Asquith was coming to dinner and he could tell him then that he meant to ask for Fisher's recall, but was not anxious to say more and so bring down protests.

[18] Arthur Basil Markham, 1866–1916. Liberal MP, 1900–16. Created Baronet, 1911. He died on 7 August 1916.

[19] Alfred Moritz Mond, 1868–1930. Industrialist and financier. Liberal MP, 1910–26. Created Baronet, 1910. First Commissioner of Works, December 1916–21. Joined the Conservative Party, 1926. Created Baron Melchett, 1928.

He was not aiming at anything for himself but only at getting what was necessary done. Six months abroad had 'cleaned' him. He had come in contact with the crude realities of life and escape from the atmosphere of scheming and intrigue. Had learned to see things more simply. He had missed the means of self-expression, but on the whole the time of absence had been one of the most contented of his life. He seemed to be indeed stronger and saner than before he went out.

Fisher sent one further exhortation on March 6:

Dear Winston,

If you dont follow my advice *then* your Future is *RUINED!* DON'T GO BACK! *Stick to* THE BOX OF THE LEADER OF THE OPPOSITION— your last words are splendid!!

'*I feel events are so grave in the Navy that my duty is* HERE *with* HEALTHY *not* HOSTILE *criticism*'!

*IT IS NOT TOO LATE!! THEREFORE* I SPEAK! ! Otherwise I would have held my tongue. Let me as First Sea Lord be a subsidiary matter —the one to see NOT ONLY the old programme completed but to take fresh gigantic steps for fresh gigantic doings with Big Conceptions that will end the War! *You Winston Churchill yourself ask for nothing! Simply you are there to help!* and feel more use at the opposition leaders box than the unwilling partner of an effete conduct of the war!!!

Yours

STICK TO THIS!

F

Don't let Asquith know.

That night Asquith and his wife dined with the Churchills at 41 Cromwell Road. Churchill made no secret of his intentions to speak in the debate. He said nothing about his detailed criticisms, but did say that he intended to demand Fisher's return. Asquith's daughter Violet Bonham Carter wrote in *Winston Churchill As I Knew Him:*

When they returned from this dinner-party Margot, who had sat next to him, told me that she had said to him that she was sorry he was going to speak in the debate and that he had replied 'with a glare in his eye': that he had 'a good deal of importance to say about the Navy'. She said that she then told him what a 'fine exit' he had made, giving up money and position, taking his place with his fellows and risking his life for his country, and added, 'Don't go and spoil it all.' Later he asked her whether she thought a proper Opposition in the House of Commons would be a good, or a bad, thing for the country. She said she could not see the elements of a good Opposition in Dalziel, Markham, Mond, Carson, etc, and added that she could not see him co-operating with the Simon group.[20] . . . She was convinced that Winston was 'dreaming of an amazing Opposition which he was to lead'.

My father told me that he had had a short private talk with Winston after dinner and feared that he was going to make a most unwise speech which could do him nothing but harm. He had done his best to dissuade him from it but evidently felt that he had failed. I said that I was surprised at not having had a word or a sign from him since he got back. My father replied, 'That doesn't surprise me in the least in view of his intentions.'

After breakfast on the morning of March 7 C. P. Scott called on Churchill, recording in his note of the conversation: 'He evidently felt he was in for a serious enterprise, said he knew he should have to face obloquy, but once launched on an enterprise he could never hold back.' Churchill told Scott that making this speech 'needed more courage than the war of the trenches'. He went on to say that he had not yet finally decided 'whether to stay or return to France. It would partly depend on how things went today. He wished he could be here a week hence for the Army Estimates. He had a good deal to say on the Army administration which was in many ways old-fashioned and unenterprising. Our Army telephones for instance—a vital matter—were mere toys compared to the Germans.' Fisher lost no opportunity during the last hours to excite Churchill's mind and seek to push him forward, having convinced himself that even the Premiership was within Churchill's grasp. On the morning of March 7, while Churchill was putting the finishing touches to his speech, Fisher wrote once more:

[20] A small group of Liberal MPs who, after Sir John Simon's resignation in January 1915, had united to oppose conscription. In May 1915 they voted against the Military Service Bill.

My Dear Winston—

Please forgive my d—d reiteration but I am terribly afraid of the Asquithian cajolery! (*am I already too late?*)

Providence has placed the Plum bang in your mouth, *Certain Prime Minister!*

You have no Rival as Leader of the Opposition and Such a Cry for assuming the position! ! ! ! so PATRIOTIC! ! ! !

'*The Navy in Danger*'

'*But not "TOO LATE" for Safety*'

Ask George Lambert to tell you the inner history of the late East End Election when BOTH the Election Machines working furiously only just avoided defeat 300 Votes! 151 men in that huge constituency could have beaten the Coalition Government![21] *There is seething and wide-spread discontent at the conduct of the War!*

But the People see no one as a new Leader!

There is the Cave of Adullam but no David has come along!

See the 1st Book of Samuel Chap 22 Verse 2

'He became a Captain over them'

'And there with him about 400 Men'!

AINT THAT A GOOD MAJORITY FOR YOU?

SO DONT GO BACK!

Never leave that Box—once you have banged it as you will this afternoon—As meek as Moses you'll say your mission is to help!

YES! Help the War!

YES! 'BIG CONCEPTIONS! QUICK DECISIONS!'

That will be your War Cry!

'THINK IN OCEANS'!

SHOOT AT SIGHT!

That will be your action!

Go in and Win!

Dont Falter

'Aut Caesar Aut Nullus'

*accept no post in this Government*

*They are doomed!*

*Fate has you in it's Grasp!*

*Dont wriggle out of it!*

*D-n Fisher!—You get*

---

[21] On 25 January 1916, in a by-election at Mile End, the Coalition candidate, Warwick Brookes, was elected as a Unionist MP with 1,991 votes. Pemberton Billing, the only other candidate, received 1,615 votes.

*Prime Minister!*
*That will end the War!*
  *Nought else will!*
The Country wants a Man!
  Every War always wants a Man!
    *Dont go back—accept nothing!*[22]

Yours
F

In the retrospect of more than half a century this letter may seem to bear the mark of lunacy. But for Churchill, cut off from the inner workings of politics, rejected, as he believed, by his former colleagues, denied any place in a Government in which he believed he could play a decisive part, this appeal from the man with whom he had worked so closely and admired so deeply did not depend for its strength upon its logic. Only five days earlier Churchill had been isolated and alone amid what he had described to his wife as 'the strain & severity' of life in the trenches, amid the remoteness of the war zone, and the ever-present chance of death. Now he was told that he was on the verge of a great personal triumph which might lead him forward to power. All the vociferous forces of faction and discontent were pressing him to go forward. He failed to see that he was about to prove to every critic and to most friends that he lacked the mature judgement of statesmanship.

[22] Fisher's letter to Churchill is reproduced in facsimile on pages 1038–41.

# 23

# Humiliation

---

TWELVE YEARS had passed since Churchill had last spoken in the House of Commons as the critic of a Government. Then, his had been the lance of youthful anger hurled, always with agility and sometimes with venom, against the Conservative Prime Minister, A. J. Balfour. It had seemed impudence for so young a Member of Parliament to attack the Leader of the ruling Party, from whose back benches he had only just migrated. The impudent young man had himself risen to be a member of the Cabinet, and an able administrator. Since 1906, whatever he had done, he had done as a member of the Government and from a position of increasing political power. When he rose to speak from the front opposition bench late in the afternoon of Tuesday 7 March 1916, it was with the accumulated experience of those twelve years behind him; but it was also with his credibility impaired by the controversies and disasters of the previous year. After twelve years, it was again A. J. Balfour whom he rose to attack.

At the outset of his speech Churchill warned: 'I shall have to strike a jarring note.' He explained that it would be 'a note not of reproach, nor of censure nor of panic, but a note in some respects of warning'. He had nothing but praise, he told the House of Commons, for the sailors at sea, or for their commanders who combined 'the utmost professional skill' with 'unflinching resolution'. His intention was to criticize the inadequacy of the ships, the guns, the ammunition and the supplies which these men had at their disposal. He spoke of the naval programmes for which he, Prince Louis and Lord Fisher had been responsible. 'How are they being executed?' he asked. 'Are they being executed at full blast—are they being executed punctually?' There was, he declared, a serious gap in the survey of the naval situation which Balfour had delivered in the House earlier that afternoon. 'I rather wish that the First Lord had found it possible,' he said, 'to give an assurance to the House that the dates to which Lord Fisher and I were working would be substantially and with inconsiderable exceptions maintained throughout the great new field of new construction.' He expressed alarm that the goals established during the early months of the war, while he was First Lord, and the enormous armada of new ships which had been laid down when Fisher returned to the Admiralty in October 1914, had not been properly pursued. 'I am bound to say,' he warned the House, 'that since I returned to this country I have received from sources, on which I must to some extent rely, impressions of a less completely satisfactory and reassuring kind than would naturally be derived from the annual statement of the Minister responsible.' He contrasted the apparent slackening of effort at the Admiralty under Balfour with what he felt convinced must be the opposite policy in Germany:

We do not know what Germany has done. An impenetrable veil, as the right hon Gentleman knows, has fallen for eighteen months over the German dockyards, naval and commercial. The right hon Gentleman says he does not know what progress is being made there. That is a serious statement—not one in connection with which I make any reproach, but it is a grave fact which we must bear in mind that we do not know what is going on there. But let us be sure of this: something is in progress there. . . .

Can we conceive that the German Government, as we know it to our cost, would be content to allow that Navy to lie impotent and derided in the Kiel Canal without any hope of action? If there were any possibility within the range of their extraordinary military intelligences by which it could be rendered a really effective factor in the course of the struggle, is it likely that they would have acquiesced in the total loss of utility and of all the efforts, organisation, and resources which have made them the second naval Power? We should be most imprudent

if we were to act on such an assumption. We are bound to assume that
Germany has completed every vessel begun before the War. It may
not be so—I dare say it is not so—but we must assume it.

It would be lamentable, Churchill warned, if, confronted by German preparations on a vast scale, 'serious and solid reasons' did
not exist for the postponement and delays in the building of
British ships. Before the war began, Parliament had sanctioned
the construction of fourteen battleships, each armed with 15-inch
guns. He wanted to know why these were not yet ready. There
was a further point which disturbed him:

We have not only reached a period in the War when all the capital
ships begun before the War can certainly be completed, but we are
just entering upon a period when new capital ships begun since the
War may be ready on either side. Here, again, I know of course what
we have done, and that secret is jealously guarded; but we cannot
tell what Germany has done. We have left the region of the known, of
the declared or defined; we have left the region of naval annuals and
almanacks; and we have entered the sphere of the uncertain. We have
entered a sphere which is within certain limits not merely uncertain
but incalculable. For this reason we cannot afford to allow any delay
to creep into the execution of our programme, because we must from
now on provide, not only against the known and against the declared
ships, but against what will be a continually increasing element of the
unknown. . . .
    The War is full of surprises to all of us; but so far the Admiralty has
kept ahead. But that has not been done—I am very anxious to couch
my argument in language which will not be offensive or vexing to my
right hon Friend, whose courtesy I have always experienced, but I
must say that it has not been done—by easy methods. It was done by
rough and harsh and even violent methods, and by a tireless daily
struggle. Remember, everything else is in movement too. We see our
own great expansion, but remember, everything else around us is ex-
panding and developing at the same time. You cannot afford to indulge even for the shortest period of time in resting on your oars. You
must continually drive the vast machine forward at its utmost speed.
To lose momentum is not merely to stop, but to fall.
    We have survived, and we are recovering from a shortage of
munitions for the Army. At a hideous cost in life and treasure we have

regained control, and ascendency lies before us at no great distance. A shortage in naval material, if it were to occur from any cause, would give no chance of future recovery. Blood and money, however lavishly poured out, would never repair the consequences of what might be even an unconscious relaxation of effort.

The House of Commons had not heard such a strong indictment of a Government Department since the war began. Violet Bonham Carter, who was present during the debate, recorded in *Winston Churchill As I Knew Him,* that everything Churchill was saying seemed calculated 'to shake the confidence of the House in the energy, initiative and determination of the present Board of Admiralty. And to arouse fears that Germany was secretly outbuilding us.'

Churchill was determined to disturb the conscience of Parliament. He felt that this was the moment in the war when the Government must choose, either to continue in the old way with loss of life and loss of opportunity going hand in hand, or to strike out in a more forceful, a more logical, a more intelligible and, ultimately, a victorious direction. He asserted that if this opportunity for a radical change were lost, Britain might lose the war:

I have come down here this afternoon to say these things with the deepest sense of responsibility. I say them because I am sure there is time to avoid all these dangers, because I am sure that it is not too late. If it were too late, silence would be vital. It is not; there is time; and I am anxious that the warning and exhortation which I am going to use, and am using, which may possibly excite resentment, but which must, nevertheless, be said, should be spoken while it is quite certain they may produce a useful effect. But I say advisedly that, though there is time, the Admiralty must not think the battle over. They must forthwith hurl themselves with renewed energy into their task, and press it forward without the loss of a day.

Churchill continued his speech with an examination of the details of the naval programme. He had already sought to create doubts about the adequacy of battleship construction; he next turned to the question of destroyers. He drew the attention of the House to the fact that when Fisher had returned to the Admiralty in October 1914, and the two of them had worked together, 'things were not only planned, but done on a scale beyond anything ever thought possible'. He feared that the programme, both of destroyers, and other small vessels, which he and Fisher had launched, had been 'allowed to fall into arrears' and that 'their delivery has been allowed to slide back from month to month'. If this were so, he went on, 'then I say the Navy and the Grand Fleet might find themselves deprived of securities and advantages which we had prepared for them, and which we deemed it indispensible they should receive'. He did not believe that Balfour's survey of naval affairs had given any indication that the naval programme was really being driven forward. 'It is no use saying, "We are doing our best,"' Churchill warned, 'you have got to succeed in doing what is necessary.' He was worried that Balfour had failed to obtain the necessary labour in the dockyards to build the ships as quickly as they could be built. At this point Asquith interrupted, 'He did not say so,' but Churchill persevered in his argument. Balfour had spoken, he said, of bringing men back from the front as if that would be a remedy for labour problems in the docks; 'and I understood', Churchill continued, 'a remedy which has not yet been adopted'. He was disturbed by the labour situation. 'I know my right hon Friend's difficulties, and the toils and burdens upon him, but he must overcome them. The resources of British shipyards are incomparable, and fully equal, if used at the highest possible speed and power. . . .' At this point Balfour interrupted. His remarks, although inaudible in the Reporters' Gallery and therefore not recorded in Hansard, made Churchill exceedingly angry. How did Balfour suppose, he retorted, that the fleet of Monitors which he and Fisher had designed—'which have been so improvidently scattered to the world'—had been brought into existence in the course of only six months? 'No one,' he told the House, 'can form any conception of the achievements which can be produced from the British yards if they are really driven to their fullest capacity.'

Churchill's speech gathered in force and foreboding as it continued. He was warning of dangers which no one had warned of in public before. He was voicing the discontent which others had begun to feel. There were, he warned, 'novel dangers requiring novel expedients'. In a naval war 'you must always be asking about the enemy—what now, what next? . . . your measures must always be governed and framed on the basis that he would do what you would least like him to do'. Churchill criticized Balfour for making no reference in his speech to the danger of submarines:

Although the German submarine campaign has up to date been a great failure, and although it will probably continue to be a failure—here again you cannot afford to assume that it will not present itself in new and more difficult forms, and that new exertions and new inventions will not be demanded, and you must be ready with your new devices before the enemy is ready with his, and your resourcefulness and developments must continually proceed upon a scale which exceeds the maximum you expect from him. I find it necessary to utter this word of warning, which for obvious reasons I should not proceed to elaborate.

From the future danger of the submarine, Churchill turned to the existing depredations of the Zeppelin, hinting that had he and Fisher remained at the Admiralty schemes of a bolder and more effective nature might have been adopted to deal with them:

A strategic policy for the Navy, purely negative in character, by no means necessarily implies that the path of greatest prudence is being followed. I wish to place on record that the late Board would certainly not have been content with an attitude of pure passivity during the whole of the year 1916. . . .

We hear a great deal about air raids. A great remedy against Zeppelin raids is to destroy the Zeppelins in their sheds. I cannot understand myself why all these many months, with resources far greater than those which Lord Fisher and I ever possessed, it has not been found possible to carry on the policy of raiding which, in the early days even, carried a handful of naval pilots to Cologne, Düsseldorf, and Friedrichshafen, and even to Cuxhaven itself.

Churchill had completed his criticisms. At times, in the interests of secrecy, he had spoken guardedly, but the culminating result was to raise serious doubts about Admiralty policy. He had made his points simply, confidently and with effect. The House had listened with a growing realization that Admiralty mismanagement could lead to defeat. Churchill had one more point to make. It was an appeal so extraordinary in its implications, so improbable in its advocate, that the House listened in stunned silence, and Violet Bonham Carter, who considered herself his friend, believed that 'he must surely be deranged'. This was his conclusion:

But I have not spoken to-day without intending to lead up to a conclusion. I have not used words of warning without being sure first that they are spoken in time to be fruitful, and secondly, without having a definite and practical proposal to make.

When in November, 1914, Prince Louis of Battenberg told me he felt it his duty to retire and lay down the charge he had executed so faithfully, I was certain that there was only one man who could succeed him. I knew personally all the high officers of the Navy, and I was sure that there was no one who possessed the power, the insight, and energy of Lord Fisher. I therefore made it plain that I would work with no other First Sea Lord. In this way the oppositions, naval and otherwise, which have always, perhaps not unnaturally, obstructed Lord Fisher's faithful footsteps, were overcome. He returned to his old place, and the six months of war administration which followed will, I believe, rank as one of the remarkable periods in the history of the Royal Navy.

I did not believe it possible that our very cordial and intimate association would be ruptured, but the stress and shocks of this War are tremendous, and the situations into which men are plunged expose them to strain beyond any that this generation have had experience of.

We parted on a great enterprise upon which the Government had decided and to which they were committed and in which the fortunes of a struggling and ill-supported Army were already involved; it stood between us as a barrier. I therefore should have resisted, on public grounds, the return of Lord Fisher to the Admiralty—and I have on several occasions expressed this opinion in the strongest terms to the Prime Minister and the First Lord of the Admiralty.

We have now reached an entirely different situation, and I have no doubt whatever what it is my duty to say now. There was a time when I did not think that I could have brought myself to say it, but I have been away for some months, and my mind is now clear. The times are crucial. The issues are momentous. The great War deepens and widens and expands around us. The existence of our country and of our cause depend upon the Fleet. We cannot afford to deprive ourselves or the Navy of the strongest and most vigorous forces that are available. No personal consideration must stand between the country and those who can serve her best.

I feel that there is in the present Admiralty administration, for all their competence, loyalty, and zeal, a lack of driving force and mental energy which cannot be allowed to continue, which must be rectified while time remains and before evil results, and can only be rectified in one way. I am sure the nation and the Navy expect that the necessary step will be taken. . . .

I urge the First Lord of the Admiralty without delay to fortify himself, to vitalise and animate his Board of Admiralty by recalling Lord Fisher to his post as First Sea Lord.

Churchill's appeal for Fisher's return destroyed in a few minutes the whole impact of his speech, turning what had been to that moment one of the most serious and skilful speeches he had ever made into an object of derision. Churchill's hammer blows of criticism were forgotten. The Government, Parliament and, on the morrow, the British public, gaped in amazement. When Violet Bonham Carter reached her father's room in the House of Commons, she found Asquith 'speechless' and Edward Marsh with tears in his eyes. Churchill, Asquith told her, had taken a 'suicidal' step by his appeal for Fisher's return. Yet Churchill had believed that this appeal would strengthen his position as a critic; it would show that the personal animosities and divisive rancour of May 1915 were over, and indicate that he wanted the Navy to be in the hands of the one man whose energy and stature were known to all: proof that he was thinking, not of himself but of the national need. Churchill was deluded. He had aroused in the House the realization that Britain could lose the war; but ending with the appeal for Fisher's return, he had blunted the impact of this warning and made himself appear absurd.

Holding a weapon which Churchill himself had delivered into its hand, the Government acted quickly. Asquith had already shown his usual skill at political manoeuvre by having asked Fisher to attend the War Council that was to meet on the following morning. Of all the national newspapers, only the *Manchester Guardian* decided to treat Churchill's speech as a serious and valid challenge to Government inertia; C. P. Scott having always looked to Fisher's return as a panacea. Churchill received no flood of congratulatory letters. No enthusiastic notes were passed to him along the benches. Violet Bonham Carter wrote to him in bewilderment, asking for a chance to talk to him. Only one correspondent, Fisher, was enthusiastic, writing on March 7:

My dear Winston,
　SPLENDID!!!
You'll have your Reward! All I entreat you now is to entrench yourself as Leader of the Opposition! and wait for the Big thing to come to you!

C. P. Scott said to me it would come! Your attitude so excellent—a helpful (*not a hostile*) critic. *Anyhow my heart is very full!* I feel the good old times are back!

　　　　　　　　　　　　　　　　　Yours
　　　　　　　　　　　　　　　　　Fisher

Don't trouble to answer. Telephone when I can see you after the Council tomorrow and *where!*

Churchill left the House of Commons immediately after his speech. He was quite unprepared for the ridicule which its extraordinary conclusion had drawn upon him. In the debate that followed only one speaker, George Lambert, tried, briefly, to take up the plea for Fisher's return; but Parliament was less interested in discussing whether Fisher should return than in castigating Churchill for having urged them to bring him back. Commander

Bellairs[1] spoke bitterly of the dangers to British policy should Churchill control it once more:

Does he mean by an attitude of activity the thing we have been accustomed to in the past, with ship after ship knocking at the Dardanelles, warning the Turks we were coming, when we had embarked on that project without any central scheme of action—is that the sort of activity he means? Does he mean we are to go and bombard Heligoland, and thereby knock out more of those capital ships he considers so necessary? Is not the Navy accomplishing at the present moment every single purpose for which it was devised?

For Churchill to demand that the Government discard its senior naval adviser and bring in someone else was, Bellairs declared, 'an intolerable situation'. 'Hear, hear!' interrupted Balfour.

The most vitriolic speech that evening came from the Admiral, Sir Hedworth Meux, whom Churchill had known for many years. This was his maiden speech:

I had not intended to interpose in this Debate until I had the pain of hearing the speech of the late First Lord of the Admiralty (Colonel Churchill). I think it is well the House should know that if the present First Lord is foolish enough to adopt his suggestion and bring Lord Fisher back to the Admiralty there will be general consternation throughout the Navy.

Some week or ten days ago I had two or three officers in the Grand Fleet say to me, 'For God's sake stop this intrigue which is going on,' and I intend to do what I can.

What is the right hon and gallant Gentleman—I was very sorry not to see him in uniform; he has often seen me in uniform, but I have never seen him—really asking the First Lord of the Admiralty to do? He is asking him to commit harikiri, and not only him, but the Government also. That is the meaning of this intrigue—to turn out the Government, nothing else.

Let us put ourselves in the place of the Grand Fleet—Sir John Jellicoe, captains and officers—when they read this Debate and see what

[1] Carlyon Bellairs, 1871–1955. Midshipman, 1886. Retired from the Navy with rank of a Commander 1902, on the failure of his eyesight. Liberal MP, 1906–9. Conservative MP, 1909–10; 1915–31. An opponent of political honours, he declined a Baronetcy in 1927.

the late First Lord has said. They will say, 'Here is a nice state of
things. What has our present First Sea Lord of the Admiralty done?
What is the matter with Sir Henry Jackson? What is his fault?' Shall I
tell you what is his fault in the eyes of the people who want to turn
him out? It is that he does not advertise.

Mr BALFOUR: Hear, hear!

Admiral Sir HEDWORTH MEUX: He does not have correspondents
and newspaper people in his place all day. That is really the reason
this agitation has been got up. It is because the present Board of
Admiralty are doing their work to the satisfaction of the Navy and not
boasting about it.

In the first few months of the War, whenever we had a success or
whenever the enemy had a slight failure, the whole of the Navy were
pained by the vulgar boasting that went on. When we read boasting
and foolish condemnation of our enemies—who, in spite of some of
their brutalities, are a gallant enemy—a quiver goes through the whole
of the Navy. Anybody in the Navy knows what an unlucky thing it
is to boast. When the present First Lord's speech is read we shall say,
'Thank heaven, at last we have got a ruler who does not grate upon
our nerves!'

The hon and gallant Member is a very old friend of mine, and I have
received many kindnesses from him, but there are limits to endurance.
When the late First Lord (Colonel Churchill) and Lord Fisher were
at the Admiralty they were at daggers drawn, and everybody at the
Admiralty knew it. Are we to have all that over again? What did the
late First Lord say about Lord Fisher when he made his exculpating
speech in this House? Did he not say that he could not get proper
guidance from Lord Fisher, and is that the man you want to bring
back?

Who has called for Lord Fisher? Has the House called for him?
The Navy has not called for him. . . .

Churchill was not present to hear this strident attack, or to
answer the serious accusation that he was privy to an intrigue
aimed at overthrowing the Government. Meux referred to his
absence at the end of his speech, in a savage passage:

I am sorry the late First Lord is not in his place, because, with all
due humility, I would like to say to him, 'Rolling stones gather no
moss.' I do not know how many posts he has had in his short and brilliant career. He has succeeded in them all. He might always have

done better had he stuck to them, but he never has, and I believe what I say now will be approved by a very large number of Members in this House. We all wish him a great deal of success in France, and we hope that he will stay there.

The Press criticisms on the morning of March 8 echoed the views of Bellairs and Meux. Although comment concentrated upon the final appeal for Fisher's return, no newspaper denied that the earlier part of Churchill's speech constituted a clear and powerful indictment of Asquith's administration. Some newspapers expressed surprise that there had been no official answer that evening to the detailed charges which Churchill had put forward. But because Churchill's criticisms had been so unexpected, because he had taken so short a time to prepare them, because he had not sought to enlist the help of a single member of the Government, his speech puzzled more people than it inspired. He had made it without enlisting parliamentary supporters or setting up a Press campaign to set the scene, believing that spontaneity and surprise would give the speech an added strength. His friends, other than Fisher, were bewildered by his action. When Riddell spoke to Lloyd George on March 8, Lloyd George, according to Riddell's *War Diary*, called the speech 'a great error':

He should have stopped after criticising the Administration. When Winston remarked, 'I am now going to make a practical suggestion,' I wondered what he was going to say. Bonar Law whispered to me, 'He is going to suggest the recall of Fisher.' I could not believe it. Of course, if his object was to ruin Fisher's chances, he did his best to achieve it; but I do not believe he would act in such a Machiavellian way. That is not like Winston. On the other hand, if he meant to improve his own position, he made a great mistake.

Churchill realized the damage which he had done to himself by insisting upon Fisher's recall. He could not decide whether to remain in London for further debates, or to return to Flanders. On the morning of March 8 Fisher appeared at 41 Cromwell Road and tried to persuade him to continue with his parliamentary criticisms. Clementine Churchill doubted whether, as a result of his speech, her husband could possibly win parliamentary support. Fisher disagreed, believing that only a few more well-directed blows aimed at naval or military policy would bring Asquith down. Churchill was inclined to agree, and believed that he still had a part to play.

On the afternoon of March 8 Balfour replied to Churchill's speech in the House of Commons. By his speech, he ensured that Churchill's humiliation was complete. Churchill's criticisms, he said, were 'very unfortunate, both in form and substance . . . inspired I know not by whom, or whence . . .'. Balfour proceeded to deal with Churchill's various points, denying absolutely 'slackness, indifference, want of push and drive', and claiming that the Navy 'is far stronger than it was at the beginning of the War, and is, I believe, stronger than it has ever been in its history'. But Balfour did not defend himself against Churchill's criticisms by rational argument. He concentrated instead upon Churchill's final appeal, using ridicule and invective:

Let me say now one word about the remedy which he proposed at the end. I do not imagine that there was a single person who heard my right hon Friend's speech who did not listen to this latter part of it with profound stupefaction.

My right hon Friend has often astonished the House, but I do not think he ever astonished it so much as when he came down to explain that the remedy for all our ills, as far as the Navy is concerned, is to get rid of Sir Henry Jackson and to put in his place Lord Fisher.

My right hon Friend has never made the smallest concealment, either in public or in private, of what he thought of Lord Fisher. Certainly the impression that we all had of what he thought of Lord Fisher was singularly unlike the picture that we should ourselves have drawn uninspired as to the character of a saviour of his country. Because, what did he say when he made what at the time he thought was his farewell speech, when he exchanged a political for a military career? He told us that the First Sea Lord, Lord Fisher, did not give him, when he was serving in the same Admiralty with him, either the clear guidance before the event or the firm support after it which he was entitled to expect. . . .

Then my right hon Friend, with the memory of that speech in his mind, had naturally to frame some explanation of advice which suggested that Sir Henry Jackson should be relieved of his office in order to put in his place the most brilliant and distinguished sailor who had, however, according to the right hon Gentleman, the defect of not giving his chief either the clear guidance or the firm support which his chief had a right to expect. It was not a very easy thing to explain, and I must honestly say not a thing which was very adequately or satisfactorily explained.

All that my right hon Friend said was that he had gone since then to the front, and that with the opportunity for calm meditation which apparently the front presents his mind was cleared.

The great ancestor of my right hon Friend, the first Duke of Marlborough, was always supposed to be more cool, more collected, more master of himself, more clear in thought amid the din of battle than he was in the calmer occupations of peace, and perhaps my right hon Friend shares this hereditary peculiarity. I venture to suggest that that clearness of thought which we all desiderate is bought at a rather costly figure if it involves a European war in order to obtain it. . . .

I cannot follow the workings of the right hon Gentleman's mind. He told us in his speech yesterday, I have not got the quotation, but it came however to this, that he told the Prime Minister when Prince Louis resigned the position of First Sea Lord that the only man he could work with was Lord Fisher.

He seemed dogged by ill-fortune. Is it not a most extraordinary and emphatic coincidence that the only man with whom my right hon Friend could consent to work at the Admiralty was the most distinguished sailor who, after five months, refused to work with my right hon Friend? . . .

I do not know if my right hon Friend is under the impression—perhaps he is—that if the change which he desires to force on the Government were accepted, I should still remain a member of the Government. But let us suppose that that is so, and that I was prepared to take my Board of Admiralty from the right hon Gentleman—rather a violent supposition—why does he suppose that Lord Fisher should behave differently to me from the manner in which my right hon Friend declared Lord Fisher behaved to him? Is it my merits? Am I more happily gifted in the way of working with people than my right hon Friend? Does he think that I could better utilise Lord Fisher's great gifts and avoid this want of harmony which rose between them and which in different circumstances might still have prevailed if Lord Fisher were still First Sea Lord? I do not know whether that is the explanation or not.

The fact remains that the right hon Gentleman, who could not get on with Lord Fisher—I will not say that, but with whom Lord Fisher could not get on—says that Lord Fisher, who according to my right hon Friend neither supported him nor guided him, is nevertheless the man who ought to be given as a supporter and a guide to anybody who happens to hold at this moment the responsible position of First Lord of the Admiralty. It is a paradox of the wildest and most extravagant kind. . . .

My right hon Friend comes forward with this suggestion. He put it in the form of a suggestion that Lord Fisher should come to the Admiralty. There is another form in which it could be put, which is equally veracious. That is that Sir Henry Jackson should go from the Admiralty. . . . I think when the right hon Gentleman comes down to this House, and, without a tittle of evidence, giving us no argument, no ground, suggests to the Government that this great public servant should be turned adrift in order to introduce in his place a man of whom I would never say anything which does not indicate my enormous admiration of the great services he has performed to his country in connection with the creation of our Fleet, but who, according to the right hon Gentleman himself, has not done that which is his first duty as First Sea Lord to do, namely, to give guidance and advice to the First Lord and his colleagues in the Cabinet, seems to me the most amazing proposition that has ever been laid before the House of Commons. . . .

I should regard myself as contemptible beyond the power of expression if I were to yield an inch to a demand of such a kind, made in such a way. . . .

Churchill was stunned by the savagery of Balfour's reply. He answered briefly and with dignity, but to no avail. Balfour, he said, was 'a master of Parliamentary sword-play and of every dialectical art'; his high position in British politics enabled him easily to rebuke those who did not have his authority, and in particular one 'who is so much younger than himself'. 'All the familiar Parliamentary devices,' he said, had been employed against him. He reiterated briefly the points which he had made in his speech on the previous day, and continued:

It is very easy to exaggerate the statements which I made, and then to protest against the form in which they were couched. But the right hon Gentleman ought, I think, not to be unduly offended or vexed at the speech which I made, because, after all, a speech is a very small thing, and a failure of any kind in this matter is a vital thing.

Do not let us be too touchy on the Treasury Bench in regard to matters of that kind. It is right that a note of warning should be sounded, and sounded in time.

Churchill then spoke of his final plea for Fisher's return:

The right hon Gentleman, of course, was very effective in dealing with my relations with Lord Fisher. I made him a present of all the rhetorical and debating retorts which he can derive from that fertile field, and I must say that I do not at all wonder that he was able to rove about in this luxuriant field, so well fitted to the special arts he exercises.

But, after all, what is the real fact? The real fact is that if we could associate in some way or another the driving power and energy of Lord Fisher, with the carrying out of Lord Fisher's programme at the highest possible speed, there is no reason to suppose that great public advantage would not result from that.

Compared with Balfour's attack, Churchill's reply made no impact at all. Balfour had triumphed. Margot Asquith wrote to him later that day from 10 Downing Street:

Dearest Arthur,

I hope & believe Winston will never be forgiven his yesterday's speech. Henry & I were thunderstruck at the *meanness* & the gigantic folly of it. I've never varied in my opinion of Winston I am glad to say.

He is a hound of the lowest sense of political honour, a fool of the lowest judgement & contemptible.

He cured me of oratory in the House & bored me with oratory in the Home!

If it's not cheek I must tell you Henry & I thought you admirable and if H had not had a deputation he said he wd have given Winston 10 of the nastiest minutes of his life he was so *disgusted*.

Everyone delighted with Hedworth.

V devoted
Margot

Margot Asquith's verdict was also for a large part the Parliamentary one. It ignored the anguish which Churchill felt at what he believed to be unpardonable neglect and apathy in high places. But ridicule, wielded effectively, had greater force than reason. By his final plea, Churchill had laid himself open to derisive laughter; it was a gesture as naïve as it was ill-considered. At noon on March 7 Churchill had believed that the challenge which he was about to make could change the course of the war. By noon on March 8 he knew that he had failed. 'My dear Lord Fisher,' Hankey wrote on March 9, 'I fear that Winston, whose conduct is in striking contrast to yours, did not do you much good. He gave AJB a chance he was not likely to miss.' In the House of Lords on March 9, Lord Charles Beresford—who had been created Baron Beresford in January—declared he would halt the mischief caused by Churchill's 'wicked statement'. Not all commentators were hostile. 'Churchill's outburst,' Lord Esher wrote to Sir Douglas Haig on March 11, 'was the culmination of a great deal of discontent in the Fleet itself. . . . It is said that the old peace methods prevail there, as elsewhere, and that the highest degree of efficiency is denied to the Grand Fleet by adherence to procedure that is unsuited to a war of this kind. That Jellicoe is short of certain types of vessels essential to him is, I fear, beyond question.'

Churchill knew that the arguments which he had put forward about the Navy were valid. He felt that equally strong arguments could be used to criticize the conduct of military affairs. He therefore decided to stay in England, and to continue his assault upon Government policy. That day he wrote to the Secretary of State for War from 41 Cromwell Road:

Circumstances have arisen which make it my duty to give undivided attention to Parliamentary and public business for some time to come. I ask you therefore to have me relieved from my command as soon as this can be done without disadvantage to the service. In the meanwhile I should be glad if my leave of absence could be extended—equally without disadvantage, as I must otherwise return to France tomorrow.

Perhaps you will if necessary show this letter to the Prime Minister.

Kitchener took this letter to 10 Downing Street. Asquith agreed to extend Churchill's leave; Churchill was no longer a threat politically either in London or in Ploegsteert. The speech had destroyed his power to harm the Government. By inviting Fisher to the War Council of March 8, Asquith had isolated Churchill even further. 'Five Admiralty officials with masses of paper to swallow me up!' Fisher wrote to Jellicoe after his first reappearance at 10 Downing Street since May 1915. At the War Council Asquith had flattered Fisher, so that he came away believing, as he wrote to Jellicoe, that although 'Balfour & Co tried a lot of red herrings to no purpose!' he and Asquith had been in agreement 'that the position of the Grand Fleet owing to lack of destroyers was "PERILOUS"!' Asquith's impression was very different. At four o'clock that afternoon he saw C. P. Scott at 10 Downing Street, at Scott's request. 'He was silent and grim,' Scott recorded in a note of the interview. Scott told Asquith that he had intended to speak to him about the Navy, but that 'a great part of what I wanted to say had now already been said by Churchill'. Scott pressed for Fisher's return. Asquith told him that when the War Council had asked Fisher what was required to make the Navy more effective his answer had been: 'a contemptuous ejaculation and gesture, casting thumb back over shoulder as though to get rid of dirt'.

Scott recorded that Asquith then rose from his seat and began 'marching to and fro', denouncing both Fisher and Churchill with vehemence. Soon afterwards Scott wrote down the gist of Asquith's remarks:

As for Churchill's speech it was a piece of the grossest effrontery. Did I know that only 3 months ago when Fisher was appointed as head of the Inventions Department both Churchill and his wife had been furious and had denounced it as an outrage, so much so that Mrs Churchill had almost cut him and his wife and would not speak to him. And now suddenly Churchill professed to have discovered Fisher's extraordinary merits and called for his reinstatement. It was a piece of 'impudent humbug'. Why when Churchill and Fisher were together they did nothing but quarrel and Fisher's resignations were a perpetual worry of his life. He had resigned 8 times before the last time. Then he actually deserted his post and went away at a time too of some anxiety. Had he not gone there would, said Asquith, have been no Ministerial crisis and no Coalition. 'He deserved to be shot,' shouted Asquith, 'and in any other country he would have been shot.'

Fisher was a spent force. The War Council, having seen this, could ignore Churchill's challenge. When the War Council was over Hankey sent Fisher a fulsome letter of praise, thanking him for 'dotting the "i's" and crossing the "t's" of Jellicoe's evidence'; he then informed him that the country owed him a debt of gratitude 'not merely for what you have done but for the patriotic manner in which you have avoided any publicity, which might help the enemy, and compelled the highest authority to take the matter up . . .'. This strong hint for continued silence was successful. Fisher decided to give up his idea of putting forward his criticisms in the House of Lords. But he still hoped that Churchill would make the running for him. Of Fisher's friends, Scott, however, influenced by Asquith's outburst, was sceptical of any chance of success for Churchill. Garvin remained optimistic, feeling that Churchill could circumvent the ridicule of his naval speech by a further attack on the Government during the Army Estimates debate on the following Tuesday, March 14. During the afternoon of March 8 Churchill asked Violet Bonham Carter to call to see him at Lady Randolph's house. She recorded her impressions in *Winston Churchill As I Knew Him*:

I found him alone there. He looked pale, defiant, on the defensive. I shall never forget the pain of the talk which followed. I knew better than to criticize, reproach or even ask the question that gnawed at me, 'What possessed you? *Why* did you do it?' I saw at once that, whatever his motive, he realized that he had hopelessly failed to accomplish what he had set out to do. . . . What he had conceived as a great gesture of magnanimity—the forgiveness of the wrongs Fisher had done to him, for the sake of a greater aim, our naval supremacy—had not been interpreted as such. It was regarded instead as a clumsy gambler's throw for his own ends. . . .

I had not seen him since our farewell luncheon at Cromwell Road in November, two days before he left for the Front. My first words were of the joy of his safe return, the miracle of the evacuation of

Gallipoli, of his own experience since—but I knew that his attention was perfunctory and his mind elsewhere.

After a pause he said: 'I suppose you are against me like the rest of them.' I said that he knew well that I could never be against him, but that I was strong against reinvesting Fisher with any sort of authority, as he had proved himself quite unfit for it. I could never trust him again and I was amazed that Winston could bring himself to do so. 'You may forgive what he has done to you. You have not the right to forgive the ruin he has brought on others and on the Dardanelles campaign.' He sheered off the Dardanelles and said that he knew from private sources that things were going badly at the Admiralty; that Fisher's fire and drive could put it out of the rut, reanimate it, speed it forward, etc. etc. 'Arthur's never been exactly a dynamo at the best of times.'

I did not pursue the argument, but after a time asked what his plans were. Was it true, as my father had told me, that he thought of resigning from the Army here and now and not returning to France? He said it was. He had come to the conclusion that it was right for him to remain here and exercise what influence he had at the heart of affairs. Many others thought so too. He had many friends and supporters (this rather militantly), including the *Manchester Guardian*. Had I read it that morning?

Fisher remained convinced that Churchill could succeed in overthrowing Asquith if he made a further effort, believing that the Army debate on March 14 offered a major opportunity for a renewed attack on the Government's conduct of the war. On March 8 Fisher wrote urging him to give up his Battalion altogether:

My dear Winston,

For Goodness sake dont hesitate! Write at once and resign! *I beg you to do this!* Garvin is absolutely confident it would be the mistake of your life to leave the House of Commons for a single day! You mark the gravity of the Naval and Military situation by remaining! Fancy losing your splendid opportunity next week on the Army Estimates. . . . Who else but you can rub Kitchener's nose in it? I assure you I am not so much thinking of your personal interests (*immense as they are! because you have the Prime Ministership in your grasp!*) but of saving the country! *Now now now* is the time to save the Country try NOT 3 months ahead! As my dear Winston you know better than I do that it's all d——d humbug Asquith weeping on your shoulder

and entreating you to go and be shot at!—I feel certain Kitchener and
Balfour felt the danger today of your stopping at home when they
discussed your letter! I *earnestly EARNESTLY* beg you to *write at
once* and resign! *The man who hesitates is lost!* If ever in this world
a Leader was wanted—it is *NOW!* and Providence has provided you
and given you an automatic opportunity. So once more on my bended
knees I implore you to write at once. Delays are Dangerous!

Yours<br>Fisher

On March 9 Fisher wrote triumphantly to C. P. Scott: 'Mc-
Kenna told me yesterday (This is most secret!) that if Winston
remained he would turn out the Government. Dead Sure. *SO
HE WILL!!!*' Churchill's speech, he wrote to Jellicoe that same
day, 'was really wonderfully good. *HE HELD THE HOUSE
ENTHRALLED.*'

Asquith, having flattered Fisher's ego and obtained his silence,
now tried to persuade Churchill to abandon his opposition.
Neither Asquith nor Churchill left any account of their meeting,
which took place on March 9 at 10 Downing Street. Immediately
after it, Violet Bonham Carter asked her father what had passed
between them and later wrote in *Winston Churchill As I Knew
Him:*

He told me that he had reminded Winston how his father, Lord
Randolph (to whom my father was devoted), had committed political
suicide through one impulsive action. He had said, 'If I can, I want to
save you from doing the same thing. You will know that nothing but
affection prompts me. It is because I care for you that I shall save
you.' He said that Winston had tears in his eyes when they parted and
that he was sure that he would go back to France. He added that it
was strange how little Winston knew of the attitude of others towards
himself. He had spoken to my father, as he did to me, of the many
ardent supporters who looked to him for leadership and my father
had said to him, 'At the moment you have none who count at all.' One
of the things which saddened my father most about this episode was
that he was always watching and hoping for an opportunity when the
climate of opinion in the Tory Party would change and enable him
to bring Winston back into the Government. Alas, 'at this moment he
has few political friends inside it or outside, nor is there a single office
he could be given'. I said the wheel must turn—'He will, he *must,*

come back some day. If only he isn't killed. . . . Supposing that he were killed—what should *we* feel, those of us who have urged him to go back?' My father said, 'I could only advise him to do what I am sure is right—right above all for his own sake.'

On March 10 an unexpected straw in the wind gave Churchill further encouragement for political action. At a by-election in East Hertfordshire the official Conservative candidate, Captain Henderson,[2] who had the support of the local Liberal organization, was defeated. The successful candidate was the airman Pemberton Billing, who stood as an independent in the interests of a strong Air policy. Pemberton Billing polled 4,590 votes against 3,559 cast for the coalition. That afternoon Fisher and Garvin went together to see Churchill at 41 Cromwell Road. To their delight, they found that he had already prepared a speech for the Army debate, which he read to them. That evening Fisher wrote to C. P. Scott, who had returned to Manchester: 'This East Herts Election is a Big Bomb. I believe the Government will soon be cleared out if our Friend remains as he should do and discourses on the Army estimates next Tuesday.' Sir Max Aitken also tried to convince Churchill to stay in London. Two weeks later, on March 24, Churchill wrote to him from Ploegsteert: 'I did not feel able after all to take yr advice; for though my instinct agreed with yours I had small but insistent obligations here wh cd not be hastily discarded for the sake of a personal opportunity. . . . I did not feel in me . . . the virtue necessary for the tremendous tasks you indicated. My interests were too evident & one cannot tell how much they sway one's judgement.' What were these 'tremendous tasks'? The leadership of a powerful opposition, drawing in dissidents from both Liberal and Conservative ranks? The overthrow of Asquith? Fisher, who saw Churchill again on the evening of March 10, did not doubt the nature of Churchill's opportunity. 'I think the Government will be turned out in about 3 weeks time,' Fisher wrote to Hankey on March 11: '*There is* SEETHING DISCONTENT

[2] Brodie Haldane Henderson, 1869–1936. Civil Engineer. Served in the Royal Engineers, 1914–18. Captain, 1914. Brigadier-General, 1918. Knighted, 1919.

*throughout the masses.'* That morning Fisher made a final appeal:

My dear Winston,

I've slept over it! I've thought of nothing else! If any specious twaddle about honour or Asquithian Jugglery persuades you not to rise from the corner of the Front Opposition Bench next Tuesday to brand the Government with the *massacre* of our *troops* and the utter *ineptitude* of the conduct of the war then I say that *YOU* become the '*Murderer*' because you are the *one and only* man who it is absolutely certain can prevent it and can voice the removal of Kitchener and so if not Prime Minister (which I am *sure* you will be) then you can be War Minister.

*NEVER* was there such an Opportunity!

*Fate has led you straight to it!*

Had you the very faintest idea when you left France that the Prime Minister with his own hand had written Jellicoe's condition as

'PERILOUS'

*Had you then the faintest idea that both 'Coalition' and 'Labour' would be utterly smashed by the Seething Discontent of the Masses?*

*GREAT OCCASIONS NECESSITATE GREAT RISKS!* To the public—Balfour has trounced *you! You've* got to trounce *him* by another flank movement! *He has got to be discredited!* Or he will be the alternative Prime Minister with Asquith as Lord Chancellor!

*VIA THE ARMY ESTIMATES YOU CAN DO IT!*

Stick at nothing!

Speak on Tuesday!

Yours

F

On March 11 Churchill rehearsed his naval criticisms in a letter to Sir Frederick Cawley,[3] the Chairman of the Liberal War Committee,[4] and an influential backbench figure:

[3] Frederick Cawley, 1850–1937. Liberal MP, 1895–1918. Created Baronet, 1906. Member of the Dardanelles Commission, 1916–17. Chancellor of the Duchy of Lancaster, December 1916–18. Created Baron, 1918. Of his four sons, three were killed in the war: Major J. S. Cawley in the retreat from Mons, August 1914; Captain Harold Thomas Cawley, MP, at Gallipoli, September 1915; and Captain Oswald Cawley, MP, in France, August 1918.

[4] The Liberal War Committee, a group of some forty Liberal MPs anxious about the conduct of the war, who wanted Parliament to take a more active

I have, after very careful consideration of all the circumstances, decided to apply to be relieved of my command in order to resume Parliamentary duties. Meanwhile I am returning to France and I wish to restate briefly the main facts about the Admiralty which compelled me to intervene in the recent debate. They are eight in number:—

1. The margin of safety is ample and unimpaired.
2. There has been preventable delay in completing the Fisher war Programme.
3. This delay affects both capital ships and destroyers required for the progressive reinforcement of the Fleets at sea.
4. A new impulse of the utmost vigour must be imparted to the whole volume of our construction, particularly to those units most urgently needed.
5. If this impulse is forthcoming there is still time fully to maintain the position.
6. For this purpose the present Board of Admiralty must be strengthened in whatever way will be most effective regardless of naval or personal feuds.
7. There has been a total lack of initiative in the tactical direction of the Naval Air Service resulting in a cessation for many months of all attempts to destroy German zeppelins in their bases and thus safeguard this country from their attacks.
8. There has been ample time to prepare and organize these counter air raids and to make all the appliances required for them;

It would appear to be the duty of your Committee to take good care that these vital facts are not overlooked.

On that same day Churchill obtained a written promise from Asquith that his eventual return would not be frustrated by any military pressures. 'As you are returning with my full approval to your military functions at the front,' Asquith wrote, 'I wish to assure you that, if hereafter you should find that your sense of public duty called upon you to return to political life here, no obstacle will be put in your way, and your relief will be arranged for, as soon as it can be effected without detriment to the Service.' That evening Fisher and Churchill met again. Fisher insisted

---

part in war policy. Several of them, including Cawley, joined Lloyd George's Government in December 1916. Its members included Dalziel, Markham, and Mond.

that it was Churchill's duty to remain in London. Pemberton Billing's by-election success was, he said, a clear indication of real public discontent with the Government. Churchill had not yet made up his mind. On the morning of March 12 Fisher wrote again:

You said last night you had not given your final answer to Asquith *so I make one more effort not to lose the war!* The very fact of Asquith's intense desire for you to go back coupled with Mrs Asquith's entreaty to F. E. Smith to use all his influence to make you go back and the considered opinion of Asquith's closest friend that you will turn out the Government if you stay and the East Herts Election to support you on Tuesday in your onslaught and the approaching Tigris disaster and possibly a yet bigger disaster that must be *momentarily* dealt with! (*No use then your coming home!*) TOO LATE! I say in view of these facts you are absolutely blind both to Patriotism as well as self-interest to return. *And it is not too late even now! A telegram will do it you know it can!*

Your speech as you rehearsed it on Friday afternoon to Garvin and me was incomparable! And you have yet to say you left France without the very faintest idea that the Navy Estimates were coming on! And you are paying £500 a year extra premium on your Life Insurance, losing £400 a year as MP because serving in the war and only getting £500 a year for your soldiering and Asquith asks you as to your material loss if you go back! A *sorry joke!*

'There's a tide in the affairs of men which taken at the Flood leads on to Fortune . . .'
*You know how to finish it! ! !*[5]
*Seize the Moment!*
Rehearse your Army speech to Carson! but *he won't back you! WE ARE GOING TO LOSE THE WAR! ! !*

That night, Churchill saw Sir Henry Dalziel, one of his few parliamentary supporters, to discuss his political prospects.

---

[5] The quotation, from Shakespeare's *Julius Caesar* (Act 4, Scene 3), continues:

> Omitted, all the voyage of their life
> Is bound in shallows and in miseries.
> On such a full sea are we now afloat;
> And we must take the current when it serve
> Or lose our ventures.

Dalziel was keen for Churchill to stay in London. But Clementine Churchill persuaded her husband that he must return at
once, if only for a short while, to his Battalion duties. By returning, he would not be able to take part in the opening of the Army
debate. He hoped that if the debate lasted long enough he might
be able to come back later and intervene at its end. On the
morning of March 13 he wrote to Dalziel:

> I daresay in about a week I shall be able to return to the House
> of Commons. You must forgive these uncertainties which arise from
> the difficulty of doing justice to two different sets of obligations.
> I am grateful to you for your help and kindness during this tiresome
> week.
> Do you think there is any chance of the army estimates running
> over into the next Parliamentary week? If so, send me a line and I will
> once again adjust my mind to the topic that I mentioned to you.

Churchill left for Flanders that morning. On his way to Dover
with his wife he rehearsed the arguments in favour of taking up
a permanent place with the parliamentary opposition. But
Clementine Churchill was sceptical of his chances. Her assessment of the political situation was right. Churchill had no influential supporters. On March 11, having heard of the moves to
attack the Government, Northcliffe had telegraphed from Paris to
the editor of *The Times*, Geoffrey Robinson: 'Stated here that
Churchill lead opposition. Don't give least support. . . .' Robinson obeyed his instructions. Several newspapers still hankered
after Fisher's return; none felt compelled to advocate Churchill's.

Churchill was not influenced by his wife's doubts. On reaching
Dover he sent Asquith a letter asking to be relieved of his command, and gave his wife a statement for the Press Association
explaining his course. Then he crossed over to France. Late that
afternoon he reached Ploegsteert, where his Battalion was in its
forward trenches. He was exhausted by the week that had
passed. He could not judge how far his speech had shattered his
chances of leading an effective opposition. He wanted more time
to reflect, and realized that it would be too precipitate to return
even during the final stages of the military debate. If he failed

then to gather sufficient support he would be in a very weak position. He felt on reflection that he had been unwise to send off his letter to Asquith, resigning his command. He wanted to wait longer, to look at the situation more calmly, to understand the nature of his support. He therefore telegraphed that night to Asquith withdrawing his letter. Asquith was relieved, and at once despatched Maurice Bonham Carter to 41 Cromwell Road to retrieve the Press Association statement from Clementine Churchill.

# 24

# 'My True War Station'

CHURCHILL RETURNED to the trenches shaken by his Parliamentary humiliation of the previous week. But he no longer doubted that his future must be a political one. He sensed that unless he returned quickly to the political arena he might be cheated of the career which he now knew was the only conceivable one for him. 'My dearest soul,' he wrote to Clementine Churchill on March 13, his first evening back in reserve, 'you have seen me vy weak & foolish & mentally infirm this week. Dual obligations, both honourable, both weighty have rent me. But I am sure my true war station is in the H of C. There I can help the movement of events. I cannot tell you how much I love & honour you and how sweet & steadfast you have been through all my hesitations & perplexity.' He was looking forward to 'a few more days reflection' in the trenches, and declared that he would not write to anyone 'or ask anyone for his advice or opinion'. 'Don't we live in a strange world,' he continued, 'full of wonderful pictures & intricate affairs. Across the troubled waters one can only steer by compass—not to do anything that is not honourable & manly, & subject to that to use my vital force to the utmost effect to win the war—there is the test I am going to try my decision by.'

After seeing her husband off at Dover on March 13, Clementine Churchill had gone at once to Carson's house at Rottingdean. On March 14 she sent her husband an account of the meeting, and of Carson's grave doubts about the wisdom of a precipitate return. 'Carson is a most important factor,' Churchill replied on March 16, '& I am impressed by his misgivings.' But he was not to be deterred in his course. 'That it is right for me to come home is certain,' he insisted. 'What is not clear is when & on what grounds.' General Furse, with whom he discussed the question of what course he should take, had been emphatic, Churchill reported to his wife, 'that my future was at home'. Furse had told Churchill bluntly that 'although it may be easier for you here with a battalion or a brigade & pleasanter, you have no right to think of that'. Churchill had played the devil's advocate. He had argued that a rapid return to politics would brand him with the mark of a changeling; but Furse had replied: 'The thing is much larger than that.'

Churchill also discussed his problems with Archibald Sinclair, to whom he unburdened himself each evening. 'Archie is a strong advocate of my staying here,' Churchill told his wife in a long letter on March 16. Sinclair saw no point in a precipitate return, or in any action without a definite reason. This was also Clementine Churchill's opinion. 'It is odd,' he told her, 'how similar are the standpoints from wh you and he both view my tiresome affairs.'

During Churchill's first week back in reserve, General Walshe was relieved of his command. A new Brigadier was needed to take charge of the Brigade. There was a chance that Churchill would be promoted to this position, on which he had once set his heart. But Generalship held no attractions for him now. 'Although this matter will in no way *determine* my action,' he wrote to his wife, 'I may as well have its decision before me before I settle.'

Churchill and his men were due to move forward again to the front line on March 20. He felt that by then he might have reached the decision to return. 'Now mind you keep in touch with Garvin, Scott, Dalziel,' he wrote in his long letter of March 16, '& don't let them drift off or think I have resigned the game. Tell them I am taking time to consider, method & occasion, but that in principle I have decided.' She might, he added, have a talk with Sir Frederick Cawley, '& even with the Fiend himself'. Clementine Churchill refused to talk to Fisher, but did everything else that he asked. Churchill appreciated his wife's efforts on his behalf. 'I cannot tell you,' he wrote on March 16, after reading of her visit to Carson, 'how much I treasure & count on yr aid & counsel. It was hard on you to set such exhausting tasks. You discharged them famously.'

On March 17 Churchill received the newspaper reports of the Army debate in which he had so wanted to take part. That night he wrote to his wife:

. . . How different I cd have made it! My conviction strengthens & deepens each day that my place is there, & that I cd fill it with credit & public advantage. Meanwhile however the actual step seems so easy to put off—so irrevocable when taken, that I continue to pause on the brink, not undecided but dilatory.

We are elated to have our little town (nameless) mentioned in Haig's daily report as a scene of artillery activity. The odd thing is that this mention occurs *the day before* the shelling took place! How history is written! . . .

One of the last things our late lamented Brigadier did was to rebuke me by memo for 'undue leniency' in punishments. I was preparing statistics to show that since I have commanded the battalion, offences as well as punishments have sensibly diminished. However this will not be necessary now.

This evening Archie & I took a stroll up the lines on our right & went to the HQrs of the battalion there. The same conditions & features reproduce themselves in every section—shattered buildings, sandbag habitations, trenches heavily wired, shell holes, frequent graveyards with thickets of little crosses, rank wild growing grass, muddy roads, khaki soldiers—& so on for hundreds & hundreds of miles—on both sides. Miserable Europe. Only a few rifle shots & the occasional bang of a gun broke the stillness of the evening. One wondered whether the nations were getting their money's worth out of the brooding armies.

Cd I help to a victorious peace more in H of C than here? That is the sole question. Believe me if my life cd materially aid our fortunes I wd not grudge it.

On March 19 Churchill learned that Colonel Trotter,[1] a friend of earlier years, was to succeed Walshe as Brigadier. Trotter's appointment made it clear, he wrote to his wife, 'that I have no prospects'. His reaction was calm: 'I do not mind this a bit,' he told her. 'If I were to stay out here, I cd hardly be better suited than where I am. A Brigade wd give me no more scope & less personal interest. There is no doubt at all in my mind as to what I ought to do.' But on March 19 Churchill delayed his decision to return in order to let Archibald Sinclair go on leave. He prized his friendship with Sinclair. In reserve the two men had spent many hours each day together trying to solve the Battalion's problems, and reflecting on Churchill's political ones. In the front line they shared the ever-present dangers. On March 19 Churchill wrote to his wife to ask her to look after Sinclair while he was on leave:

I want him to stay at Cromwell & you & Goonie to cherish & nourish him. He is all alone in the world,[2] & very precious as a friend to me. I am telling him to come straight to you on arrival—so get my room ready for him in good time. He will tell you all about our life out here; & my disturbing moods. In order not to interfere with his much needed rest & change, I have put off once again the hour of decision. It wd have been vy hard on him to cut him from his longed-for holiday. . . . He will arrive about 5 pm on 22nd. I think you had better engage him a temporary servant. . . . You must write me every day. I shall be vy much alone while Archie is away.

Churchill returned to Laurence Farm and the front-line trenches on March 20; his desire to return to politics was clamant. That day he explained his feelings to Garvin, in order to put Garvin's mind at rest about his intentions:

[1] Gerald Frederick Trotter, 1871–1945. Entered Army, 1885. Major, Grenadier Guards, 1914–16. Brigadier-General commanding the 27th Infantry Brigade, 17 March 1916 to 4 July 1916. Commanded 51st Infantry Brigade, July 1916–May 1917. Commanded British Military Mission (Instructional) to the USA, 1917–18. Gentleman Usher to George V, 1919–36.

[2] Sinclair's mother (formerly Miss Mabel Sands of New York) died in November 1890, within a month of his birth; his father (Clarence Granville Sinclair) died in 1895.

I have not in any way altered my view that I shd return to the H of C as soon as possible. On the contrary reflection makes me more than ever convinced that my duty is there. In principle therefore I am decided. But time & occasion still present difficult questions: for to be useful when I come home I must return under good conditions. Also here the days pass easily away absorbed in exercise & small affairs; and one cannot help being reluctant to terminate finally associations so simple & so honourable. Meanwhile I have written to Carson and shall have time to receive an answer from him.

You shd I think continue as occasion serves to prepare the way for the formation of a stronger opposition, & for an increase in the influence of the H of C. These Army debates for instance seem to me to have been quite lifeless & the armies' needs wh claim attention to have found little or no expression. Also the Naval issue shd not pass out of sight—tho' no doubt some of the work that was required is done.

I will write to you again shortly: meanwhile pray write to me. Do not I beg you suppose that I am incapable of facing the perplexities & risks of the Front Opposition Bench, or that I shall shrink from decision. But I am naturally reluctant to quit this scene (the more so oddly enough that I can do so at any moment) and especially am I anxious when I do return to do so in circumstances wh will be most favourable to my usefulness. The decision is for me alone: but to some extent my friends—none a better friend than you—can create & dispose these circumstances.

Fearing that his friends in London might mistake his wife's cautious attitude for his own, Churchill wrote to her on March 21: 'Be careful not to use arguments or take up an attitude in conflict with my general intention, & do nothing to discourage friends who wish for my return. On the contrary labour as opportunity serves to create favourable circumstances.' Clementine Churchill believed that a sudden return to London would stimulate her husband's critics without encouraging his friends. 'With patience and waiting for the right and good opportunity,' she wrote on March 21, the future 'is all yours'. On the following day she wrote again. C. P. Scott had called to see her, and was, she reported, 'very anxious that your return should not make an unfavourable impression'. While at 41 Cromwell Road, Sinclair had told her that her husband might still get a Brigade somewhere else in the line. *'That* is what I *hope*,' she wrote; and she reiterated C. P. Scott's belief that 'the right opportunity should be waited for'. Churchill was certain that it was futile to wait. He believed that if he returned at once he could still make a forceful impression on Parliament. On March 22 he wrote to his wife, rehearsing the arguments against his return, but then declaring:

. . . I do not think any reason is needed beyond the general reason —wh is the true one—that I think it right to resume political & Parlt duties wh are incompatible with holding a military command. It wd of course be a good thing to have some local reason for a break—such as our division going out of the line, or my being offered promotion; but this advantage must be weighed agst opportunities in England. I cannot decide yet. The broad facts may with confidence be submitted to the public. Let us see what they are.

1. I resigned my office & gave up a salary of £4,300 a year rather than hold a sinecure at this time.

2. I shall have served for nearly five months at the front, almost always in the front line, certainly without discredit—discharging arduous & difficult duties to the full satisfaction of my superiors & to the advantage of my officers & men.

3. I have a recognised position in British politics acquired by years of public work, enabling me to command the attention (at any rate) of my fellow countrymen in a manner not exceeded by more than 3 or 4 living men.

4. The period of our national fortunes is critical & grave: and almost every question both affecting war & peace conditions, with wh I have always been foremostly connected, is now raised. I cannot exclude myself from these discussions or divest myself of responsibilities concerning them.

Surely these facts may stand by themselves as an answer to sneers & cavillings. At any rate I feel I can rest upon them with a sure & easy conscience. Do not my darling one underrate the contribution I have made to the public cause, or the solidarity of a political position acquired by so many years of work & power. Gusts of ill-feeling & newspaper attack sweep by. But public men who really are known by the mass of the nation, do not lose their place in public counsels except for something wh touches their private character & honour. My command of the 6th RSF will certainly not unfavourably affect these general conclusions.

Churchill exaggerated the strength of his position. He did not realize the extent of feeling against him. But even with his belief in his own indispensability, he could not resolve the dilemma of when he should act. 'Next time I come home,' he wrote to his wife on March 23, 'it will be with a set purpose & a clear course, & with no wild & anxious hurry of fleeting moments & uncertain plans.' 'When you do return,' his wife warned on March 24, 'the reason should be apparent to the man in the street, tho' he need not necessarily agree with it.' She believed that it would be damaging to his career 'if it got about that you had returned becos' you were dissatisfied with your prospects of promotion and irked by the smallness of your duties in your present position'. She felt that his resignation speech of the previous November 'did not give the impression that you meant to return home after you had made a sufficient interval between your position as a member of the government and as a member of the opposition'. She received support for her view from Carson, who wrote to Churchill on March 23:

. . . I think myself, speaking quite candidly, that having stated in yr resignation you were going to take up active service in the field it will give lots of grounds for criticism if you come back without some opportunity of showing the grave necessity you feel for such a step —& above all things it wd be so hard for yr causes & usefulness if the country got the impression you acted spasmodically or without sound and deliberate judgement. . . .

Clementine Churchill sent this letter on to her husband on March 24. 'You see how anxious he is,' she wrote, 'that you should not blunt or break yourself as an instrument by a premature return.' Churchill rejected Carson's advice. On March 26, as soon as the letter reached him, he wrote to his wife:

. . . Of course if C chooses he can make my path smooth; but smooth or rough I mean to tread it. I am absolutely sure it is the right thing to do—& all these fears of taunts & criticisms shd be treated as if they were enemy's shells—i.e. they shd not deter one from any action wh is necessary in the general interest. As Furse says 'It is bigger than that'. Have a good confidence & do not easily lend yourself to the estimate formed by those who will never be satisfied till the breath is out of my body. All this dawdling is wrong. Manoeuvering for position is only a minor part of war; a strong army & a good cause & plenty of ammunition drives ahead all right. . . .

Nothing will now turn me from my intention. The more I feel myself cool & indifferent in danger here, the more I feel strong for the work that lies before me. . . . If Carson & his whole committee advised against my return—protested even—still I shd come—& at once.

Not all the advice which Churchill received was opposed to his return. When C. P. Scott wrote on March 24 he expressed none of the reservations which he had expressed to Clementine Churchill two days before. Scott was enthusiastic to see Churchill back in the House of Commons:

. . . I rejoice that you intend to return shortly & I cannot doubt that, so far as the political opportunity is concerned, the need for your presence is immediate. The Opposition—that is the party of energy & of concentration—is leaderless & waits for you to lead it. Any day may bring great events—the reconstruction of the Ministry, or a military folly or misfortune. . . . People may say what they like about you, as they have said & will say, but as long as you do the right thing with a single eye to the public safety nothing can hurt you. Personally—if it's worth while to speak of so small a matter—I have often found myself in antagonism to you & expect I shall again, but that doesn't prevent me from seeing that you may be able to render a great service to the country & from desiring that, with the least possible delay, you shd take the work in hand. Your place is here, not there. . . .

On March 22 Churchill read in the newspapers of the attack made on the Government's air policy by the newly elected Pemberton Billing. 'Our present position in the air,' Billing had told the House of Commons, 'is one that reflects credit neither on our Government, nor on those officers whose duty it has been to prepare, to look forward, and to endeavour to gain for this country supremacy in the air'; and he demanded the creation of an Air Board which would promote an active and unified air policy. 'Billing's air speech strikes me as vy good,' Churchill wrote to his

wife on March 25, '& it must disturb the complacency of the Govt
—if anything cd.' But Billing had no political strength: Clementine Churchill saw this at once, and told her husband so.

Churchill was driven forward—his wife exhausted—by this daily
barrage of uncertainty and doubt. 'These grave public anxieties
are very wearing,' she wrote to him on March 23; 'When next I
see you I hope there will be a little time for us both alone. We
are still young, but Time flies, stealing love away and leaving
only friendship which is very peaceful but not very stimulating
or warming.' Churchill, shaken by this sad confession, replied on
March 26:

. . . Oh my darling do not write of 'friendship' to me—I love you
more each month that passes and feel the need of you & all your
beauty. My precious charming Clemmie—I too feel sometimes the
longing for rest & peace. So much effort, so many years of ceaseless
fighting & worry, so much excitement & now this rough fierce life here
under the hammer of Thor, makes my older mind turn—for the first
time I think to other things than action. Is it 'Forty & finished' as the
old devil's Duchess wrote? But wd it not be delicious to go for a few
weeks to some lovely spot in Italy or Spain & just paint & wander about
together in bright warm sunlight far from the clash of arms or bray
of Parliaments? We know each other so well now & cd play better than
we ever could.

Sometimes also I think I wd not mind stopping living vy much—I
am so devoured by egoism that I wd like to have another soul in another world & meet you in another setting, & pay you all the love &
honour of the gt romances. Two days ago I was walking up to the
trenches & we heard several shells on our left, each shot coming nearer
as the gun travelled round searching for prey. One cd calculate more
or less where the next wd come. Our road led naturally past the
ruined convent (where I have made the 'conning tower') and I said
'the next will hit the convent'. Sure enough just as we got abreast of it,
the shell arrived with a screech and a roar & tremendous bang &
showers of bricks & clouds of smoke & all the soldiers jumped & scur-
ried, & peeped up out of their holes & corners. It did not make me
jump a bit—not a pulse quickened. I do not mind noise as some vy
brave people do. But I felt—20 yards more to the left & no more tan-
gles to unravel, no more anxieties to face, no more hatreds & injustices

to encounter: joy of all my foes, relief of that old rogue, a good ending
to a chequered life, a final gift—unvalued—to an ungrateful country—
an impoverishment of the war-making power of Britain wh no one wd
ever know or measure or mourn.

But I am not going to give in or tire at all. I am going on fighting to
the vy end in any station open to me from wh I can most effectively
drive on this war to victory. If I were somehow persuaded that I was
not fit for a wider scope I shd be quite content here—whatever happened. If I am equally persuaded that my worth lies elsewhere I will
not be turned from it by any blast of malice or criticism.

During the last week of March, Churchill wrote to several
friends in England seeking their advice: to F. E. Smith, to Edward Goulding, to Max Aitken, to Carson again and to Sir George
Ritchie, the Chairman of the Dundee Liberal Association. On
March 27 he dined with General Lipsett. 'He has gone out of his
way to be helpful to me out here,' Churchill wrote to his wife on
the following day, 'even coming out with me on a prowl in No-
man's-land to see if there were any possibilities to bringing off an
enterprise agst the German trenches.' They talked about Churchill's future. 'I was interested,' Churchill reported, 'to hear him
repeat almost word for word Carson's opinion.' Lipsett's arguments for delay had impressed him. But he still could not believe
they were the right ones. Once more he explained his reasoning
to his wife:

. . . His view is that by waiting a month here a good occasion might
be found that wd save 2 or 3 months waiting at home before effective
work wd be open to me. 'Of course you ought to go home: but you
must get the barbed wire cut first.' Cd not Carson or the Liberal war
cte [committee] ask you to come etc! You are familiar with all this.
Do not suppose I do not feel the force of it. But what if these good
conditions cannot be obtained while I remain out of touch—with all
my means of action & communication paralysed? Frankly I do not think
any really responsible or influential body of MP's are likely to take the
responsibility of inviting me to return, without knowing what I mean
to do or say. And on the other hand if I wait for a Ministerial crisis,
will it not look as if I had come back like a sultan hastening unbidden
to a feast. Whereas in spite of all the crabbing abuse wh has always

beset me, I cd undoubtedly from the box at Westminster, exercise an influence & command attention to matters of vital urgency & import, wh wd in itself justify retrospectively the step I had taken. Nothing cd I think deprive me of my hold on the public attention. Even a controversy about whether I shd or shd not have come home wd only increase the interest in what I said: and the need for justice & Parly expression is so great & widely felt & so real & so recurring that everything will come right. Therefore if, as I expect, it will not be possible to get the barbed wire cut beforehand, I shall nevertheless try to make my way through it. . . .

This was Churchill's last confident assertion that he could brave the difficulties of a return to politics alone. There now arrived from England several letters which made it absolutely clear that if he came back too soon his position would not only be weak but hopeless. On April 3 he received Sir George Ritchie's assessment of Dundee opinion, written on March 28. Churchill could not ignore the views of a man so close to political realities in the constituency upon whose votes he depended. Ritchie stressed bluntly that many of his constituency supporters regarded the Fisher speech as 'unfortunate'. Dundee opinion, he wrote, was 'quite solid that nothing should be done to cause division'; indeed, 'no movement which would endanger the unity of the Country or the stability of the present Government would have the slightest chance of success'. Ritchie felt that if Churchill opposed Asquith publicly, it would 'put a weapon into the hands of your Enemies who would hurl the charge of instability at you and use it for all it was worth to thwart your advancement'.

Churchill was influenced by Ritchie's letter. He knew that it was based upon careful inquiries and genuine goodwill. 'It makes a serious impression upon me,' he wrote to his wife on April 3. She tried to reinforce Ritchie's advice, sending her husband a letter which Garvin had sent her on March 28, and which argued against precipitate action. Garvin had written:

. . . no instant conquests are to be looked for. The less they seem to be sought—when so many enemies are on the qui vive to impute feverish ambition—the sooner they will come. Something like a definite programme of the course to be pursued should be mapped out and adhered to. Then the occasions will lend their aid.

It would be well worth Winston's while to spend a month after leaving the army before reappearing in the House. That would put him back again on the old basis of thorough mental preparation which is his strength; and to the deliberation would attach the sense of power.

If he comes back to play a rather lone hand for a few months, he owes it to himself that people should not be *too* certain of what he is going to say and that his criticisms should have measured power by recognising where the Government have done well, or rather less ill, in some respects than in others. As I am never tired of saying, to be obstructive one must be just. It's absolutely true. So much for 'the lone hand' which in a few months would make him much sought after by several sections.

Garvin speculated on the possibility of Churchill joining with Carson, or alternatively of waiting for the possibility of an autumn Election. He continued:

Above all, no hurry. Too much is at stake for the whole of after-life. A month after coming home to study the whole situation, to see people and things as it were from the outside, to make sure of what ground is firm under foot before the quiet vibrating decisive intervention begins. I have *no fear* for the ultimate result: at the worst adversity for six months, a year, two years! What does that matter to the only man of high political rank who has the priceless advantage of being only 41.

Garvin echoed Clementine Churchill's concern for the man himself, for his reputation and for his personal position. Churchill understood such concern. But he was consumed by the desire to return at once to active political life, believing that this could not harm his reputation.

Garvin had ended his letter with an immediate suggestion: 'I believe Northcliffe would take for the Times a series of articles on the "needs of the army", done as Winston could do them.' Churchill was excited by this idea. Because neither of Northcliffe's main daily newspapers, *The Times* and the *Daily Mail*, were sympathetic to Churchill, he moved cautiously, enlisting the support of Northcliffe's brother, Lord Rothermere, who encouraged him to follow up Garvin's suggestion. On April 3 Churchill sent his wife a letter for Northcliffe which he asked her to send on once she had read it: 'It can only do good or do nothing,' he told her. But she did not like it, and explained why. 'If it goes,' she warned him on April 6, 'it will form part of your biography in after times and after the way Lord N has flouted you I cannot bear that you should write to him in that vein. Besides I do not think it is as well-expressed as some of your letters. I am sure it is no use writing private letters to great journalists—Even if they do, in consequence decide to run you, they feel patronizing and protective about it and the support then lacks in genuine ardour.' Clementine Churchill realized, on reading his letter to Northcliffe, that her husband did not intend to remain at the front much longer. In her own letter she tried to explain her feelings:

My Darling own Dear Winston I am so torn and lacerated over you. If I say 'stay where you are' a wicked bullet may find you which you might but for me escape. . . .

If I were sure that you would come thro' unscathed I would say: 'wait wait have patience, don't pluck the fruit before it is ripe. Everything will come to you if you don't snatch at it.' To be great one's actions must be able to be understood by simple people. Your motive for going to the Front was easy to understand. Your motive for coming back requires explanation.

That is why your Fisher speech was not a success—people could not understand it. It required another speech to make it clear. . . .

Darling don't be vexed with me for writing so crudely. If to help you or make you great or happy I could give up my life it would be easy for me to do it.

Clementine Churchill knew how much her husband was the victim of depression. She had seen him depressed to the point of resignation after his return from Antwerp. She had seen depression settle upon him after his removal from the Admiralty. She had watched while the obsession with Gallipoli threatened to cloud his judgement and alienate his colleagues. In her letter of April 6 she warned him of the danger that if he returned too soon from the trenches, and failed to obtain political office, he risked embittering himself yet again. She was afraid that this time he would not be able to shake off the brooding and the introspection, but that, as she wrote bluntly, he would 'rehearse all the past events over and over again and gradually live in the past instead of in the present and in the great future'.

Clementine Churchill continued to send her husband warnings against too swift a return. She feared that his hatred of Government inaction was an insufficient reason, and might appear to many purely opportunistic. She felt that his isolation in Flanders had led him to exaggerate the public need for his return. Nor did she share his optimism at the effect of Billing's challenge. 'Mr Pemberton Billing does not make headway,' she had written to him on March 29 'tho' I agree with you in thinking his speech good. The newspapers are chary of taking him up. People seem to think he has an axe to grind (being an unsuccessful aeroplane constructor) and so he is suspect. I am afraid he is rather a flashy young man. . . . I really don't think he has harmed the Govt one bit. It needs something far more stern and weighty. He is just out to make people's flesh creep!' But Churchill could not bear to be deflected from his path. 'How completely out of action I am!' he wrote to his wife on March 30. 'How wasted all my knowledge, training, life, energy! Believe me I do all that I can do here usefully. But it wd be folly to continue—now that I see clearly another field opening out.' Clementine Churchill recognized the intensity of his feelings. 'His intention of coming home,' she wrote in her reply to Garvin on March 29, 'is gradually hardening and becoming definite. In fact he has now ceased to discuss the pros and cons. The remaining difficulty with him is the time for taking the step. . . . He may return quite suddenly.'

April 1 was Clementine Churchill's birthday. She was thirty-one; but, she wrote to him, if victory were imminent and he both safe and content, she would feel no older than twenty. But contentment was impossible for him. That same day Sir Arthur

Markham, one of his few Parliamentary supporters, wrote urging him to return at once:

My dear Churchill,

You have doubtless many friends & advisers urging you to take a certain decision either to remain in France or return. I will add one more word if I may, though I do not suppose it will influence your decision. I am quite clear your duty is in the House of Commons & that you can do more effective work there for your country than command-ing a regiment. No one doubts your courage & that any decision you arrive at will not be influenced by public opinion. To be candid your reply to Balfour was unfortunate, you would have done better to have left him alone or to have remained here pursuing the course you had taken to its logical end; at all events this view is held by most people. All that I want is to see effective opposition for the good of the coun-try. Carson certainly is in better health but if you returned you could both with your voice & pen render I am convinced better service to the country than by remaining in France. The govt drift day by day indecision being their key note, & our poor country has bad days ahead. You ought to be the vigilant watch dog to urge them to make war. I would rather see a multitude of mistakes where we had the initiative than we always should let the Germans have the same. The man who makes no mistakes never makes anything; we all make mistakes. Come back; those who want you, will help you to fight your battle in the House.

> Best of wishes, Yrs sincerely
> Arthur B. Markham

'My mind is unchanged about returning,' Churchill wrote to his mother on April 3; 'It is only a question of how & when. I ex-pect to decide vy soon now. . . . I will let you know when I come to any decision. Meanwhile try to get hold of Donald of the Daily Chronicle & without telling him my plans try to make him friendly & well-disposed. After all he is a Fisherite—so he ought to be pleased.' 'How & when', he could not decide. 'I am still wait-ing to hear further from Carson,' he wrote to his wife on April 6, '& I suppose he is still waiting to see how the situation develops.' Later that day he wrote to her again, for he had heard from F. E. Smith of further grumblings in the Cabinet about conscription.

'Try to keep in touch with LG,' he asked her, '& with BL through Max. I don't expect myself that this will come to anything. A [Asquith] will toe the line about compulsion when he sees they mean to have it. He delays these things in order to be able to give them away at the last minute. But I am not in any hurry now, & will certainly "wait & see".'

Throughout April Churchill tried to discover what issues would threaten to bring Asquith's Government down, who were the politicians willing to exploit them, and whether they would be willing to let him work with them, and join them in any new ad-ministration. He believed that his principal hope lay in Lloyd George's defection. *Keep in touch with LG,*' he begged his wife on April 7. It was over the growing demand for conscription that a serious crisis was most likely to arise. Churchill believed that the Tories, led by Bonar Law, Curzon and Lansdowne, might leave the Coalition if Asquith refused to introduce conscription immediately. 'A vy big situation wd be open then,' he told his wife, 'but I am by no means certain how it would affect me.' On April 3 he had written to Curzon to encourage a firm line over conscription. 'Surely there is only one course now with regard to the married man,' he wrote, '—universal compulsion with nec-essary exemptions. I hope you are pressing this.' Churchill asked Curzon for 'one of your promised letters'; but it never came.

Churchill had great faith that F. E. Smith would represent his interests in London, writing to him on April 6: 'Keep in touch with LG . . . keep him up to the mark about me.' Two days later he wrote again, realizing how much he depended upon F. E. Smith for the successful advocacy of his cause. He was convinced that if Asquith's Government fell, its successor would have need of him. He also believed that the help which he had given Lloyd George during the Marconi affair in 1913 had put Lloyd George politically in his debt. His letter to F. E. Smith of April 8 was frank; so much so that he wanted it burnt, writing:

. . . Generally speaking LG is the key to my position at the mo-ment. However a new system might be formed, it seems to me that LG and I shd be together. If he came in to what must be in substance a Tory Administration, he wd need above all Liberal associates. I think you shd get hold of Rufus [Lord Reading] betimes and put to him vy plainly the personal obligation wh exists. He has always recognised it, and wd have gt weight on that point in that quarter.

I have a feeling that BL and LG have a supreme chance now, if they have the resolution to act. It does not seem to me material whether BL is first or LG War or *vice versa*. Either place wd afford the basis of an effective war organisation—compared to wh nothing matters. Munitions will seem to be the easiest opening for me, tho' of course you know my wishes, if they are attainable.

The party of the future might be formed. I am sorry the crisis comes now—if it does: but in that case it is to you I must look and do look with entire confidence that you will set my affairs first in yr thoughts. Burn this wh is for your secret eye alone.

At a time when Churchill most needed a platform, he had to abandon his plan to write for the Northcliffe press. 'I have heard from Goulding, who I got to sound Northcliffe through a discreet channel,' he wrote to his wife on April 9, 'that the latter was vy hostile to the plan. This wd be serious.' 'The opportunity wh existed after the Navy Row has passed,' he added; 'I think I missed a chance through indecision.' But a new opportunity presented itself unexpectedly on April 10, when Churchill received a letter from Carson, written four days earlier, no longer trying to keep him at arm's length:

. . . I think myself things are coming to a crisis here over the question of universal military service, and my Committee, which is growing very strong, is determined that we should raise the question on a definite motion before Easter, and are indeed growing very dissatisfied with the way everything is drifting. It might be worth your while to consider, when a day is fixed for this, whether it would not be your duty to come over, but you will see how things develop in that direction within the next few days. I am not so sure myself that it will be possible for the present Coalition Government to continue its existence as at present, but I will write to you again if there is any information that I think may guide your judgment.

Fired by Carson's change of mood, Churchill wrote immediately to Lloyd George, to discover if his discontent over the repeated delays to bring in conscription had reached the point of breaking with Asquith:

Secret
My dear David,

It seems to me from what I hear that the situation we had in view before the Derby efforts, & again at Christmas is now again maturing. A decision on the recruiting question is now vital, & the repeated postponements cannot surely be tolerated longer. I think that Asquith will probably give way again at the last moment and thus the crisis will be averted for the time. But if not the moment for you to act has come. We are jeopardizing our chances of winning by a continuance of a Governing instrument wh never acts except upon political expediency, wh never initiates anything, & wh utterly fails to do justice to the resolution & spirit of the country. You have let several good chances go by in hope of a better. I cannot judge events & forces vy thoroughly from here, but I am inclined to think that this is the best opportunity that has yet offered: & that unless a decision to adopt universal compulsion is taken forthwith you ought to resign. The party of the future might then be formed: & in that party we shd be strong enough to secure those special political interests & principles with wh we have been identified after the war is over, as well as driving the war forward with the utmost vigour.

I intend vy shortly to return to the House and I am only delaying from day to day on account of small ties out here wh are being adjusted. I am not however in any hurry & wd much rather return on general grounds at my leisure than on the eve of a crisis. I hold the PM's written promise I shall be relieved whenever I wish. Events however may force my hand. . . .

I shd like vy much to hear from you as soon as you feel able to write freely, & no doubt you can find a safe hand to carry your letter. On the whole I believe our interests are likely to lie together in the near future as they have done so often in the past, & certainly we have a common object wh overrides all others.

Yours vy sincly<br>Winston S. Churchill

Hoping to secure the support of the Liberal Press for a new alignment in which he would have a part, Churchill also wrote on April 10 to C. P. Scott:

My dear Scott,

. . . The possibilities of a change in the character & leadership of the Government make me anxious to interchange thoughts with you upon the general & ultimate consequences of such an event. My feeling is that everything that may be necessary to win the war shd be done apart altogether from political peace time opinions: but that it must also be an honourable understanding that after the war our Liberal position on all these questions must be in no way prejudiced, save in so far as the world is changing round us. We have the gt causes of the harmony of the European family of nations, of the rights of nationalities including Ireland, & of a sound & peace tending economic system to safeguard, and we shall need to stand together to discharge these obligations well. Do not let us therefore worry about anything that we may feel necessary to be done now—so long as it is temporary & emergency in its nature. On the other hand we must be strong enough in any new arrangement to secure respect for these enduring interests. You have a considerable part to play at this juncture. See Carson: see Cawley: see also Lloyd George. Show the last if you will this letter.

The numbing hand of Asquith is over everything, and all initiative & energy seem paralysed. All the time however our money (which is not limitless) and life & limb are being consumed on a cruel scale. If they cd see themselves the actual spectacles they wd perhaps sense themselves. . . .

Try now with your influence to knit together the forces that may best serve us in the present catastrophe, and preserve our political conceptions, after we have weathered the storm.

Yours vy sincerely<br>Winston S. Churchill

On April 12 Clementine Churchill begged her husband to change his mind about returning. She did not share his belief in the imminence of a crisis, nor of the ability of Carson, Lloyd George or C. P. Scott to assuage the enmities which her husband had created both as First Lord, and by his continual criticism of Coalition lethargy:

. . . You say in your letter to me: 'You are deluded if you think that by remaining here and doing nothing, I shall regain my influence on affairs.' That is not what I do think.

What I do think is that remaining there you are in an honourable, *comprehensible* position until such time as a portion at least of the country demand your services for the state. If you come back before the call you may blunt yourself. People will always try to deny you power if they think you are looking for it. To gain a share of war direction you are contemplating a terrible risk, the risk of life-long disappointment and bitterness. My Darling Love—For *once only* I pray be patient. It will come if you wait. Don't tear off the unripe fruit which is maturing tho' slowly or check its growth by the frost of a premature return.

I could not bear you to lose your military halo. I have had cause during the 8 years we have lived together to be proud and glad for you so often, but it is this I cherish most of all. And it is this phase which when all is known will strike the imagination of the people: The man who prepared and mobilized the Fleet, who really won the war for England—in the trenches as a simple Colonel. It would be a great romance.

You say you want to be where you can help the war most. If you come home and your return is not generally accepted as correct soldier-like conduct you will not be really able to help the war. You *are* helping it now by example. You are always an interesting figure, be a great one my Darling. You have the opportunity. . . .

Do not be alienated from me by what I write. If I hide what I feel from you the constraint would be unbearable.

Churchill could not take his wife's advice. 'Well,' he replied on April 15 from Laurence Farm, 'there is no use going over the old ground again, nor in darkening this page with my reflections.'

Churchill was not deflected by the weakness of his position. He was determined to return to the centre of policy-making. His feelings about the war intensified during April, strengthening this determination. The prolonged bloodbath of Verdun seemed, he had written to F. E. Smith on April 6, 'to vindicate all I have ever said or written about the offensives by either side in the West.'[3]

[3] The Germans launched an attack on the French fortress of Verdun on 21 February 1916. After four months of intense fighting and artillery bombardment, 650,000 French and German soldiers had been killed, but Verdun remained in French hands. In his book *Verdun*, published in 1930, General Pétain wrote of the young French soldiers returning from the fortress: 'In their unsteady look one sensed visions of horror, while their step and bearing revealed utter despondency. They were crushed by horrifying memories.'

On April 14 he wrote to his wife setting out the 'definite opinions' he had formed about the war:

First we must now make up our minds that there is no chance of
our winning in 1916. That is the beginning of wisdom—we must make
our plans for a combined attack in the summer of 1917: & meanwhile
only bicker on all the fronts, while improving our armies, piling up
munitions and arming the limitless manhood of Russia. Let the Germans attack if they will. Above all no premature offensive by France,
or still more by England alone.

My advice wd therefore be with variation the same as last year. No
offensive in the West, destroy Turkey. That is all we have the
strength to do this year. Next year victory may be won.

Unhappily I expect the exact opposite of all this will be done: and
we shall end the year after bitter losses no further forward than we
are today.

I greatly fear the general result. More than I have ever done before,
I realize the stupendous nature of the task; & the unwisdom with wh
our affairs are conducted makes me almost despair at times of a victorious issue. The same leadership that has waited on public opinion
& newspaper promptings for so long, will readily be the exponent of
an inclusive peace—if that mood is upward in the nation.

Do you think we should succeed in an offensive, if the Germans cannot do it at Verdun with all their skill & science? Our army is not the
same as theirs; and of course their staff is quite intact & taught by
successful experiment. Our staff only represents the brain power of
our poor little peacetime army—with wh hardly any really able men
wd go. We are children at the game compared to them. And in this
day to day trench warfare—they lose half what we do in my opinion.
On the sea the submarine menace is by no means at an end. Balfour's
easy & airy slumbers have after 11 months left us in a worse position
than before. Then the danger was new & unfamiliar. I see a lot of
ships sunk each day, & they no longer publish any weekly summaries:
but far more than in our time. Yet think of the advantage they have
over us in resources. Yet no one complains.

You know how often I have been right about this war. I feel now
that only a supreme effort of patience, & wisdom, with furious energy
straining at the leash will save our cause. Alas I am powerless even
to utter my warnings.

Asquith was finding it increasingly difficult to retain the loyalty of his ministers. On April 13 Lloyd George and C. P. Scott
had tea with Sir George Riddell. According to Riddell's *War
Diary* Lloyd George spoke bitterly against the Coalition. 'There
is no grip,' he asserted; 'Asquith and Balfour do not seem to realize the serious nature of the situation.' Lloyd George declared
that he might resign and praised Carson for 'managing his little
group with great skill'. The discontent mounted. On April 18
Lord Milner appealed in the House of Lords for compulsory military service. He was supported by Lord Morley, who had resigned on the eve of war in protest against British involvement,
by Lord Charles Beresford, and by Lord Derby, whose voluntary
recruiting scheme Asquith had tried to use as an alternative to
compulsion. On April 20 Sir Henry Wilson wrote to Milner: 'If
ever a man deserved to be tried and shot that man is the PM.
. . . We hope that you and Carson and LG have, at last, got him
by the throat. No mercy please.' That same day Asquith offered
to explain his recruiting policy to Parliament. But he insisted that
his explanation must take place at a Secret Session.

As soon as Lord Milner emerged as a focal point of dissent,
Churchill's chances of being called upon faded considerably. Ten
years had passed since he had publicly and savagely attacked
Milner's conduct of affairs in South Africa. But time could not
heal all wounds, and these were deep ones. Milner refused to
forgive Churchill for what had passed. Carson tried to act as an
intermediary, but in vain. Nor did Churchill receive sufficiently
full accounts of how the various centres of dissent were grouping
to appreciate their objectives or gauge the part he might play.
Until March he had appeared to the dissenters a possible and
indeed valuable ally, articulate and persuasive; since his Fisher
speech many critics of the Government saw him as a dangerous
companion, erratic and unpredictable. Clementine Churchill
sensed this new hostility. After a dinner party at 10 Downing
Street in the second week of April she talked to Lord Reading.
'He fears your coming back unless sent for would be injurious
to your reputation,' she wrote on April 14. There were other Ministers at the dinner. 'Grey terribly aged and worn-looking,' she

wrote, 'Kitchener thinner and sad. AJB wan and white, but still purring away.' As for the conscription crisis, Asquith 'seems quite unconcerned. . . . He is like morphia.'

On April 15 Churchill wrote to his wife from Laurence Farm that General Furse, his Divisional General, was coming to dine with him. Many Generals had become disillusioned with the Coalition. 'His only relaxation,' Churchill wrote of Furse, 'is to wish for the downfall of Asquith who he thinks is the cause of all our evils.' Churchill told his wife of his own state of mind: 'when I am not consumed with inward fury at the damnable twists wh I have been served with and chewing black charcoal with all my might, I am buoyant & lively . . .'.

On April 18 Churchill learned of the Secret Session, and decided to seek leave to return to London. This he was granted; but he had to promise to return to his Battalion the moment the debate was over. He reached London on April 19. On April 20 Sinclair wrote encouragingly from Ploegsteert: 'Good luck to you Samson, and if you find your strength has returned, stay where you can most effectively contribute to the damnation of the Philistine.' On reaching London Churchill received a letter dated April 16 from C. P. Scott, replying to his own letter of April 10 and informing him that Lloyd George was on the verge of resignation. Upon this belief Scott had based a plan in which Churchill had a leading part. Lloyd George's departure, Scott believed:

. . . will be the beginning of a new chapter in the history of the war & of our politics. At once, with him & Carson outside the Govment there will be the beginnings of a real Opposition. You will, I take for granted, join them—as soon, I hope, as Parliament meets after the Easter recess—and together you will be formidable & all the more independent and energetic elements in the House will by degrees rally round you. The effect on the Govment will be immediate & in the long run decisive—A real reconstruction will for the first time become possible—one which shall be not merely a re-shuffling of the old elements with the old palsied spirit still pervading it, but one in the construction of which those at present outside it will have had the chief voice & on which they will be able to impose a new policy—

That is an occasion surely large enough & hopeful enough to recall you to your true place—I desire your return the more because I agree so deeply with the general policy outlined in your letter. There will be those in any combination, old or new, who will be opposed to some of its main ideas & who will be prepared to substitute a tariff war for a war of armies &, so far as in them lies, to divide Europe into two permanently hostile camps—That way lies the destruction & death & the ruin of all our hopes for the future of our country & of the world. Anything rather than that, & if there is to be union it must be a union on terms & in the hope & resolve of a better England which, even during the war, we may join to build up. This part of your letter I read to Lloyd George today & he cordially concurred in the policy expressed. On that basis we can join hands. . . .

Churchill was excited by Scott's plan. He saw Lloyd George, who discussed the possibility of resigning, and of their common action. But in the third week of April, determined to preserve his Coalition, Asquith bowed to the Cabinet's pressure and agreed to an extension of compulsion. Lloyd George had therefore no cause to resign. Scott's hopes for a 'real Opposition' were destroyed. 'Churchill is very sick at the idea of the thing going through quietly,' Frances Stevenson noted in her diary on April 19. 'He is all for a split, and for the forming of a vigorous opposition, in which he would take an active part.' Churchill found himself, not an engineer of Asquith's most serious parliamentary challenge of the war, but a spectator of events which could not bring him advantage. He decided, however, to seek further release from his military duties, and asked for an extra two weeks leave to follow on immediately from the Secret Session. Haig sent a message to say that he had no objection; his Deputy Military Secretary, Major Vesey,[4] wrote enthusiastically to Churchill on April 23: 'Good luck to you in your work during the next few weeks. I am sure you can do a good deal at home for the Cause.'

[4] Ivo Lucius Beresford Vesey, 1876-    . 2nd Lieutenant, 1897. Major, War Office 1914–15; GHQ France, 1915–16. Director of Recruiting and Organization, War Office, 1919–23. Knighted, 1923. Director of Organization and Staff Duties, Air Ministry, 1923–9. Major-General, 1928. Director of Staff Duties, War Office, 1931–34. General, 1937. Chief of General Staff, India, 1937–9.

No record survives of what was said during the Secret Session of April 25. 'If only your speech had been reported,' Clementine Churchill wrote three days later, 'I feel the Press would urge your recall.' But secrecy, as Asquith realized, acted to the Government's advantage. The Press was necessarily silent, and the public never found out who had spoken, or to what purpose.

On April 27 Parliament met in open session. This was the moment of public confrontation. To his extreme anger, Churchill could not be there. That morning he had received a telegram from Brigadier-General Trotter informing him that General Furse 'does not sanction extension while you are commanding 6 R Scots Fus and your battalion is in trenches'. Churchill returned at once to Ploegsteert. 'It is such a waste having him in a dugout,' Jack Churchill wrote to Lady Randolph that night, 'and it reflects very much on the jealous fools who keep him there. . . .' The debate on conscription took place in Churchill's absence; he could neither influence it, nor gain advantage from it. On April 27 the Government introduced a Bill for a further extension of partial military service. Carson rose as the leader of the opposition and was so successful in demanding a more comprehensive measure that Asquith abandoned the Bill. Five days later the Government accepted the principle of full compulsory service. On May 3 a new Bill was introduced in the House of Commons, making all men between the ages of eighteen and forty-one subject to compulsory enlistment. For fear of civil unrest, Ireland was excluded. On May 25 the Bill received Royal assent. The compulsionists had won. Carson was triumphant. But Asquith remained Prime Minister.

Clementine Churchill was angry that her husband had been recalled so abruptly and unexpectedly to the front. Despite her strong pleas for him not to return prematurely, she now recognized the tremendous opportunity which joint opposition with Carson offered him. 'If only you had been here yesterday & spoken,' she wrote to him on April 28. Her disillusionment with Asquith was complete: 'The Government are in a shameful position,' she wrote. Churchill did not fret. He had made up his mind to leave the Army altogether, convinced that another opportunity for opposition would soon present itself. Plans were being discussed at GHQ to amalgamate the 6th Battalion of the Royal Scots Fusiliers with the 7th Battalion, as there were no longer enough men in either to form two effective fighting units. The amalgamated force was likely to be commanded by the Colonel of the 7th Battalion, Lieutenant-Colonel Gordon,[5] a regular officer, so that Churchill had no immediate prospect of further front-line employment. Hakewill Smith later wrote to the author that at about this time Churchill had gone to St Omer to see Sir Douglas Haig. On his return he had told the officers of his Headquarters Staff 'that Haig had offered him command of a Brigade; but had said that he could do much more for the war effort by returning to Parliament and using his energy and skill to get conscription through the House. Winston added that he had seen the force of Haig's arguments and had reluctantly agreed to return to England.'

The amalgamation of the Battalions seemed to Churchill an ideal opportunity to quit the trenches. On April 29 he wrote to his wife from Laurence Farm: 'The military were pleased & placated by my return. It is probable that the battalion will be broken up within 10 days, & that we shall not return to the trenches after we leave them on Wednesday morning.' In his postscript Churchill asked his wife to 'explain the position' to Carson, Garvin and Scott, on whom his political hopes centred increasingly. Lloyd George remained in the Cabinet, gaining in power and confidence; he had no need of Churchill's support.

Churchill waited impatiently for confirmation that his Battalion was to be dissolved. 'The Government is moribund,' he wrote to his wife on May 1. 'I only trust they will not die too soon.' Clementine Churchill had become equally impatient for a decision. 'Let me hear that you are coming home for *good* to take up your *real* work,' she wrote from Blenheim Palace on April 30. She was now an active partisan of his swift return. On May 2 Churchill

[5] Edward Ian Drumearn Gordon, 1877–1942. 2nd Lieutenant, Royal Scots Fusiliers, 1899. Major, January 1915. Lieutenant-Colonel commanding, 6th/7th Battalion, Royal Scots Fusiliers, June 1916–January 1918; 1st Battalion, January–July 1918. Retired, 1919.

sent her his final letter from Laurence Farm. With his hopes for a rapid return to politics fulfilled, his fretfulness was gone, and he was willing to contemplate relaxation. 'Wd it not be vy nice to go to Blenheim for the Sunday,' he wrote: 'If you arrange this, please get me 3 large tubes of *thin* white (not stiff) . . . also 3 more canvasses: and a bottle of that poisonous solution wh cleans the paint off old canvasses.'

The time had come for Churchill to leave his Battalion. On May 3 he and his men moved out of Ploegsteert, where they had served for more than four months. Dry billets were found a few miles behind the lines. On May 6 Churchill wrote formally to his Corps Commander, Sir Charles Fergusson: 'I do not seek a new appointment at the present time. I desire to attend to my Parliamentary & public duties which have become urgent. I request therefore that I may be permitted to proceed to England on leave as soon as my command is broken up & that I may await further orders there.' Churchill's request was granted.

During his final days with the 6th Royal Scots Fusiliers Churchill made every effort to help those whose future was uncertain as a result of the Battalion's amalgamation. 'He took endless trouble,' Captain Gibb recorded: 'he borrowed motor-cars and *scoured* France, interviewing Generals and Staff-officers great and small, in the effort to do something to help those who had served under him. Needless to say, the orderly-room was seething with applications of all sorts, possible and impossible, but he treated them all with the utmost patience and good humour.' On May 6 Churchill gave his officers a farewell lunch in Armentières. That afternoon the Battalion entrained for Bethune, and for a rest in reserve, out of the war zone. On May 7 General Furse sent Churchill a note of farewell. 'It seems to me peculiarly up to you and to Lloyd George,' he wrote, 'to concentrate all your efforts on breaking such a futile Govt—and that, immediately. How can anyone suppose that the same men in the same large flat bottomed tub can do any better in the future than they have done in the past? . . . I wish you the best of luck in a task of enormous difficulty and honour.' On the morning of May 7 the Battalion was inspected by Major-General McCracken,[6] the officer commanding the 15th Division to which it was to be transferred. At two that afternoon Churchill summoned his officers to the Orderly Room. 'He told us,' Gibb recalled, 'that he had come to regard the young Scot as a most "formidable fighting animal", and he touched on his other connections with Scotland in the most appreciative fashion. As he rose to shake hands, the Adjutant spoke up and told him what we were all thinking, and what it had been to us to serve under him. . . . I believe every man in the room felt Winston Churchill's leaving us a real personal loss.'

[6] Frederick William Nicholas McCracken, 1859–1949. 2nd Lieutenant, 1879. Major-General, 1914. Inspector of Infantry, December 1914–March 1915. Commanded 15th Scottish Division, March 1915–June 1917. Knighted, 1917. Lieutenant-General commanding Scottish Command, 1918–19.

# 25

# 'I am learning to hate'

CHURCHILL'S RETURN to London in May 1916 was marked by no upsurge in his political fortunes. Asquith, by accepting compulsory service, had prevented the conscriptionists from destroying the Coalition. Lloyd George, with whom Churchill had hoped to form the nucleus of an opposition, remained in the Cabinet. Of the dissident Tories, Lord Milner still refused to be reconciled to Churchill, and Carson's opposition had been temporarily weakened by Asquith's conscription success. As for Lord Fisher, everyone whom Churchill met spoke disparagingly of the old Admiral, and there seemed no future in a Fisher–Churchill alliance.

Having chosen to resume his Parliamentary duties, Churchill had every intention of speaking as soon as possible, although his wife advised him to bide his time. On May 9, only two days after his return, he spoke in the Commons for the first time since the Secret Session; and for the first time publicly since his Fisher speech. The issue was a serious one, but the occasion unsuited to a major assault on Government policy. In April 1916, the Easter Rising in Dublin had been suppressed by armed force; Asquith therefore decided that, given the excited state of Irish feeling, Ireland should be excluded from compulsory service. A clause was inserted into the Military Service Bill which allowed Ireland to keep the system of voluntary recruitment. Asquith gave the House of Commons only a brief time to debate the Bill, and the Irish exclusion clause received little attention. But Carson, as the champion of Ulster, spoke against special privileges designed to placate the southern catholics, and Churchill, fearing that a shortage of men would create grave danger for the Allies, spoke likewise against the Irish clause. Both he and Carson knew that they could not change Government policy. But, like Carson, Churchill wanted to make his protest known. 'It is a time when men are urgently needed,' he told the House of Commons, 'and from the British and Imperial point of view the desirability of obtaining fresh and extended supplies from Ireland is clear and patent to the minds of everyone.' Churchill's experience of trench warfare had convinced him of the paramount need for more men. 'This is a time for trying to overcome difficulties,' he insisted, 'and not for being discouraged or too readily deterred by them.' At that moment there was an interruption. An Irish Nationalist MP, Laurence Ginnell,[1] cried out in anger: 'What about the Dardanelles?'

Here was the challenge which would recur month by month and year by year, never to be shaken off. Suddenly Churchill realized that well-argued speeches on subjects about which he felt strongly were not enough to re-establish his political position. He needed to clear his name of a crippling charge. The conscription debate continued. Churchill could not interrupt his speech in order to discuss the Dardanelles. No clever repartee, no brief digression, could answer the allegations which had been built up against him. He knew that it would need a searching enquiry to make the facts known. All he could reply to Ginnell's outburst, almost all he could ever say unless the Government agreed to publish the facts, was a lame: 'I am afraid I should be out of order if I were to deal with that matter.' He continued with his speech. Ireland was the subject, of Ireland he must talk. But the cry, 'What about the Dardanelles?' echoed about the Chamber like a widow's curse.

During Churchill's first week back in London Fisher sent him a letter of welcome. 'This moment I've seen in the paper you are

[1] Laurence Ginnell, 1854–1923. A Barrister. Nationalist MP, 1906–18. One of the founders of the London Irish Literary Society.

back,' he wrote on May 10; '*Welcome home* for *good I hope!*' A year had passed since Fisher's resignation. 'My dear Fisher,' Churchill replied affectionately on May 14, 'This accursed year has now come to an end, & please God there will be better luck for you & me in the next, & some chance of helping our country to save itself & all dependent on it. Don't lose heart—I am convinced destiny has not done with you yet. Yours ever W.' Fisher replied that day: 'A Big Change is imminent but will it be in time?' He was wrong; no change in Asquith's strength was either imminent or likely. The only organized Parliamentary opposition group, the Unionist War Committee led by Carson, did not feel itself strong enough to divide the House.

On May 17 Churchill rose again to speak from the opposition benches, this time about an Air Department which the Government had agreed to establish. A Conservative MP, William Joynson-Hicks[2] had brought in a motion calling upon the Government to take without delay 'every possible step to make adequate provision for a powerful Air Service'. Churchill believed that he himself could revitalize the Air Service, enthuse the pilots, and give their frail craft mastery of the air. He had watched with anger the growing German air superiority above his own trenches at Ploegsteert. He listened with apprehension to the Government's plans, which were outlined in the Commons by the Under-Secretary of State for War, Harold Tennant, who explained that an Air Board would be set up, with powers to coordinate the air policy of the Admiralty and War Office. Tennant added that Asquith had invited Lord Curzon to accept the presidency of the Board, and that Curzon had accepted. Churchill was dissatisfied with what Tennant had outlined as the Air Board's functions and powers. 'The House will have heard with some feelings of disappointment,' he said, 'the announcement of my right hon Friend of the change which is proposed by the Gov-

2 William Joynson-Hicks, 1865–1932. Known as 'Jix'. Churchill's successful opponent at the by-election in North-West Manchester, 1908. Conservative MP, 1908–10; 1911–29. Keenly interested in aeronautics. Chairman, Belgian Field Ambulance Service, 1914–18. Created Baronet, 1919. Postmaster-General and Paymaster-General, 1923. Minister of Health, 1923–4. Home Secretary 1924–9. Created Viscount Brentford, 1929.

ernment. After the many months that this matter has been under discussion, and the repeated postponements in bringing it before the House, we had hoped that a real solution, or a real effort towards a solution, would have been set forth in the Government statement.' Churchill did not criticize the choice of Curzon as President, although many of his listeners knew how much he himself had hoped to be offered the post. He criticized, not the man but the nature of his task. 'Lord Curzon, without adequate powers, will not succeed in altering the present state of affairs,' he declared, 'and in the choice of a policy, judging by the impression made upon me by the statement to which we have just listened, the Government have followed no principle whatever, except the familiar principle of postponing until the last possible moment and then following the line of least resistance.'

Churchill felt the need to defend his own record in the matter of air defence. Without defending each of his Admiralty policies which had been under attack, he could not see how he would ever again be accepted as a serious contender for high office. He believed that the aerial successes won while he was at the Admiralty had been based upon policies which his successor, A. J. Balfour, had subsequently neglected; and that the public had never been given the facts about all that he himself had achieved. He defended his record as First Lord:

It is commonly supposed that the Admiralty before the War, at some more or less distant period before the War, under my impulsion rushed into the business of Home defence, snatched it away from the proper authorities, and then mismanaged and neglected it. That is not the truth. The contrary is the truth. Until a month after the war had begun the sole responsibility for the defence of all vulnerable points in England, by gun fire, seaplanes, or any other method against aerial attack, rested with the War Office. . . .

A month after the War had begun—3rd September, I think, was the actual date—Lord Kitchener asked me whether the Admiralty would undertake the general duty of Home defence against aerial attack. . . .

I carefully stated that the Admiralty could not be responsible for Home defence, but could only be responsible for doing the best possible with the material available. On this basis, which was formally accepted by the Government, the Admiralty undertook, very reluctantly for the most part, the thankless—and as it seemed then almost hopeless task. . . . Our available guns and aeroplanes were forthwith disposed to what we considered the best possible advantages, and overseas air bases in France and Flanders were established, and those have proved an effective and almost absolute parry to the attack of German Army Zeppelins coming from Belgium and the Rhine.

The series of offensive enterprises against the Zeppelin sheds began, and on this quest, in spite of their slender resources, the naval arm went to Düsseldorf, to Cologne, and Friedrichshafen, on Lake Constance, and even to Cuxhaven, in the North Sea. Six Zeppelins, it is believed, were destroyed either in the air, or in their sheds by a handful of naval pilots acting, what the First Lord of the Admiralty would now call, 'outside their normal sphere'.

It would be hard to show that all allied airmen and pilots had during all the War succeeded by this method in destroying so many. Moreover, within a few weeks of the Admiralty becoming responsible very large orders were placed for aerial guns and the proper kind of ammunition, and searchlights, and immense orders were distributed for aeroplanes to the utmost productive limit of every aircraft factory in any part of the world not already occupied with Army work. . . .

Such were the circumstances in which the Admiralty became responsible for Home defence, and the manner in which we endeavoured to discharge that responsibility, and I think I am justified in telling them to the House and to the country.

The criticisms levelled at Churchill covered, as he knew, every aspect of his work at the Admiralty; even the phrases which he had used in his speeches. He had once referred to the pilots of the Royal Naval Air Service as 'hornets'. This description had subsequently been criticized as derogatory to the pilots, and this criticism had been raised again earlier in the debate of May 17. Churchill spoke strongly in his own defence:

My hon Friend the Member for Brentford (Mr Joynson-Hicks) has twitted me this afternoon with my phrase about 'hornets'. I am very glad to come to the 'hornets'. The main defence of England against Zeppelins has consisted since the War began in that formidable 'swarm of hornets' of which I spoke in 1913—that is to say, aeroplanes with skilful pilots held ready with bombs and guns to attack any Zeppelin which approaches our shores. This defence has been effective, up to date, in preventing any attack by Zeppelins coming here by daylight, or even by moonlight.

Churchill continued his defence, angry that his concern to build up the Royal Naval Air Service had become the subject of criticism by those who felt that he should have concentrated his efforts on the Navy:

But for the aeroplane service we had created before the War there would have been nothing to stop Zeppelins from raiding us every fine day; and if they were able to come in daylight they would be able to find their way with certainty to the vital and vulnerable points —to our arsenals, to our magazines, to our oil tanks, to our dockyards, to our munition works, and to drop their bombs with accuracy and deliberation from altitudes beyond the reach of any anti-aircraft gun which, at any rate, existed during the first year of the War.

Our aeroplane defence has restricted Zeppelin attacks to a few nights in certain months, and even then those attacks can only be delivered erring and almost blindfold. The proof of the triumph of the aeroplane is that after twenty-two months of war no object of any military or naval importance among the thousands which exist scattered broadcast throughout the country has yet been struck by any Zeppelin bomb.

Churchill was so embittered by being a victim of misrepresentation, so depressed by the accusations of his rashness and negligence, so convinced that his achievements placed him above almost all his leading contemporaries in foresight and perseverance, that he felt forced to defend himself in detail; otherwise, he believed, he would never be called to office again. Because of the increased German Zeppelin raids, his critics had begun to ask why the Admiralty had refused, while he was First Lord, to build its own airships which could have been the counterpart to the Zeppelin. Churchill's preference for aeroplanes was denounced as a fatal error; proof that he did not understand the realities of national defence. This was a serious indictment, which, if it could be sustained, might greatly damage his political future, certainly for as long as the war lasted. He defended his decision:

. . . who is to pretend that it was in our power, even if we had begun, say, in 1912, to create a Zeppelin fleet approaching in quality or numbers the German Zeppelin fleet—the product of ten years' expense and experiment on the most lavish scale.

Why, Sir, even if any Government had entertained the project— and no Government I have ever seen would have done—even if any Parliament had voted the funds necessary, we could not have hoped to compete with Germany successfully in rigid airships in the time available. We had not the art, we have not the native stores of aluminium which would be accessible in time of war. Our attempts to build experimental machines have been baulked until some months after the beginning of the War by continuous delay and disappointment.

Nearly 100 aeroplanes and their sheds can be obtained for the price of one Zeppelin and its shed.[3] What folly it would have been for us to have squandered the hard-won, grudged, and exiguous money which had to be secured for air defence on Zeppelins, fewer in number, inferior in type, and certainly ineffective for the purpose in hand —the defence of the civil population from Zeppelin raids.

What would our situation have been at the sudden outbreak of war if we had been found with a handful of these frail and feeble monsters, so easily broken by the accidents of weather, instead of with an Army Aeroplane Service, out of which the immense expansion of the present time has developed, or of a Naval Wing which in the emergency guarded securely every vital point in our Islands, and set the military free to go abroad? We should indeed have thrown away the substance for the shadow.

We are all surfeited nowadays with that kind of wisdom which comes after the event, but I do not in the least shrink from applying that unfair test to the policy pursued by the Admiralty and the War Office, partly under my responsibility and with my full agreement, in regard to the building of a Zeppelin fleet before the War.

Suppose by the stroke of a wand we could step back with full

[3] A Zeppelin could cost as much as £500,000. This sum included the cost of the shed and its land, which, because of the Zeppelin's size (and lack of manoeuvrability while on the ground), was much greater than for an aeroplane.

knowledge to the year 1912, and suppose that the £8,000,000 or £10,000,000 necessary to establish a good Zeppelin fleet were placed at our disposal as an addition to the ordinary Estimates which were, in fact, voted. Should we be wise to build one? With £10,000,000 you could have had sixty or seventy submarines; you could have had fifty destroyers; you could have had another twenty-five light cruisers; you could have had an Aeroplane Service of absolutely overwhelming strength; you could have had 2,000,000 rifles, which would, perhaps, have meant 3,000,000 more men in the field during the great struggle of last autumn; you could have had 1,000 heavy guns, applied in the earlier stages of the War, might have ruptured the German lines in France.

Is it not clear that, even if we are going to use the light of our present knowledge on the decisions which should have been taken before the War, a great many other competing things would have had to be considered before we came to the question of spending £10,000,000 on Zeppelins? Are we quite sure, after twenty-two months of war, that the Germans themselves might not have made a more formidable investment of the large sums of money which they have spent on their Zeppelins?

At any rate, the story is not yet finished. Events unfold from day to day, and I, for my part, am quite content to await the final judgement which will be passed on these matters when the War can be surveyed in retrospect as a whole.

Churchill had no intention of answering his critics and then sitting down. Confident of his case, he moved into the attack. The true remedy for Zeppelin raids, he said, was to counter-attack the German Zeppelin sheds. This had been his policy as First Lord. He believed that it had succeeded, but that Balfour had not followed it up:

. . . I can only repeat what I said three months ago—why has it been discontinued?

Why, after a whole year of limitless money, of accumulated experience, and of multiplying resources, has it not been possible to continue this system of attack upon the enemy's air bases?

Why has it not been possible to construct the special types of machines that may be required for each particular objective? . . .

No doubt the difficulties have increased, and the enemy's means of defence is continually improving. All the more condemnation to you, I say, for losing so much valuable time, and perhaps for letting such precious opportunities slip by!

Churchill did not accept that the remedy lay in an Air Board such as Asquith had just set up. These plans, he declared, were a feeble subterfuge:

They seem to be a mere attempt to parry the demand for an Air Ministry by setting up another Advisory Committee with Lord Curzon, instead of Lord Derby, at its head. There is, I gather, to be a Joint Board, and the members of this Board may advise the president, but he need not take their advice, and the president may advise the Admiralty and the War Office, but they need not take his advice. . . .

And if their advice, suggestions, recommendations etc, bear no fruit with the two fighting Departments, who, after all, are busy carrying on the War, and apt to give rough answers on these matters, then the president, I understand, may complain to the War Council—

Here Churchill was interrupted by Bonar Law; but he continued with his charge, pointing out that if Curzon's powers as President of the Air Board were limited to giving general advice, without the power to carry it through into action, he might as well just give it as an advising Cabinet Minister. He warned of the futility of setting up an Air Board without executive powers:

I know the public Departments, and especially the military Departments, of this country well, and I know what their attitude is towards a body which has the opportunity to inquire, to criticise, to offer advice, and to make complaints, but which has not the right to their allegiance and the power to exact obedience to orders.

Either the arrangements now proposed will lead to nothing effective, which will be the case if Lord Curzon shows the great qualities of tact which are likely to be required of the holder of the new office which is created, or—I say quite frankly—they seem to me likely to lead to a first-class row.

If he is going to make his work a reality, it is perfectly clear there will be very great differences, and much friction—the friction which you have been unable to overcome yourselves in making these proposals—will be created. In both cases, whether they produce no result, or whether they lead to trouble, they will lead to delay . . .

Can anyone feel that the proposals are put forward by the Government in the sincere belief that they will really open the way for the conquest of aerial supremacy for this country? Yet I cannot think it difficult.

Churchill had his own solution; an Air Ministry with full departmental powers:

No doubt we shall hear from the Government of the difficulties that stand in the way of an Air Ministry, of the resistance of this and that highly-placed official, and the prejudices of the Departments. No doubt we shall be told of the practical difficulties of calling it into existence in the middle of a great war, as if far greater difficulties have not been overcome, and far greater prejudices worn down, in the creation of a Munitions Department.

I cannot think it difficult myself either to devise or to bring into operation a unified organisation, or to divide on natural and well-marked lines the services of training and supply on the one hand, from the tactical employment of units afloat and in the field on the other hand.

I proposed to the Prime Minister a scheme on those lines nearly a year ago.

Soon, Churchill believed, the Air Service would be 'the dominating arm of war'. It should therefore—'and the sooner the better' —be a 'unified, permanent branch of Imperial defence, composed exclusively of men who will not think of themselves as soldiers, sailors or civilians, but as airmen . . .'.

Churchill knew that he could not change Government policy by his speech, or blot out the hostility which had accumulated against him. But he had no intention of remaining silent. A growing disgust with Government policy, a mounting frustration at his own lack of power, drove him on:

Complete, unquestionable supremacy in the air would give an overwhelming advantage to the artillery of the Armies that enjoyed it. It would confer the greatest benefits upon the Fleet that enjoyed it.

You have not got, in spite of what the right hon Gentleman has said, that complete supremacy now. You have not even got equality. On the contrary, in many respects the Germans have the advantage, and you have lost the superiority which, at the outbreak of war, it was admitted we possessed. But you can recover it. There is nothing to prevent your recovering it.

At sea, the increased power of the defensive in mines and submarines has largely robbed the stronger Navy of its rights. On land, we are in the position of having lost our ground before the modern defensive was thoroughly understood, and having to win it back when the offensive has been elevated into a fine art. But the air is free and open. There are no entrenchments there. It is equal for the attack and for the defence. It is equal for all comers.

The resources of the whole world are at our disposal and command. Nothing stands in the way of our obtaining the aerial supremacy in the War but yourselves. There is no reason, and there can be no excuse, for failure to obtain that aerial supremacy, which is, perhaps, the most obvious and the most practical step towards a victorious issue from the increasing dangers of the War.

It fell to Bonar Law, the Colonial Secretary, to answer Churchill's attack. He reacted as Balfour had done two months before, ignoring Churchill's serious charges but scoring a debating point: 'I really do not understand my right hon and gallant Friend', he said. 'He is in favour of an Air Ministry. Did that never occur to him as a good thing earlier, when he himself was a Member of the Government?' Churchill replied that he had put before Asquith early in June 1915 proposals of that character. Bonar Law replied cheaply: 'If I remember correctly, that was after the right hon and gallant Gentleman had left the Admiralty'; and to Churchill's stunned gasp, went on in similar mocking vein: 'I really do not understand my right hon and gallant Friend. If there was one man who, if an Air Ministry was the right thing, had the power to establish it, it was my right hon and gallant Friend. . . .'

Bonar Law's ridicule was effective. Few MP's were interested in Churchill's defence, or stirred by his anger. The Government's military and air policies were not altered on account of Churchill's criticisms. But he continued to speak in every debate about the war; to defend his own record, to attack that of his successors, to demand a more coherent war policy, and to argue that the endless squandering of human life without plan, or purpose, or prospect of victory, was a wicked policy. On May 23, six days after his attack on the Air Board, he rose again from the opposition bench, speaking immediately after the Prime Minister, as the first opposition speaker. Asquith had asked the House of Commons for a Supplementary Vote of Credit of three hundred million pounds, the identical sum which Parliament had already voted a month before. As during the Air debate, Churchill spoke from a position of political weakness and personal isolation. His speech did nothing to advance his political fortunes. Asquith ignored it; the Tories were not won over by it; no powerful group of dissident backbenchers rallied to him as a result of it.

Churchill appealed for a policy which would enable all able-bodied men to take their place in the fighting line, which would end the discrimination which sent some to the front and some to a leisured post, and which would draw upon the great reserves of manpower which remained neglected or untapped. He was afraid that as a result of the influx of conscripted men, inequalities and unfairness would be created, and the rights of the men themselves neglected. He wished to dwell, he told the House, not on technical matters, but 'on the men who are paid and maintained with the money which Parliament is asked and is willing to vote'. He begged the House to realize that compulsion was a major event. 'We have now reached a point,' he declared, 'when the need of the State is so grave that it has been necessary to compel by law to serve in the field the willing and the unwilling, the married and the unmarried, the young student and the old war-broken soldier, the head of a business and the father of a family.' Parliament, he believed, 'would not have taken these measures if it had not been convinced that they were indispensable to preserving the life of the State in the most serious and deadly crisis in its history'.

Churchill insisted that the men who were conscripted should be used in the most effective, least wasteful manner, and that every other possible source of manpower outside Britain 'should be simultaneously used to its utmost extent'. He drew attention to 'five large reservoirs of men', which he believed were being neglected, thereby throwing an unfair burden on the men in the trenches. The first reservoir was the officers and men who, although actually in France 'in the prime of their military manhood', never, or only seldom, went under enemy fire. Churchill told MPs that he had seen while at the front 'one of the clearest and grimmest class distinctions ever drawn in this world—the distinction between the trench and the non-trench population'. He believed that this distinction ought to be ended at once:

. . . the trench population lives almost continuously under the fire of the enemy. It returns again and again, after being wounded twice and sometimes three times, to the front and to the trenches, and it is continually subject, without respite, to the hardest of tests that men have ever been called upon to bear, while all the time the non-trench population scarcely suffers at all, and has good food and good wages, higher wages in a great many cases than are drawn by the men under fire every day, and their share of the decorations and rewards is so disproportionate that it has passed into a byword.

I wish to point out to the House this afternoon that the part of the Army that really counts for ending the War is this killing, fighting, suffering part.

The second reservoir of manpower of which Churchill spoke was 'the Army at home', created by the massive response to Kitchener's appeal for volunteers. Many of the volunteers had proved unfit for military service, but had been kept on in the army, forming, as Churchill explained, a 'very large accumulation in our depots, in our hospitals, in our camps, in our training schools, of men who have never been and will never be fit to be put into the field'. Why, he asked, had these men been taken away from productive work in factories and mines, shipyards and other useful employment, drawing army pay and carried on the army's ration strength:

No man should be retained who is not going to be of use. There is no need to try to swell mere numbers now for paper purposes. No man need be taken until he is required, and no man should be taken who can do more to beat the Germans by staying at home than by serving as a soldier.

I have never looked on compulsion as a means to sweep a vast mass into the military net, though it is perhaps the only way in which large aggregate numbers can be obtained. I have regarded compulsion not as the gathering together of men as if they were heaps of shingle, but the fitting of them into their places like the pieces in the pattern of a mosaic. . . .

The case of every man, the employment of every man now in uniform, should be subjected to at least as severe a scrutiny as the case of every man not yet joined. . . .

We hear a great deal, and this is the moral of what I have been saying in the House, about 'comb this industry', or 'comb that', or 'comb this Department or that', but I say to the War Office, 'Physician, comb thyself.'

Churchill then spoke of the third neglected reservoir of manpower, 'the Armies in the East', amounting in all to half a million men. He hoped that one day Parliament would be told why so great an allied Army had ever been sent to the eastern Mediterranean at all: he wanted the story told—'the fullest information and the publication of documents'—as soon as possible. Meanwhile, he asked: 'What have they been doing all these months? What are they doing now? We have a great Army in Egypt. What is it doing? Who is it fighting? We have another great Army at Salonika. What is it doing? Who is it fighting & who is it going to fight? Who can it get at to fight, except the Bulgarians, who do not want to fight?' There were, Churchill believed, enormous tasks which the troops idle in the East could perform:

Used in time, and sent in time, there is no military object in the Eastern theatre which the forces which are now accumulating in the East could not have achieved. But what have they done? What are they doing? Are they threatening Constantinople? Are they helping the Grand Duke? Are they relieving the pressure upon Verdun?

In all these tremendous events they have borne and are bearing absolutely no part. The Government is open to obvious and serious criticism every day that passes without these forces being made to play their part against the enemy.

. . . every day that these Armies are discovered sitting behind their defences and not holding their fighting weight in the conflict, there is a gross and grave misuse and maldirection of our limited military resources, for which there can be no excuse and no adequate explanation.

Churchill's fourth and fifth reservoirs of men, which he likewise accused the Government of neglecting, were those African and Indian troops who had volunteered for service in the Imperial Army, but had not been allotted a war station. He wanted a military camp set up in Egypt, or somewhere else with a suitable climate, 'where African troops raised in various parts of the Continent would be assembled, drilled and trained, and then passed into the war as individuals or as units in whatever capacity they were best fitted for, and in whatever theatre of war and against whatever enemies the climate and their religion rendered it most suitable for them to be employed'.

Many MPs saw Churchill's proposals as no more than the time-wasting exercises of a man frustrated because he no longer had a part to play in the war. But Churchill spoke with a conviction which, while made more bitter by frustration, drew its strength from his contempt for what he was certain were misguided and dangerous policies:

I would not venture to put such an argument to the House but for the grave situation. I say to myself every day, What is going on while we sit here, while we go away to dinner, or home to bed? Nearly 1,000 men—Englishmen, Britishers, men of our own race—are knocked into bundles of bloody rags every twenty-four hours, and carried away to hasty graves or to field ambulances, and the money of which the Prime Minister has spoken so clearly is flowing away in its broad stream. Every measure must be considered, and none put aside while there is hope of obtaining something from it. . . .

Suppose you get only 100,000 men for your theatres of war. Is that nothing? Suppose you get only 20,000 men. Is that nothing? In this War you will find that at the very best you will have to pay a life for a life. Every man counts, and his case must be counted against the case of someone whom, perhaps, you know. . . .

Here let me point to the great difference which has been made by the enactment of national service in this country.

If we were keeping our manhood out of the struggle and trying to get it fought for us by subject races and mercenary armies, all the old arguments and reproaches with which history is familiar would apply. But when we are engaging every class, when the last man and the last shilling are to be claimed, we have a right and are bound to claim similar exertions, or whatever exertions are possible, from the dependencies which share our fortunes.

The doctrine of equality of sacrifice is not limited by the confines of the United Kingdom.

Churchill turned finally to the aspect of the war which worried him most, the wastage of human life by futile offensives. He had heard so often from the officers of his own Battalion, from the Generals at their headquarters, and from his friends at the front, of the grotesque slaughter of men during the battle of Loos. He did not want further unnecessary bloodshed:

Many of our difficulties in the West at the present time spring from the unfortunate offensive to which we committed ourselves last autumn. My right hon Friend knows that this is no new view of mine taken after the event.

Let us look back now. Only think if we had kept that tremendous effort ever accumulating for the true tactical moment. Think if we had kept that rammer compressed ready to release when the time came—if we had held in reserve the energies which were expended at Loos, Arras, and in Champagne—kept them to discharge at some moment during the protracted and ill-starred German attack on Verdun! Might we not then have recovered at a stroke the strategic initiative without which victory lags long on the road?

Let us not repeat that error. Do not let us be drawn into any course of action not justified by purely military considerations. The argument which is used that 'it is our turn now' has no place in military thought. Whatever is done must be done in the cold light of science. . . .

When you are able to gather round the frontiers of Germany and Austria armies which show a real, substantial preponderance of strength, then the advantage of their interior situation will be swamped and overweighed, and then the hour of decisive victory will be at hand. This hour is bound to come if patience is combined with energy, and if all the resources at the disposal of the Allies are remorselessly developed to their extreme capacity.

Churchill had spoken with passion. He did not believe that Britain could win the war by hurling men continuously to their deaths, and he despised the Government for trying to do so. The premature offensive against which he warned took place on the Somme within six weeks of his speech. On 1 July 1916, the first day of that offensive, twenty thousand men died and sixty thousand were wounded north of the Somme, for gains that were small, and to no perceptible advantage to the Allied cause. Yet no Cabinet Minister replied to Churchill's charges; and the reply which was given, by the Under-Secretary of State at the War Office, Harold Tennant, began with a sneer which echoed Balfour and Bonar Law, and confirmed the pattern for all official answers to Churchill's subsequent appeals. 'There is one thing,' Tennant said, 'which I envy my right hon and gallant Friend, and that is the time which he has in order to prepare his very carefully thought-out speeches. I wish I had the same opportunity.'

Churchill needed political allies, but these were hard to find. George Lambert, the only MP to have openly supported Churchill's appeal for Fisher's return in March, wrote on May 25 asking if Churchill intended to speak again against the wastage of manpower in the War Office debate of May 31. 'If so,' Lambert wrote, 'I will come up and support you by speech or vote.' Churchill hoped that Lambert's offer of support might tempt a wider alliance of opposition.[4] He therefore sent Lambert's letter to Carson, asking: 'Surely the W.O. vote ought to be made the occasion for pressing for a sound policy of Army Administration. Do your people contemplate any action?' But Carson's Unionist War Committee had no plans to force a vote on May 31. They were guarding their strength. Churchill therefore acted alone. He spoke in

---

[4] Lambert did not know that in August 1914 Churchill had pressed Asquith to remove him from his post as Civil Lord of the Admiralty, and to give the office to his cousin, Lord Wimborne. Asquith had refused to make the change. 'L is not very competent,' he had written to Venetia Stanley on August 9, 'but to boot him out at this moment wd be cruel.' Haldane had also intervened on Lambert's behalf, writing to Churchill on the same day: 'It would be a humiliation for him at such a period.'

the House of Commons again, at length and in great detail, on
May 31. In his conclusion he again attacked Government policy:

We feel ourselves grappling with the most terrible foe that ever
menaced freedom. Our whole life energies are required. We are trying our best, but are we at present developing the full results of the
great effort made by the nation? I cannot think so. . . .

I say the nation has responded to every call, and the force which
we have exerted in this War is far greater than any Ally had a right to
expect or than any enemy had a right to take into its calculation; but
the fact remains that full use has not yet been made and is not now
being made of the nation's strength or of the Army's strength, or of
the Empire's strength.

We are the only great reserve of the Allied cause, and a proper use
of our resources will enable us increasingly to come to the succour of
our superb Ally with an Army which grows increasingly in strength
and power as our latent resources are realised, and becomes a support for all the losses and exertions to which she has been put.

No one who subjects the present organisation of the Army, either in
the field or at home, to searching and dispassionate scrutiny can believe that every measure to that end is being taken at the present
time.

Churchill's lone opposition brought him no nearer to high office. He was entirely cut off from Government policy-making. He
had no access to the inner sources of discontent. He could not
see the telegrams from Ambassadors, the reports from Generals,
the estimates drawn up at the War Office and the Admiralty. He
knew little of the arguments which were dividing the Cabinet,
of the policies in dispute, or of the strategies being devised for
future assaults. He had no power to move forward from his belligerent but isolated position to one where his return to the Cabinet might be considered. As soon as the debate of May 31 was
over he sat down to write to Fisher, who was likewise isolated
from the power he so desired:

My dear Fisher,
    Let us meet. You must not be downhearted. I am vy confident that
things will right themselves in time. Nothing counts but winning the
war. Gt care is needed. I do not deal with the Navy at the moment;

because I am gathering strength and now that I am installed here I can measure the situation much more surely than under the disadvantages of a flying visit.

But what a shameful year of cowardice, inertia, futility and insolence has the Arthur Balfour regime presented.

The dead hand lies heavy on our noble fleets: & they even kiss it. *Courage* as the gallant French say.

Yours ever
W

The public was impressed by Churchill's parliamentary protest.[5] Many soldiers and soldiers' wives, wrote to express their gratitude that he had spoken out so frankly about the wastage of manpower. One letter, typical of many, came from a servant in the Officers' Mess at the Buller Barracks, Aldershot, H. C. Waterlow,[6] who begged to be given an opportunity to serve overseas. The work which he and his fellow servants were doing, he claimed, could easily be done by women, by men over age, or by those who were unfit. He told Churchill that the male staff at the Barracks, all of military age, consisted of five officers' servants, five clerks, seven waiters, seven kitchen men, six general cleaning men, two men to clean silver, two to wash china, two to attend boilers, one to wash glass, one to clean knives, one for the wine cellar and one for the stores. 'Imagine a club, or a small hotel,' he wrote on June 7, 'with an average of fifty members or visitors, keeping a staff of forty-seven to attend to them.' Mrs Gillespie, the mother of a lieutenant in a Highland Regiment, wrote that her son[7] had been badly wounded at Loos, being hit in no less than five places, twice seriously in the head; but that after six months at home he expected to be sent out again to

[5] Churchill's army speeches of May 23 and May 31 were published on 13 July 1916 by Macmillan as a 32-page penny pamphlet *The Fighting Line*. Five thousand copies were printed.

[6] I have been unable to find further biographical details about H. C. Waterlow.

[7] Five commissioned Gillespies from Highland regiments fought at Loos: two in the Gordon Highlanders, two in the Highland Light Infantry, one in the Seaforth Highlanders. I cannot discover which one was Mrs Gillespie's son.

France. 'Seeing that there are *hundreds* of *thousands* of fit & willing men anxious to go out and do their bit,' she wrote on June 14, 'I certainly consider this returning of wounded men an absolute scandal. These men have been through the mill, and in *few* cases have they much heart for going out again.' In the postscript she wrote: 'I may say I expect to have five sons serving by next month.' An earlier appeal, dated May 31, came from Glasgow:

To the Honourable Colonel,

I the Wife of Lance Corp Thomas McKee[8] 7759 I Coy 2nd Scottish Rifles Humble pray your Honour to Interest yourself in my sad case my husband has did his duty for 3 years & four months in South Africa and as soon as this war broke out although time expired went and gave his service for King & Country till shot through the throat at the charge of Neuve Chappel they have sent him to France again from me & his 6 little children & I would nobley make the Sacrifice. But there are so many young men trained for the Past 18 Months who have never Been sent to France to do their Bit my whole 5 Brothers are doing there duty 3 in France one a prisoner in Wattenberg Germany & one at Deal. I asked him not to Leave us again & so many young ones at Home. But he only said I am sorry I did not think they would send me again But I must obey my Superiors. I most humbly pray that your honour will help me & my 6 children.

Mrs Thomas McKee

Asquith knew of the general impact of Churchill's speeches. He had no desire to see Churchill's concern for the soldiers lead to a growth of anti-Government feeling, and two attempts were at once made to involve him in a semi-official manner in the Government's affairs. Curzon asked him to attend a meeting of the Air Board in order to give his opinion of what ought to be done; Balfour, when the first official news of the Battle of Jutland on June 1 had shaken public confidence, asked him to draft a more inspiring communiqué which might steady the public's nerve.

---

[8] I have been unable to trace any further biographical details about Lance Corporal McKee. According to the Ministry of Defence, his records were probably among those destroyed by fire during the blitz of 1940, when the Army Records Centre, Arnside Street, Southwark, London, SE1, was bombed and three-quarters of its records destroyed.

Churchill attended Curzon's Board, and drafted Balfour's second communiqué.[9] But these minor contributions did not satisfy his hunger to be involved once more in Cabinet policy.

By the end of May Churchill had come to realize that there was only one way in which he could ensure his return; that there was one indispensable step to take, without which his denunciation of Government policy could not be effective. The cry 'What about the Dardanelles?' must be answered. The public would have to be shown the details of what had happened, of what it had been about; and would have to be satisfied that it had not been a lunatic offspring of Churchill's irresponsibility, but, as he believed, a central and carefully thought out part of Government policy. Churchill pressed Asquith to allow the principal documents to be published, as fully as military security would allow. Asquith agreed, and on June 1 Bonar Law announced in the House of Commons that documents relating to the Dardanelles would be laid before Parliament as soon as possible. Churchill was determined to exploit this opportunity for vindication to the full, writing to Asquith on June 2:

Private

My dear Prime Minister,

Wd it not save your time, if you sent Hankey to me to arrange what shd be published about the Dardanelles & Gallipoli operations? I wd explain to him my views with wh I think you will be in general agreement. The series of papers wh I wish to have published cd then be printed provisionally & circulated with those wh others affected may choose. It may be that a few additions will then be thought necessary.

---

[9] Other than writing this communiqué, Churchill had no part in the Battle of Jutland. There is no contemporary correspondence about it in his papers. On hearing of the battle he had gone at once to see Lord Fisher, who was likewise only a spectator. But in 1927, in volume 3 of *The World Crisis*, Churchill entered into the Jutland controversy, devoting 62 pages to the battle, many of them critical of Jellicoe's conduct. He ended his account: 'The ponderous, poignant responsibilities borne successfully, if not triumphantly, by Sir John Jellicoe during two years of faithful command, constitute unanswerable claims to the lasting respect of the nation. But the Royal Navy must find in other personalities and other episodes the golden links which carried forward through the Great War the audacious and conquering traditions of the past.'

I shd be ready with my papers to see Hankey on Monday morning —if you think this course convenient. . . .

The main point I wish to establish from them is my demand on behalf of the Admiralty on the 27th of Feb for the immediate despatch of the 29th Division & two Territorial Divisions in addition to the other troops. I also think that the decision of each War Council meeting about the Dardanelles shd be shortly stated, with the names of those who were present. This last I think vy important. Nearly everyone of consequence was present when the original decision to begin a purely naval attack was taken. I presume that I may refresh my memory from the records of any meeting in wh I was concerned. . . .

Yours sincerely
W

Fisher was also determined that his story should be told fully. At 1.30 on the afternoon of June 2 he presented himself at 10 Downing Street and handed in the following letter:

My dear Prime Minister,

I see in the Times of this morning that the Government have undertaken to publish papers about the Dardanelles and Gallipoli operations. I have no objection in principle to such a publication provided the papers give a fair representation of the facts, and I presume I shall be consulted as to any selection that may be made.

Certain striking facts must be incorporated in these published papers that do not of course appear in the written records; but nevertheless they are vital and verifiable by the Participants in the Drama—such, for instance, as my abruptly rising from the War Council Table at 10 Downing Street on January 28th, 1915, and going to the window, determined to terminate my service at the Admiralty, and Lord Kitchener following me to that window with his professional remonstrance appealing to me to continue and carry through the Dardanelles operations, which caused me reluctantly to resume my seat!

There are also other vital incidents not recorded in writing . . .

Fisher appended to his letter a large selection of documents which he had already had privately printed.

Churchill's excitement during the first week in June was intense. He was determined that the story should be published as fully as possible. He wanted every shift and twist in the War

Council's decisions, and his own repeated appeals, first for Allies, then for troops, to be made known. In search of documentation he entered into correspondence with Fisher and saw Sir Ian Hamilton, who since his recall to London in October 1915 had little hope of high military command in the field. Fisher, Hamilton and Churchill, each desperate for an active part in the war, made a natural triumvirate, but a feeble one. Each looked to past events for vindication. But those conducting the war were concerned with the present and future. They had not the time to focus on retrospective problems, to reconstruct arguments which had no relevance to the urgent needs of the war. Yet for Fisher, Hamilton and Churchill, only a re-examination of the past seemed to offer any hope of employment in the future. Asquith envisaged the publication of certain selected documents; they wanted the story told in such detail that every subtle shift of policy could be displayed. Fisher continued to have printed documents and reflections which he felt were to his advantage. Hamilton began to dictate to his secretary, Mary Kaye,[10] an elaborate narrative of events, based upon recollection and documents. On June 5 Churchill dined with Hamilton at his home in Hyde Park Gardens. Together they went through some twenty telegrams which Hamilton had sent to the War Office from Gallipoli, in which he had pleaded for high explosive shells to be sent to him at once, instead of the shrapnel shells which had proved too feeble. Together they examined Hamilton's protests at the holding up in Egypt of a whole Army meant for the Dardanelles on the pretext that Cairo was in grave danger from a possible attack by tribesmen in the Libyan desert. Hamilton later wrote in *Listening For The Drums* of how he had impressed upon Churchill that these appeals, 'had all been bottled up by K of K and not one had been shown to the Cabinet when he had met them during the campaign and professed to expound the situation'.

[10] Mary Forbes Kaye, 1895–    . Personal Secretary to Sir Ian Hamilton, 1916–47. Married George Eustace Ridley Shield, 1925. Sir Ian Hamilton's Literary Executor, 1947–    .

Churchill was appalled at this evidence of Kitchener's neglect. He felt certain that the public would be amazed by the contrast between his own repeated warnings and Kitchener's neglect. This, he decided, would be the central, unanswerable theme of his case, so well-documented that Kitchener would be unable to controvert it. Churchill asked Hamilton to call on him the next morning at 41 Cromwell Road. He wanted to go through these damning telegrams again, checking that nothing had been omitted, and finalizing the statement which he intended to make as part of his submission of evidence. At midday on June 6 Hamilton drove to Churchill's house. The two men pored once more over the documents. Suddenly they heard a noise in the street. Somebody was calling out Kitchener's name. In *Listening For The Drums* Hamilton recorded the sequel: 'We jumped up and Winston threw the window open. As he did so an apparition passed beneath us. I can use no other word to describe the strange looks of this newsvendor of wild and uncouth aspect. He had his bundle of newspapers under his arm and as we opened the window was crying out, "Kitchener drowned! No survivors!"'

On the previous day Kitchener had left Scapa Flow on board HMS *Hampshire* for a secret mission to Russia, yet another attempt by Asquith to remove him from London. The ship had struck a mine, and sank in a few minutes beneath the icy waters of the North Sea. Kitchener's death sent a wave of horror across the country. The hero had gone; and while those in Government knew that he had for many months been edged away from power, for the British public it was a disaster. There could no longer be any question of Churchill's evidence, or of anyone's evidence, about the Dardanelles depending upon criticism of Kitchener. A legend had been born, which Asquith's Government could not allow to be tarnished; a legend of military skill and wise counsel. 'The fact that he should have vanished,' Hamilton wrote in his book, 'at the very moment Winston and I were making out an unanswerable case against him was one of those *coups* with which his career was crowded—he was not going to answer!'

Hamilton and Churchill went upstairs to lunch. Among the others present were Clementine Churchill and her mother, Lady Blanche Hozier.[11] The two men went into the dining-room. Hamilton later recorded: 'Winston signed to everyone to be seated and then, before taking his own seat very solemnly quoted: "Fortunate was he in the moment of his death!"' It was, Hamilton recorded, 'a nightmare lunch—no small talk—Winston said K might yet turn up but I told the company that he always had a horror of cold water, and that the shock of the icy sea would at once extinguish his life.'

The Secretary of State for War was dead; the struggle for his succession began at once. Lord Milner saw this as his opportunity to lead a phalanx of Tory dissidents forward into the citadel of Government. Asquith thought otherwise, and acted accordingly with his usual skill, delaying the new appointment for over a month, but letting it be known that he was most likely to move Lloyd George from the Ministry of Munitions to the War Office. Churchill believed that Lloyd George's departure from Munitions would be his opportunity. Some months previously Lloyd George had already suggested that he might take charge of the heavy gun department of the Ministry. He believed he could take the whole responsibility into his hands.

On June 7, the day after Kitchener's death was announced, Churchill called to see Lloyd George at the Ministry of Munitions. As he was going into Lloyd George's room, Lord Northcliffe came out. When Northcliffe saw Churchill he said, chaffingly 'I suppose you have come after LG's job.' Many years before, Northcliffe had given Churchill a small white china bust of Napoleon, which had become a most prized possession, and stood upon his desk facing him when he wrote. Stung by Northcliffe's jest, he felt that his desperate desire to serve his country was being turned into an object of jest and derision. Returning home, he wrote to the Press Lord:

[11] Lady Blanche Ogilvy, 1852–1924. Daughter of the 10th Earl of Airlie. She married Sir Henry Hozier, who died in 1907. Mother of Clementine, Nellie and William.

Private
Dear Northcliffe,

You will I am sure understand why I send back this statuette.

I accepted it as a token of friendship and even when much unfair and ill-informed attack robbed it of that significance, I still regarded it as the gift of a courteous gentleman.

I can do so no longer.

Yours v. fthfy.
Winston S. Churchill

Northcliffe sent Churchill's letter to Lloyd George, commenting: 'I think it must be a matter of Health.' Lord Rothermere telegraphed asking Churchill to accept his brother's apology. Northcliffe sent the little Napoleon by special messenger to Blenheim Palace, asking Churchill to receive it back, and writing:

Dear Churchill,

I am sorry that you took a purely chaffing remark so seriously. I had no desire whatever to wound your feelings.

The attitude of my public newspapers toward public men has nothing to do with my private disposition toward individuals. Had I thought that the remark would have wounded you, I would not for a moment have made it; and I ask you to accept an expression of my regret for having said it.

Yours sincerely
N

Churchill replied on June 9:

Dear Northcliffe,

I accept your expression of regret in the spirit in wh it is offered, & I am vy glad indeed that you are able to remove from my mind a painful impression.

I shall not think about it any more. Let my words be forgotten too.

Yours sincerely
WSC

Kitchener's death, Northcliffe's jibe, the impending vacancy at the Ministry of Munitions, each made it more imperative to Churchill that the facts about the Dardanelles should be published fully and quickly. On June 8, while at Blenheim Palace, he wrote to Asquith:

. . . You will readily understand my wish that the truth shd be known. Not a day passes without my being the object of unjust reproach & now that poor Kitchener is gone I cannot see that the fortunes of the Ministry will be in any way prejudiced. The genesis of the operation is the vital point & your interest in showing that it was soberly & carefully entered upon is the same as mine. . . .

Only the facts can tell the tale: and the public ought now to have them.

Churchill tried to show Lloyd George how concerned he was about munitions. On June 8 he wrote asking him to see his friend Pelham Burn, 'one of the best young Colonels in the army who has been through the whole war' and who was in London on leave. 'You can only learn the truth,' Churchill wrote, 'by talking to the men who really do the work. Please send for him. . . .' On June 13 Lord Reading dined with Churchill at 41 Cromwell Road. They discussed the possibilities of Churchill succeeding Lloyd George as Minister of Munitions. As soon as the dinner was over, Reading sought out Lloyd George, and on the following day sent Churchill an account of their meeting. 'LG was at No 10 when I got back from you,' wrote Reading, 'I saw him afterwards. In a word he thinks it is premature to press you for the post in question—but is very sympathetic and as you wish it, notwithstanding his own views he will push it. Nothing could be better than his reception of the suggestion.'

Churchill knew that Lloyd George's goodwill was not enough. Asquith had no reason to bring him back into the Government while the stigma of the Dardanelles remained upon him. The Government would only invite continued controversy if it had to explain to the public why someone whose judgement it had been taught to distrust was to come back. For the rest of June Churchill pressed upon the Prime Minister the need to publish the Dardanelles documents immediately. But Asquith was becoming increasingly reluctant to have the documents published. On June 20 Churchill learned from Hamilton that the Admiralty

were 'jibbing' at the publication of the naval side of the story.
That day he wrote to Fisher: 'The refusal on the part of the Government to publish now would be very prejudicial to them. So
will the publication.' Churchill correctly assessed the Government's dilemma. The publication of documents might help him
to escape from further unfair attacks; but it might equally well
bring unwelcome controversy to Asquith. Yet Churchill continued
with his pressure, supported by Carson and Dalziel. On June 21
he described the situation, and his own mood, to his brother, who
was then serving in France at the Headquarters of the Anzac
Corps:

. . . The Press is amazingly vicious & I count only on the publication of the Dlles papers to turn their mood. These will much embar-
rass the Government. I am sorry that the end of poor old K shd have
come at this moment. For his own sake it was a good exit—the glory
had departed, the clouds were gathering & night drew near. . . . I
am quite resigned to a further period of detachment & do not care vy
much one way or the other. But for the war, I wd not dream of acting
with these people. . . .

On June 19 Hankey had written to inform Churchill that Asquith had decided not to allow him to use the War Council minutes in the documents which he was selecting for publication.
Asquith believed, Hankey wrote, that if these minutes were published, 'it would be very difficult to resist a pressure to publish
proceedings in regard to other aspects of the war which might
not be in the public interest'. Asquith also feared, Hankey explained, that if the remarks of senior Ministers were 'liable to
publication', future discussion might be hampered. Churchill replied direct to Asquith on June 22, pointing out that it was only
from the minutes of the War Council that any clear idea could
be obtained by the public of how the policy had been evolved,
and of his own part in it. It was necessary, he said, to publish the
text of what the War Council had discussed on 28 January 1915
in order to show 'the strong support of the naval project given
by you, Grey, Kitchener & A. Balfour . . .'. He also demanded
that all the War Council minutes for February should be pub-

lished, showing as they did 'my disclaimer of responsibility if a military disaster occurred through adequate troops not being sent in time'. He felt that it was important that the public should know that his disclaimer 'was not an ordinary incident of discussion, but that I asked formally & at the time that my dissent shd be placed on record'. Surely, he continued, Asquith could see 'that this fact is vy important for a true judgement on the event'? Churchill was afraid that if Asquith refused to allow the publication of the War Council minutes, even in some paraphrased form, the public would never learn of his real part in the evolution of the Dardanelles campaign. 'I am sure,' he ended his appeal, 'your sense of fairness wd not acquiesce in its suppression.'

Hankey's letter to Churchill about the impossibility of publishing the War Council minutes indicated a change in Asquith's attitude towards the whole question of letting the story be told. Realizing this, Churchill mobilized the few forces at his disposal in an attempt to hold the Prime Minister to his pledge. On June 26 Dalziel asked in the House of Commons when the Government would publish the despatches of the Gallipoli campaign. Asquith replied that 'a considerable period must elapse before these papers are likely to be ready'. Churchill believed that delay was a euphemism for cancellation; but when he put this view to Edward Marsh, who was then working in Asquith's private office, Marsh consulted Masterton Smith and replied on July 4 that there was nothing 'sinister' about the hold up in the production of the documents, and that the Admiralty were not trying in any way to prevent publication. 'There are hundreds of telegrams to be gone through,' Marsh wrote 'besides those which figure in your file—the War Staff is at work on them, but it is a matter which *must* take time, & of course they haven't much to spare.' Churchill persevered in his quest for vindication. On July 7, the day of Lloyd George's formal appointment as Secretary of State for War, he wrote to Lloyd George, asking him to allow the documents which he wanted from the War Office files to be published with as few 'omissions and suppressions' as possible. On July 8 he wrote to Asquith that he would be glad to hear from him about whether or not he could quote in his evidence the verbatim minutes of the War Council. He added:

. . . I am also anxious to obtain from you an assurance that dilatory measures will not be allowed to prevent the publication being made while Parliament is sitting. More than six weeks have already passed since the promise to lay the papers was made to the House of Commons: and if I may judge from reports that have reached me there are some indications that an obstructive attitude is being adopted.

I propose therefore unless I hear from you some reasons to the contrary to put a series of questions on the notice paper.

Four days later Asquith wrote to tell Churchill that the Government had decided not to publish the Dardanelles documents at all. It was a bitter blow. Asquith claimed that his decision had been taken on the grounds of security. But Major-General Callwell, whom Asquith had instructed to go through the War Office files, explained to H. A. Gwynne on July 13 that 'if the papers were laid at all the truth would have to be told about there not being sufficient men available to keep Hamilton up to strength'. On July 13 Dalziel and Carson asked formally in the House of Commons when the documents were to be laid before Parliament. Asquith replied that publication had now been abandoned, as it would not be in the national interest. Churchill wrote at once in protest to Asquith:

. . . I cannot agree that this decision is justified in the public interest. The pledge of the Government was freely given by the Colonial Secretary speaking with your full and direct authority. The circumstances of the case, the nature of the documents, and their bearing on the course of the war must have been present in your mind, although perhaps there were some which you have over-looked or forgotten. The pledge to publish was not given at my request, though as you know I have always wished that the whole truth should be made known to the nation and to the Dominions, and that nothing essential should be concealed. It was given to the House and we have been left for more than six weeks in the expectation that it would be fulfilled. I do not think that in these circumstances it ought to be departed from on any vague and general ground. Papers have been submitted to you by me and I understand by other persons affected.

There may be passages in these papers which affect allied or neutral powers. Certainly they are few and far between. There is no reason why they should not be omitted, or expressed in a different way by mutual agreement. There may be technical matters which if desired could be suppressed without impairing in any way the proper presentation of the facts of the case.

It is unfair to the House—I do not speak of individuals—that objections founded on a few passages or documents which are not material, and would not be claimed as material to the case by the persons concerned, should be used as a bar to prevent any publication at all. . . .

Churchill was not alone in being angered at Asquith's reversal of the Government's pledge to publish the Dardanelles documents. An increasing number of MPs began to press for a full-scale debate. In an attempt to deflect criticism, Lloyd George suggested that the Government should appoint a secret committee of the House of Commons to enquire into the Dardanelles operation. He discussed his suggestion privately with Churchill, proposing that the report of this committee should be allowed to replace the earlier proposal that the documents themselves should be put before Parliament. Churchill did not approve of this change:

My dear Lloyd George,

. . . First the Government have given a definite promise to the House that the authentic documents shd be published. The matter is one wh therefore concerns the House of Commons, & I have no right to express an opinion on their behalf.

Secondly altho' the pledge was given by Mr Bonar Law, the Prime Minister had intended to give it himself personally & was only prevented from doing so by the unexpected prolongation of the debate on other matters.

Thirdly the pledge of the Government was given after prolonged consideration & with full knowledge both of the facts and of the suitability of the documents for publication at this juncture. In consequence of the pledge of the Government I submitted to the Prime Minister a series of documents wh I conceive are necessary among others to the exposure of the truth, & wh except in minor and immaterial details & passages to the excision of wh no objection cd be taken, cd in any judgment be made public without detriment to the State. These papers had been circulated to the Cabinet more than a year ago. They have been examined lately by an impartial general[12] chosen by the Government, who has reported that their publication in the main wd not be injurious to the State, but that it wd reflect upon the Government. In these circumstances I can well understand the desire of the Government to substitute for a publication of authentic documents on wh the nation can judge, a secret inquiry of indefinite duration by a body selected by themselves.

The personal aspect of this matter is not vy important, except in so far as it affects the behaviour of colleagues to one another. But the public aspect is serious. The nation & the Dominions whose blood has been poured out vainly have a right to know the truth. The Government had decided of their own accord that the truth cd be told & had given a formal promise to Parliament: & now as the time draws nearer they shrink from the task.

If a Committee is appointed I will of course attend and assist its labours in any way that is possible. But the first witness who shd be called before them is the Prime Minister, who alone cd have co-ordinated the naval and military action & given to the war-policy of the country the necessary guidance & leadership. Such a Committee however can be no substitute for the laying upon the table of the House of the papers wh the Government have promised: nor cd I allow it to prejudice in any way my freedom of action & discussion if need & opportunity arise. . . .

Churchill's appeal was in vain. He was angry and depressed not to be allowed to put before Parliament a full documentary statement of what had occurred. Without evidence in profusion, without the clear authenticity of the documents themselves, he knew that he would always remain the scapegoat. Every mistake that had been made, every aspersion that had been cast, every taunt that had been thrown would be a rope holding him back from his chance of exercising power at the centre of na-

[12] The General was Callwell. In his book *The Dardanelles*, published in 1919, he concluded: 'Cabinets, War Councils, Dardanelles Committees, and kindred executive gangs are generally composed entirely, or almost entirely, of persons, who if they have any knowledge of war at all, are merely furnished with that modicum of it that is so dangerous a thing . . . governments should leave the contriving of military and naval operations to those who understand them.'

tional affairs. On July 15 he went to Blenheim Palace with his family, hoping to calm his mind by painting. But he could not do so. In his depression he even thought of returning to the western front as a battalion commander. That evening he wrote to his brother:

Is it not damnable that I should be denied all real scope to serve this country, in this tremendous hour? I cannot tell how things political will turn out: but great instability prevails and at any moment a situation favourable to me might come. Meanwhile Asquith reigns supine, sodden and supreme. LG made a half-hearted fight about Munitions. He is very much alone and none too well qualified for the particular job he has claimed. But very friendly according to the accounts I get from various trustworthy sources.

The Govt have decided to repudiate their pledge to publish the D'Iles papers. My dossier was more than they could face. There will be a row, but there are many good arguments in the public interest against publishing: and many more good arguments in the Government interest!

Tho' my life is full of comfort, pleasure and prosperity I writhe hourly not to be able to get my teeth effectively into the Boche. But to plunge as a battalion commander unless ordered—into this mistaken welter—when a turn of the wheel may enable me to do 10,000 times as much would not be the path of patriotism or of sense. There will be time enough for such courses. Jack my dear I am learning to hate.

# 26

# Cast Aside

---

ON JULY 18 the House of Commons debated whether or not the
Dardanelles documents should be put before them. Asquith announced that 'the presentation of these Papers must be postponed', and trusted that the House would agree 'that the pledge
to publish them cannot for the moment . . . be fulfilled'. The
reason, he said, was that the Admiralty, the War Office and the
Foreign Office were 'unanimously of the opinion that the publication at the present time of papers could not be made . . . without omissions so numerous and so important that the papers
actually presented would be incomplete and misleading'. A long
debate ensued. Carson took the lead in criticising the Government's decision. Two days later Asquith announced that the most
the Government would agree to was to set up a select committee 'to inquire into the conduct of the Dardanelles operations'. Its chairman was Lord Cromer; its other members
Field-Marshal Lord Nicholson,[1] Sir William Pickford,[2] Admiral
of the Fleet Sir William May,[3] Sir Frederick Cawley, James

---

[1] William Gustavus Nicholson, 1845–1918. Lieutenant, Royal Engineers,
1865. Major-General, 1899. Chief of the Imperial General Staff, 1908–12.
Field-Marshal, 1911. Chairman of the Commission on Indian Army Expenditure, 1912–13. Created Baron, 1912.

[2] William Pickford, 1848–1923. Judge of the High Court of Justice,
1907–14. Knighted, 1914. Lord Justice of Appeal, 1914–18. Created Baron
Sterndale, 1918. President of the Probate Division, Admiralty Court, 1918–19.

[3] William Henry May, 1849–1930. Lieutenant, Royal Navy, 1871.
Knighted, 1904. Second Sea Lord, 1907–9. Commanded the Home Fleet,

Clyde,[4] Captain Gwynn[5] and Walter Roch.[6] This was the outcome which Churchill feared: the committee would undoubtedly
publish a fair report; but it would be opinions, not documents;
fragments of evidence, not substantial fact. The debate that followed Asquith's announcement was a turbulent one. Many MP's
shared Churchill's fears that a Commission of Inquiry would be
inconclusive and inadequate. When Asquith proposed that the
House adjourn, Churchill spoke with bitterness that it had not
been found possible to publish the documents, 'as was originally
intended and promised by the Prime Minister, in the name of
the Government'. He told the House how, very soon after the
Government had made this promise to publish, he had noticed 'a
dilatory and destructive tendency'. But he had to accept Asquith's proposal. It was better than nothing. He hoped that the
Commission of Inquiry would be given every encouragement to
publish as many documents as possible. It was not the solution
that he had wanted; but he realized that his political future depended upon the story being known, at least in part. He preferred truncated evidence to no evidence at all. He did not wish
to remain the scapegoat for ever.

As soon as Asquith announced his decision to set up a Commission of Inquiry on the Dardanelles, Churchill began to
prepare a statement to make before it. He was determined to include as many documents as possible in his own evidence. For
five months, from July to November 1916, he worked at his statement, assembling documents, rehearsing arguments and drafting
increasingly elaborate narratives.[7] The need to make the state-

---

1909–11. Commander-in-Chief, Plymouth, 1911–13. Admiral of the Fleet,
1913.

4 James Avon Clyde, 1863–1944. Solicitor-General, Scotland, 1905–6. Liberal Unionist MP, 1909–18. Lord Advocate, Scotland, 1916–20. Conservative
Unionist MP, 1918–20. Lord Justice-General of Scotland, 1920–35.

5 Stephen Lucius Gwynn, 1864–1950. Author and journalist. Nationalist
MP, 1906–18. Joined the Leinster Regiment as a Private, January 1915; Captain, July 1915. Served in France with the 16th Irish Division, 1915–17.

6 Walter Francis Roch, 1880–1965. Liberal MP, 1908–18.

7 'Let me say at the outset,' Churchill wrote on the first of several hundred
pages of handwritten notes for his evidence, 'that I take full responsibility

ment as comprehensive and as convincing as possible, became his preoccupation.

During July Churchill found a journalistic outlet, writing four articles for Lord Rothermere's *Sunday Pictorial*. He was excited at how much he was to be paid, writing to his brother on 15 July, 'I get 4 or 5 shillings a word for everything I write: and apparently even at this price the newspaper is the gainer. *Sunday Pictorial* circulation is 448,000 in a single day. This beats all records in journalism.' The four articles earned him £1,000, and appeared on four successive Sundays in July. The first two described different aspects of the coming of war in August 1914. On the second Sunday Lord Haldane sent Churchill a note of approval. 'These articles contain far the most penetrating and accurate analysis of the situation before the war that I have ever seen,' wrote the former Secretary of State for War, '& I agree with every word you have written in them. . . . What you yourself did will always be historical.' Churchill's third article described the state of the Navy at the beginning of the war, and the role of the Navy in British power. His final article described the changing nature of the war in Europe. 'The chaos of the first explosions,' he wrote, 'has given place to the slow fire of trench warfare: the wild turbulence of the incalculable, the sense of terrible adventure have passed. . . . A sombre mood prevails in Britain. The faculty of wonder has been dulled; emotion and enthusiasm have given place to endurance; excitement is bankrupt, death is familiar, and sorrow numb. The world is in twilight; and from beyond dim flickering horizons comes tirelessly the thudding of guns.' On July 31 Churchill sent Jack Seely copies of his articles, together with a survey of the political position:

---

for all the proceedings of the Adm$^y$ in these affairs during my tenure. I have no complaint to make in regard to any officer serving under the Bd of Adm$^y$ whether afloat or ashore . . . in what I am about to say I do not seek to transfer responsibility to any officer serving under the Admiralty. If I cite the opinions & advice of Admirals & others of high expert authority it is not to relieve myself of responsibility, but to show that that responsibility was properly & carefully discharged.'

My dear Jack,

. . . There is gt uncertainty here & the position of the Government is not good. Asquith in particular seems to be on the road to pay his debts. L.G. is vy affable and I see a good deal of him. . . .

You know my views on the offensive too well for me to repeat them here. I trust you will not expose yourself needlessly to danger when not on duty: Look after Jack (my other one) if you come near Anzac H.Qrs.

Archie has had a good rest, but now has succeeded in getting ordered to France as a Squadron commander in the 2nd L. Guards. I am vy fond of him & shall always remember yr kindness in letting me have him when I was at the war.

Let me know if there is any way in wh I can serve you. It is vy painful to me to be impotent & inactive at this time: but perhaps a little later on I may find a chance to be useful.

The Dardanelles Commission will require some of my attention in the near future. I am hopeful that the truth may be published. But failure & tragedy are all that are left to divide.

This is a morose letter—but do not let it depress you. . . .

Your devoted friend
W

Churchill wanted to be heard in Government circles, and at the Cabinet table. He feared a repetition of the Somme offensive, and further bloodshed for objectives which he believed were both ill-considered and unobtainable. He put these fears into a memorandum. F. E. Smith agreed to write an introduction to it, and to have it printed for the Cabinet. Churchill's memorandum, dated August 1, concluded:

So long as an army possesses a strong offensive power, it rivets its adversary's attention. But when the kick is out of it, when the long-saved-up effort has been expended, the enemy's anxiety is relieved, and he recovers his freedom of movement. This is the danger into which we are now drifting. We are using up division after division— not only those originally concentrated for the attack, but many taken from all parts of the line. After being put through the mill and losing perhaps half their infantry and two-thirds of their infantry officers, these shattered divisions will take several months to recover, especially as they will in many cases have to go into the trenches at once.

41. Churchill
leaving for the
Front, early 1916

42. Sir Archibald Sinclair and Churchill, Armentières, 11 February 1916

43. Captain Gibb, Adjutant, 6th Royal Scots Fusiliers, April 1916

44. Lieutenant Napier-Clavering, Royal Engineers, 1916

45. 2nd Lieutenant Hakewill Smith, 6th Royal Scots Fusiliers, April 1916

46. 2nd Lieutenant McDavid, 6th Royal Scots Fusiliers, April 1916

47. Captain Spiers (third from left), Churchill, General Fayolle (on right) and a
German prisoner (in cap, behind General Fayolle), 29 December 1915

48. Violet Bonham Carter, Clementine Churchill and David Lloyd George, Ponders End, 3 February 1916, at the opening of a canteen for munitions workers

49. German shell exploding above Ploegsteert Wood, 1916

50. Ploegsteert Church, spring 1916

51. British trench in the Ploegsteert sector, after a snowfall, January 1916

52. Churchill, 1916

53. Clementine Churchill, 1915

54. Churchill, summer 1916

55. David Lloyd George, 1916

Thus the pent-up energies of the army are being dissipated, and if the process is allowed to go on, the enemy will not be under the need of keeping so many troops on our front as heretofore. He will then be able to restore or sustain the situation against Russia.

There were some politicians and soldiers who suspected an ulterior motive in Churchill's hostility to the strategy of the Somme offensive. On August 1 Hankey recorded in his diary a talk with Sir William Robertson, the Chief of the Imperial General Staff: 'Robertson told me that F. E. Smith was writing a paper to show that the big offensive in France had failed. I suspect that Ll George & Winston Churchill are at the back of it. Personally I think it is true but it is a mistake to admit it yet.' F. E. Smith circulated Churchill's memorandum to the Cabinet on August 1. The reaction was one of scepticism. Ministers did not want to believe that the Somme offensive should be halted. A copy of the memorandum reached Haig at St Omer within a week; he too was unwilling to accept any limitation to his policy of continual attack. To Northcliffe, who was visiting St Omer, Haig strongly defended the offensive. Northcliffe wrote to Geoffrey Robinson on August 8, from Paris: 'Let me once more say and urge that what is taking place on the Somme must not be measured in metres. It is the first time we have had a proper scientific attack. There are no complaints of bad Staff work, no complaints of lack of ammunition, no muddling. . . . If we wrote communiqués as well as the Germans, we would lay much more stress on the German losses, which are *known* to be immense.' Robinson accepted Northcliffe's judgement. Churchill's criticisms met with no response in *The Times*.

The summer passed. Churchill's opinion was not sought again by the Government. He sat for his portrait by William Orpen.[8] In 1964, a few months before his death, Churchill dined alone with one of his former Private Secretaries, John Colville,[9] who later recorded, in a letter to the author:

[8] William Orpen, 1878–1931. Painter. Knighted, 1918. The portrait, which was Churchill's favourite portrait of himself, passed first to his son Randolph and then to his grandson Winston.
[9] John Rupert Colville, 1915–    . A grandson of Lord Crewe. Entered the Diplomatic Service, 1937. Assistant Private Secretary to Neville Chamber-

His memory had already faded and conversation was exceedingly difficult. During the first two or three courses at dinner I tried every subject in which I knew him to be interested, without success. . . . Finally, over the savoury, I looked at the Orpen, which was hanging in the dining room behind his chair, and made the not very original remark that it was far and away the best portrait of him which had ever been painted. Suddenly his brain cleared. His voice became exactly as it had been years before. He replied, 'I am glad you think so. I gave him eleven sittings, which is more than I have ever had time to give any other painter. It was in 1916, at a very unhappy time of my life when I had nothing whatever to do. Rothermere gave me the portrait, which was very generous of him, and almost my only occupation was to sit to the artist.' His mind then clouded over again and we had no coherent conversation for the rest of the evening.

On July 24 Asquith introduced the Supplementary Vote of Credit for 1916, asking the House of Commons to vote a further £450,000,000 for the prosecution of the war. Churchill was Asquith's principal critic, speaking immediately after the Prime Minister:

We have not had from the Prime Minister what he alone can give and what his moving these Votes would enable him to give, namely, a broad survey of, or at any rate some reference to, the general progress of the War and the state of the great enterprises for the furtherance of which this money is asked. . . .

Very grave and important events have taken place in the two months that have passed. I had certainly looked forward to hearing from the Prime Minister, in asking for this immense sum of money, some reference to events like the naval battle off Jutland, or the brilliant tactics of General Brusiloff,[10] or the sustained and magnificent defence made by our Allies at Verdun. Even if it were not possible to

lain, 1939–40; to Churchill 1940–1 and 1943–5; to Clement Attlee, 1945. Private Secretary to Princess Elizabeth, 1947–9. Joint Principal Private Secretary to Churchill, 1951–5.

[10] Alexei Alexeievich Brusilov, 1853–1926. Commanded the Russian Armies south of the Pripet Marshes, 1916–17. His successful offensive, launched on 4 June 1916, was halted in September through lack of artillery munitions, having at one point advanced 70 miles. Supreme Commander of the Russian Armies, May–July 1917. Put his services at the disposal of the Red Army during the Russo-Polish war, 1920. Inspector of Cavalry, 1923–4. Head of the State Horse-breeding Establishment, Moscow, 1924–6.

comment on the other operations which are now in progress, I believe a statement from the Prime Minister on this subject would be bound, as on other occasions, both to instruct the country and to encourage and to gratify our Allies.

Churchill used the opportunity of this debate to speak caustically against Asquith for not appointing a Secretary of State for War during the thirty days between Kitchener's death on June 6 and Lloyd George's transfer to the War Office on July 7. Throughout that month, Asquith himself had acted as Secretary of State for War; he had therefore been responsible for the conduct of War Office policy both during the final three weeks of preparation and the first disastrous week of battle on the Somme. Churchill attacked Asquith for undertaking this responsibility:

It was impossible that the War Office in time of war should be conducted by the Prime Minister in the odd hours that he could snatch from his own laborious duties, and from adjusting the recurring crises of the Coalition Government. When the office became vacant it ought to have been filled within forty-eight hours in the interests of the War. It ought not to have been left vacant, with only such time as the right hon Gentleman could spare from his already most severe labours. It was not at all a satisfactory event, and I think it is one of those cases which illustrates the undue importance which is attached at the present time to mere political adjustments as compared with effective, energetic means to prosecute the War.

Churchill then raised, in more detail and with added evidence, the points which he had made two months before about the misuse and wastage of manpower. He addressed himself to the new Secretary of State for War, Lloyd George:

What has been done to provide, as far as possible, substitutes for young, fit, military males who are at present engaged in noncombatant services far from the front? What has been done to afford relief to war-worn soldiers, and particularly to wounded men, who are sent back time after time to the trenches which others have never visited at all?

Does my right hon Friend know—I am informed that it is the case and it seems so extraordinary that I put it in interrogative form—that wounded men on being discharged from hospital are immediately placed in what is known as category A? That is to say, they go back to their depots and home units as fit for service.

One would have thought that when a wounded man recovers from injury he would have been put at the bottom of the roster of trained and fit men, and would only have gone out after the whole of the list had been exhausted. . . .

I have heard nothing which indicates that any attempt is being made to use the manpower of India, or India's great resources effectively in the War. The India Office attitude is one of general apathy and obstruction.[11]

What about Africa? I asked before what use was the Government making of the African population, whether for war or for labour? There are the natives of East Africa about whom encouraging reports are spread by those who are acquainted with the country and with the military quality of these men. There are possibilities in South Africa. There is the native population of Nigeria. There are the native populations of the Soudan. All those great fields ought to be developed to the fullest possible capacity, and merely to say, 'Oh, there are great difficulties,' and 'It is difficult to find officers and interpreters,' and so on, is not dealing with the subject as its urgency and importance require.

I am going to ask the right hon Gentleman whether anything has been done to reduce redundant administration training staffs at home.

I am quite certain, if he looks into the condition of some of those large fortresses at home, with depots in them, he will find great overlapping, great confusion and complication of machinery, undue multiplication of persons engaged in the training staff proportionate to the number of recruits they are turning out and handling, and generally the possibilities of reduction in the staffs, which will both save the public purse and liberate more men for the fighting front. . . .

All these matters are serious and urgent. I make no apology for bringing them before the House. We are fighting for our lives, and any useful means of advance towards the strengthening of our war

[11] Between 1914 and 1918 India provided one soldier for every 225 of its inhabitants; New Zealand, 1 for every 5; Great Britain, 1 for every 7; Australia, 1 for every 10; Canada, 1 for every 11; South Africa, 1 for every 44. Of the 1,400,000 Indians under arms, 850,000 left India for the war zones.

effort is legitimate, and Parliament ought to give its attention to these matters.

Churchill turned to another contentious matter, that of military honours. 'I am not concerned,' he said sarcastically, 'with the honours and rewards of the Staff and of the higher ranks, because, I believe, they are tolerably well provided for at the present time.' His concern was with those men 'on whom we depend for our lives'. 'It is the privates, the non-commissioned officers, and the regimental officers,' he explained, 'whose case requires the sympathetic attention of the House and of the Secretary of State. Honour should go where death and danger go, and these are the men who pay all the penalties in the terrible business which is now proceeding.' Churchill went into further details about awards and decorations. The House was impatient with such minutiae. But Churchill persevered in his attack. 'People who never themselves go into danger,' he said, 'talk airily about cheapening the British standard of decoration and reward. If you gave three or four times, or even five or six times, as many as you have given to the lower ranks of the Army, I am certain you could do it without conferring any reward upon a man who would not have gained the highest possible distinction, or, at any rate, marked distinction and notice, in any previous war.' Churchill believed that honours, properly bestowed—not 'handed out with the rations' as many officers joked—would make a difference 'to the lives, the hopes and encouragement' of the men at the front. As for the Military Medal, which had just been introduced, he was annoyed that 'the distribution has been so limited and so niggardly, and the cases in which it has been given promptly so rare and exceptional, that it has practically made no sensible impression at all upon the immense armies we have now got in the field'. Churchill had further advice for the new Secretary of State for War. It concerned promotions. 'I wonder if my right hon Friend is aware,' he asked, 'that promotion in the battalions at home is much quicker than promotion in the battalions at the front?' It was, he believed, 'a very anomalous state of affairs that one man should be a year or a year and a half in the trenches, in continual danger, and should actually make slower progress up the military ladder than his brother who has joined a Home service battalion and has not been ordered to the front'.

Churchill believed that these were important matters. 'Let us never forget,' he urged, 'how much these things are thought of by the people who are risking everything for us.' But he realized that he was amid a hostile audience which did not want to hear such detail. 'I do not believe,' he said, 'that people in this country have any comprehension of what the men in the trenches and those who are engaging in battles are doing or what their sufferings and achievements are.' It was his contention that, despite the obvious lack of parliamentary interest in front-line problems, 'the trench population, these fighting men, are the people who require the care and attention of the House and the Secretary of State'.

Churchill continued his speech by outlining several practical suggestions about the system of communications at the front, a system whose inadequacies he had himself witnessed. He wanted preparations to be made at once for the winter, 'so that our men will have as good a chance as the Germans, so that they may have as much comfort in their life in the trenches as the Germans, so that they will not lose more life than the enemy, and in order that the lines can be held by as few troops as possible, and our Armies have the utmost possible rest during the winter months'. He pressed for a more extensive and elaborate system of light railways to enable trench stores to be brought up more quickly and easily to the front, and kept in constant repair. He then raised the question of the inferior quality of British trench lights. The German light, he said, burned brighter and longer, and went much further; the British light could not even reach the German lines, and the Germans could strengthen their front-line wire without interruption. 'These are very important things for the successful conduct of the War,' he pleaded, 'and there is no excuse for these lights not being as good as the German lights. . . .' Churchill went on to express his anger that the Government had delayed so long in introducing steel helmets, one of which he himself had worn throughout his six months in the trenches. 'Many men might have been alive to-day,' he said, 'who have perished, and many men would have had slight injuries who to-day are gravely wounded had this proposal not been put aside in the early stages of the War.'

During his speech Churchill made one reference to the Admiralty. Here too he was concerned at the unnecessary risk which the men at sea were forced to run. 'The Admiralty,' he insisted, 'ought to press on night and day with every form of new construction. . . . That is, the construction which saves the lives of our men, and does not expose them to needless and hopeless peril.'

In his reply, Lloyd George spoke appreciatively of Churchill's criticisms. They would, he said, be carefully examined, and, where justified, followed up. He subsequently encouraged Churchill to call on him at the War Office whenever he wanted to raise some point of military policy; he listened to Churchill's suggestions and in many cases acted upon them. With Lloyd George at the War Office, Churchill's position as a critic was much weakened. He knew that in any change of Government he would depend almost entirely upon Lloyd George's support for a Cabinet position. Nor did he regard Lloyd George as lacking in the qualities needed to effect a drastic change in war policies.

During August, Lloyd George and Churchill saw much of each other, and talked freely of politics. Christopher Addison recorded in a note of August 4, later published in his memoirs *Four And A Half Years:*

On Tuesday (August 1) had breakfast with L.G.. Churchill and Reading came in. The chief gossip was of Government reconstruction. Churchill, with whom the wish is father to the thought, considered the P.M. would welcome the opportunity of becoming Lord Chancellor and so get rid of his private financial difficulties. I do not see this happening, unless he is obliged: neither, I think, did Reading. The P.M. will sit tight and things will drift on longer.

Lloyd George and Churchill began again to discuss foreign affairs, with the same acerbity as in the summer of 1915. Both were still critical of what they regarded as Grey's lack of foresight, and Asquith's lethargy. Shortly before the German–Bulgarian–Austrian attack on Rumania of 1 September 1916 Lloyd George explained the military situation in detail to Churchill, who recorded in *The World Crisis*: '. . . after we had mutually alarmed each other in a long talk at Walton Heath, he wrote a serious though belated warning to the Prime Minister.' But the warning itself, that the French and Russian Governments should be urged to be more active on Rumania's behalf, came to nothing. Nor could Lloyd George's confidences give Churchill a sense of real participation in war policy.

Churchill tried to find solace in painting. In mid-August he spent a weekend at Hurstmonceux Castle in Sussex, the home of Claude Lowther.[12] Violet Bonham Carter was also there. In *Winston Churchill As I Knew Him* she recalled how Churchill painted in silence, totally absorbed by the canvas:

The spell was only broken once that day by the dull distant thunder of the cannonade in France. He broke off then, laid down his brush and spoke with bitterness of his position; of the unfair attacks upon him for the failure in Gallipoli, of his desire for a public enquiry, in which he could have the chance of vindicating himself, of the Government's duty to lay the relevant papers before Parliament; of his sense of unjust exclusion from the great world struggle in which he knew that he could play an essential part, of all the ideas he could pour into it, now running to waste in the sand. 'They don't want to listen to me, or use me. They only want to keep me out.'

On August 13, while at Hurstmonceux, Churchill wrote to Seely:

[12] Claude Lowther, 1872–1929. Conservative MP, 1900–6; 1910–18. Served with the Imperial Yeomanry in South Africa, 1900. In August 1914 he raised a battalion of Sussex men, known as Lowther's Lambs, whom he commanded in France. In 1915 he raised three more battalions.

My dear Jack,

I think it probable that Asquith will out last the session—& then there is a six weeks holiday. His position is however not at all good. The Tories outside the Gvt despise him: the Irish have lost faith in him & many of the Liberals are estranged or sore. There are vy hostile forces at work in the Cabinet and at any time a collapse is possible.

Meanwhile the Dlles Commission will occupy my immediate attention; & I am hopeful that my case may command their respect when it is fully unfolded. It is a pretty good commission.

When will you come home for a spell of leave? I want vy much to talk to you & learn all yr news. I see a good deal of French and we dwell pleasantly 'upon the days that are no more'. A. Balfour dozes placidly upon the Admiralty throne, & the art of doing nothing with mighty rewards is carried to its finest perfection.

On the whole it looks as if Austria was hard hit. We ought to concentrate all efforts on her destruction. Germany can no more stand without Austria, than we & France cd conquer without Russia. Looking back on this war one sees that its gt decisions arose out of the interplay of forces wh had escaped from human direction—the turn at the Marne—the check on the Yser—the non extinction of Russia as a belligerent in the autumn of 1915; Brusiloff's lightening stroke now—All are imponderable—Why did the Germans attack Verdun? Surely it has been their undoing. Fancy both Germany & Austria coming to the West against us & Italy, & letting that half dead bear rise with renewed & perhaps illimitable strength. Turkey shows weakness now wh is as unexpected to me as her strength was last year. She must have been vy nearly cooked at Gallipoli. A little more energy & resolution, a clear determined policy, & we might so easily have done her in.

Good luck to you my dear—count on me if the moment comes when I am worth anything again.

I can hear the guns here (Sussex) quite plainly thudding away. I am sorry there was no sphere for me out there. It is painful being here idle. But I must just wait. Perhaps another chance of being of some use will come.

Yours always
W

Churchill continued to speak on military affairs. But the military debates no longer provided him with the opportunity he had earlier expected from them. It had been easy to attack War

Office policy while Kitchener was responsible for it. But as soon as Lloyd George went to the War Office, a less defective policy was adopted; nor did Churchill relish attacking the one senior political figure sympathetic to his aspirations.

In August the Government introduced a Special Register Bill to determine who would be entitled to vote, should there be a wartime election. Under this Bill, soldiers in France were to have been excluded. On August 16 the President of the Local Government Board, Walter Long, spoke on behalf of the Government. He said that although the Bill had certain weaknesses, it should nevertheless still be passed. Churchill replied with a short, sarcastic speech:

> This is what he now says to us: That the Bill is an unseaworthy Bill, an illogical Bill, a bad Bill . . . all these defects, all these evils! Therefore what? Therefore pass it! Pass it at once. Pass it with scarcely any study. Pass it with very little discussion. But pass it with general acclamation!
>
> Surely, Sir, when measures of consequence are put forward in such a very half-hearted fashion, and with such evident lack of conviction behind them, those who make themselves responsible for them should not blame the House if it asks for reasonable time and opportunity, and if it declines to pass propositions of this character without reasonable time and opportunity for considering them.

Churchill's principal complaint was this: 'Is it not perfectly clear that the soldiers who are fighting our battles ought not to be excluded?' But Asquith was determined that the Bill should be passed without further delay, and used the official Whip to press Parliamentary opinion behind it. Churchill again protested. This, he declared, was a flagrant misuse of the Government's Parliamentary powers. Bonar Law, in a sharp and personal reply, which ignored the substance of Churchill's criticism, tried to demolish his credibility by mockery:

> I really do not think that any of us who have listened to this Debate have much reason to be proud of the display which the House of Commons is making. The right hon Gentleman who has just spoken has given us two very valuable lessons, which came with great effect from

him. One is, that we should all conduct ourselves with becoming modesty, which is good advice wherever it comes from. The other is that we are committing an unpardonable offence in proposing to put on the Government Whips for a Government Bill.

It may be worth while to note in passing that this is the same right hon Gentleman who told us yesterday that all that the House of Commons wanted the Government to do was to give a lead and say what they wanted.

Churchill was stung by these remarks, writing to Max Aitken on August 18: 'It is a pity Bonar shd be *personal* in rejoinders to me. I do not make personal attacks on him or try to decry his personal behaviour or qualities. Surely the wide field of political argument shd afford sufficient scope at the present time, when everything is so uncertain.'

Each debate led to bitterness. Churchill was unable to win the respect of the Tory leaders. The future of Asquith's Government was unclear; the speculation about his successor unnerving. Old wounds began to smart again, old sores to fester; and in such an atmosphere Churchill suffered. A letter which Lord Derby wrote to Lloyd George on August 19 reflected the Tory hostility. Derby had heard that Churchill often called to see Lloyd George at the War Office:

I know your feelings about him and I appreciate very much that feeling which makes you wish not to hit a man when he is down, but Winston is never down or rather will never allow that he is down and I assure you that his coming to the War Office as he does is—not to put it too strongly—most distasteful to everybody in that office. If as I hope there will be a new Party formed at the end of the War which shall break down all the old Party ties, Winston could not possibly be in it. Our Party will not work with him and as far as I am concerned personally nothing would induce me to support any Government of which he was a member. I like him personally. He has got a very attractive personality but he is absolutely untrustworthy as was his father before him, and he has got to learn that just as his father had to disappear from politics so must he, or at all events from official life.

Churchill continued to try to influence the House of Commons. On August 22, in the main speech of the Adjournment debate, he warned the House that all was not going well with the war, despite frequent Government assertions to the contrary. He wanted the Government to intervene in every aspect of war-direction. 'We cannot go on treating the War,' he warned, 'as if it were an emergency which can be met by makeshifts. It is, until it is ended, the one vast, all-embracing industry of the nation, and it is until it is ended the whole aim and purpose of all our lives.' He believed that there was only one solution: 'Everything in the State ought now to be devised and regulated with a view to the development and maintenance of our war power at the absolute maximum for an indefinite period. If you want to shorten the War, do this. If you want to discourage the enemy, let them see that you are doing it. If you want to cheer our own people, let them feel that you are doing it.' The most effective method of disheartening Germany, he asserted, was to make it quite clear that 'her most formidable antagonists, for so we are now coming to have the honour to be, are coldly, scientifically, and systemati-cally arranging their national life for the one supreme business in hand'.

Churchill begged the Government to control the rise in food prices. He warned that if prices continued to rise a collapse of civilian morale was inevitable. Prices could be kept low, he in-sisted, only if the State took control of the shipping industry and eliminated the profits which shipowners were making as a result of war conditions. Churchill declared emphatically that although the country was able to accept 'every hardship and every sacri-fice', he strongly believed that 'the people of this country do re-quire to know that the sacrifices and sufferings they endure arise solely from the needs of the War and of the action against the enemy and that they are not added to by any lack of grip and energy in dealing with the freight problems here or by the ac-cumulation of extortionate profits in the hands of private indi-viduals'.

Churchill had seen each of his recent speeches dismissed by Government spokesmen with cheap sneers and sarcasm. In ap-pealing at the end of this speech for resolute Government ac-tion, he implored the House of Commons to take his criticisms seriously, even though Ministers would try to dismiss them. 'Ministers are often offended with discussions which take place in this House . . .' he warned. 'The slightest opposition renders them indignant, and they are always ready to attribute mean motives to those concerned in it.' Their duty was to take positive action. 'Let the Government show,' he concluded, 'that they do not merely hold the offices of State, but that they hold the key to the solutions of the difficulties with which they are confronted; that they do not need to be pushed by the House of Commons and by the Press into action on so many occasions, but that they can go forward spontaneously with good and well-thought-out arrangements; that they are really the leaders of the country in its hour of peril. . . .'

From the beginning of June, when Asquith had first promised to put the Dardanelles documents to Parliament, to the end of July, when the Commission of Inquiry was set up, and on through the late summer and autumn, each of the participants assembled his evidence and prepared to be examined by the Commission. Churchill became increasingly embroiled in the past. At the end of July, Fisher asked him for help in preparing his own evidence for the Commissioners. 'My dear Fisher,' Churchill replied on August 1, 'I really feel gt diffidence in doing what you ask me. Although I greatly appreciate the confidence you show in me, I am sure it is much better that in the first instance you shd do it yrself. Then we can discuss it.' Three days later Fisher sent Churchill his first draft. It was not at all hostile to the enterprise. 'The gt kindness & goodwill of yr paper touches me,' Churchill replied at once. 'I will come & talk to you about it next week. You must set yrself more on public grounds for every action & you can I think do more justice to yr own case. But it has the compulsive buoyancy of truth.' Churchill discussed his own evidence with Hankey on several occasions. On August 3 Hankey wrote in his diary: 'In the evening Churchill called to see me & ranted for an hour about the Dardanelles, so that I got home very late.'

On August 10 Churchill and Fisher met to discuss the progress of their respective statements. Fisher was anxious that Churchill should continue to help him with his evidence. Churchill rehearsed to the Admiral a possible line of argument to support his hostility to the Dardanelles. On the following morning Fisher wrote:

My dear Winston,

   You were most convincing last night!

   *Impossible for me to equal it!* So please telephone to Phillips[13] on your return (Gerrard 301) & tell him to send shorthand writer and dictate just as you said it so convincingly last evening. Dont fail! What I enclose puts it on the wrong basis yet I would wish to bring out how you fought for me and how I reciprocated your affection!

   All the telegrams & letters I enclose were sent me by Crease (*just as you see them*) as being what he had put by! I never kept letters received or copies of letters sent—I am not sure now that this is not a happy thing! They cant call for what I have not got! So please let me, say next week, have your last evening's excellent narrative.

                                                                Yours
                                                                Fisher

   The two men met again on August 15. Churchill again helped Fisher with his draft, and promised to write down a line of argument for him. A few hours after their meeting Fisher wrote enthusiastically:

3.30 *A.M.!!!*
Private

                        'The Early Bird *catches the worm*'
Dear Winston,

   I did not emphasize the following point yesterday evening made by my acute Duchess[14] LONG SINCE!:—

   She has ALL ALONG maintained (*the war being our* ONE *object!*) that your case can be infinitely better stated for YOUR benefit by MY case being put forward on the one sole ground that I was originally

[13] James Faulkner Phillips, 1871–1933. Deputy Librarian, Admiralty, 1908–31; Librarian, 1931–2. Fisher's Secretary at the Board of Invention and Research, 1915–18.

[14] Nina Mary Benita Poore, 1878–1951. She married, 1901, the 13th Duke of Hamilton, an old shipmate of Fisher's. She was Lord Fisher's friend and ardent supporter. She and her husband made the Admiral welcome at both Hamilton Palace in Lanarkshire and Balcombe Place in Sussex. Vice-Patron, Royal Society for Prevention of Cruelty to Animals, 1903–25.

drawn to you by your WAR ATTRIBUTES (*unpossessed by any other member of the Government*).

'*Celerity*'
'*Courage*'
'*Audacity*'
'*Imagination*'

So I clung to you! clung against my convictions!

If on that text you unfold my case to the young woman Phillips sends you on application (Gerrard 301 Extension 5) then you'll make a good thing of it!

Yours
Fisher

'I think also YOU made an excellent point,' Fisher wrote in his postscript, 'of enlarging on the Armada of 593 vessels & my reluctance to leave that task unfinished. . . . Also I see the Force of your remark about bringing in the Falkland Islands, slurred over in all recent emanations from Authority!'

Because Churchill and Fisher had renewed their friendship, Churchill did not build up his evidence, as he might have done, on the basis of Fisher's erratic behaviour between October 1914 and May 1915. Instead, he tried to make their two cases fit together, modifying the fierce conflict which had in reality done so much harm to the planning of the enterprise. Fisher's mental collapse, to which Asquith, Hankey and Churchill had each referred with such conviction in May 1915, and the megalomania of the resignation demands which Fisher had sent Asquith on 19 May 1915, were not referred to once during the six months of the Commission's sittings.

By the middle of August Churchill's evidence was almost ready. On August 12 he had written to the Chairman of the Dardanelles Commission, Lord Cromer, setting out his intentions. The letter was confident in its tone and comprehensive in its demands:

My dear Lord Cromer,

As I expect that the meetings of your Commission are about to commence, I write to say that I desire at an early stage in the proceedings to place the Commission in possession of certain documents and information, and to make a general statement to them in regard to the

Admiralty's share in these transactions. I presume that the Prime Minister will probably wish to come before you first, but I should be quite ready to follow him with reasonable notice.

My evidence will be given in three separate phases: (1) the genesis of the Naval and Military operations and their conduct, down to the conclusion of Sir Ian Hamilton's first attempt to carry the Peninsula in the early days of May. (2) The proceedings leading to the Battle of Suvla Bay in August. (3) The policy and conduct of the operations from after the Battle of Suvla Bay to the evacuation of the Peninsula in January 1916.

It is with the first of these phases that I am now alone prepared to deal in detail. I was much less closely concerned with the other two stages, and considerable research among the papers and documents is required to enable me to present the case as I see it to the Commission. If agreeable to you, I should therefore prefer to confine my evidence to the first phase at the present time: but in regard to this I wish to deal both with the naval & military operations & their co-ordination.

With regard to the procedure of the Commission, I presume that I shall be at liberty to be present during the course of the Enquiry. I have a number of witnesses to bring before the Commission. I propose to conduct the case, so far as I am concerned, myself, and not to ask leave to employ Counsel.

Yours sincerely<br>Winston S. Churchill

Churchill sent a draft of his evidence to a Liberal MP, Alexander MacCallum Scott,[15] who in 1905 had written Churchill's biography, and who was just about to publish another biographical volume, *Winston Churchill in Peace and War*. On August 25 MacCallum Scott sent his suggestions, including advice about the way Churchill should deal with the renewal of the indecisive naval attack of 18 March 1915:

. . . I suggest you should not emphasise or over-elaborate your own personal view, or insist over much that you would, if it had been left to you alone, have ordered the attack to be renewed. I think you

[15] Alexander MacCallum Scott, 1874–1928. Secretary, the Liberal League against Aggression and Militarism, 1900–3. Liberal MP, 1910–22. He published a biography, *Winston Spencer Churchill* in 1905 and a revised edition, *With Winston Churchill in Peace and War*, in 1916. He joined the Labour Party in 1924.

were right; but after all you were not the technical expert, & the Committee is not inquiring into what you might have done under other circumstances but what was done under existing circumstances.

As far as the Commission is concerned the important fact is that the naval attempt was then broken off in view of definitely promised military operations.

You would have preferred pressing the naval assault to the final test but in view of the decision of the technical experts & of your colleagues you deferred.

At all events, I think this part of the story wants careful handling.

During August Lloyd George helped Churchill to obtain material from the War Office files. The Admiralty provided copies of many of the naval signals that had passed between the Admiralty and the officers at the Dardanelles. But a serious problem was caused by Asquith, who still refused to give Hankey permission to send Churchill a complete set of the War Council minutes. Asquith could only suffer if the evidence of his own support for the Dardanelles, or of Kitchener's vacillations, were to become known, and be used as a lever against him by Government critics. Without this essential evidence Churchill's case was incomplete, and in parts much weaker than it might otherwise have been. By the end of August Churchill had done what he could from the materials at his disposal. On August 30 he wrote to Fisher:

My dear Fisher,

I have been working at my statement of the Admiralty case & have vy nearly completed it. I will send it you when it is ready & we can then discuss particular points & documents. . . . I think you will be pleased with it.

I send you a copy I got from the WO of Kitchener's statement to the War Council of May 13. It will certainly be produced. He was vy angry about the Queen Elizabeth being withdrawn.

The Admiralty papers wh they are putting in consist entirely of Oliver's & Jackson's plans with the reports from the Admirals. You and I do not seem to have existed! I think they are behaving well. In addition there are the telegrams.

Grey has authorised me to have my papers printed at FO & this will

be a convenience. I don't expect to be called before Sept 20 or there-
abouts. So there is plenty of time.

Yes indeed stagnation, apathy & playing for safety are the orders of
the day.

Yours vy sincerely
Winston S. Churchill

The Foreign Office printer worked quickly. On September 8
Churchill received several copies of the first selection of his evidence. He sent one set at once to F. E. Smith, together with
the draft of a covering letter which he intended to give to the
Commission. To F. E. Smith he wrote:

My dear Fred,

. . . In this letter I have put down what I believe I can prove by
documents and witnesses. I have drafted it so that Fisher will probably
be able to say, 'I do not disagree with any of the statements of fact,
but I must add, etc, etc.' I want you to consider the case from an advocate's point of view. I am under no obligation to put in all these
documents, and the question of how big a target should be exposed
spontaneously is important. . . .

The great question of tactics seems to be whether I should confine
myself exclusively to the Naval part and avail myself of my formal
and recorded disclaimers of responsibility for the Military operations.
There is no doubt, I think, that the Naval part is very solid, but on the
other hand the case as I present it in my draft is the true case.

Another question is whether I should not very early point out that
the kind of crude misconceptions which have generally been widely
current about the inception of the Naval operations, eg that it was an
amateur scheme without proper expert backing, rushed through the
War Council without consideration or even with concealment; that the
Navy began unbeknown to Lord Kitchener and at dates that the Army
did not expect, etc—and should I then when these allegations have
been demolished ask the Commission to clear away these misconceptions decidedly? . . .

If you are in London Monday or Tuesday perhaps we could have a
talk about these things, and I could then show you some alternative or
additional documents about which I am at present undecided. . . .

Yours always
W

It was difficult to reconstruct the past, particularly as much of the evidence was locked away in archives to which Churchill had no access. There were only a few people with whom he could consult. When he sent a draft of his evidence to Sir Graham Greene, the Secretary to the Admiralty, Greene replied on September 9, advising him to moderate his criticisms of Kitchener. 'Although,' Greene wrote, 'so far as I am able to judge your comments are just, I am inclined to think that, having regard to the fact that he is no longer alive and able to speak for himself a little more reserve in referring to him would improve the general impression gained from hearing or reading your memorandum.' Churchill could not challenge the Kitchener myth; he was defeated before he could even present his defence.

Churchill continued his collaboration with Fisher, sending drafts of his evidence to the Admiral, and checking Fisher's drafts. On September 16 he sent Fisher an outline of how he thought Fisher should present his evidence to the Commission:

1. Definite long formed opinion against it.
2. Desire not to close the mind against *new* developments.
3. Overwhelming political need and pressure.
4. Unanimity at the Admiralty and on the spot for it.
5. Me!
6. Loyal and resolute conduct of the operation up to the point where the Admiral on the spot pulled up.
7. Then determination not to go further and desire to break off—if possible.
8. Consequent disagreement with me.
9. Hopeless military indecision and delay.
10. Conviction that you could not put your heart into the further measures—your utility for the time exhausted.
Above all sombre, silent, sphinx.

Churchill ended his letter on a personal note. 'Ah how cruel it is,' he wrote, 'to feel what we could do for these mugs! . . . Still I have not given up hope yet—that things may come right for us both.'

Some of Fisher's friends thought Churchill's collaboration with him unwise, and even Churchill wondered whether it should continue. But F. E. Smith was opposed to any secrecy or concealment. On September 20 Churchill wrote to Fisher:

FE saw no objection to our having a talk or to yr seeing the statement & documents I propose to hand in. On the contrary he thought it right that misunderstanding shd be eliminated where possible between persons who have been responsible for such momentous affairs, so that the truth cd be made clear without confusion or unfounded reproaches. I intend to show Asquith what I am going to say beforehand in pursuance of this advice.

But beset as we are by foes it is better to proceed with the utmost caution. I think you have chosen very wisely in Garvin. I will see him in the first instance and show him what I have prepared. We can postpone our talk till afterwards: & it may not be necessary in the end.

I will send for G today.

Freddy is such a loyal friend that his advice must always be weighed even when it is not endorsed by others.

On September 21, after he had spent an evening with Fisher going through the Admiral's evidence, Garvin wrote to Churchill:

My dear Winston,

. . . The Admiral seems strongly inclined now to discard his 'preamble' and to adopt the alternative statement of his case—with letter January 3rd 1915 and Baltic project for its corner-stones. A vast improvement. I have put to him the point about his offer to go out in Command. He and I are to meet again at Edward Goulding's (Wargrave) for a few hours, and I hope to get him again on Tuesday or Wednesday and to bring him to close quarters with your case. Really he is very amenable and magnanimous. He is convinced that if you were both together again, you could do the Baltic yet and above all *execute now* the letter of January 3—with modifications of course—so as to solve the Balkan–Constantinople business, where the military hitch promises to become again serious & prolonged! ! ! I must see you after I have seen him, next Monday.

Yours ever
JLG

On September 19 the Dardanelles Commission met to consider Churchill's letter of August 12. On the following day Lord

Cromer informed him of their decisions, which were not what Churchill had anticipated:

. . . As regards procedure, you say, 'I presume that I shall be at liberty to be present during the course of the enquiry.' The Commissioners have decided, in respect of all such meetings as are held in secret, not to admit anyone. They are, therefore, unable to comply with your request. But I may add that the evidence of all the witnesses will be printed, and that, should it appear desirable, for whatsoever reason, that any witness who has been already examined should be placed in possession of the evidence of other witnesses, a copy will be confidentially sent to him. Thus, on the one hand, the Commissioners will have an opportunity of recalling a witness should they think it desirable to do so, and, on the other hand, a witness who has been already examined will have an opportunity of requesting that he may be recalled in order to furnish any further explanation which he may wish to make, resulting from the evidence of subsequent witnesses. . . .

A second letter from Cromer on September 21 seemed to imply that the evidence considered by the Commission might not be as detailed as Churchill had wanted. 'As regards the Admiralty papers,' Cromer wrote, 'a very large number of telegrams were put at our disposal. I have not myself seen them but I believe they contain nothing but telegrams. A great many of these deal with points of detail which, for our purposes, are unimportant.' Cromer did not explain how he judged what was unimportant before any of the evidence had been taken. Another member of the Commission, Sir William Pickford, had gone through the file of telegrams, and, Cromer told Churchill, 'selected all those which are of real importance'. This was before a single witness had been examined.

On September 28 Churchill appeared before the Commissioners. He read his statement and answered their questions. He told them that five distinct truths could be drawn from the factual evidence. These were, he said:

1. That there was full authority;
2. That there was a reasonable prospect of success;
3. That greater interests were not compromised;

4. That all possible care and forethought were exercised in the preparation;

5. That vigour and determination were shown in the execution.

The evidence that Churchill produced to substantiate these
points was voluminous; but it was never published. When the
enquiry was over the Government agreed to publish only a general report. The documents, the submissions and the cross-
examination were not made public.

On one of Churchill's visits to the War Office in the summer of
1916 Lloyd George had told him that a small number of the new
'tanks', with the development of which Churchill had been so
closely connected, were to be used on the Somme. Churchill was
shocked at the idea of the premature use of what he believed
would be a decisive weapon if held back until it could be used
in quantity, and with an element of surprise. He therefore asked
Asquith to see him. Asquith listened so patiently to Churchill's
tactical arguments that he came away believing that the tank
would not be used until there were sufficient numbers to make an
immediate impact; probably early in 1917. But Churchill's arguments had not prevailed. On 15 September 1916 the first few
tanks went into action, without any decisive effect, and the element of surprise was lost. 'My poor "land battleships",' Churchill
wrote in his letter to Fisher of September 16, 'have been let off
prematurely and on a petty scale. In that idea resided one real
victory.' Churchill was angered by what he believed to have
been a shortsighted policy. But he was also disappointed to gain
no political advantage from the widespread public excitement
at the appearance of a new weapon of war. Few people knew
how closely he had been connected with its development. When
Arthur Conan Doyle[16] wrote to him at the end of September
with praise for his efforts with the tank, Churchill replied on October 1:

[16] Arthur Conan Doyle, 1859–1930. Historian and novelist. Inventor of
Sherlock Holmes. During the First World War he was gathering material for
his six-volume history *The British Campaign in France and Flanders,* published at intervals between 1915 and 1920.

I am vy much obliged to you for yr kindness in writing to me about the caterpillars.

There are plenty of good ideas if only they can be backed with power and brought into reality. But think what a time it took—from February 1915 when I gave the original orders—to Sept 1916 when the first use was made of these machines! And even then I think it wd have been better to wait & act on a much larger scale—having waited so long.

The caterpillars are the land sisters of the monitors. Both are intended to restore to the stronger power an effective means of the offensive. The monitor was the beginning of the torpedo-proof fleet. The caterpillar of the bullet proof army. But *surprise* was the true setting for both.

On October 12 Lloyd George was questioned about the invention of the tank in the House of Commons. He explained that the suggestions had come from D'Eyncourt and Hankey, but that 'these suggestions would never have fructified had it not been for the fact that Mr Churchill, who was then First Lord of the Admiralty, gave practical effect to them by making the necessary experiments, setting up committees for carrying the suggestions into effect, and by putting the whole of his energy and strength towards materialising the hopes of those who had been looking forward to an attempt of this kind'. Lloyd George's praise did not reduce Churchill's isolation.

Press hostility had not diminished since Churchill's return from the trenches. On October 11 H. A. Gwynne, the editor of the *Morning Post,* sent General Rawlinson details of an intrigue which he believed he had uncovered. 'French, Winston, Smith and Lloyd George are all working hand in hand though with different objects,' he wrote. 'Lloyd George is, I think, merely trying to get the Army in the hollow of his hand, and be able to order it about as he did the Ministry of Munitions. The others want to get rid of DH [Haig], but do not have any anxiety about the outcome. I have got satisfactory assurances that the plot will fail entirely, and that it may recoil on the heads of those who planned it. . . . I have taken care that the right people shall be prepared for all the ramifications of this dirty little trick.' To Asquith,

Gwynne wrote that same day of 'a sort of plot whose ramifications I am not altogether able to trace. There seems to be on the
part of the War Minister, Mr Winston Churchill, Sir F. E. Smith,
and Lord French, a common agreement in regard to the capabilities of the Commander-in-Chief of the British Armies in France;
and I am about justified in saying that I perceive indications that
the form which this understanding is taking is that of exalting
the French system of tactics and strategy at the expense of our
own.' Churchill's most severe public rebuke came on October 13,
when a leading article in Lord Northcliffe's *Daily Mail* challenged
his criticism of the renewed offensive in France, and warned him
not to pit himself against Haig, or against the Chief of the Imperial General Staff, Sir William Robertson:

> There is no Cabinet Minister or ex-Cabinet Minister, not even the
> most eminent, the most gifted, the most eloquent, the most energetic
> and most popular, whom this country would allow at this time of day
> to interfere with the plans of these two men. We have had more than
> enough of that sort of thing in the present war. The country has seen
> a Cabinet Minister who had just intelligence enough to know that
> Antwerp and Constantinople were places of importance and yet was
> mad enough to embark on adventures in both places with forces and
> methods that were insanely disproportionate to the enterprises upon
> which our unfortunate sailors and soldiers were launched in each case.
> In the Dardanelles affair in particular a megalomaniac politician risked
> the fate of our Army in France and sacrificed thousands of lives to no
> purpose.
>
> His duty at the time when he dragged his too pliant officers and
> experts with him into these reckless and hopeless 'gambles' was simply
> to supply the Navy with men and with material, and to be answerable
> to the House of Commons that it was so supplied. He had no other
> function whatever, and, if his naval colleagues had been men of the
> stamp of Sir Douglas Haig and Sir William Robertson, he would not
> have been allowed to exercise any other function.

Asserting in italics, '*Ministerial meddling means military muddling*', the article continued: 'No politician who remembers the
contemptible fiasco of Antwerp and the ghastly blunder of Gallipoli need expect either patience or forgiveness from the British

public if he interferes with the soldiers in charge of our operations. . . .' Churchill was familiar with these accusations. He realized that he had little chance of returning to office if, while the
whole Dardanelles episode was still being enquired into, he could
be pilloried in this way in an influential daily newspaper. On October 17 he wrote to Lord Cromer to protest both about the article in the *Daily Mail* and about the methods adopted by the
Dardanelles Commission to obtain evidence:

Whether this article is a proper one to have appeared while matters
of this character are sub judice is a question which I do not now refer
to; but it shows very clearly the kind of attack to which I am exposed
and from which I have every right to defend myself before the Commission. I am doing so however under considerable disabilities. I am
not able to examine myself the principal witnesses upon whom I rely
to establish the Admiralty case. Many of the questions which are essential to elicit the facts have not yet been put to them. On the other
hand adverse witnesses have had a number of leading questions put
to them the result of which has been to obtain from them evidence
which is open to direct challenge without my having any opportunity
of cross-examination. Other questions have been put to witnesses
which they have no competence to answer, and their answers are
recorded as authoritative pronouncements. I need not point out to the
Commission (for it is recognised I believe in nearly every civilised
system or procedure) the misleading effects which are certain to follow from very suggestive legal questions when wholly uncorrected by
cross-examination. The result of this is that the Commission has not
yet been placed in a position to do justice to the Admiralty case especially in its professional and technical aspect.

Churchill persisted with his defence, trying to ensure that the
Commission was fully informed of what had actually taken
place at the Dardanelles. On October 19 he wrote to its Secretary, Grimwood Mears,[17] that he intended to bring forward 'sufficient evidence and argument' to prove three points:

[17] Edward Grimwood Mears, 1869–1963. Gave up his practice at the Bar
on Government request to investigate allegations of German atrocities in Belgium, 1914–15. Secretary to the Royal Commission appointed to enquire
into the causes of the Easter Rising in Ireland, 1916. Secretary to the Darda-

(a) That at no time during the Dardanelles operation was the margin of safety of the Grand Fleet compromised or reduced in the slightest degree.

(b) That the ammunition reserves of the Admiralty were in all respects sufficient both for the needs of the Grand Fleet and the Dardanelles operation as planned.

(c) That the old battleships of the Majestic and Canopus class were really *surplus* to all requirements of the Fleet of blue water fighting and were therefore available to be risked in bombarding or in a similar operation.

That day Churchill also wrote to Admiral Oliver, who had been summoned to give evidence to the Dardanelles Commission. 'I think you should be able to give evidence broadly as follows,' Churchill wrote, and then outlined the points which he wished Oliver to stress:

That, like other Naval officers of high standing who have been captains of ships, you have yourself a good general knowledge of naval gunnery and its possibilities. . . .

That you have, during the course of this war, repeatedly made plans or revised plans for bombarding operations of all kinds. . . .

That in Commodore de Bartolomé you had a gunnery specialist of very high order with whom you were in frequent consultation, at regular meetings and at other times.

That your plans were prepared with all possible care and thought in accordance with the directions of the First Lord and First Sea Lord, in close conjunction with the work which was being done by Sir Henry Jackson, and that, of course, the full and accurate information of the Admiralty Intelligence Department was at your disposal.

That you adhere to the general soundness of these plans so far as the calculable factors are concerned, the chief of these being the destruction of permanent forts.

That the degree of Turkish resistance which would be encountered was an incalculable factor, though there were good reasons (vide Doris' proceedings on the Syrian Coast, etc.) for believing that the

nelles Commission, 1916–17; he agreed to become Secretary on condition that he was given a knighthood for his services. Knighted, 1917. Assistant to Lord Reading, Washington, 1918–19. Chief Justice, Allahabad High Court, India, 1919–32.

Turkish resistance would not immediately be of the most efficient character.

That the amount of opposition from mobile guns and its effect upon sweeping the Kephez minefield was also an incalculable factor.

That, for that reason, a gradual method of advance was prescribed, from which we could at any time withdraw, and from which we did, in fact, withdraw.

Oliver agreed to give evidence as Churchill suggested. In a private note on Churchill's letter he commented: 'If all the requirements they consider essential to success had to be met before an operation was undertaken no big operation of war would ever be undertaken. Most operations consist in making the most of a lot of bad conditions.'

On October 27 Hankey wrote in his diary: 'Winston Churchill called in the afternoon. . . . He seems quite satisfied that he made good his case.' That day Churchill wrote to Captain Spiers: 'I am slowly triumphing in this Dardanelles Commission, and bit by bit am carrying the whole case. I am really hopeful that they will free me from the burden wh cripples my action.' On October 28 Churchill wrote to Asquith, pointing out how much of the evidence given to the Commission by the naval experts vindicated his judgement. But he was disappointed by Grey's evidence, which he felt was 'pretty thin'. 'After all,' he reminded Asquith, 'it was a great Foreign Office need that the Admiralty were endeavouring to meet.' The Dardanelles Commission continued to sit throughout November. Churchill absorbed himself in studying the evidence which they took almost every day, and in seeking, where he felt it necessary, to rebut the accusations as they were made against him. In the whole of the British Press there was only one friendly article. It appeared on November 12 in the *Sunday Pictorial*, signed by the proprietor himself, Lord Rothermere:[18]

[18] On the following day Rothermere's second son, Vere Sidney Tudor Harmsworth (born 1895), was killed in action in France, while serving as a Lieutenant, Royal Naval Division. His eldest son, Harold Alfred Vyvian St George Harmsworth (born 1894) died of wounds received in action in France on 12 February 1918.

In the minds of some writers Mr Churchill appears to exercise an omnipresent and ubiquitous influence. They see his shadow in every glass. They search for traces of his identity in any anonymous writings that may for the moment attract more than usual attention. The public departments which he administered in the past are suspected of still echoing his views. Individual Ministers are thought to be susceptible to his influence, while any suggestion in any quarter to the effect that Mr Churchill has performed great and enduring services to the nation is seized upon as evidence of some concerted intrigue to restore him to power.

. . . the attacks on Mr Churchill continue, the object apparently being to discredit him utterly as a politician in the estimation of the public, and to prevent him at any future time from taking any useful share in the public life of the nation.

The majority of these attacks I believe to be sincere and devoid of personal animus. They are based upon the belief that Mr Churchill is by record and temperament unfitted to play any conspicuous part in the councils of the people. A man's character and temperament are expressed by his record in life, by the things which he has done and the things which he has not done, and it is, I believe, because Mr Churchill's opponents are only in partial possession of the facts concerning his administrative career at the Admiralty that they regard him as temperamentally unfitted for the most serious duties of public service.

There followed a detailed examination of Churchill's record at the Admiralty, and the statement that 'it is to Mr Churchill's credit that the outbreak of war after a century of peace found every ship, great or small, of our enormous fleets ready and at their war stations'. Such an achievement, Rothermere concluded, 'may never be repeated in history. It was one of those great specific acts of statesmanship which shape and decide the destinies of wars and peoples. It was an achievement which is alone sufficient to secure for Mr Churchill and all others concerned a grateful recognition in the records and the minds of their countrymen.'

During October, Sir Edward Carson had been busy organizing an effective opposition to Asquith. Over a hundred and fifty

Conservative MPs had become associated with his Unionist War Committee, which had been set up at the beginning of the year, and was as critical of Bonar Law as of Asquith. On every possible occasion members of Carson's Committee spoke in Parliament of the need for greater state control: shipping, food distribution and coal were three areas where they believed direct state intervention was necessary in the interests of the proper prosecution of the war. Churchill had sympathy with many of their demands.

On November 8 Carson led the dissidents in their first concerted challenge to the Government, using a debate on the disposal of enemy property in Nigeria as the point of attack. The Government proposed to sell the captured property to any buyers except citizens of enemy countries; Carson demanded that it should be sold only to British buyers. Bonar Law, who defended the Government's policy, insisted that the vote would be one of confidence in the Government. The vote went in the Government's favour. But of those Conservatives who voted, sixty-five supported Carson, as against seventy-one who voted for the Government. Had Carson been supported by only four more Tories, Bonar Law, under the pledge he had given the Conservatives on joining the Government in May 1915, would have had to resign, and the Coalition would have collapsed. Among the others who voted with Carson were eleven Liberals, including Churchill.[19] Bonar Law at once took measures to protect his position and that of the Coalition, meeting with both Carson and Lloyd George to devise some scheme of reconstruction. Both Bonar Law and Lloyd George were willing that Asquith should remain Prime Minister, but both wanted the daily direction of war policy to be in other hands.

On the evening of November 20 C. P. Scott went to see Churchill at 41 Cromwell Road. He spent two hours alone with him, noting two days later:

[19] The Liberals who voted with Carson included Frederick Handel Booth (one of Churchill's critics at the time of the Friedrichshafen raid), Leicester Harmsworth (brother of Lord Northcliffe and Lord Rothermere), Sir Alfred Mond (the only Privy Councillor other than Churchill) and Walter Roch (a member of the Dardanelles Commission).

He was evidently suffering acutely from his enforced inactivity. 'What fools they are,' he said, smiting the arm of his chair. 'They could get more out of me now in two years of war than in a hundred afterwards.' I urged him to make a business of Parliament and make himself a figure there, but he said the papers (with the exception of the Manchester Guardian) would not report him and on the contrary ill natured remarks were always made, as that 'there were few members present and no one troubled to come in' or 'what a contrast with the old days when his rising was the signal for the House to fill' and so on. Therefore he preferred to find his public in the press. Then at least every word he wished to say was printed and it took him no longer to write an article for the 'Sunday Pictorial' for which he got £250 than to prepare a speech which was not reported. After Xmas he meant to start a new series of articles in which there would be some very plain speaking.

At present he was the best abused man in the country. He was determined, however, to stick it out. He could effect nothing by going back to the Army so he must just 'wait in that chair'—a large and comfortable one—till his chance came. The mistake he had made was in not allowing enough for the power of the press, at a time of suspended party activity, to attack and ruin an individual. He had great hopes from the forthcoming report of the Dardanelles Commission which he had reason to believe would go far to clear him on that issue. . . .

Speaking of the possibility of a reconstructed Ministry he said no change would be material which did not involve a change in the Premiership. Lloyd George, 'with all his faults', was the only possible alternative Prime Minister. I asked if in case George formed a ministry he could count on being included. He said he thought so—that George would desire it and that it would be in his interest.

But when C. P. Scott spoke to Lloyd George's Parliamentary Secretary, David Davies,[20] on November 22, Churchill's chances of office seemed less certain. 'Didn't I think he had had his chance?' Davies asked Scott: 'And when a man had had his chance and missed it ought he not to be set aside?' Davies went on to say that Churchill was 'anathema in the Army', and that if Lloyd

[20] David Davies, 1880–1944. Liberal MP, 1906–29. Commanded 14th Battalion Royal Welch Fusiliers, 1914–16. Parliamentary Private Secretary to Lloyd George, 1916–17. Landed proprietor and company director. Created Baron, 1932.

George were involved in giving him office he might incur a share of the unpopularity which would result. Scott did not pass back this gloomy intelligence to Churchill, who seemed unaware of how slim were his chances of gaining advantage from Asquith's fall.

On November 26, when Bonar Law, Lloyd George, Carson and many of those who had been Churchill's Cabinet colleagues in 1914 were concentrating upon the political crisis, Churchill himself published in the *Sunday Pictorial* his first public account of what had happened at Antwerp over two years before. The attack in the *Daily Mail* had stirred him to action. He sensed that the Dardanelles Commission of Enquiry would not publish enough evidence to vindicate, or even to explain, his actions. He therefore began the process of self-defence for the policies over which he had been criticised, not only the Dardanelles, but Antwerp and all naval policy. This process was to take up much of his time in the years to come. But his Antwerp article could not make any serious impression on the public during a week of intense political speculation about the future of the Coalition.

On November 27 Churchill received a further communication from the Dardanelles Commission. It was a copy of the statement submitted to them two days before by one of Kitchener's former Private Secretaries, Sir George Arthur.[21] Churchill was incensed at what he regarded as its blatant falsifications. Arthur had told the Commissioners that, on some unspecified date, Kitchener had been 'invited to a Conference by the First Lord of the Admiralty when the passage of the Dardanelles was the subject of discussion' and that 'he protested vigorously against such an undertaking by the Navy without very strong and very careful support from & co-operation with the Army'. For two days Churchill brooded upon this new challenge to his own honesty.

[21] George Compton Archibald Arthur, 1860–1946. 3rd Baronet, 1878. Entered Army, 1880. Private Secretary to Lord Kitchener, 1914–16. Assistant to the Director of Military Operations, War Office, 1916–18. On several missions to France; he acted as interpreter between Sir Douglas Haig and General Nivelle before the battle of Arras, March 1917. His publications include *Life of Lord Kitchener* (3 vols, 1920) and *Concerning Winston Spencer Churchill* (1940).

Then, on November 29, he sent his answer. Bitterness broke through in every paragraph:

The only 'Conferences' held on this subject were the various meetings of the War Council the records of which are before the Commission. On no occasion either in Council or in conversation did Lord Kitchener express views of the kind attributed to him by Sir George Arthur. If he held such opinions it was his duty to have expressed them at the War Councils in place of the diametrically oppositive views which he expressed both by speech and in writing. The documentary evidence I have laid before the Commission and the records of the War Council are conclusive on this point. Further, Lord Kitchener was in almost daily consultation with the Prime Minister and the Prime Minister has deposed that 'Lord Kitchener was strongly in favour of the Naval undertaking'. . . .

If it were necessary I have no doubt that negative evidence from all the naval and political personages concerned could be adduced to prove first that no such Conference took place and secondly that no such protest was made by Lord Kitchener as is described by Sir George Arthur. I hardly imagine however that in view of the evidence before them the Commissioners will wish to embark on this process. If they decide to do so I would ask their leave to marshal the evidence; and if expressions of Lord Kitchener's opinion made to a responsible person at unnamed dates are to be admitted in evidence I conceive myself in a position to produce evidence that Lord Kitchener expressed private opinions in an entirely contrary sense during the period when the Naval attack showed good prospects of succeeding. . . .

All the facts stated by Sir George Arthur are untrue and without foundation, but I desire to repeat what I have said on several occasions to the Commission—that I take full responsibility for the advice given by me in the name of the Admiralty to the War Council in regard to the Naval operation. I have never tried to throw any of this burden upon Lord Kitchener. As a principal person next to the Prime Minister concerned with the direction of the war, and as a great soldier acquainted with gunnery and quasi-military problems such as the attack of Forts, etc, he no doubt has his responsibility, but I wish to bear my responsibility as the head of the Admiralty so far as I may properly do so myself. In the same way I conceive that the prime responsibility for the inception and conduct of the military operation rests subject to the

War Council with the Secretary of State for War. As the Commission know, this last point is one to which I attach importance. . . .

Churchill then raised the question of the origin of the rumours which had been circulating against him:

I have for the last eighteen months been the subject of persistent and damaging attacks in the public press and elsewhere in connection with the Dardanelles operation. It is hardly conceivable that such attacks would have been maintained with so much confidence, if they had not been founded and nourished on statements purporting to emanate from the highest authority of the character of those now brought before the Commission by Sir George Arthur. I cannot believe that Lord Kitchener himself had anything to do with the circulation of such untruthful and unfounded allegations, but that they have been made from time to time by persons in his entourage has long been suspected by me and this suspicion cannot but be confirmed by Sir George Arthur's statement.

Before the Commission began its labours I was frequently asked whether I was in a position to disprove the charge that Lord Kitchener was throughout opposed to the whole Dardanelles policy. There is no doubt that this impression was sedulously fostered and is even now widespread. The fact that at the close of the first phase of the Dardanelles operations which the Commission have now under review, I was removed from my Office as First Lord of the Admiralty while Lord Kitchener was simultaneously invested with the Order of the Garter and continued to be Secretary of State for War until his lamented death has no doubt been accepted as an unanswerable confirmation of such statements. . . .

November 30 was Churchill's forty-second birthday. He spent it at home with his wife and family. It was a year since he had ceased to be a Cabinet Minister. Nearly eighteen months had passed since he had last been the head of a Department of State. His correspondence with the Dardanelles Commission and his articles on the early history of the war took up much time; but they were not what he wanted to use his time for. While he fell back into an angry contemplation of the past, political developments continued on a turbulent course. Conservative and Liberal Ministers alike were discussing how to reduce Asquith's powers, and even to remove him altogether. Some saw Bonar Law, others saw Lloyd George, as the likely successor. Churchill was not consulted about the political upheaval, and was seldom informed of its course. On December 2, the day on which Lloyd George wrote to Bonar Law that 'the life of the country depends on resolute action by you now', Max Aitken met Churchill in London. He recalled in *Politicians and the War* how Churchill was 'almost wistfully eager for news'. Churchill was in a remote position. Yet his career seemed to depend upon the outcome of the political struggle. If Asquith remained in any position of power, or if Bonar Law became Prime Minister, it was unlikely that he could expect any upsurge in his political fortunes. But if Lloyd George emerged either as Prime Minister, or as the real focus of power, he was convinced that there would be a place for him in the new Government. Lloyd George knew the full extent of Churchill's capabilities; he understood his burning desire to help the nation at war, shared his dislike of sloth, humbug and deception, and appreciated his skill at inspiring those who feared defeat. But the only supporter of Churchill's claims who wrote on his behalf was Sir Abe Bailey, a South African mine owner who wrote on December 2:

Dear Mr Lloyd George,
    Am just off after being held up for four days & I only hope to God everything goes right & you are elected Prime Minister. Then there is a chance. I shall be awfully sorry if Winston's brain & push have to be left on the shelf for I know & so do you that he is full of ideas, & good ones too. I have no friendships except for the Empire & it is having those feelings that I shall for one deplore the loss of his valuable services. He will I know assist *you* in any case.
    Goodbye, good luck & God bless your work.

                                               Yours most sincerely
                                                    Abe Bailey

On December 3 Asquith agreed to the joint demands of Lloyd George and Bonar Law for a small War Committee, led by Lloyd George, on which Asquith would not serve, although he would remain Prime Minister. Lloyd George told Churchill of this enormous concession by Asquith. Churchill was sceptical, doubting that it would really serve the purpose of a more vigorous direction of the war. In *The World Crisis* he later wrote of how both he and Carson had felt that Lloyd George's position would be a weak and possibly a dangerous one under such a scheme:

On him would fall all the brunt of battling with the naval and military Chiefs. . . . The appeal in all cases would have been to the Prime Minister who, free from the friction of the discussions of the War Committee, yet fully informed on every point, would have been able to decide with final authority. On the other hand, Mr Lloyd George, publicly appointed to preside over the Committee actually directing the conduct of the war, would have been held responsible for every misfortune that occurred and there were bound to be many.

It was Asquith, not Lloyd George, who changed his mind, rejecting the arrangement to which he had already agreed. Lloyd George thereupon resigned. On December 5 Bonar Law, Curzon, Austen Chamberlain and Lord Robert Cecil likewise submitted their resignations. Faced with the immediate dissolution of his Government, Asquith tendered his own resignation to the King at seven o'clock that evening. Two and a half hours later the King received Bonar Law at Buckingham Palace, and asked him to form an administration. Lloyd George was in favour of Bonar Law doing so, and willing to serve under him. That evening Lloyd George and Aitken were due to dine with F. E. Smith at Grosvenor Gardens. Churchill had not been invited; but in *Politicians and the War* Max Aitken gave an account of how, at this late hour of the crisis, Churchill was drawn in:

Birkenhead [F. E. Smith] and Churchill were at the Turkish Bath of the Automobile Club that evening, and Birkenhead had rung up George to remind him of a dinner engagement. He mentioned that Churchill was with him and Lloyd George immediately requested that Churchill should be asked to come too. This suggestion, probably quite carelessly made, produced on Churchill's mind the natural impression that he was regarded as one of the new set of war administrators who were about to grasp the helm. Surely Lloyd George would not ask him to be included in a dinner party on this night of all others if he did not mean to offer him a real post—and a real post to Churchill meant nothing but war-service. . . .

At the dinner, Aitken recalled, the conversation 'turned entirely on the personnel of the new Ministry' and all present—Lloyd George, F. E. Smith, Max Aitken and Churchill—took part in the conversation 'on terms of equality'. Lloyd George had to leave in order to meet Bonar Law on his return from Buckingham Palace. He asked Aitken to accompany him. During the drive he explained to Aitken that enormous pressure was being brought to bear to exclude Churchill from any new administration, and that if Lloyd George himself were to become Prime Minister, even he would not be prepared to run the risk involved in giving Churchill Cabinet office. Aitken's account continued: 'Lloyd George asked me to convey a hint of this kind on my return to the party. . . . He thought Churchill too confident of high office in the new regime. A refusal would be awkward. It would be better if Churchill were dashed a bit first.'

Aitken therefore returned to F. E. Smith's house; he himself expected some position, perhaps a substantial one, in the new administration, and therefore, as he recalled:

I smiled on Churchill as a senior colleague might on an aspiring junior. I still, so to speak, walked warily—but I walked. Churchill also had every reason to suppose that he was sure of high office. We discussed as allies and equals the personnel of the new Government. Churchill suggested that I might be made Postmaster-General—a task suitable to my abilities.

Then I conveyed to him the hint Lloyd George had given me. . . . these are the exact words I used: 'The new Government will be very well disposed towards you. All your friends will be there. You will have a great field of common action with them.'

Something in the very restraint of my language carried conviction to Churchill's mind. He suddenly felt he had been duped by his invitation to the dinner, and he blazed into righteous anger. I have never known him address his great friend Birkenhead in any other way except as 'Fred' or 'FE'. On this occasion he said suddenly: 'Smith, this man knows that I am not to be included in the new Government.'

With that Churchill walked out into the street. . . .

On the evening of December 5, after leaving Buckingham Palace, Bonar Law asked Asquith if he would agree to serve under him. Asquith refused. On the following afternoon, at a meeting of Balfour, Bonar Law, Lloyd George, Asquith and the Labour leader Arthur Henderson at Buckingham Palace, Bonar Law said that if Asquith would not serve under him, he would give up the attempt to form a Government, and that Lloyd George must do so. The Conference broke up. When it was over Asquith again refused Bonar Law's offer. That evening Bonar Law returned to Buckingham Palace and told the King that he declined to try any longer to form a Government. The King then asked Lloyd George to form a Government, and that evening Lloyd George became Prime Minister, with Bonar Law as Chancellor of the Exchequer. Balfour agreed to serve as Foreign Secretary,[22] Lord Curzon as a member of the War Cabinet. Lord Milner and Arthur Henderson also joined the War Cabinet. Lord Derby became Secretary of State for War, Walter Long Colonial Secretary, Dr Christopher Addison Minister of Munitions. F. E. Smith remained Attorney-General and Lord Robert Cecil Minister of Blockade. At a discussion on the personnel of the new Ministry held at the War Office on December 6, Addison drafted a list of possible Ministers. Churchill was not in the list. But Lloyd George wrote in the margin '? Air Winston'. No Air Ministry was established, however; nor did Lloyd George offer Churchill any place in the new Coalition.

Lloyd George wanted to give Churchill a place in his Government. But he had been unable to overcome the strong Conservative opposition to Churchill's inclusion. In his *War Memoirs* he recalled that when he had asked Bonar Law: 'Is he more dangerous *for* you than when he is *against* you?' Bonar Law had replied: 'I would rather have him against us every time.' The attitude of the Conservative Leader was shared by almost all his followers, and by *The Times* and the *Morning Post*, both for so long his implacable adversaries. Churchill's exclusion became a

[22] Of Balfour at this time Churchill wrote in *Great Contemporaries:* 'He passed from one Cabinet to the other, from the Prime Minister who was his champion to the Prime Minister who had been his most severe critic, like a powerful graceful cat walking delicately and unsoiled across a rather muddy street.'

certainty when, on December 7, Austen Chamberlain, Walter Long, Lord Robert Cecil and Curzon pressed upon Lloyd George, as a condition of their own entry into his Cabinet, that Churchill should be excluded altogether from the administration. Without the support of these four Conservatives, Lloyd George could not have formed a Government. He therefore bowed to their veto. Churchill felt humiliated and betrayed; his critics rejoiced. The public, declared *The Times*, 'learn with relief and satisfaction that Mr. Churchill will not be offered any post in the new Administration'.

The implacable hostility and suspicion of the Conservatives, Asquith's refusal to allow the facts about the Dardanelles to be published, and the isolation imposed by a year without office, combined to keep Churchill from power. Lloyd George's Cabinet colleagues were confident that they could deal with the war without his guidance. That his outspoken public criticisms of Asquith during the previous six months may have helped their cause did not mitigate their hostility or reduce their mistrust. Nor did they consider that his long experience of naval warfare and organization gave him any claim to return to the Admiralty. Carson was appointed First Lord, the post Churchill had wanted for himself.

From May 1915 to December 1916 Churchill had believed that if he had been called upon to direct the nation's affairs, he would have made an effective war leader. He was convinced, he wrote to his wife on 28 January 1916, that he could use power 'better than any other living Englishman to determine the war policy of Britain'. He was confident that he had the ability to drive forward the machinery of Government with vigour and cohesion, and that his ideas for national organization and naval, military and aerial strategy could have averted the disasters and broken the stalemates of 1915 and 1916. Churchill's confidence in his abilities was absolute; as a Cabinet Minister he had shown this confidence to his colleagues, and it had always been a striking feature of his public speeches. It was a strong and vaunted confidence, applauded at first both by his colleagues and by the public, who appreciated and were often inspired by his combination of faith in the outcome of the war and recognition of the difficulties still to come. But to be accepted fully, to be trusted and rewarded, such confidence needed to be set against successful results. The series of failures at the Dardanelles and Gallipoli, however much they could be explained by errors other than Churchill's own, or, as he had come to explain them, by his lack of overall authority, set up a barrier between the confidence which he felt in himself, and the public assessment of him. Nor was it the Dardanelles alone that kept this barrier in place, depriving him of the power which he believed he could use effectively, and relegating him to political impotence. Irrespective of particular successes or failures, in spite of such explanations and documentation which he was able to give, Churchill's contemporaries found in his activities insufficient claim on their respect and trust. He was believed by many to be wanting in certain essential qualities of statesmanship; and was judged more deficient in these qualities by the winter of 1916 than he had been in the autumn of 1914. His wartime work at the Admiralty, for which he believed himself entitled to the praise and support of his fellow-countrymen, was interpreted in such a way as to confirm in many minds the doubts that had already been formed during the previous decade, and to create doubts where none had earlier existed. Churchill believed that his war policies and war-making zeal had been both unique and beneficial, making him indispensable to any successful wartime administration, and qualifying him for the highest public office. But for others his war policies, and the enthusiasm with which he entered into them, created suspicion and even fear, destroying his chances of directing the war from 10 Downing Street, the Admiralty or the War Office. Any other place he regarded as insufficient challenge to his abilities, and as a waste of his energies.

Churchill did not understand why it was that he created mistrust where he expected to secure approval. He believed that his abilities and achievements were such that only a malicious critic would deny them. Clementine Churchill realized why he did not inspire trust. She saw how far his strident confidence frightened those with whom he worked and to whom he had to look for support. She alone of those closest to him told him of his faults; others, like Asquith and Lloyd George, added to his self-deception by frequent praise and encouragement when they were with him, but by severe censure on him in their private talk and correspondence. Clementine Churchill cautioned him directly. In her letters to him she stressed the danger to his career of the impatience and scorn which he often showed towards those who disagreed with him. She rebuked his tendency to take provocative or unexpected measures without regard to the likely reaction of others. She stressed how much he harmed himself by acting upon ideas which he had not given others time to accept, or which he had failed adequately to explain. She warned him that these weaknesses of character were accentuated by his often brusque and dictatorial manner, and by his overriding impatience. She saw clearly that the ideas which he produced with such extraordinary energy and conviction were seen by others as lacking in judgement; and that the more fiercely he pressed forward with a course of action, the more lacking in perspective he appeared to those colleagues without whose support he could not act.

These criticisms were all justified; Clementine Churchill understood her husband's failure to convince others. But there was a deeper failure than that. Churchill had always to be at the centre; he wanted to be responsible for the principal decisions of the war, and to be known to be. He believed that risks had to be taken and failed to understand why others were repelled by his evident relish for warmaking. While he had been at the Admiralty he had insisted upon swift and bold decisions. Those who hesitated to accept those decisions sensed his disapproval. Those who wanted to wait longer upon events found his scorn direct, outspoken and galling. He showed little sympathy for those who could not make up their minds, or who did so with reservations. As 1915 progressed, his arguments at the War Council became increasingly ineffective. Because of his forceful and assertive manner he often appeared to his colleagues over-simple and over-dramatic. At times his counsel was weighty and sober, but at times it seemed hasty and immature. Unable to explain his diverse moods, his growing obsessions or his seemingly dictatorial approach to dissent, Churchill's contemporaries found themselves making frequent and caustic reference to his ambition, which, they felt, overrode consistency. Asquith and Lloyd George, whose respective patronage had been essential to Churchill for him to remain in Government or return to it, both felt that the imaginative, constructive, hard-working colleague of pre-war years was being eaten up by personal ambition, and that his judgement had been impaired.

The doubts felt by Asquith and Lloyd George kept Churchill from office for nearly two years. These doubts were widespread, making his emergence as a war leader impossible. He believed he could govern the country effectively in time of war; few other people shared this belief. He had no national following and no regional support. No influential section of the Liberal Party considered him their leader. No significant political groups regarded him as their spokesman. The hostilities which he had aroused by the end of 1915 cut him off from all but a small group of isolated allies of no political strength. Churchill craved the allegiance of large numbers, both in Parliament and outside it. He believed that his foresight and his abilities, if fully known by his fellow-countrymen, would win that allegiance for him. But faith in his powers of leadership was held by few; by a small family circle, and by friends who had been captivated by his driving force. They alone felt that his consuming self-confidence, his impatience and his brooding were a necessary counterpart to his positive qualities, and did not undermine them.

Churchill could not dispel the doubts and distrust which he had created. All the faults to which people pointed seem to spring from an egoism which would be dangerous if allowed to control, or even influence, a War Cabinet. Only an overriding concern with self seemed adequate to explain the different phases of his wartime career: his excitement at the preparations for war, his exhilaration when it came, his personal involvement in the siege of Antwerp, his desire to give up the Admiralty for a military command, his growing obsession with the Dardanelles, his gnawing impatience with his reduced powers at the Duchy of

Lancaster, his appeal for Fisher's return to the Admiralty in
March 1916 and his brooding concern for vindication over each
of the disasters of his nine and a half wartime months as First
Lord. The selfishness and irresponsibility which these concerns of
his seemed to indicate could be set against substantial achievements in naval policy, and wisdom and foresight in counsel. But
the mistrust which Churchill aroused prevented these compari-
sons from being made, and his substantial achievements failed to
create public confidence.

During 1916 Churchill saw that he could do nothing to curb
the continuous criticisms of his past actions, or to allay suspicions
about his motives. He came increasingly to fear that his contemporaries would never recognize what he believed were the
extent of his achievements, and of his capabilities. He felt that
these had come to be blotted out of the public mind by malice,
partisanship and prejudice. His bitterness against Asquith for not
publishing the documents about the Dardanelles was acute; his
dislike of the Press for condemning him without the evidence was
severe. He became convinced that only when the archives of the
Admiralty and the War Council were made public would his
true worth be known. He believed that, although contemporaries
belittled his achievements, historical research would show his
actions to have been prudent, wise and remarkable. He fell back
upon the belief that, despite the harsh judgement of his contemporaries, the judgement of history would support him. Cut
off from power, denigrated, condemned, Churchill saw history
as the final refuge of his reputation. But his immediate career,
and his influence on the course of the war, depended entirely,
not upon the historical, but upon the contemporary verdict; that
verdict, in December 1916, was outspokenly hostile and seemingly irreversible.

# Facsimiles

First draft
London
15 April 1878

25. 8. 14

My dear Grey,

Don't jump: but do
you mind my sending
this the personal message
to Enver. I have measured
this man & am sure
it will do good. But
of course your "NO" is
final.

Yours ever

L

I know that Sir E Grey who has
already been approached as to possible
terms of peace if Germany & Austria
has stated that if Turkey remains
neutral an agreement to respect
the integrity of her territory must be
a condition of any terms of peace that
affect the Near East.

2 . 1. 15

My dear Churchill

You have no doubt
seen Buchanan's telegram about
the Russians & Turks if not Fitzgerald
is taking it over.
Do you think any naval actions
would be possible to prevent Turks
sending more men into the
Caucasus & thus demanding
Constantinople.

Yours very truly
Kitchener

10, Downing Street,
Whitehall. S.W.

Lord Fisher

In the King's name,
I order you at once
to return to your post.

H.H. Asquith

15 May 1915

Dec: 28th

My darling

Your letter from Dover just arrived & I am sending it on at once to H.Q. coupled with an invitation to luncheon. It seems centuries since you left & a thick pall of fog has settled round me thro' which I can neither hear nor see the conflict. Something good must come of it — If as I fear the F.M keeps his pledge, at any rate we get Conscription

Tomorrow I go to Alderley till Monday
I am absolutely worn out with
Emotions & the Excitement of seeing
you & I must have a few days'
rest. I can't sleep for anxiety &

I send you one or two letters
& a cutting. I know nothing, but I
feel the break-up is not yet; this
futile government will fumble on
for a few more months..

I could not tell you how much
I wanted you at the Station. I was
so out of ~~the~~ breath with running
for the train. Your loving
Clemmie

with much hesitation.

Tuesday Morning. 36 Berkeley Square

My dear Minister.

Please forgive my d—d reiteration
but I am terribly afraid of the Asquithian
cajolery! ( Am I already too late? )
Providence has placed the Plum bang
in your Mouth! Certain Prime Minister!
You have no Rival as Leader of
the Opposition and such a Cry for
assuming the position!!! So Patriotic!!!!

"The Navy in Danger"!
"— But not too late for Safety".

Ask George Lambert to tell you the inner history
of the late East End Election when but the Election Machine

looking furiously on just avoided defeat
300 votes! 157 men in that large Constituency
would have beaten the Coalition Government!
There is. Seething and Wide-Spread
discontent at the Conduct of the War!

But the People see No One as a
new Leader !

There is the Cave of Adullam but
No David has Come along.!
See the 1st Book of Samuel Chap 22 Verse 2
"He became a Captain over them"
"And there with him about 400 Men"!
Arn't that a good majority for you?

So dont go back!

3

Never leave that Box. once you
have banged it as you will this
afternoon. As meek as Moses
you'll say your mission is to help!
Yes! Help the war!
Yes! " Big Conceptions! Quick Decisions!
That will be your War Cry!
" Think in Oceans"!
Shoot at Sight!
That will be your action!
Go in and Win!
Don't Falter
" Aut Caesar Aut Nullus "
accept no post in this Government they

4

They are doomed !

Fate has you in it's Grasp !

Dont wriggle out of it !

D-n Fisher!— You get
Prime Minister !

That will End the War !

Nought else will !

The Country wants a Man !

Every War always wants a Man !

Dont go back. Accept nothing ! Yours

7.3.16.

THE TURKISH EMPIRE,

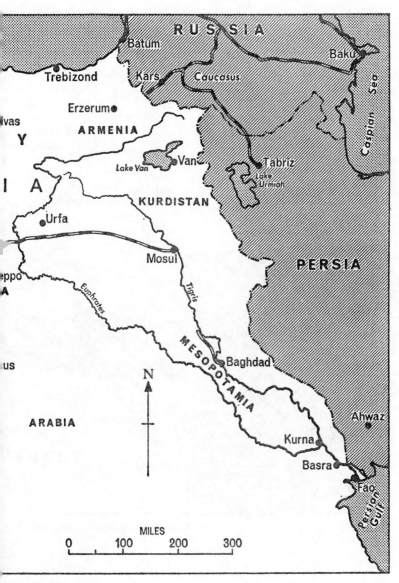

AUGUST 1914

THE GALLIPOLI PENINSULA AND THE

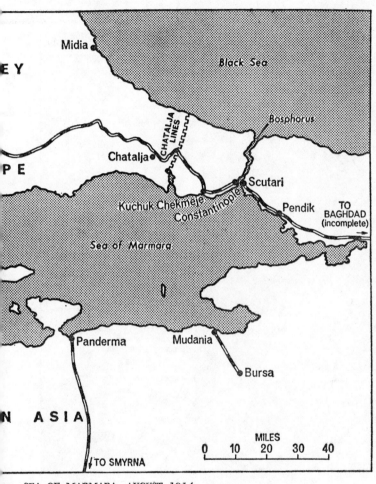

SEA OF MARMARA, AUGUST 1914

THE ALTERNATE WAR ZONES DISCUSSED IN
JANUARY 1915

# Index of
# Documents Quoted

In this Index I have listed, in chronological order, the 1446 documents quoted in full or in part in this volume. I have given the date on which each document was written, the page on which it is cited in this volume, and the archive in which I found it. For all documents from the Churchill papers, or from the Admiralty, Air Ministry, Foreign Office and War Office papers, I have given specific file references. Whenever the document can be found in the Churchill papers as well as in other collections, I have given the Churchill papers file number.

For six of the documents cited, I have taken the text from a published version, having been unable to find the original source; for two documents, my reference was a facsimile copy printed in a published book. Whenever the date of a document is uncertain, I have indicated this by square brackets.

Churchill to Milne, p. 78. Copy, Churchill papers: 13/31

Asquith to Venetia Stanley, p. 78. Montagu papers

Churchill to all British Ships, p. 78. Milne papers

Churchill to Milne, p. 78. Milne papers

Churchill to Milne (Italian neutrality), p. 79. Milne papers

Churchill to all British ships, p. 79. Milne papers

Churchill to all naval Commanders, p. 80. Milne papers

Walter Long to Churchill, p. 81. Spencer-Churchill papers

[4] Aug. 1914 Beatty to Churchill, p. 60. Copy, Beatty papers

5 Aug. 1914 Carson to Churchill, p. 82. Churchill papers: 2/64

Churchill to Grey, p. 158. Grey papers

6 Aug. 1914 Churchill to Kitchener, p. 84. Kitchener papers

7 Aug. 1914 Gretton to Churchill, p. 82. Spencer-Churchill papers

Kitchener to Churchill, p. 85. Churchill papers: 13/43

8 Aug. 1914 Fisher to Hankey, p. 63. Hankey papers

Benckendorff note, p. 272. Copy, Churchill papers: 13/37

9 Aug. 1914 Clementine Churchill to Churchill, pp. 83, 89. Spencer-Churchill papers

Churchill to Prince Louis, p. 87. Admiralty papers: 137/452

Churchill to Clementine Churchill, p. 89. Spencer-Churchill papers

Asquith to Venetia Stanley, p. 968. Montagu papers

Haldane to Churchill, p. 968. Churchill papers: 28/152

11 Aug. 1914 Churchill to Clementine Churchill, p. 90. Spencer-Churchill papers

Grey to Greene, p. 93. Copy, Churchill papers: 13/43

### SEPTEMBER 1914

### DECEMBER 1914

17 Dec. 1914
Fisher to Esher, p. 227. Esher papers
Churchill to Asquith, p. 239. Asquith papers
Asquith to Churchill, p. 239. Copy, Asquith papers
Churchill note, p. 239. Asquith papers
Churchill to Kitchener, p. 239. Kitchener papers

18 Dec. 1914
Asquith to Churchill, p. 239. Churchill papers: 26/1
Churchill to Kitchener, p. 240. Copy, Churchill papers: 26/1
Asquith to Venetia Stanley, pp. 240, 241. Montagu papers
Kitchener to Churchill, p. 240. Draft, Kitchener papers
Grey to Bertie, p. 425. Copy, Grey papers

19 Dec. 1914
Kitchener to Churchill, p. 241. Churchill papers: 26/1
Churchill to Kitchener, p. 241. Copy, Churchill papers: 26/1
Guest to Churchill, p. 241. Churchill papers: 26/1

20 Dec. 1914
Asquith to Venetia Stanley, p. 242. Montagu papers
Fisher to Jellicoe, p. 264. Jellicoe papers

21 Dec. 1914
Asquith to Venetia Stanley, p. 156. Montagu papers
Churchill to Kitchener, p. 242. Copy, Churchill papers: 26/1
Churchill to Fisher, p. 258. Fisher papers
Fisher to Churchill, p. 264. Churchill papers: 29/1
Knox to War Office, p. 311. Copy, Churchill papers: 26/5

22 Dec. 1914
Churchill to Fisher, p. 312. Fisher papers

23 Dec. 1914
Churchill note, p. 155. Draft, Admiralty papers: 116/1351

25 Dec. 1914
Fisher to Churchill, p. 261. Churchill papers: 13/43

27 Dec. 1914
Asquith to Venetia Stanley, p. 311. Montagu papers

28 Dec. 1914
Churchill to French, p. 243. Copy, Churchill papers: 26/1

4 Jan. 1915    Fisher to Balfour, p. 325. Balfour papers
Fisher to Churchill, p. 325. Churchill papers: 13/56
Fisher to Churchill, p. 327. Churchill papers: 13/56
Churchill to Fisher, p. 328. Copy, Churchill papers: 13/56

5 Jan. 1915    Carden to Churchill, p. 325. Churchill papers: 13/65
Asquith to Venetia Stanley, pp. 325, 326. Montagu papers
Churchill to Asquith, p. 682. Churchill papers: 13/44

6 Jan. 1915    Churchill to Carden, p. 327. Copy, Churchill papers: 13/65

7 Jan. 1915    War Council, Secretary's notes, p. 328. Cabinet papers: 22/1
Asquith to Venetia Stanley, p. 331. Montagu papers
Churchill to Asquith, p. 331. Copy, Churchill papers: 26/2

8 Jan. 1915    Churchill to French, p. 243. Copy, Churchill papers: 26/2
War Council, Secretary's notes, p. 332. Cabinet papers: 22/1

9 Jan. 1915    Fisher to Churchill, p. 335. Churchill papers: 13/56

10 Jan. 1915   Margot Asquith diary, p. 335. Countess Oxford and Asquith papers

11 Jan. 1915   Churchill to Jellicoe, pp. 262, 337. Copy, Churchill papers: 13/46
Churchill to French, p. 336. Copy, Churchill papers: 26/2
Carden to Churchill, p. 339. Churchill papers: 13/65

12 Jan. 1915   Fisher to Tyrrell, p. 337. Foreign Office papers: 800/220
Churchill to Fisher, p. 342. Copy, Churchill papers: 8/78
Fisher to Oliver, p. 341. Oliver papers

## MARCH 1915

## MAY 1915

15 Oct. 1915     Churchill memorandum, p. 705. Churchill papers: 21/42

Margot Asquith to Hankey, p. 707. Hankey papers

18 Oct. 1915     Spender to Churchill, p. 706. Churchill papers: 21/43

Margot Asquith to Kitchener, p. 708. Kitchener papers

19 Oct. 1915     Churchill to Kitchener, p. 710. Copy, Churchill papers: 21/43

20 Oct. 1915     Churchill memorandum, p. 706. Churchill papers: 2/99

22 Oct. 1915     Churchill to Asquith, p. 710. Draft, Churchill papers: 21/37

Hankey diary, p. 712. Hankey papers

24 Oct. 1915     Goulding to Churchill, p. 712. Churchill papers: 2/67

Churchill memorandum, p. 713. Cabinet papers: 42/3

27 Oct. 1915     Churchill to Asquith, Kitchener and Balfour, p. 713. Copy, Churchill papers: 21/45

30 Oct. 1915     Churchill to Asquith, p. 730. Copy, Churchill papers: 2/67

31 Oct. 1915     Monro to Kitchener, p. 715. Copy, Churchill papers: 2/68

[?] Oct. 1915     Carson to Lloyd George, p. 709. Lloyd George papers

Harcourt to Churchill, p. 712. Churchill papers: 21/37

Churchill statement, p. 713. Churchill papers: 21/43

## NOVEMBER 1915

1 Nov. 1915     Drummond to Margot Asquith, p. 711. Countess Oxford and Asquith papers

## JANUARY 1916

## JUNE 1916

2 June 1916 Churchill to Asquith, p. 972. Copy, Churchill papers: 2/74
Fisher to Asquith, p. 973. Copy, Churchill papers: 2/74

7 June 1916 Waterlow to Churchill, p. 970. Churchill papers: 2/71
Churchill to Northcliffe, p. 976. Copy, Churchill papers: 2/71

8 June 1916 Northcliffe to Lloyd George, p. 977. Copy, Northcliffe papers
Churchill to Asquith, p. 978. Copy, Churchill papers: 2/74
Churchill to Lloyd George, p. 978. Lloyd George papers

[8] June 1916 Northcliffe to Churchill, p. 977. Copy, Northcliffe papers

9 June 1916 Churchill to Northcliffe, p. 977. Copy, Churchill papers: 2/71

14 June 1916 Reading to Churchill, p. 978. Churchill papers: 2/71
Gillespie to Churchill, p. 971. Churchill papers: 2/71

[15] June 1916 George V minute, p. 147. Royal Archives

19 June 1916 Hankey to Churchill, p. 979. Churchill papers: 2/74

20 June 1916 Churchill to Fisher, p. 979. Fisher papers

21 June 1916 Churchill to John Churchill, p. 979. John Churchill papers

22 June 1916 Churchill to Asquith, p. 979. Copy, Churchill papers: 2/74

## AUTHOR'S RECORDS 1966–71

Field-Marshal Earl Alexander of Tunis: conversation with the author, 28 Dec. 1968, p. 176

Mr Frank Ashton-Gwatkin: conversation with the author, 14 Feb. 1970, p. 95

Mr Ralph Bingham: letter to the author, 11 July 1966, p. 731

Mr J. R. Colville: letter to the author, 11 May 1970, p. 989

Air Vice-Marshal Sir John Cordingley: letter to the author, 27 Dec. 1968, p. 102

Mr Robert Fulton: letter to the author, 20 Dec. 1968, p. 830

Major-General Sir Edmund Hakewill Smith: conversation with the author, 22 Dec. 1966, p. 795 *et seq.;* letter to the author, 3 Jan. 1971, p. 949

Sir Ralph Hawtrey: letter to the author, 10 Nov. 1968, p. 611

Mr Reginald Hurt: letter to the author, 8 March 1970, p. 847

Mr Jock McDavid: conversation with the author, 15 March 1967, p. 798 *et seq.;* letter to the author, 5 March 1970, p. 796; conversation with the author, 24 May 1970, p. 831

The 10th Duke of Marlborough: conversation with the author, 7 Oct. 1969, p. 86

M. André Maurois: letter to the author, 6 Jan. 1967, p. 825

Mr C. J. F. Mitchell: conversation with the author, 6 March 1969, p. 183

Major F. D. Napier-Clavering: conversation with the author, 21 Nov. 1968, p. 845 *et seq.*

Mr Stewart Owler: letter to the author, 5 Feb. 1970, p. 189

Major-General Sir Edward Louis Spears: conversation with the author, 4 May 1970, p. 789

Baroness Spencer-Churchill: conversation with the author, 7 Aug. 1969, pp. 540, 613

Mr Henry Stevens: letter to the author, 14 April 1969, p. 172

# Index

## Compiled by the Author

Churchill, Winston Leonard Spencer

MILITARY EXPERIENCES DRAWN ON BY:

to devise new methods of mechanical warfare (Dec 1915), 747–50; to assert importance of extending conscription to Ireland (9 May 1916), 953; to stress need for British air supremacy (17 May 1916), 954, 961; to advocate proper use of conscripts (23 May 1916), 963–4; to compare the trench population with the non-trench population (23 May 1916), 964; to allege 'gross and grave misuse' of military manpower (23 May 1916), 966; to oppose the Somme offensive, 968, 988, 990–1; to criticize the Government's military policy (24 July 1916), 991–4; to advise against premature use of the tank (Sept 1916), 1110–11

VISITS ABROAD OF:

his first wartime visit to France (10 Sept 1914), 129–30; his second (16 Sept 1914), 138; his third (22 Sept 1914), 148, 150; his fourth (26 Sept 1914), 152; his fifth (6 Dec 1914), 238; his sixth (29 Jan 1915), 374; his seventh (16 March 1915), 456; his eighth (5–10 May 1915), 535, 537–8, 539, 546, 547; at the siege of Antwerp, (4–6 Oct 1914), 169–85

HOPED-FOR MISSIONS ABROAD OF:

to the Calais Conference (July 1915), 648; to the Dardanelles (July 1915), 652–7; to the Balkan capitals (July 1915), 655; to Russia (Oct 1915), 713, 773$n$; to East Africa (Nov 1915), 716, 718–19, 722

MOODS OF:

'geared up & happy' (20 July 1914), 80; seeks reassurance from Lloyd George (23 Aug 1914), 108; 'Unless we win, I do not want to live any more. But win we will' (24 Aug 1914), 108; 'gloomy & dissatisfied' (Clementine Churchill, 26 Sept 1914), 153; 'very depressed' (Asquith, 8 Oct 1914), 189; cast down by criticisms of his action at Antwerp (Oct 1914), 198–202; 'It is vain to look backwards', 202; 'I have not seen him so despondent before' (Captain Richmond, 24 Oct 1914), 210; 'a rather sombre mood' (Asquith, 27 Oct 1914), 211; 'vexed by trifles' (28 Dec 1914), 243; disappointed by lack of public enthusiasm for the Friedrichshafen air raid (Nov 1914), 250–1; elated by Falkland Islands victory (Dec 1914), 261; 'his most bellicose' (Asquith, 17 Aug 1914), 275; 'violently anti-Turk' (Asquith, 21 Aug 1914), 277; 'I would not be out of this glorious delicious war for anything' (reported by Margot Asquith, 10 Jan 1915), 336; disappointed by limited results of Dogger Bank action (24 Jan 1915), 354–5; impatient with Asquith, Grey and Kitchener (7 Feb 1915), 375; 'the stresses and strains' of the war (15 Feb 1915), 383; 'I wish you had heard what I had to say before assuming that I was in the wrong' (17 Feb 1915), 388; disappointed at failure to obtain troops for the Dardanelles (24 Feb 1915), 405; 'immense and unconcealed dudgeon' (Asquith, 26 Feb 1915), 412; 'breast high about the Dardanelles' (Asquith, 1 March 1915), 420; determined to renew

Coalition (*cont'd*)
'forced on' by Lloyd George in
May 1915, 690; many Generals
disillusioned by (April 1916),
946

Coke, Sir Charles: 723

Colenso, battle of (15 Dec 1899):
363

Collet, Charles Herbert: bombs German Zeppelin shed at Düsseldorf
(22 Sept 1914), 149

Cologne (Germany): British air raid
on Zeppelin sheds at (22 Sept
1914), 149; second air raid on (9
Oct 1914), 189–90, 205; Churchill refers to air raids on, 903, 956–
7; MAP, 148

Colombo (Ceylon): 360

Colonial Office: Grey protests to
about Churchill's actions, 398–9;
Lloyd George suggests sending
Churchill to (May 1915), 575;
Churchill willing to go to, 578;
Cabinet Ministers reported reluc-
tant that Churchill should go to,
582; Asquith implored not to send
Churchill to, 589

Colville, John Rupert: records a
conversation with Churchill about
'a very unhappy time of my life',
989

Committee of Imperial Defence:
Kitchener a member of, 54n; its
plans for national emergency, 55;
General Wilson's demonstration to
(1911), 76; discusses Dutch neutrality, 158; Churchill a member
of, 179; recommends military
landing at Haifa (1909), 305;
examination of possible joint military and naval attack on Dardanelles (1906), 393; Fisher insists
on Sir Arthur Wilson being dismissed from, 580; Churchill wants
special sub-committee of, to report on future of Gallipoli (Oct
1915), 697

Compulsion, *see* Conscription

Conan Doyle, Arthur: Churchill

writes to about the 'tank' (Sept
1916), 1010

*Concerning Winston Spencer
Churchill* (Sir George Arthur):
1019n

Congleton, 5th Baron (Henry Bligh
Fortescue Parnell): killed in action at Ypres (18 Nov 1914),
768n

*Conqueror* (British battleship): col-
lision with *Monarch* (27 Dec
1914) impairs naval margin, 363

Conscription: pre-1914 campaign
for, 98; Churchill argues in favour
of, at Cabinet (26 Aug 1914),
110; the growing pressure for
(June 1915), 630; Kitchener attacked for his opposition to (Oct
1915), 707–12; Curzon appeals to
Churchill for support over (Nov
1915), 762; its advocates gain in
strength (Dec 1915), 781–2; the
growing crisis over (Jan 1916),
853–7; the renewed crisis over
(April 1916), 938–41, 945–8;
Churchill on the need to make
proper use of, 963–5

Conservative Party: and the coming
of war, 69–70; attitude to
Churchill, 81–2; and Home Rule,
134–8; critical of Churchill's visits
to France, 150, 546–7; critical of
Churchill's actions at Antwerp,
201; Churchill describes certain
members of as '*swine*', 239; believes Asquith did not reconvene
Parliament (Oct 1914) in order
to avoid questions on Antwerp,
244; critical of Churchill's policy
on the collier question, 382; finds
it difficult to attack War Office
while Kitchener is Secretary of
State, 416; and criticism of Gallipoli landings, 533; denied equal
part in prosecution of the war,
600–1; and Churchill's hopes of
support from during the political
crisis of May 1915, 611–12; the
growing call for conscription,

*Goliath* (British battleship): needed at Dardanelles, 515; sunk at Dardanelles (12 May 1915), 548

*Good Hope* (British cruiser): sunk at battle off Coronel (1 Nov 1914), 231, 259

Gordon, General Charles George (1833–85): 433n

Gordon, Edward Ian Drumearn: to command amalgamated 6/7 Royal Scots Fusiliers, 949

Gosford, 4th Earl of (Archibald Brabazon Sparrow Acheson): shocked to learn Churchill not yet a Brigadier (Feb 1916), 851

Goulding, Sir Edward Alfred: urges Churchill not to resign from Cabinet (Oct 1915), 712; Churchill asks his wife to keep in touch with (Jan 1916), 865; acts as an intermediary between Churchill and Fisher (Feb 1916), 889; Churchill seeks advice of (March 1916), 933; Northcliffe informs of his hostile attitude to Churchill (April 1916), 940; Fisher and Garvin discuss Dardanelles Commission evidence at home of (Sept 1916), 1008

Grand Fleet, *see* First Fleet

Granet, Edward John: suggests British air raid on Friedrichshafen, 247

Grant Duff, Evelyn Mountstuart: wants Britain to apologize for alleged violation of Swiss neutrality by naval aviators, 250–1

*Great Contemporaries* (Winston S. Churchill): quoted, on sending of Fleet to North Sea, 53; on Asquith's letters to Venetia Stanley, 68n; on Asquith's behaviour in the political crisis of May 1915, 615; on Balfour during the political crisis of December 1916, 1025

Greece: naval rivalry with Turkey, 269; possible British ally against Turkey, 279, 293; possibility of action against Austria, 281; provision of troops to fight Turkey from, 282; Churchill sees 'brilliant but fleeting opportunity' for (31 Aug 1914), 283; troops from considered essential in Gallipoli landings, 285; Churchill wants pro-British policy towards, 291; Asquith expects (31 Oct 1914), to join Allies shortly, 300, 304; Fisher wants as Allies' military arm against Gallipoli, 306; lack of troops from, ends British discussions for seizing Gallipoli, 308; Lloyd George wants as ally against Austria, 316; importance of in British plans for the defeat of Turkey, 317, 323, 334, 340; little disposed to help Serbia, 369; Churchill believes could be persuaded to join Allies, 370; Austrian aim to overawe, 374; possibility of troops of to help Serbia, 379; Balfour on inducements to, 406; Churchill appeals for immediate naval help from (1 March 1915), 420; Kitchener wants Gallipoli Peninsula handed over to after the war, 426; Churchill wants military support from (4 March 1915), 431; Russians refuse to allow as an ally against Turkey, 434–5; Churchill angered by loss of assistance from, 443; Fisher wants Britain to seize the Fleet of, 445; Churchill seeks in vain to overcome Russian veto on help from, 453; forced to buy wheat from the United States because of Turkish closure of the Straits, 459; will not get Smyrna after the war unless they join the Allies (April 1915), 499; and effect of the Gallipoli landings on, 532; and the Austrian attack on Serbia (Oct 1915), 698; MAPS, 323, 694, 1042, 1046

Greene, Conyngham: 93

Hankey, Maurice Pascal Alers (*cont'd*)
nelles Committee (7 June 1915), 633; chosen by Kitchener to accompany Churchill to Gallipoli, 655; goes to Dardanelles by himself, 658; at Suvla Bay (8 Aug 1915), 662, 666; reports (30 Aug 1915) on hopes for success at Anzac, 671; and the origin of the tank, 682, 1011; Churchill wants as Secretary to a special committee to decide future of Gallipoli (Oct 1915), 696–7; and the ministerial attacks on Kitchener (Oct 1915), 707–8; suggests sending Churchill on mission to Russia (22 Oct 1915), 712–13; reports Cabinet unanimous that Kitchener should leave War Office (1 Nov 1915), 714; and speculation on Churchill's future career (Nov 1915), 716; and effect of Churchill's departure from the Cabinet, 736, 766; Fisher writes to about anti-Asquith feeling (Jan 1916), 878–80, 884; and Churchill's appeal for Fisher's return to the Admiralty (March 1916), 913, 915, 918–19; and the proposed publication of Dardanelles documents (June 1916), 972, 979–80; and Churchill's criticisms (Aug 1916) of the Somme offensive, 989; and Churchill's evidence to the Dardanelles Commission, 1001, 1015

Harcourt, Lewis: wants to annex German East Africa as a centre for Indian emigrants, 440; wants acquisition of Turkish port of Marmarice, 441; suggests giving the Holy Places of Palestine as a mandate to the United States, 487; believes Fisher 'has triumphed' (18 May 1915), 579; Emmott implores Asquith not to replace as Colonial Secretary by Churchill, 589; seeks Duchy of

Lancaster patronage, 622; hopes Churchill will not resign (Nov 1915), 712; a possible Viceroy of India (1916), 858

Hardinge of Penshurst, 1st Baron (Charles Hardinge): complains that Royal Navy is not doing enough to track down the *Emden*, 209; orders action against Turkey at head of Persian Gulf, 306–7; his successor as Viceroy of India discussed, 335; hopeful about attack on Dardanelles, 429; informed of territorial plans for the partition of Turkey, 452; on advantage to India of a British victory at the Dardanelles, 458

'Harlot of Europe', the: Churchill describes Italy as, 549n

Harmsworth, Harold Alfred Vyvian St George: died of wounds received in action in France (12 Feb 1918), 1015n

Harmsworth, Leicester: votes against the Government in the Nigeria debate (Nov 1916), 1017n

Harmsworth, Vere Sidney: killed in action in France (13 Nov 1916), 1015n

Harper, (?)William: in armoured car skirmish near Cassel, 125

*Hawke* (British cruiser): torpedoed (15 Oct 1914), 261

Hawtrey, Ralph George: recalls a pre-1914 conversation between Churchill and Lloyd George, 611

Hay, Ian, *see* Beith, John Hay

Hazebrouck (France): 447; Churchill attends lectures at, 809, 810; Churchill entertains his officers at, 815–16; Churchill meets Lloyd George and Bonar Law at, 874–5; MAP, 797

Hearn, Gordon Risley: discusses trenchworks with Churchill, 845

Heligoland (German island): possible British base, 66, 67; Sir Arthur Wilson plans attacks on, 226; MAP, 66

Jackson, Sir Henry Bradwardine: King suggests as possible First Sea Lord, 222; studies effect of bombardment of outer forts of the Dardanelles, 304; discusses with Churchill and Fisher best method of forcing Dardanelles, 305; in favour of systematic bombardment of Dardanelles, 326; member of Admiralty War Group, 341; and planning of naval attack at Dardanelles, 346, 348–50; argues need for a 'strong military force' to assist navy at Dardanelles (15 Feb 1915), 385; favours annexation of Lemnos, 429; his plan for attacking Bosphorus forts being sent to Admiral Carden, 432; urges (11 March 1915) immediate military support for the navy in Dardanelles attack, 443; advises annexation of Alexandretta, 459; supports Fisher's refusal to order de Robeck to make a second naval attack without military assistance, 477–9; on Committee to consider British territorial needs in Turkey, 507–8; with Churchill in Paris during Anglo-Italian negotiations (5–8 May 1915), 535; favoured by Admiralty officials as possible First Sea Lord, 585, 587; Churchill advises as First Sea Lord (21 May 1915), 595; succeeds Fisher as First Sea Lord, and concurs in submarine reinforcements to Dardanelles, 623; examines merits of western and Gallipoli fronts (Oct 1915), 698n; proposes bombardment of Bulgarian port (Oct 1915), 703; and Churchill's appeal for Fisher's return to the Admiralty in place of (March 1916), 907, 909–11

Jade River: Churchill wishes to block German bases at mouth of, 257

Jaffa (Turkey): Churchill proposes French naval command at, 361

Japan: Churchill eager to bring in as an ally, 93–5; naval help sent to Indian Ocean, 209; Churchill and Fisher seek naval assistance of, against von Spee, 231; navy of has effective command of Pacific, 255; Churchill wants naval force sent to Mediterranean by, 283; possibility of transit of Russian troops for Gallipoli Peninsula through, 287; Churchill wants rifles from, to arm 150,000 Russians (Oct 1915), 713

Jeffreys, George Darell: Churchill trains in Grenadier Guards' Battalion of (Nov–Dec 1915), 729–31, 732, 735; offers to make Churchill his second-in-command, 766; and Churchill's impending promotion to command a Brigade, 769; 'austere', 784

Jellicoe, Sir John Rushworth: becomes Commander-in-Chief of the First Fleet, 59, 62, 75, 89; Clementine Churchill's advice on, 60–1; Churchill informs of fall of Namur, 108–9; Fisher's prediction that he would become Commander-in-Chief in 1914, 119; provides Churchill with pistols, 140; wants to suppress news of sinking of *Audacious*, 211–12; Gwynne urges Asquith to put in Churchill's place as First Lord, 215; 'a splendid man of business', 216; Fisher urges Churchill to trust implicitly, 217; Fisher declares *'shoot the pessimists'* to, 227; Kitchener does not interfere with, 240; Asquith describes face of, 252n; ordered to send two battle cruisers to South America, 259; learns why it is not wise 'to terrorize Admirals for losing ships', 262; Fisher describes Admiralty

Malta (*cont'd*)
to, 568; Churchill wants Gallipoli Peninsula troop reinforcements assembled at (June 1915), 637

Malta Conference (1912): Churchill impressed by Kitchener at, 56

*Manchester Guardian:* praises Churchill for troop transportation, 87; for frankness, 88; for his London Opera House speech (11 Sept 1914), 133; for his Liverpool speech (21 Sept 1914), 143–4; its editor hears Churchill and Lloyd George criticize further offensives on the western front (Sept 1915), 689–90; welcomed by Churchill as an ally (Dec 1915), 755; supports Churchill's appeal for Fisher's return to the Admiralty (March 1916), 905, 916; said to be the only paper to report Churchill's parliamentary speeches (Nov 1916), 1018

Marconi affair (1912): Lloyd George's 'failure' in, 635; Churchill's belief that Lloyd George owed him a debt as a result of, 787*n*, 939

Marine Brigade: to form part of Royal Naval Division, 99, 103; sent by Churchill to Ostend, 109; sent by Churchill to Dunkirk, 130; bus drivers enlist in, 131

Marix, Reginald Lennox George: at Dunkirk air base, 123; on bombing raid from Antwerp to Cologne (22 Sept 1914), 149; on raid from Antwerp to Düsseldorf (9 Oct 1914), 190, 205

Markham, Sir Arthur Basil: supports Churchill's criticisms of Asquith (March 1916), 892, 894; a member of the Liberal War Committee, 919–20*n;* urges Churchill's return from the trenches to Parliament (April 1916), 938

Marlborough, 1st Duke of, *see* Churchill, John

Marlborough, 9th Duke of (Charles Richard John Spencer-Churchill): reconciliation with Churchill, 85–6; Colonel-in-Chief, Oxfordshire Hussars, 130; acts as War Office messenger, 447; and the crisis of May 1915, 598–99, 611; informs Churchill of Admiralty complacency (Feb 1916), 881

Marlborough, 10th Duke of, *see* Blandford, Marquis of

Marlowe, Thomas: 193

Marmara, Sea of: *Goeben* in, 273; Limpus suggest sending torpedo craft into, 279; Churchill recalls importance of sending a fleet into, at earliest possible moment, 281; Churchill instructs War Office to draw up plans making it possible for fleet to enter, 284; plan for a joint Anglo-Greek fleet to enter, 286; British plan to enter, 339, 349; Kitchener believes Anzac troops 'good enough' for a cruise in, 404; Balfour believes ships alone will secure allied command of, 410; Turkey's principal arsenals on shore of, vulnerable to naval bombardment, 423; Admiral Carden's instructions (5 March 1915) in the event of his entering, 432–3; Admiral de Robeck reluctant to enter (25 March 1915), 482–3; Churchill believes arrival of ships in, will cut off Turkish army on Gallipoli Peninsula, 483; de Robeck's plans to penetrate, 507, 510; Jack Churchill envisages British ships within two weeks of Gallipoli landings, 527; Churchill wants further naval effort to penetrate (Aug 1915), 670; MAP, 1044–5

Marmarice (Turkey): Lewis Harcourt suggests annexation of, 441; MAP, 1042

Marne, Battle of (Sept 1914): 127–8, 167, 296